The New York Times

BOOK OF
HEALTH

The New York Times

BOOK OF
HEALTH

How to Feel Fitter,
Eat Better,
and Live Longer

JANE E. BRODY
and Reporters of
The New York Times

Edited by Nicholas Wade

Introduction by Jane E. Brody

TIMES BOOKS

RANDOM HOUSE

All of the essays in this work originally appeared
in *The New York Times*

Library of Congress Cataloging-in-Publication Data
Brody, Jane E.
The New York Times book of health : how to feel fitter, eat
better, and live longer / Jane E. Brody and the reporters of
the New York Times.
p.   cm.
Includes index.
ISBN 0-8129-2858-X
1. Health.   2. Medicine, Popular.   3. Physical fitness.
4. Nutrition.   I. New York Times.   II. Title.
RA776.B7748   1997
613—dc21   96-47065

Random House website address:
http://www.randomhouse.com/
Printed in the United States of America on acid-free paper
2   4   6   8   9   7   5   3
First Edition
Book design by Mina Greenstein

ACKNOWLEDGMENTS

Modern medicine is based on science, but physicians and health experts must wrestle every day with problems for which science as yet has provided few or sketchy answers. Even these answers are subject to change as new findings from the laboratory or clinical trial refine some theories and overthrow others.

Thus health is not a settled subject. The years from 1990 to 1996, while I was the *New York Times*'s science and health editor, seem to have been particularly tumultuous. This selection of articles, from the latter half of that period, takes readers to the forefront of many debates and fields of inquiry. Though written to report daily events, the articles are here grouped by subject matter and gain a coherence that is seldom possible in a newspaper.

The midwives of this book were Mitchel Levitas of *The New York Times* and, at Times Books, Steve Wasserman (now of the *Los Angeles Times*) and Elizabeth Rapoport. The unseen hands that commissioned or helped shape many of the articles belong to Katherine Bouton, former deputy science editor, and to her successor James Gorman. To the reporters whose works are anthologized here belongs the credit for whatever insights and instruction the reader may find.

—Nicholas Wade

LIST OF CONTRIBUTORS

LKA	Lawrence K. Altman
NA	Natalie Angier
SB	Sandra Blakeslee
JEB	Jane E. Brody
MB	Marian Burros
DG	Daniel Goleman
DGr	Denise Grady
GK	Gina Kolata
WEL	Warren E. Leary

CONTENTS

SECTION THREE

The Many Benefits of Exercise
The Fountain of Youth: Can It Be Just Perspiration?

SECTION FOUR

The Science of Eating Right
Nutrition: The Never-Ending Debate

SECTION FIVE

Vitamins and Other Supplements
The Bad News About Vitamin Megadoses

SECTION SIX

Protecting the Heart
The Heart's Worst Enemy: Affluence

SECTION SEVEN

Averting Cancer Risks
The Body's Superb Defenses Against Cancer

SECTION EIGHT

Stages of Life—Pregnancy and Birth
The Human Life Cycle

SECTION NINE

Stages of Life—Childhood
The Vulnerable Years

SECTION TEN

Stages of Life—Menopause
The Diminuendo of the Hormones

SECTION ELEVEN

Stages of Life—Aging
Coping with Age

INTRODUCTION

Confused about health? Nearly everyone is these days. Despite extensive research utilizing some of the most sophisticated study methods available, many of the major health questions of our times still evoke memories of that famous Clairol ad: "Does she or doesn't she?" Should you, or shouldn't you, for example, take vitamin supplements, eat a low-fat diet, keep your weight at its college low, exercise vigorously three or more times a week? Can you protect your heart by eating fish, prevent cancer by eating vegetables, keep your bones strong by taking calcium?

There are also myriad debates about the benefits and risks of many medical procedures that are already in widespread use as well as those not yet widely adopted but often recommended by most experts and major health organizations. Should every woman 40 and over have an annual mammogram? Should every fetus be monitored electronically during labor and delivery? Is a mother who fails to nurse her baby compromising its development? Is hormone replacement at menopause safe and desirable, and for how long? Should men also consider supplementing their waning supply of testosterone as they age?

Then there are the many societal issues that can have a major impact on personal health. Can children be taught to eat better, exercise more and resist tobacco, drugs and alcohol, or are we doomed to raising one generation after another of Americans prone to chronic health problems precipitated by bad habits acquired during childhood and adolescence? Can the dismal rate of childhood immunizations be boosted, or will future generations be plagued by outbreaks of devastating yet preventable ills such as polio, whooping cough and measles? Can our youngsters' brains be protected from the permanent damage that can be caused by overexposure to lead? Should every child have his or her cholesterol level tested, and if so, then what? What can we do to protect our aging society from chronic disease and disability so that many more than now do can truly enjoy their golden years? Should there be societal campaigns to enhance the nutrition, exercise habits and hormone balance of the elderly? Can our highways be improved to reduce the risk of accidents caused by sleepy drivers? Should helmet laws be extended to adults who ride bicycles? Can prescription practices be improved to protect elderly patients against inappropriate medications, toxic reactions and drug overdoses?

You will find within this book detailed discussions of these and scores of similar issues, discussions that reflect the latest in medical research and the considered opinions of the world's best experts in the various areas. All are articles that were published originally in *The New York Times* since January 1993 and so represent the latest information and thinking about critical health issues. This book can help you to make wise choices about how to live your life healthfully, based on the best-available and most up-to-date medical evidence.

The discussions here can also give you the tools to evaluate future issues and disputes when new medical findings and advice are given a public airing. We are living in unprecedented times, when the world's leading medical publications—from the *New England Journal of Medicine* and *The Journal of the American Medical Association* to the British journals *Nature* and *The Lancet*—compete for public attention and each week invite the news media to publicize scientific reports that they publish. As a result, you and I and millions of others who pay attention to medical news are continually being bombarded by findings that may be difficult to interpret and advice that seems to change every other week.

You can learn from the material included here how to integrate new findings into current dogma and make the best possible sense of new information as it comes along. You can learn how and when to act when confronted with a new finding: how to assess its validity, generalizability and applicability to your personal life. Should you give up drinking coffee when a widely publicized study from a prestigious medical institution links coffee drinking to an increase in pancreatic cancer? Or should you wait to see whether anyone else can confirm the finding? Should a small increase in the risk of developing breast cancer prompt a woman to abandon postmenopausal hormones? Should a scare about one vaccine prompt parents to question the safety and wisdom of all vaccines for children?

As you might guess by now, this is no ordinary health book that gives you pat answers about anything and everything that might ail you. There are plenty of those tomes, both good and bad, and this book makes no attempt to compete with them and provide information about every conceivable ailment. By their very nature, the various books published by one institution can be misleading because they usually reflect one voice, not the full spectrum of medical opinion. In medicine, there is not always one version of the truth. And new truths often grow from issues raised by iconoclasts who buck the tide of dogma and ask questions that force researchers back to the bench to look for firmer documentation. Sometimes they find it, other times not. And when they do not, medical advice must change accordingly.

Besides, most of the health books now on bookshelves quickly become outdated because medical science is in a constant state of flux and—as I have already noted—because many of the most pressing health matters facing this turn-of-the-century society do not have cut-and-dried answers. Medical science is continually evolving, changing and growing, and the advice that ensues must likewise be modified. The articles herein reflect those changes. Reliable advice must be based on good science, and good science means continuing research that utilizes ever more refined methods for arriving at the truth. Quackery remains the same year after year because it is based on wishful thinking, not solid research.

The story of beta-carotene is a case in point. It began with epidemiological observations that groups of people whose diets were rich in this nutrient, a precursor of vitamin A, also had lower-than-expected rates of various cancers, including the rate of lung cancer among smokers. Laboratory studies on test animals seemed to add weight to these observations, and together they prompted millions of people to start downing daily supplements of beta-carotene. But when very large, well-controlled studies were undertaken in which some participants were randomly assigned to take beta-carotene supplements and others got a look-alike placebo each day for years, the presumed protection offered by beta-carotene dissolved like a soap bubble. In fact, in two studies beta-carotene users developed more cancers than nonusers did. Forget beta-carotene supplements, at least for now, became the researchers' clarion call. For you, it's back to that old familiar standby: eat your fruits and vegetables. And for scientists it's back to the drawing boards to determine whether beta-carotene itself is responsible for our initial observations, whether it must interact with scores of other carotenoids in foods in order to protect health, or whether it is merely an indicator nutrient that in itself is not exceptional but rather reflects the overall benefits of a diet rich in fruits and vegetables.

Medical science does not always progress in a straight line. Along the way there are many arguments among researchers as to what is appropriate advice to give the public and when it should be given. In this book you will find disputes about medical advice laid out like dirty laundry, with the advice outlined in some articles contradicted days, weeks or months later by articles suggesting something entirely different. This is the way science—good science—progresses. Sometimes scientists take two steps forward, only to have to take one step back when new findings indicate that a prior conclusion may have reached too far. And sometimes, as in the children's game, "Mother, May I?" and with supplements of beta-carotene, the retreat must be back to the starting line when new research reveals a flaw in logic or method or an erroneous or too-hasty conclusion.

None of this means, however, that you should abandon all hope of adopting health-promoting living habits until science comes up with rock-solid conclusions. You should not use the debates in this book as an excuse to return to devil-may-care practices. It would not be wise, for example, to return to a high-fat diet while medical researchers grapple with defining the full benefits of a regimen low in fat or to resume an overindulgence in saturated animal fats while scientists go back and forth about the benefits of vegetable and fish oils. Nor would it be wise to abandon an exercise regime because some activities may expose you to the risk of injury. Far more people die in bed than on tennis courts and bike paths. A sprained ligament or sore muscle is far less serious than a heart attack.

None of us can afford to wait until every *i* is dotted and every *t* crossed before deciding how best to live our lives. Your choice must be made now, on the basis of the best information currently available. And within these pages, you should find just such information.

—JANE E. BRODY
Personal Health columnist,
The New York Times

Good Health Versus Bad Habits

HEALTH ADVICE IS EASIER TO GIVE
THAN TO FOLLOW

American hospitals offer the most sophisticated medicine available. But in American homes, the best practice is far from standard. Their occupants eat too much fat and take too little exercise. And the trend is getting worse by the year. The share of the American population that is seriously overweight rose from a quarter of all adults in 1980 to more than a third a decade later.

It is not for lack of good advice that Americans follow these bad habits. Health experts are so used to being ignored that some of them try to water down their prescriptions to what they think a patient might be coaxed to swallow.

Even so, their advisees have mostly turned a deaf ear. Many Americans work so hard and frenetically that they simply don't have time to exercise hard three times a week. Fast foods are as much a necessity as a convenience. What is the point of affluence if it doesn't offer temptations?

It is all too easy to understand the better course but choose the worse, especially if a distant benefit must be weighed against an immediate pleasure. We are all such experts at the moral equivalent of discounted cash flow—valuing distant rewards at far less than the same goodies right now—that we can perform the calculations without a conscious thought. A slice of triple-layer chocolate fudge cake now sounds better than slicing the putative risk of heart trouble 10 years hence.

The articles that follow describe the impasse between Americans and their health advisers.

Why Bad Health Habits
Drive Out the Good

DESPITE widely publicized advice about what to do, how to do it and why, most Americans—even those strongly convinced that they must do something about their bad habits—abandon health-promoting behaviors before they have had a chance to prove their worth. This is readily apparent from the lack of progress being made in reaching the *Healthy People 2000* goals established by the surgeon general in 1990.

Between 1980 and 1991, Americans' consumption of dietary fats dropped a mere 2 percentage points—from 36 percent to 34 percent of calories, still far from the goal of 30 percent set for the year 2000. Saturated fat intake is down from 13 percent to 12 percent of calories, but the goal is 10 percent. These declines may look like progress, but in reality there was little or no reduction in the consumption of health-damaging fats, because Americans increased their caloric intake.

At the same time, the percentage of Americans who engage in regular physical exercise has increased only slightly (from 22 percent in 1985 to 24 percent in 1991 for light to moderate activity, and from 16 percent to 17 percent for vigorous activity), and the share of totally sedentary Americans has not budged from its baseline of 24 percent in 1985.

And, of course, overweight, a consequence of consuming more calories but not using more, has risen dramatically. The number of adults who are overweight, defined as at least 20 percent more weight than is desirable for optimal health, rose from 26 percent in 1980 to 34 percent a decade later. In other words, in 1980 one out of three adults was—and now one in two is—overweight.

Even for smoking, where the progress has been greatest, the goal for 2000 is far from realization. While 29 percent of American adults were smokers in 1987 and the number has dropped to 25 percent, the goal is 15 percent.

Why, when nearly everyone knows what to do to live more healthfully, do so many Americans continue to have bad habits? And even when people do make changes with the very best intentions of maintaining them, why do so many backslide, regaining lost pounds, indulging once again in fatty foods, resuming smoking or abandoning exercise? Such questions are being addressed by an interdisciplinary network of health researchers convened by the John D. and Catherine T. MacArthur Foundation, based in Chicago. The researchers are beginning to understand why so many people continue to engage in health-damaging behaviors and how they can be encouraged to replace them with health-promoting ones.

SHORT-TERM SACRIFICES, LONG-TERM GOALS. "When people are faced with a short-term gain—the pleasure of smoking or eating a high-fat food, for example—it's hard to suppress the desire for the sake of a long-term gain," said Dr. Paul Rozin, a health psychologist at the University of Pennsylvania in Philadelphia and a member of the MacArthur group. "At a distance, the sacrifice may look like a minor price to pay, but when confronted with the reality, it seems much more costly."

Dr. Donald A. Redelmeier of the University of Toronto said that people tend to act in proportion to their worries, and long-term threats, however large, are less worrisome than immediate dangers, however small. Thus, to help people change, the emphasis should be primarily on a habit's current adverse effects and the immediate benefits of change. For smoking, the short-term rewards of stopping include increased stamina, greater resistance to respiratory infections, less phlegm and coughing and less odor from clothes and breath. For those who start exercising, immediate benefits may include less fatigue, greater energy, improved sleep, reduced stress and a loss of unwanted inches.

TOO MUCH INFORMATION. "People are besieged by information about what they should and should not be eating," Dr. Rozin said. "If they did it all, it would cripple their lifestyle." People are continually bombarded by new findings, but they have no sense of what is really important. "They don't distinguish between a risk that might take one hour off life versus a risk that might cost them a year of life," he said.

People also hear too much contradictory evidence, prompting many to decide, "I don't believe any of it." A more appropriate response is to wait to see how it all develops before taking any action, Dr. Rozin says.

CATEGORICAL THINKING. People tend to oversimplify, concluding that things are "safe" or "dangerous" regardless of quantity. Thus, in one study people rated a teaspoon of ice cream as having more calories than a pint of cottage cheese. When told that residues of a pesticide were much less likely to cause cancer than one raw mushroom a day, many decided they could no longer eat mushrooms.

Many people believe that one cannot consume too many vitamins, that trace amounts of sugar or salt make a food unhealthful or that eating even a small amount of animal fat is dangerous. If people adopted this all-or-nothing attitude across the board, Dr. Rozin said, "they would never drive or walk on the street again, activities that are more dangerous than most of the things we're trying to modify in our diet."

When placed in a rational perspective, healthful eating does not require supreme sacrifices or the permanent abandonment of a beloved food. Meaningful dietary changes can be made without losing the pleasure of eating.

MORALITY AND TASTE. People who are offended by meat or cigarettes find it much easier to be vegetarians or nonsmokers, Dr. Rozin said. Likewise, those who learn to enjoy exercise look forward to it and are far more likely to stick with it. "Our job now is to find ways to help people get their likes in line with what they should like, and vice versa," he said.

TOO MANY CHOICES. "As the number of available options increases, paradoxically the status quo becomes increasingly attractive," Dr. Redelmeier said. "When a person is given only one choice, it's more tempting to go ahead and do it. If a physician gives a patient seven pieces of advice, chances are the patient will follow none of them. But if he's given only one thing to do, he's more likely to do it." However, when a dieter is confronted by only one tempting dessert, chances are it will get eaten. But if instead the dieter reads through the entire dessert menu and finds several tempting choices, he or she is better able to resist them all, Dr. Redelmeier said.

[JEB, February 1995]

The Health Cost of Seven Bad Habits

AS if he were a medieval artist depicting the depravity of the seven deadly sins, Dr. Lester Breslow, a California public health specialist, has created a solemn portrait of self-destruction. The weapons are seven unwholesome habits he first identified more than a quarter century ago.

By following the fates of nearly 7,000 adults living in California's Alameda County over three decades, he proved that the more of these poor health habits people practiced in 1965, the greater their chances were of dying within 10 years.

And now his latest study shows that even fewer people than thought escape the ravages of their health "sins." In a study conducted with his son Norman, a statistician at the University of Washington in Seattle, Dr. Breslow has shown that the unhealthy habits portend not only early death for many but chronic and costly disabilities for those who survive.

Two of the poor health practices, as Dr. Breslow calls them, obesity and physical inactivity, are reminiscent of the ancient sins of gluttony and sloth. The others include both the predictable—smoking and drinking too much alcohol—and the surprising—sleeping too much or too little, eating between meals and skipping breakfast. On the basis of studies he and others did in the 1960s, Dr. Breslow cited these seven things as likely to predict an early death.

His first Alameda County report revealed in 1972 that in combination these poor health practices could double a person's chance of dying prematurely. Now, in his latest paper, published in a recent issue of the journal *Preventive Medicine,* Dr. Breslow reports that even when the practices do not lead to an early death, they increase the risk that a person will suffer one or more physical or medical limitations that can degrade the later years of life.

The Breslows' study found that those Californians whose lives in 1965 were characterized by six or seven of the poor health practices were twice as likely to be disabled 10 or more years later as were their neighbors with no more than two of these habits.

Even without taking age or initial health status into account, among those with no poor health habits or just one, 12.2 percent were disabled, and for those with two or three poor health habits, 14.1 percent were disabled. In contrast, 18.7 percent of those with four or more poor health habits were disabled.

Dr. Jonathan Fielding, chairman of the board of the nonprofit California Wellness Foundation and chief health policy planner for Johnson & Johnson, said Dr. Breslow's newest study was "critically important" at a time when the nation is trying to revamp its approach to health care.

"The results really say that how you live determines how long you will live without your state of health interfering with the things you want to do or forcing you to make changes in your life to accommodate your health problems," he said in a telephone interview.

Dr. Breslow, a professor emeritus at the School of Public Health of the University of California at Los Angeles, is perhaps his own best advertisement for the merits of disease prevention. Noting that he has avoided all seven of the poor health practices for most of his life, the 78-year-old researcher, who retired in 1980, said he worked "only eight days a week." He also swims, continues to eat sensibly and maintains a normal weight.

"With people of the United States now living typically into their 70s and 80s, the personal and social importance of maintaining health into the later years is mounting," the Breslows wrote. "People are increasingly concerned about how to avoid disability during their longer lives."

But are people concerned enough to make changes in the living habits that undermine their chances of continued good health? And can young people be enticed to lead "cleaner" lives when the wages of their health sins may not be exacted until decades later?

According to the latest survey of American health practices, the decades-long trend toward healthier living habits has taken a turn for the worse. In December 1992, Louis Harris & Associates polled 1,251 randomly selected adults in a survey by telephone conducted for Baxter International, a Michigan producer of health care products and services. The survey included many of the same questions the Harris poll takers have been asking every year for a decade.

The 1992 survey showed that compared with the findings in 1991 or, say, 1983, more Americans were overweight, and they were eating less carefully, exercising less and getting less sleep. In 1992, 66 percent of Americans were found to be overweight, up from 63 percent in 1991 and 58 percent in 1983. Only 33 percent said they exercised vigorously three or more times a week, down from 37 percent the year before. Fewer of those questioned were "trying hard" to eat less cholesterol, fat and sodium and to eat more fiber than in 1991.

And, as an indication that their lives had become more stressful, in 1992 only 50 percent of respondents said they got as much as seven to eight hours of sleep a night, down from 64 percent in 1983.

"These survey results represent disturbing trends in the nation's health behaviors," concluded Dr. James S. Todd, executive director of the American Medical Association, a traditionally conservative organization that has belatedly jumped on the preventive-medicine bandwagon.

But for some of the health practices Dr. Breslow has been studying, the survey findings were encouraging. Cigarette smoking, the nation's single most damaging and costly habit in terms of health, was practiced by only 24 percent of adult Americans, and 70 percent of them said they wanted to quit. In the 1960s, when Dr. Breslow began the Alameda study, half of Americans smoked regularly.

The survey also found a rise in the number of people who said they drank alcohol either moderately or not at all and a decline in the number who said they consumed more than three drinks on any given day.

In questioning Alameda County residents about how much they slept or whether they ate breakfast or ate between meals, Dr. Breslow said he did not mean to suggest that sleeping too much or too little, snacking and skipping breakfast were deadly habits in themselves on a par with smoking or excessive drinking. Rather, he said, "I believe these poor health practices are indicative of a chaotic lifestyle" and that people who follow them are likely to pay inadequate attention to their overall well-being.

As the years passed, to the surprise of nearly all Dr. Breslow's colleagues, the study showed that snackers, breakfast skippers and people who slept more or less than seven to eight hours a night were more likely to die prematurely or to suffer life-limiting disabilities.

"Regularity in one's living habits seems to be important to health and longevity," Dr. Breslow said. He also urged health care policy planners to recognize that "people do not choose their health habits in a vacuum; rather, they are strongly influenced by their social environment."

"We have to address the environmental and social influences on people's health practices, influences like cigarette advertising and the ease with which teenagers can buy cigarettes," he said.

[JEB, May 1993]

Health Experts Advise Less Advice

AMID the deluge of health advice, health news, health tips and health warnings that swells ever larger each year, a number of public health experts and medical researchers are calling for a time-out. The public, they contend, should be told not just what the latest study says but also what it does not say, and how certain it is that the conclusion is correct.

The most recent debates illustrate the problem, these experts say. In February 1995, the Centers for Disease Control and Prevention issued a statement saying any exercise was good, even the most modest activity. Then in April 1995, a study by Harvard University researchers concluded that only people who exercised regularly and strenuously would live longer.

Advice about the relationship between diet and heart disease has also been held up to question. A recent study found no evidence that eating fish protects against heart disease, contradicting a widely held but poorly substantiated belief that fish contains some specifically heart-healthy component. And a recent review of studies on low-fat diets found no evidence to support the national goal of reducing dietary fat to 30 percent of calories as a way of reducing heart disease rates.

About a year ago, the purported link between antioxidant vitamins and cancers was questioned. A large study of smokers found that those who took vitamin E and beta-carotene had the same lung cancer rate as those who did not take the vitamins, and a second study found that vitamin C, vitamin E and beta-carotene offered no protection against precancerous growths on the colon.

The problem, said Dr. Jules Hirsch, an obesity researcher at Rockefeller University in New York, is that some researchers and officials have overstated the case for healthful habits, reasoning that the public wants advice. Many people, he said, want to hear that there is a magic set of foods that will protect them from heart disease or cancer or obesity, or that modest exercise will prolong their lives. "It's such an attractive thing to be able to do something for yourself," Dr. Hirsch said. But as advice proliferates, "it's gotten all out of proportion to the facts of the matter."

Dr. E. H. Ahrens, Jr., a professor emeritus at Rockefeller University, agreed and added that doctors themselves must share the blame. "Doctors want to recommend something," he said. "So in the lack of anything very interesting to do, they advise people to change their diets. There is a sort of basic premise in medicine to do something good for people. If you have that feeling, and here's a patient coming to you for help, you've got to say something: 'Take a multivitamin, eat in moderation.' If that physician thinks he's going to get a happy relationship by recommending a low-fat, low-cholesterol diet, he's going to do it."

But much of the fervently repeated health advice "is ludicrous," said Dr. Donald Louria, chairman of preventive medicine and community health at the New Jersey Medical School in Newark. With the proliferation of guidelines and advice, he said, "we are grotesquely overselling to the American people." And he cautioned, "The danger of that is that they will not believe the stuff we have that's documented."

Dr. Suzanne Fletcher, a professor of ambulatory care and prevention at Harvard University Medical School in Boston, said that with much of current knowledge about health and disease prevention, "We're in a position of 'Don't just do something, stand there.' And it's hard to do that."

But, she added, experts should exercise extreme caution, because "if you're making recommendations for everyone, you have to be darn sure you're not hurting people" in some way. "And I think we have to have a rather broad view of the word 'hurt' to include whether we are hurting people not only physically but also emotionally," she said. "Are we creating a feeling among people that they're not healthy or that they don't have healthy behavior?"

These experts do not think that everything the American public has been told is questionable. Cholesterol levels are linked to heart disease risk, and indirect evidence strongly suggests that people with high cholesterol levels who reduce them, whether by very low-fat diets or drugs, do protect themselves from heart disease. Studies have proved that those who already have heart disease and lower their cholesterol levels with drugs reduce their risk of dying from heart attacks or strokes.

High blood pressure does predispose people to strokes and heart attacks, and people with high blood pressure should take drugs to reduce it. And what often sound like the most boring, prosaic recommendations—to wear seat belts when riding in an automobile, to wear a helmet when riding a bicycle or Rollerblading and to refrain from smoking cigarettes—are among the best-documented, most effective health advice for the greatest number of people.

The confusion comes in, said Dr. Walter C. Willett, a professor of epidemiology and nutrition at the Harvard School of Public Health, because often little distinction is made in public health advice between firmly grounded facts and wishful thinking. As a result, when studies come out contradicting conventional wisdom, many people throw up their hands, concluding that they cannot believe anything scientists say.

For example, Dr. Willett said, the recommendation to eat a 30-percent-fat diet to protect against heart disease is not based on facts. Research has not proved that there is an ideal amount of fat to be aimed for in the diet. This was apparent even in a pivotal study in the search for dietary advice, the Seven Countries Study, which was published in 1980.

The study correlated heart disease rates with dietary fat in different countries and found that heart disease rates tended to be lower in areas where less saturated fat was eaten. But, Dr. Willett noted, it also found that the lowest heart disease rate was in Crete, where the diet was 40 percent fat. It may depend on what kind of fat is eaten, Dr. Willett said, but much more research needs to be done on that question.

Dr. Willett said cancer prevention was another example "where

we've given a lot of strong advice without good data to back it up."
He said that the link between high-fat diets and cancer was tenuous
at best. Studies within populations have repeatedly failed to find a
relationship between fat intake and cancer incidence. And comparisons of populations in different countries may neglect other factors
contributing to low cancer rates.

For example, Dr. Willett said, in rural China, where the population eats little fat and has a low breast cancer rate, people also have
limited amounts of food in general and the average age of menar-
che is 18. The later the onset of menstruation, the lower the cancer
rate.

On the other hand, Dr. Willett said, there are so many studies indicating that fruits and vegetables are beneficial in protecting
against cancer that "some of them are going to hold up."

Yet, said Dr. Louria, even with the fruit-and-vegetable connection, many experts go too far, hypothesizing that they know what
the ingredient is that protects against cancer.

"What everyone is doing now is saying that in essence we know
what it is—vitamin E or carotene or vitamin C," Dr. Louria said.
But, he added: "In point of fact we have no idea whether that's true.
It might be other carotenoids or flavonoids or some other substance."

Some public health experts said it might be better simply to tell
the public where the uncertainties were, to emphasize the limits of
studies that compare populations or that lack control groups and to
say that if a hypothesis is unproven, then people will have to weigh
the evidence themselves and decide what they want to do.

But that approach can backfire, as the National Cancer Institute
learned in 1994, when it decided to withdraw its advice that women
in their 40s have mammograms, telling them instead that they
should look at the data and decide for themselves. The institute
concluded that there was no evidence that women under 50 bene-
fited from mammograms, but that younger women might choose,
as individuals, to have the breast cancer screening test anyway.

That decision set off a firestorm of criticism from those who
wanted the institute to take a firm stand. Some said the institute
should have flatly told younger women not to have mammograms.
Others, equally adamant, wanted the institute to stand by its previous recommendation that younger women have the tests.

The mammogram debacle "shows what risks you take trying to be honest," said Dr. Barnett Kramer, associate director of the Community Oncology and Early Detection Program at the cancer institute. But he said he believed the institute had done the right thing. "It gets down to levels of evidence," he said. "It gets down to where you're willing to draw the line."

Dr. Fletcher, who headed a panel that evaluated the mammogram evidence for the cancer institute, agreed that there was a danger in going against the tide and declining to give guidelines when the evidence was not there. But, she said: "I don't see any way around that. I think we have to keep working to educate the public and tell them what we know and what we don't know."

The message Dr. Fletcher would like to see is that science is incremental. "People want to know about scientific advances, and I think we should tell them," she said. "But we should communicate the level of our certainty." The problem now, Dr. Fletcher said, is that "we tend to communicate more certainty than we have.

"And that's when people become cynical," she said.

[GK, May 1995]

Defying Advice, Americans Get Fatter

AMERICAN adults may be more aware of the need to exercise and count calories than they once were, but more of them than ever are overweight.

The number of overweight adults, which had remained stable at about a fourth of the adult population from 1960 through 1980, suddenly jumped to a third of all adults between 1980 and 1991 and to one-half by 1996, according to a recent study by the National Center for Health Statistics in the Centers for Disease Control and Prevention.

For purposes of the study, obesity was defined as being 20 percent or more above a person's desirable weight. That is about 25 pounds for an average 5-foot-4-inch woman and 30 pounds for an average 5-foot-10-inch man.

The increase in obesity rates continues despite a growing awareness that it has a negative effect on health and despite the continued growth of the diet industry, now estimated to have revenues of $40 billion to $50 billion a year.

Although the study confirms what experts have said they suspect, it is the first time the growth of the problem in the 1980s has been measured. The data on American weight patterns have been collected in several government surveys that began in 1960. The studies are designed to determine the relationship between diet and health and help the government run its food assistance programs.

The latest study found that the groups with the highest proportion of overweight people were black non-Hispanic women, at 49.5 percent, and Mexican-American women, at 47.9 percent. Those levels represent increases of 12.2 percent and 15.7 percent, respectively, compared with the 1980 rates. Although the percentage of white non-Hispanic women who were overweight was lower, 32.4 percent, obesity in that group increased at a much higher rate, 35.6 percent, from 1980 to 1991.

The study offers additional support to health and nutrition professionals, who argue that a national campaign to reduce obesity is essential to contain health care costs.

Dr. Philip R. Lee, assistant secretary of health in the Department of Health and Human Services, said: "The government is not doing enough. It is not focused. We don't have a coherent across-the-board policy. We are in the process of developing one."

"The problem with obesity is that once you have it, it is very difficult to treat. What you want to do is prevent it," added Dr. F. Xavier Pi-Sunyer, a professor of medicine at Columbia University. Despite the relationship between obesity and chronic diseases of the heart and other organs, obesity is usually defined not as a disease, but as a condition that will yield to good old-fashioned willpower.

Neither the federal government, the insurance industry nor the medical profession devotes many resources to preventing obesity. But the food industry spends $36 billion a year on advertising designed to entice people to eat, the Agriculture Department says.

Federal expenditures for nutrition education are minuscule. For example, the government allots states $50,000 each for nutrition education in schools. The annual advertising budget for Kellogg's Frosted Flakes is twice the budget for the National Cancer Institute's entire "5 a Day" program, which promotes the consumption of fruits and vegetables.

Obesity cost the nation an estimated $68.8 billion in 1990, according to a study by Dr. Graham A. Colditz, an associate professor of medicine at Harvard Medical School. His study, which appeared in 1994 in *PharmacoEconomics,* an international journal devoted to evaluations of drug economics and quality, drew its estimates from the costs of medical problems that have been linked to obesity, including cancer, cardiovascular disease, adult-onset diabetes and gallbladder disease.

Few insurance companies or health maintenance organizations will reimburse the cost of medical or nutritional counseling to help patients lose weight. The health care bills being considered by Congress either do not include preventive-nutrition programs and reimbursement for nutrition counseling or make those services optional.

"There is no commitment to obesity as a public health problem," said Dr. William Dietz, director of clinical nutrition at the New England Medical Center in Boston. "We've ignored it and blamed it on gluttony and sloth." Experts agree that the root causes of obesity in this country—a sedentary lifestyle and an abundance of food—are very difficult to change. "It's what I call the 3,700-calorie-a-day problem," said Dr. Marion Nestle, chairwoman of the Department of Nutrition at New York University and managing editor of the 1988 *Surgeon General's Report on Nutrition and Health.*

The Department of Agriculture reports that the American food supply produces 3,700 calories a day for every man, woman and child in this country. Women need only about half that number of calories, and men need about two-thirds of that. But people are constantly bombarded with advertisements that encourage them to eat far more than they need, Dr. Nestle said. "Advertising budgets for food that no one needs are astronomical. Compared to what is spent on nutrition education, it's laughable."

Health experts say the level of physical activity among Americans has decreased because people watch television and ride in automobiles instead of walking and because of the disappearance of physical education classes from school programs.

"TV-watching figures are shocking," said Michael Jacobson, executive director of the Center for Science in the Public Interest, a nutrition advocacy group in Washington, D.C. "Adults watch between four and five hours a day; children watch three to four hours a day. Only 36 percent of elementary and secondary schools offer physical education classes."

Dr. Dietz said television's contribution to obesity was compounded because watching television is often accompanied by eating food, especially snacks that are high in calories and fat. "Just turn off the television, and almost anything you do will be less sedentary," Dr. Dietz said. "And if you turn off the television, you are less likely to consume food."

In the last few years, there has been a tendency to say that since diets do not work, people should give up dieting and should be allowed to attain their biologically natural weight. This attitude frustrates researchers in the field.

"We have got to stop saying that diets don't work, that obesity doesn't matter," said Dr. George Blackburn, an associate professor at Harvard and director of the school's Center for the Study of Nutritional Medicine at Deaconess Hospital in Boston.

"There is an antidieting movement out there," said Dr. Pi-Sunyer. "But weight is not like body temperature; it keeps climbing. And there are so many mixed messages out there. People are confused."

The experts agree that it will be difficult to change attitudes. Dr. Jacobson said that states should require schools to provide daily physical education classes and that any health overhaul should include communitywide strategies to promote health. He suggested that the Clinton administration sponsor an annual national "No-TV Week," encouraging children and adults to exercise instead of watching television.

"In order for the Public Health Service to address the problems, they have to do more than just educate," Dr. Nestle said. "They need to look at more structural changes: restrictions on children's television advertising, major campaigns in schools, some of the same incentives that have been used to get people to stop smoking."

[MB, July 1994]

Why Weight Gain Is Health's Loss

EXTRA POUNDS ARE
EXCESS POUNDS

As people mature, their bodies tend to fill out and edge toward stoutness. The lithe figures of youth yield to the portly and matronly. What could be a more natural process? Gaining extra pounds in middle age is even blessed by official tables of desirable weight.

Unfortunately, this indulgence is not supported by new findings on the relationship between health and weight. The official tables were based on surveys that included smokers, who often weigh less as well as having bad health, and the smokers' presence masked the benefits of low weight. When smokers are excluded, as was done in the new studies, the message is clarified: for your individual best shot at longevity, don't gain weight. Heart disease and even cancer are more likely to strike earlier at those who are overweight.

The risk is not enormous. For the relationship between extra weight and disease to show up at all, thousands of people must be enrolled in studies and followed over many years. The results of these large-scale studies have now started to flow in. As the articles in this chapter explain, the developing picture is clearly one that links excess body weight to shorter life span.

The data from the new studies allow statisticians to put numbers on the risk of extra weight. (The numbers are, of course, averages that apply to large groups of people; individuals will vary on either side of the average.)

Thus a large-scale study of nurses suggests that the best weight for a woman to be, throughout her life, is whatever she weighed at age 18. For every 2.2 pounds of weight she gains, the risk of suffering a heart attack rises by 3.1 percent.

Those numbers are not as scary as they may sound. A healthy middle-aged woman has little chance of having a heart attack. So a 3 percent increase in a very small risk is still a very small risk. It's the direction of the numbers, not their absolute size, that people will probably wish to note.

If the message of the new health studies to the tubby is a little censorious, the word to the obese is quite different. New findings from the laboratory are at last starting to pick apart the delicate mechanism by which body weight is controlled. It turns out that the body's fat cells release into the bloodstream a hormone known as "leptin," which by its level in the blood signals the brain to stop gaining fat reserves.

In many people who are obese, the signaling mechanism is defective for genetic reasons. Perhaps because they produce a dud version of leptin or because their brain cells don't respond properly to the leptin signal, their fat-controlling mechanism is fundamentally flawed. Far from being fat because of greed they don't wish to curb, as others often assume, they are fat because of a genetic fiat they can no more control than the color of their eyes.

For people who are obese by an accident of genetics, the new findings hold a double source of hope: that scientists' understanding the leptin system will lead to effective treatment and that society's understanding of their condition will help dissolve the discrimination they often face.

At present scientists have merely gained the threshold of figuring out the body's fat control system. It may well prove a subtle mechanism with many other components besides leptin, and much time and effort may be required to produce fixes for its defects. But when and if that happens, weight control will at last gain a scientific basis.

In Midlife, the Leanest Men Survive

THIN is not just in. For middle-aged men, at least, it is also the route to a longer life, according to a 27-year study of more than 19,000 graduates of Harvard University.

The findings, published in a recent issue of *The Journal of the American Medical Association,* strongly suggest that increases in so-called desirable weights for men, which have been made over the last three decades, are unjustified and are likely to result in higher death rates, especially from heart disease.

In contrast to previous large studies of the relationship between body weight and death rates, the new study showed no increased risk of death among the leanest men. Rather, these men had the lowest death rates, 40 percent lower than those of the heaviest men.

With respect to deaths from heart disease, the relationship to body weight was even stronger. The heaviest men, those 20 percent or more above the desirable weights published in 1983 by the Metropolitan Life Insurance Company, had death rates two and a half times as great as those for the leanest men.

The 1983 table listed "desirable" weights that were significantly higher than those in the 1959 Metropolitan Life table. In 1990, the U.S. Department of Agriculture published yet another table listing even higher weights as desirable. For example, for a man 5 feet 10 inches tall, the 1959 table recommended an upper weight limit of 172 pounds; in 1983, this rose to 179; and in the 1990 table it became 188 pounds. Yet, the new study showed, the lowest death rates for a man of that height were associated with weights under 157 pounds.

According to Dr. I-Min Lee, epidemiologist at the Harvard School of Public Health and Brigham and Women's Hospital in Boston, the previous studies, which formed the basis for the higher weights recommended in recent tables, failed to take into account the effects on life expectancy of cigarette smoking and the possibility that some of the leanest men were thin because they were sick and would soon die.

In the study of the Harvard men, Dr. Lee and her colleagues were able to analyze data separately for men who had never smoked. Smokers as a group tend to be significantly thinner than nonsmokers and former smokers, but they are also more likely to die from many causes, including heart disease and cancer. Furthermore, the researchers excluded the deaths that occurred during the first five years of follow-up to reduce a possible bias that some men were thin because they were dying. When both these potential biases were accounted for, Dr. Lee said in a recent interview, the thinnest men had the lowest death rates.

"We found a direct relationship between weight and mortality, with the heavier men at all ages being more likely to die," she explained. "So I believe the upward trend in desirable weights is not justified."

Dr. Lee said further, "Men who are overweight and lose some weight will lower their risk somewhat, but to be at the lowest risk, they really have to be quite thin."

She added that she could not predict which was worse for mortality, staying overweight or repeatedly losing or gaining weight, since an earlier study she did showed that weight cycling, or yo-yo dieting, was itself a hazard to health and life.

"The best thing is to lose the excess weight and keep it off, which is obviously easier said than done," she remarked. But she cautioned smokers against using the excuse of a potential weight gain to justify continuing to smoke. She said: "Cigarette smoking is a much greater risk. Any weight you may gain with quitting doesn't put you at the same risk as if you continued smoking."

[JEB, December 1993]

Aging, Not Pregnancy,
Piles the Pounds On

CONVENTIONAL wisdom says that women gain weight with every baby they have and that their postpregnancy weight stubbornly remains, a silent reminder of the price they paid for having children.

But a new study has found that pregnancy's effects are fairly modest and that most women gain large amounts of weight simply with the passage of years.

The study, by Dr. Delia E. Smith and colleagues at the School of Medicine of the University of Alabama at Birmingham, followed 2,788 women aged 18 to 30 for five years, recording how their weights changed, whether their waists grew larger in proportion to their hips and whether they had any pregnancies. The study was published in a recent issue of *The Journal of the American Medical Association*. The research is part of a larger study that now has seven years of data on men and women.

The researchers say the seven-year study of men, who were 18 to 30 when the research began, show that men also get much heavier as they age.

"It was surprising in the sense that it appears to be a well-established belief that what contributes to women's overweight during young adulthood is pregnancy," Dr. Smith said. With the new findings, she said, it is clear that pregnancy is only part of the explanation.

In the five-year study of women, pregnancy resulted in a seven-pound excess weight gain on average for black women and an extra four pounds for white women, but aging alone was responsible for an even larger weight gain. Black women in the study who had no pregnancies gained an average of 12.79 pounds and those who had a baby gained 19.40 pounds, Dr. Smith reported. White women who had no pregnancies gained an average of 5.95 pounds, and those who had pregnancies gained 9.92 pounds. Only the first pregnancy made a difference to the women's excess weight gains.

Both white and black women who had babies ended up with larger waists in proportion to their hips—what is usually referred to as an apple, as opposed to pear, shape. That shape is associated with a greater risk of heart disease and diabetes. But, Dr. Smith said, it was not clear whether the women's weight was redistributed or their abdominal muscle tone was poorer.

Dr. Smith said she and her colleagues searched for reasons the women who had babies got heavier. She said that she accounted for differences in exercise and even looked at whether the women who got pregnant stopped smoking, reasoning that a halt in smoking, rather than pregnancy, might have made them gain weight. But no other reason was found to account for the extra weight on the women who had had babies.

Dr. Smith also could not explain why only the first baby made women heavier. "One possibility is that it's a threshold effect," she said. The pregnancy effect, whatever causes it, might be like a switch that is thrown on once, with the first pregnancy, and then remains in that position afterward.

In the seven-year study of men and women, Dr. Smith and her colleagues found that black men gained more weight than white men but that men had just as much of a problem with growing heavier as women had. Black men gained an average of 17.6 pounds over seven years and white men gained 13 pounds, Dr. Smith said.

Dr. Adam Drewnowski, who directs the human nutrition program at the University of Michigan, said that metabolism did slow down every year, so if a person kept eating the same amount of food, pounds would accumulate. For example, he said, one national study showed that young girls just before puberty can eat from 1,800 to 2,000 calories a day, but by the time they reach 65, they can consume only 1,200 calories a day to maintain their weight.

But, Dr. Drewnowski said, the amount of weight gained by the participants in Dr. Smith's study was remarkable, and the fact that pregnancy contributed only slightly to the overall weight gain helped demolish the long-standing conviction that pregnancy made women grow heavy and stay that way.

Dr. Drewnowski said the greatest strength of the study was that it followed women for years rather than asking them to recall their previous weights and the effect that pregnancy had on their weight. In such retrospective studies, he said, people may not accurately remember what they really weighed.

"You look at the past through rose-colored glasses," Dr. Drewnowski said. "You say, 'I was skinny then and look at me now.' " Studies like that may have led to an exaggerated impression of how much weight women permanently add to their bodies after a pregnancy, he said.

But the study also raises questions about why black women started out heavier and gained more weight during the study and more after pregnancy than white women, said Dr. Jules Hirsch, an obesity researcher at Rockefeller University in New York.

"That's one of the $64,000 questions," Dr. Smith said. Researchers have suggested that genetics plays a role, as do diet and exercise patterns and cultural standards of attractiveness. "My best bet is that it's a combination of factors," Dr. Smith said.

[GK, June 1994]

Putting on a Little Weight

Average weight gain in a five-year heart study of several hundred women, 18 to 30 years old at enrollment, adjusted for baseline weight, education, smoking status, physical fitness, baseline physical activity and change in activity.

	No children	First child	More than one child
Black women	12.79 pounds	19.40 pounds	10.80 pounds
White women	5.95 pounds	9.92 pounds	7.28 pounds

Seven-year weight change in men 18 to 30 years old, in a follow-up of the same heart study.		
Black men	17.63 pounds
White men	13.0 pounds

Sources: The Journal of the American Medical Association; Dr. C.E. Lewis and Dr. D.E. Smith/University of Alabama at Birmingham

The Midlife Weight Gain Looks
Less Acceptable

WOMEN who gain 10 to 40 pounds in midlife, an amount considered acceptable and even desirable under current guidelines, have a seriously increased risk of suffering a heart attack, a new study has found.

In a 14-year study of nearly 116,000 women, researchers from the Harvard School of Public Health and Harvard Medical School found that weight gains of even 11 to 18 pounds in adult life resulted in a 25 percent greater chance of suffering or dying of a heart attack compared with that faced by women who gained less than 11 pounds after the age of 18. With each increment of weight, the study showed, the coronary risk rose—to a 60 percent increase for weight gains of 18 to 25 pounds, and to a 200 to 300 percent increase for weight gains above 25 pounds. The findings were published in *The Journal of the American Medical Association.*

Overall, there were 1,292 nonfatal or fatal heart attacks among the 115,818 women in the study. The rate for the leanest women with the lowest risk was 106 heart attacks per 100,000 woman-years. (One woman-year represents the experience of one woman over the course of one year.)

"The current guidelines are very misleading to women," Dr. Walter C. Willett, the study's principal investigator, said in an interview. "We found that excess weight accounted for nearly 40 percent of the heart disease experienced by the women we studied. And two-thirds of that risk was from weight gained after age eighteen. There's no reason to think it's good to gain weight at age thirty-five, as indicated by the guidelines."

He and his coauthors stated, "The guidelines provide false reassurance to the large fraction of the population who are not defined as overweight, but who are at substantially increased risk of coronary heart disease." The lowest risk was found among women whose weights were below, but not excessively below, the range of desirable weights in the current guidelines.

These guidelines, issued in 1990 by the U.S. Departments of Agriculture and Health and Human Services, established 130 to

167 pounds as an acceptable weight range for an adult 35 and older who is 5 feet 6 inches tall. The lower end of the weight range is suggested to apply to women and the higher-end weight to men. Adults from 19 to 34 are advised to weigh considerably less, 118 to 155 pounds.

The current range for women in midlife represents an increase from the 1985 guideline, which suggested that 118 to 150 pounds was an acceptable weight range for a 5-foot-6-inch-tall woman over 25 (for men of this height, the 1985 range was only slightly higher, 121 to 154 pounds). The 1985 guidelines, which were based on the 1959 Metropolitan Life Desirable Weight Table, did not suggest that it was desirable to gain more weight in midlife.

"The current guidelines strongly imply that it's good to gain weight as women get older," Dr. Willett said. "But we found that the lowest risk of developing coronary heart disease was in women who were underweight according to the current guidelines. They were lean and fit at age twenty and they remained so into midlife and beyond."

The same is true for men, said Dr. William Castelli, director of the Framingham Heart Study. That study, which has followed thousands of residents of Framingham, Massachusetts, for more than 40 years, showed that significant weight gain after 25 was "a bad risk factor" for both men and women, Dr. Castelli said.

"In fact," he added, "I think excess weight is the worst coronary risk factor for men and women because it leads to unfavorable changes in blood fats, blood pressure and blood sugar, all of which increase the risk of heart attack." Dr. Willett noted that even at weights "generally not considered to represent overweight" there were bad effects on blood pressure, blood sugar and blood fats.

Dr. JoAnn Manson, codirector of women's health at Brigham and Women's Hospital in Boston and a coauthor of the new study, said, "If anything, weight gain in men is worse than it is for women because men tend to put on weight in the upper body, which is associated with high blood pressure, diabetes, coronary heart disease and stroke." Women more commonly gain weight below the waist, which has less of an effect on coronary risk factors.

The government offices that advise Americans about diet are acutely aware of these matters. William Grigg, news director of the Public Health Service, said that when the fourth edition of "Dietary Guidelines for Americans" is published at the end of this year, "the new weight advice will reflect the concerns of Dr. Willett and others about the advisability of gaining weight with age."

Dr. Castelli said, "It is folly to tell Americans it's okay to weigh more when the people who meet the ideal weights in the old 1959 Metropolitan Life table do the best." This table listed "desirable" weights for men and women by height and frame size based on actuarial data from the insurance company. The weights in the 1959 table are close to those recommended by the Public Health Service in the dietary guidelines published in 1985.

Both Dr. Castelli and Dr. Willett said they believed that the current weight guidelines were improperly developed. They pointed out that the data on which the guidelines were based failed to take into account the fact that there were many smokers among the thinnest people and that smokers have much higher death rates than nonsmokers. The data also failed to consider that many people lose weight when they have a fatal illness, they said, and these people should have been omitted from the study.

"When you control for smoking, you find that thinner people live the longest," Dr. Castelli said. "Skinny smokers have nine times the death rate of skinny nonsmokers. Many smokers are reluctant to quit because they say they'll gain weight, but if they did quit and got fat, they would still cut their death rate in half in the next thirty years."

The findings by Dr. Willett and his colleagues were derived from their continuing Nurses' Health Study, which in 1976 enrolled 121,700 women from 30 to 55 years old who were registered nurses. Of that group, 115,818 had no known coronary disease and were not pregnant at the time, and these are the women from whom the new findings were derived.

The women's weights at the start of the study and the amount of weight they had gained since the age of 18 were directly linked to their chances of suffering a heart attack during the follow-up period. In making this association, the researchers first took into account other factors that were independent of weight but could influence the women's coronary risk: age, smoking habits, menopausal status, the use of postmenopausal hormones and parental history of heart disease.

Dr. Willett said the nutrient composition of the women's diets, notably the percentage of calories from fats, had little effect on their weights. "People may lose weight on a low-fat diet, then gain it back again by eating more carbohydrates," he said. "Overeating is, of course, part of the problem of weight gain, but controlling overeating is almost always doomed in our food-focused society."

The crucial factor in controlling weight gain, Dr. Willett maintains, is exercise, not dieting. "People who exercise regularly can maintain their weight," he said, adding that very few of the nurses in the study had a regular exercise regimen.

"Women aged 20 to 50 are very busy with their families and careers and they don't take optimal care of themselves," he said. "They're not carving out that twenty minutes a day for exercise." He suggested instead that they build activity into their life's routines like "riding a bike to work or pedaling a stationary bike while watching TV" and make modest adjustments in their diets.

He noted that among the nurses studied, 80 percent were lean at 18, so their excess weight in midlife was not predetermined by adolescent obesity. Overall, for every 2.2 pounds of weight the women gained after 18, their risk of suffering a heart attack rose by 3.1 percent. But for the relatively few women who lost weight after 18, there was no increase in coronary risk.

[JEB, February 1995]

Just How Perilous Can 25 Extra Pounds Be?

A recent report linking moderate overweight and modest weight gain to an increased risk of death in midlife threw millions of American women into a tizzy. Even those who have accepted their ample bodies or middle-age spread and who scoff at fashion-model thinness were alarmed to learn that those 25 pounds they had put on since high school or the extra weight they had carried all their lives might kill them.

While there is no debate about the risks to health and life associated with frank obesity, defined as weighing at least 30 percent more than is desirable for one's height and frame, moderately overweight people have long assumed that their main concern was a cosmetic one. Now, it seems, they should be more worried about their health and life expectancy than about how they look.

On the basis of new findings from a 16-year study of 115,000 female nurses and similar findings from a continuing study of 19,000 men who graduated from Harvard, about 300,000 deaths a year in this country can be attributed to overweight. This projection, made by the study's principal author, Dr. JoAnn E. Manson of Brigham and Women's Hospital and Harvard Medical School in Boston, may even be a conservative one, since the women and men being studied are better educated, more affluent and presumably more health-aware than the average American, and are therefore likely to have lower death rates.

Furthermore, most of the women in the nurses' study have yet to reach the age when heart disease, the health problem most powerfully influenced by overweight, emerges as the leading killer. At the time the data were analyzed, the women's ages ranged from 46 to 71 and cancer was their main cause of death. Dr. Manson said she was astonished to discover that nearly one-third of the 2,586 deaths from cancer—especially cancers of the breast, colon and endometrium—could be attributed to overweight.

The new study examined two questions: the risks from gaining weight (22 pounds or more) after the age of 18 and the risks related to being heavier than the leanest women. Among women who had never smoked, those who weighed about 15 percent less than the average American woman of the same height were least likely to die during the study. For example, the average American woman is 5 feet 5 inches tall and weighs 150 to 160 pounds, which the new study suggests is about 30 pounds too many to maximize one's chances of living to a healthy old age. Those who weighed less than 120 had the lowest death rates, but chances of an early death were 20 percent higher among those who weighed 120 to 150 pounds and 30 percent higher among those who weighed 150 to 160 pounds. In other words, even women of average weight and those mildly overweight have higher death rates than the leanest women.

Although previous studies have concluded that the leanest men and women have higher death risks than those slightly heavier, most of these studies did not separate former smokers from people who had never smoked and some did not take into account the possibility that an undiagnosed illness might have accounted for thinness in many of the people who died during the studies.

In the new study, which took account of those factors, at greater weights, the risks of "dying prematurely," or sooner than the leanest women, jumped more dramatically—by 60 percent among those 5 feet 5 inches tall and weighing 161 to 175 pounds; by 110 percent among those weighing 176 to 195 pounds; and by 120 percent among those weighing more than 195 pounds.

Similar risks were found among women who gained weight as adults. Compared with those who gained less than 10 pounds after age 18, those who gained 22 to 40 pounds experienced a 70 percent increase in cardiovascular deaths and a 20 percent increase in cancer deaths. Those gaining more than 40 pounds were seven times as likely to die of heart disease during the study and 50 percent more likely to die of cancer.

What do such numbers mean to the millions of Americans whose college blazers no longer meet in the middle? First, it is helpful to realize that a woman's risk of dying in midlife is not great. Heart disease is not a common occurrence among women under 65, so even a sevenfold increase in cardiac deaths for a woman in her 50s is still a low risk of dying. Of the 4,726 deaths that occurred among the nurses, only 881 were due to cardiovascular disease. Cancer, on the other hand, is the leading killer of middle-aged women—there were 2,586 cancer deaths during the study—so even a relatively small increase in risk can be meaningful. Keep in mind, too, that the study measured deaths, not incidence of disease; far more women are likely to have been afflicted with weight-related illnesses than to have died as a result.

Furthermore, a small increase in the risk of disease and death among the mildly overweight is likely to mean more to society at large than to each individual. A 20 percent increase in premature deaths, and an even greater increase in nonfatal illness, occurring among more than 100 million middle-aged adults adds up to a lot of lost years of productive life and some very big medical bills for society to absorb. But to slightly pudgy individuals, a 20 percent increase in an initially low risk may not seem like much.

First, do not panic. If you have put on a dozen or more pounds since high school but still weigh within a desirable range (less than the equivalent of 150 pounds for a 5-foot-5-inch woman or man), the increase in your risk of premature death is quite small and may not warrant any attention to the actual numbers on the scale as long as you adopt health-promoting living habits and do not smoke. Dr.

Tim Byers, a preventive-medicine specialist at the University of Colorado School of Medicine in Denver, said: "I would worry less about body weight and more about behaviors like food choices and physical activity. If a person is eating a diet low in fat and rich in vegetables, fruits and whole grains, being moderately overweight is less likely to have adverse consequences."

If, however, you are more than moderately overweight, even if you have not gained since age 18, your risk of an early death is substantially increased and attention to actual poundage is warranted. This does not mean going on a crash diet, swallowing formulas or taking pills and potions purported to promote weight loss. Rather,

Healthy Weight Ranges for Both Sexes

Draft guidelines submitted by an advisory committee to the Department of Health and Human Services and the Department of Agriculture; the ranges apply to all ages and no longer allow for a 15-pound gain in middle age.

The higher weight ranges apply to people with more muscle and bone in proportion to body fat.

HEIGHT (without shoes)	WEIGHT (without clothing)	HEIGHT (without shoes)	WEIGHT (without clothing)
4 ft. 10 in.	91–119 lb.	5 ft. 9 in.	129–169 lb.
4 ft. 11 in.	94–124 lb.	5 ft. 10 in.	132–174 lb.
5 ft. 0 in.	97–128 lb.	5 ft. 11 in.	136–179 lb.
5 ft. 1 in.	101–132 lb.	6 ft. 0 in.	140–184 lb.
5 ft. 2 in.	104–137 lb.	6 ft. 1 in.	144–189 lb.
5 ft. 3 in.	107–141 lb.	6 ft. 2 in.	148–195 lb.
5 ft. 4 in.	111–146 lb.	6 ft. 3 in.	152–200 lb.
5 ft. 5 in.	114–150 lb.	6 ft. 4 in.	156–205 lb.
5 ft. 6 in.	118–155 lb.	6 ft. 5 in.	160–211 lb.
5 ft. 7 in.	121–160 lb.	6 ft. 6 in.	164–216 lb.
5 ft. 8 in.	125–164 lb.		

it involves adopting an eating and exercise plan that you can stay on for the rest of your life.

Scores of studies have clearly demonstrated that people are more likely to lose weight and keep it off on a diet that is low in fat, moderate in protein and high in fiber-rich foods like unrefined starches, fruits and vegetables. High-fiber foods are filling and satisfying and are less likely to lead to overeating than when people eat high-fat foods.

Add exercise to the equation and you will burn more calories during workouts and between them as well. Most long-term studies have shown that without regular exercise, few people are able to keep off lost pounds. Furthermore, even if you lose no weight through exercise, increasing your activity level can diminish your risk of developing several leading killer diseases, especially heart disease, hypertension, diabetes and some cancers.

[JEB, September 1995]

The Body Adjusts Its Weight to a Preset Goal

IN a new study that helps explain one of the givens of obesity—that the body has a weight that it naturally gravitates to—researchers have found that all people, fat or thin, adjust their metabolism to maintain that weight.

The body burns calories more slowly than normal after weight is lost and faster than normal when weight is gained, the study found. This means it is harder both to lose and, perhaps surprising to some, to gain weight than to maintain the same level. In the study, researchers found that in volunteers who gained weight, metabolism was speeded up by 10 percent to 15 percent, and in those who lost weight, metabolism was 10 percent to 15 percent slower than normal. The volunteers, both female and male, ranged in age from their 20s to their 40s, but the effect on metabolism was independent of age and sex.

The researchers also found that the way the body adjusts its metabolism is by making muscles more or less efficient in burning calories. Their findings mean that a 140-pound woman, for example, who has lost 15 pounds to achieve that weight will burn about 10 percent to 15 percent fewer calories when she exercises than a woman who maintains that weight effortlessly. Conversely, if a 140-pound woman gains 15 pounds, she will burn about 10 percent to 15 percent more calories when she exercises than a woman who has always weighed 155 pounds.

The study, conducted by researchers at Rockefeller University in an unusually rigorous manner, was published in a recent issue of the *New England Journal of Medicine*. Dr. Jules Hirsch, physician in chief at Rockefeller and the senior author of the study, said the findings showed that obesity, rather than being an eating disorder, is "an eating order." Obese people, he said, eat to maintain the weight that puts their energy metabolism precisely on target for their height and body composition.

One myth the study demolishes is that excessive dieting deranges the metabolism. The study showed equally perturbed metabolisms in those who gained and lost weight, whether they had ever dieted and whether they were fat or lean.

Another myth the study debunks is that obese people have unusually slow metabolisms. The only people in the study who showed sluggish metabolisms were those who were trying to maintain a body weight that was lower than their natural weight.

The researchers suggest that the best way to help dieters in the future might be to understand what makes the muscles more or less efficient with weight gain or loss, rather than focusing on diets and psychological counseling.

"I'd say this is a landmark investigation," said Dr. Albert Stunkard, a psychiatrist and weight-loss expert at the University of Pennsylvania School of Medicine. Calling the work "first rate," he said the group's data were so carefully gathered and the study so thorough that "what they are proposing is almost certainly right."

Dr. William Ira Bennett, a psychiatrist at Cambridge Hospital in Cambridge, Massachusetts, who wrote an editorial accompanying the paper, praised the work, saying "what it shows is very, very interesting" particularly because it was done on humans, not laboratory animals, on which so much of the work on obesity and metabolism has been done.

Weight control is an obsession for many Americans and a big

business in this country, but Dr. Rudolph L. Leibel, an author of the study, said what was surprising was how little weight people actually gain. Data from the Framingham Heart Study, an ongoing study of more than 10,000 people in Massachusetts, showed that adults increased their weight, on average, by just 10 percent over 20 years.

For a man to gain 20 pounds over 30 years, he would have had to consume about 60,000 calories more than he needed, Dr. Leibel said. But, he pointed out, those extra 60,000 calories are a minuscule fraction of the 300 million the man had to consume just to maintain his weight. "It's frightening how fine that control is," Dr. Leibel said.

Most people find it easier to gain weight than to lose it. Although it is easy to eat just an extra 200 or so calories a day, resulting in added pounds, it is much harder to subtract 200 or so calories. "It's painful; it hurts to be in negative energy balance," Dr. Leibel said.

Dr. Leibel said he and his colleagues, Dr. Hirsch and Dr. Michael Rosenbaum, began their study because they wanted to understand why it was that the hardest part of dieting was keeping the weight off.

The group recruited 18 people who were obese and 23 who had never been overweight. They were required to live at the clinical center at Rockefeller while their diet and activities were carefully controlled.

For the first four to six weeks, the volunteers ate only a liquid diet that kept their weights absolutely stable. The researchers knew each subject's energy intake and knew that their body weight was not changing, which meant that the subjects were expending the same amount of calories they were taking in.

Then the volunteers purposely gained weight by eating 5,000 to 6,000 additional calories a day until they were 10 percent above their normal weights. Gaining weight was difficult for everyone.

"Some people might imagine that obese people, given free rein to eat as much as they want, would have a field day," Dr. Leibel said. "But that was absolutely not the case. If anything, the obese subjects had a harder time gaining the extra ten percent and were more uncomfortable with it."

After the subjects had added 10 percent to their body weight, they were fed liquid formula for four to six weeks with enough calories to keep their weight stable. The researchers repeated the metabolic studies and found increased metabolism.

Then the volunteers lost weight, by consuming 800 calories a day. When they were 10 percent below their normal weights, the researchers maintained them there for four to six weeks with a liquid formula and repeated the metabolic studies, which this time showed a decreased metabolic rate.

The normal-weight volunteers, who were mostly students, received $40 a day for participating, Dr. Leibel said. The obese volunteers were not paid but were promised that at the end of the study, the researchers would keep them on a special diet at the clinical center until they no longer were fat. Some spent a year there after the end of the study, Dr. Leibel said. Most reduced to within 20 percent to 30 percent of the recommended weight for their height and build, and some got down to that weight, but none was able to maintain the weight loss. Inexorably, their weight crept up again.

"This tells you why the recidivism rate with obesity is so enormous," Dr. Leibel said. "Even at a weight loss of 10 percent, the body starts to compensate."

The investigators also studied what the body does to change its metabolism. They found that about 65 percent to 70 percent of calories burned each day are used to keep up the routine body functions—the pumping heart, the working kidneys, the metabolizing liver. About 10 percent to 15 percent are spent eating and assimilating food. And the rest, about 15 percent to 25 percent, are spent by the muscles' exercising.

Now, Dr. Leibel said, "we need to figure out what the heck is going on in muscle." One possibility is that the muscle fibers themselves may change their composition slightly. The red muscles, which are used for long-distance walking or running, for example, use fewer calories to do their work. The white muscles, used for sudden bursts of energy in activities like lifting weights or sprinting, burn more calories. When a person's weight is 10 percent or more above his or her natural weight, Dr. Leibel speculated, that person "may shift from predominantly red to predominantly white fibers, or have enzymes that do that."

But, Dr. Bennett said, the answer for dieters is not in the immediate offing. "Over and over again, people have been told there's an answer, and it's a terrible betrayal to have people think we are close," he said.

For now, Dr. Bennett added, "the key thing is to use the muscles." He added: "I'm speaking from personal experience. I bought a car five years ago and gained 30 pounds."

[GK, March 1995]

A Fat-Signaling Hormone Helps Set Weight

SCIENTISTS call it the set point: that vexing and seemingly immutable weight that even the most assiduous dieters keep drifting back to. But the actual mechanism of the body's set point, or fat-setting thermostat, has long been elusive.

The recent discovery of a fat-signaling hormone has given new insight into the body's system of fat control and suggested promising new practical approaches to the treatment of obesity. It may help solve the puzzles of how the body knows how much fat it has and why a person's weight seems always to be forced back to the set point.

The research, published in three papers in a recent issue of the journal *Science,* indicates that the fat cells of mice secrete a hormone into the bloodstream and that by monitoring the amount of this hormone the brain can estimate how much body fat is present.

The scientists found that the mice strive to maintain a constant level of the hormone, called leptin, and do so by maintaining the appropriate amount of body fat. Injected with supplements of leptin, the mice would shed fat. Humans are thought to have the same biological mechanism, since they make a hormone almost identical to leptin.

"The idea here is that there is something akin to a thermostat that regulates body fat," said Dr. Jeffrey Friedman, a molecular geneticist at the Howard Hughes Medical Institute at Rockefeller University in New York and a discoverer of leptin. A set point, like the temperature setting on a thermostat, would be the body fat level that the brain maintains to keep leptin concentrations optimal.

The idea of leptin as a signaler of body fat can help explain why some people are naturally fatter than others. For example, some people may have fat cells that are genetically disposed to make meager amounts of leptin. Their bodies would need to create more fat cells in order to contribute the right amount of leptin to the bloodstream. Others may be genetically predisposed to respond weakly to the hormone, perhaps because the receptor molecules on their brain cells, where leptin exerts its signals, only feebly bind the hormone. These people too would need more fat cells for the brain to feel it had received the right signal for its fat-thermostat setting.

The notion of a leptin as a body fat regulator may also lead to an understanding of how body weight is inherited. Identical twins reared apart turn out to weigh almost exactly the same. Children who were adopted resemble their biological parents in terms of body weight, rather than their adoptive ones. What may be inherited is an ability of fat cells to make leptin at a particular rate or an ability of the brain to respond to the hormone.

The effects of leptin on metabolism and food intake may also explain the finding that body weight is maintained not just by the regulation of appetite but also by adjustments in metabolic rates. Mice that have too much leptin greatly increase their metabolic rates and decrease their food intake until they lose enough fat to bring their leptin levels into line. The hormone is thought to act on the hypothalamus, the part of the brain that controls appetite and metabolism.

People also adjust their metabolic rates and food intake when their body fat is greatly altered. The extreme example of what may turn out to be a severe leptin deficiency comes from studies of people who weigh at least double what they should who participated in research requiring them to live on a hospital ward for a year or more while their food intake was carefully controlled. Their weights plummeted to what was considered ideal for their heights, but their bodies became deranged. Their metabolisms were sluggish and they were always cold. They were obsessed with thoughts of food. The women stopped menstruating. Although they looked normal, they behaved as though they were starving.

The idea that there might be a signaling hormone like leptin first came from studies conducted more than three decades ago. Dr. Douglas Coleman of Jackson Laboratories in Bar Harbor, Maine, hooked up genetically fat mice to normal, lean mice so that both could share a blood supply.

One strain of fat mice seemed not to make enough of the signaling substance. When one of these mice was attached to a thin mouse, it acquired the thin mouse's signaling hormones and lost weight.

Another strain of fat mice seemed unable to respond to its fat cells' signal. The animals were grotesquely obese because their brains, starved for the signaling hormone, were directing their bodies to make more and more fat. When Dr. Coleman hooked one of these mice to a thin mouse, the thin mouse was overwhelmed by the fat-signaling hormone in the fat mouse's blood. In response, the thin mouse stopped eating and literally starved to death.

These findings suggested that a factor in the animals' blood was controlling body weight. But no one could isolate the mysterious factor. The reason, as is now known, is that leptin is produced in vanishingly small quantities.

Dr. Friedman, Dr. Stephen Burley and their colleagues at the Howard Hughes Medical Institute used the tools of molecular genetics to find the gene that codes for the fat-signaling substance.

As soon as the obesity gene was found, this group as well as researchers at Amgen, Inc., a biotechnology company in Thousand Oaks, California, and at Hoffmann–La Roche, Inc., a pharmaceutical company in Nutley, New Jersey, created copious quantities of the rare protein in genetically engineered bacteria. That enabled them to conduct the recently published experiments showing just how powerfully leptin controls body weight.

Some of the most persuasive evidence that animals attempt to maintain a constant level of leptin in their blood comes from an experiment in which the investigators asked what would happen if a lean mouse was given as much leptin in supplement form as its own fat cells normally make. Dr. Friedman and his colleagues first calculated that a normal mouse has 12.5 micrograms of leptin per gram of body weight. Then they injected mice with that amount of leptin. The researchers reasoned that the only way the animals could get back down to 12.5 micrograms of leptin per gram of body weight would be to shed all of their fat. And that is exactly what they did. Within four days, the mice went from their normal 12.2 percent body fat to 0.67 percent body fat, and they maintained that level for the two weeks that they were being injected with leptin.

Dr. Richard Atkinson, an obesity researcher at the University of Wisconsin in Madison, said that it was astonishing that the animals lost so much fat. "When you are talking about 0.67 percent body fat, that means that the animals have no adipose tissue," he said. He explained that about 1 percent of body fat is bound up in cell membranes and therefore, when the mice got down to 0.67 percent fat, "that means they completely got rid of their body fat." The implication is that leptin injections act like a sort of "virtual fat," as Dr. Friedman put it. By giving a particular amount of leptin, researchers are tricking an animal's body into thinking it has just added an equivalent amount of fat. The animal responds by losing its own fat until its blood leptin levels are back to where they started.

If humans respond in a similar way to leptin injections, it might be possible for doctors to calculate how much leptin an obese person would need to maintain a more healthful amount of body fat and treat the person indefinitely with that amount of leptin. It would be akin to the treatment for diabetes, with daily injections of a hormone.

Despite the elegance of the leptin hypothesis, researchers caution that environment also plays a role in human obesity. An obesity hormone that controls fat levels "does not account in my mind for the remarkable increase in obesity that has occurred even in this decade," said Dr. Theodore van Itallie, an obesity researcher at Columbia University's College of Physicians and Surgeons in New York. Nor, he said, "does it account for the fact that people moving from one country to another will change their weights."

Dr. Claude Bouchard, an obesity researcher at Laval University in Quebec, noted that "obesity has doubled in this century and gene frequencies have not changed significantly." The implication is that many people are susceptible to becoming obese when they are living in a conducive environment, perhaps one where high-calorie foods are abundant and it is easy to avoid exercise.

Researchers suspect that leptin might still provide the clue. For example, Dr. Friedman said, it is possible that fat cells adjust their leptin production in response to different dietary compositions. Fat cells might also make less leptin as people grow older, inducing individuals to gain weight as they age.

Fat cells might make more leptin in response to exercise, Dr. Atkinson said, which may explain why people who exercise regularly and vigorously may maintain lower body weights. If fat cells do become more or less efficient in secreting leptin in different circumstances, researchers might be able to advise people how best to lower their set points, helping them to lose weight and keep it off by forcing their bodies to produce more leptin naturally. Leptin injections would be a last resort for the morbidly obese.

The leptin discovery, Dr. van Itallie said, "could be an absolutely extraordinary advance in understanding why some people are vulnerable to obesity."

He added, "Obviously, the therapeutic implications are enormous."

[GK, August 1995]

Women Pay a Price
for Being Obese

WOMEN who are fat suffer enormous social and economic consequences, a new study has shown. They are much less likely to marry than women of normal weight and are more likely to be poor and to earn far less.

Fat men are also less likely to marry than men of normal weight, but they seem just as well off financially, the researchers found.

The findings are from an eight-year study of 10,039 randomly selected people who were 16 to 24 years old when the research began. It is the first study to document the profound social and economic consequences of obesity by following a population for years.

The researchers, led by Dr. Steven L. Gortmaker of the Harvard School of Public Health, said discrimination against obese people might account for their results.

Fat women were disproportionately found in lower socioeconomic classes, and some researchers say this is because poor women are more likely to eat fat-laden food and junk foods and to get less exercise than richer women. But, Dr. Gortmaker and his colleagues wrote, "our data suggest that at least some of this relation may be a socioeconomic consequence of being overweight."

The study, published in a recent issue of the *New England Journal of Medicine*, defined obesity as the top 5 percent of people on an index in which weight is related to height. A typical obese woman in the study was 5 feet 3 inches tall and weighed 200 pounds; a typical man was 5 feet 9 inches tall and weighed 225 pounds.

The study found that fat women were more likely to lose socioeconomic status independently of their families' social status or income and independently of how well the women scored on achievement tests when they were adolescents. The fat women were 20 percent less likely to marry, had household incomes that were an average of $6,710 lower and were 10 percent more likely to be living in poverty.

The effects of obesity on men were more modest. The most significant finding was that obese men were 11 percent less likely to marry. But comparisons among all men in the study at various heights with those a foot shorter found that the shorter men were 10 percent more likely to live in poverty and had household incomes that averaged $3,037 less. Previous studies have found that taller men seem to have an advantage in the business world.

Some investigators said they hoped that the findings would wake up the medical community and society to abiding prejudices that can sour the lives of fat people. The results should be "a clarion call," said Dr. Albert J. Stunkard, an obesity researcher at the University of Pennsylvania who was the coauthor of an editorial on the findings in the same issue of the journal. Discrimination against fat people, Dr. Stunkard said, "is the last fashionable form of prejudice." He and others said fat people were too often derided as gluttonous slobs who could be thin if they really wanted to. This attitude, Dr. Stunkard said, is used to justify rampant discrimination. But it is particularly unfair, he noted, because study after study has shown that virtually all obese people cannot permanently reduce and that their weight is not their fault. "Blaming the victim," he said. "That's what it is." The researchers said discrimination against fat people was so profound that Congress should consider extending legal protection to them.

Some fat people said the findings reflected their everyday experiences. Frances White, the president of the National Association for the Advancement of Fat Acceptance, said that employers were often prejudiced against fat women, like herself, but that they were seldom direct.

"Most of us find that this sort of discrimination is very covert," she said. "It's much like racial discrimination. Nobody wants to own up to it."

Ms. White, who lives in San Francisco, recently got a job as a membership coordinator at a local Public Broadcasting System. For two and a half years before that, she worked at temporary jobs, looking for something more permanent.

"I have a wonderful résumé and years of experience," Ms. White said. "I can write a résumé tailored to each job that is absolutely perfect." She said prospective employers often would be enthusiastic about her application until they saw her.

She said employers would call her and say: "You're exactly what we want. When can you come in?" But, she said, things often changed when she walked into an office for an interview.

"All of a sudden, they would get this look on their face," she said. " 'Oh, you're Frances White.' Then they'd give me a cursory interview and say, 'We're thinking of going with a more entry-level person' or 'We're rethinking our staffing needs.' "

Dr. Susan C. Wooley, an obesity researcher and codirector of an eating disorders clinic at the University of Cincinnati, said that she hoped that the new study would alert people to the plight of obese women but that she feared it would not. The problem, she said, is that many people believe that the women could be thin if they really wanted to.

Dr. Wooley said she feared that people would conclude that the new data showed "how important it is to treat obesity." But she said: "They still won't get it. You can't solve social problems by trying to alter victims."

[GK, September 1993]

Learning to Like Yourself Even If You Can't Lose Weight

GIVEN the difficulty of losing weight, psychotherapists have come up with a treatment aimed at easing the psychological suffering that comes with being overweight.

The therapy is not meant to discourage people from trying to lose weight, nor to deny the very real increased health risks that added pounds bring. Instead it seeks to ease emotional suffering. But, the results show, once overweight people get over the acute self-consciousness that keeps them, say, from exercising in public, they are often better able to keep to their fitness regime.

"About 95 percent of people who lose weight in university-based clinical weight-loss programs have gained it back five years later," said Dr. Kelly Brownell, director of the Yale Center for Eating and Weight Disorders. "There's a collision between biology and culture. For some people there are biological barriers to losing weight at all, while others aspire to unrealistically lean ideals."

While other studies have come up with somewhat more optimistic estimates of the numbers of people who keep lost pounds off—as high as 25 percent—the odds against lasting weight loss are daunting. "The genetic research suggests that some people just have to live with being overweight," Dr. Brownell said.

"Of course this does not mean you should stop encouraging people to lose weight," Dr. Brownell added. Pointing to the public health problems, like heart disease and diabetes, that plague overweight people, "having obese people simply accept their weight is like telling smokers to keep smoking," Dr. Brownell said. "But what's needed are ways to tell more precisely who can and cannot lose weight, and help those who cannot to accept themselves as they are."

The approach has gained indirect support from a report this month in the *New England Journal of Medicine* that described the metabolic adjustments that make substantial and lasting weight loss a losing battle for so many people.

"Obese people are stigmatized and discriminated against," said Dr. Thomas Cash, a psychologist at Old Dominion University in Norfolk, Virginia. "We help them with the emotional costs of these prejudices." His book describing the program, *What Do You See When You Look in the Mirror?*, was published in January by Bantam Books. "We say, do the healthy things—and one of those is to learn to accept your body in a world that does not," Dr. Cash said.

For the chronically overweight, embarrassment, self-recrimination and obsession with their appearance are "an element of suffering in their lives that they can be freed from, whether or not they lose weight," said Dr. James C. Rosen, a psychologist at the University of Vermont, who reported results from the new therapy program in the March issue of the journal *Behavior Therapy*.

People who are extremely overweight can experience such acute embarrassment that they avoid socializing, or they spend hours preoccupied with arranging their clothes in the mirror or weighing themselves, Dr. Rosen said.

The 51 women in the treatment program were, on average, 52

percent over their ideal weight. The least overweight was about 25 pounds over her ideal weight, and one woman weighed more than 400 pounds. The program had no effect on their weight, nor was the purpose of the therapy to help them shed pounds. Instead, it focused on freeing them from self-reproach, endless rumination about their appearance and their reluctance to appear in public.

A woman who had put on 30 pounds, for example, had not gone to a family gathering in the next two years for fear of what her family would say. And another never undressed in front of her husband and would not let him touch her stomach, creating difficulties in their sex life. The therapy, by changing the women's attitudes toward their appearance, solved these problems.

There was also an indirect effect on the women's fitness: many of the women who had refrained from exercising—especially in public—now felt free to do so. "One woman, who was about 30 pounds overweight, was otherwise quite attractive and elegant," Dr. Rosen said. "She and her husband would vacation in the Caribbean every winter, but she would never put on a bathing suit or go near the water. After being in the program, she was at ease going to the beach and swimming."

The treatment, conducted in groups of four or five, began with the women's reviewing the crucial experiences—like being teased, criticized or rejected for being overweight—that led to their negative feelings about their bodies. For one woman, for example, it was the time in high school gym class when she could not do pull-ups and the other girls taunted her, calling her "Fatso."

Part of the program focused on helping the women counter their own thoughts of self-depreciation and judgment—for example, "that because I'm fat, people at work also think I'm dumb," Dr. Rosen said.

The women were also encouraged to spend time alone studying themselves in the mirror from head to toe, "moving from the easier to the more offending locations, calmly and objectively, without bad-mouthing their body," Dr. Rosen said.

The exercise, done in private, was a prelude to the women's becoming more revealing of their bodies in public. In later stages of treatment, the women purposely took risks in exposing themselves. One woman preoccupied by the fatness around her neck, for example, started to wear her long hair pulled up rather than covering her neck. Then she wore a necklace to draw more attention to her neck.

"Finally she was able to wear low-cut blouses with her hair up, and bright attention-getting jewelry around her neck," Dr. Rosen said, signifying that she had got over her fears and inhibitions about being judged.

"Most overweight people put too much emphasis on their looks, and so ignore other good qualities in themselves," said Dr. Janet Polidy, a psychologist at the University of Toronto. "The preoccupation with weight leads to unrealistic views of yourself. You end up feeling bad if your scale says your weight is up a bit this morning. You shouldn't be judging yourself by how much you weigh every day—that's not a way to lead your life."

[DG, March 1995]

The Many Benefits of Exercise

THE FOUNTAIN OF YOUTH: CAN IT BE JUST PERSPIRATION?

"Why are you putting on your running shoes?" says one man to his companion when they are surprised by a tiger. "You can't possibly outrun it." "No, but I can outrun you" is his friend's cold reply.

Early humans probably led lives of strenuous exertion, whether in escaping from saber-toothed tigers, as hunters and gatherers or as hardscrabble farmers of the first primitive crops. Our bodies are designed by evolution to have the capacity for hard labor. They are not designed for the fat-laden, perspiration-free lifestyles led by 60 percent of Americans.

It's a plausible hypothesis that exercise is good for the body. But establishing how much benefit can be expected from how much exercise is a subtle matter and still far from resolved. As with the relationship between health and weight, it requires expensive long-term studies with many participants to develop a clear picture of how exercise affects health and longevity.

Readers of the following articles will find the facts on which to make their own decisions about the value of exercise and about how much is enough. They will not find a pat prescription, because none can truthfully be given at present. A debate is under way as to how much exercise is needed to achieve any health benefit.

Before this debate, the standard advice was to take at least 20 minutes of vigorous, aerobic exercise three times a week. The advice was based largely on a study of a large group of Harvard men that showed that those who reported exercising most vigorously also tended to live the longest.

This advice still seems good; the new issue is whether moderate exercise can achieve many of the same benefits or whether only vigorous exercise will work. Those in the business of giving public advice are keenly interested in the answer because most of the American population find vigorous exercise to be something they somehow just cannot fit into their regular timetable. If working up a sweat is really so unpleasant, would moderate exercise do nearly as well? Does the prescription of only vigorous exercise (for which alone there is a proven basis) perhaps discourage people from moderate exercise, which might well carry many of the same benefits?

As the following articles make evident, the study of physical fitness is a science with many pitfalls, even for experts. In February 1995 the federal Centers for Disease Control and Prevention, abetted by the American College of Sports Medicine, took the plunge and recommended moderate exercise as being good enough to attain better health. No need to get the heart pounding, said the government's committee of experts. Just 30 minutes a day of walking or climbing stairs or yard work will yield major health benefits.

But just a month later another large study of Harvard graduates was published, and it seemed to flatly contradict this soothing message. The participants who reported taking moderate exercise lived no longer than the slouches who took none at all; only those who took vigorous exercise had pushed the envelope of longevity, the new study concluded.

There is a difference, of course, between good health and life span. Even though people who enjoy good health would also be expected to live longer, it could be that moderate exercise improves health, as many studies suggest, but without extending life span, or by doing so to such a small extent that the Harvard study did not pick it up. Or the Harvard study could just be wrong. Or the government experts could be wrong. Science doesn't yet have clear answers.

Meanwhile, there are many indications, even if not yet hard proof, that moderate exercise enhances the body's functions and the mind's sense of well-being. Any amount of exercise is almost certainly better than none.

Exercise: Some Pleasant
Side Effects

THE effects of exercise on resistance to illness, from the common cold to cancer, have long been surrounded by controversy and conflicting evidence. While few would dispute the value of fitness in warding off heart disease and osteoporosis, when it comes to the immune system the facts are not nearly so clear. Nonetheless, millions of people believe that regular exercise keeps them healthier.

Many avid exercisers insist that their fitness routine helps them ward off colds and recover more quickly from the minor illnesses they do get. Unless they are too sick to move, they tend to keep running, cycling, swimming or whatever when others with similar symptoms would lie low.

Since 1985, the American Cancer Society has recommended regular exercise as part of its 10-step program to prevent cancer. Although the evidence supporting this advice is far less established than, say, that for stopping smoking, the society concluded that exercise cannot hurt and preliminary evidence suggests that it may help to ward off certain common cancers.

Meanwhile, these are some findings worth considering:

• Regular moderate exercise appears to help ward off minor infectious ailments, but exhausting exercising impairs the immune response. Some studies have found that runners who are committed to regular exercise have fewer infectious illnesses, but following heavy training or after running a marathon, runners tend to experience more illness than others. Likewise, a study of 61 conditioned athletes on a university crew team found more frequent and more severe upper respiratory infections among them than among 126 unconditioned cadets in the university's Reserve Officers Training Corps. In other words, for exercisers who overdo it, the damaging effects of stress can outweigh the benefits of physical activity.

• Moderate exercise, both in experimental animals and in people, often—but not always—results in a temporary increase in blood levels of various immune cells and substances that may improve resistance to infection. For example, men who worked out on an indoor bicycle had an immediate increase in the number of circulating white blood cells that destroy foreign microbes and that stimulate production of antibodies and other substances that attack invaders.

• One substance that rises after exercise is endogenous pyrogen, the protein that causes fevers. A temporary increase in body temperature is a common result of physical activity, and this "fever" may help to squelch an infection before it can take hold.

• Many of the beneficial immunological changes are more likely to occur in unconditioned people who exercise than in those who are already very fit. On the other hand, laboratory animals that are "conditioned" before being exposed to a disease-causing virus are less likely to get sick and die if they are then exercised to exhaustion.

So should you exercise when you feel sick? On the basis of available evidence, Dr. Edward R. Eichner, a professor of medicine at the University of Oklahoma in Oklahoma City, suggests this: if symptoms are restricted to the upper respiratory tract—specifically, the nose and throat—try a "test drive" at half speed. If the activity clears your head and you feel peppy enough and not in pain, it should be all right to finish the workout. But do not exercise if symptoms are below the neck or bodywide, like fever, muscle aches, loss of appetite or hacking cough. Your body will recover faster with rest.

With cancer the evidence is somewhat clearer, though hardly conclusive. Although exercise increases blood levels of natural killer cells that fight off cancer cells, researchers believe other mechanisms play a far more important role.

Several studies among men and women have indicated that those who are physically fit or who are physically active have lower death rates from cancer. A study of more than 10,000 men and 3,000 women examined at the Institute for Aerobics Research in Dallas found that those who were most fit on a treadmill test had much lower cancer death rates in the ensuing eight years. There was a 4-fold difference in cancer deaths among the men and a 16-fold difference among the women.

The strongest evidence for a protective effect of exercise involves colon cancer, a leading cause of cancer deaths among Americans. In tracking deaths among more than 17,000 Harvard alumni, Dr. Ralph Paffenbarger Jr. found that those who said they exercised at moderate to high levels had 25 to 50 percent fewer cases of colon cancer than the least active men in the study. The main benefit of exercise to the colon is believed to be the increased rate at which body wastes and any cancer-causing substances they may contain pass through the colon in physically active people.

For women, exercise, particularly during the teenage and young adult years, seems to be associated with lower rates of breast cancer and various hormone-related cancers of the reproductive tract. Dr. Rose Frisch at the Harvard School of Public Health found that among nearly 5,400 female college alumnae, those who had been college athletes or who trained regularly had about half the risk of later developing breast cancer that nonathletes ran. Nonathletes also had higher rates of cancers of the uterus, ovary, cervix and vagina.

The main benefit of exercise in reducing cancer risk in women is believed to be a lower lifetime exposure to estrogen, which can stimulate growth of cells in the breasts and reproductive organs. Physical activity can change the hormone ratio and reduce body fat, which itself increases the amount of cancer-stimulating estrogens in the blood. As the cancer society says, exercise will not hurt and it may help, so get moving.

[JEB, July 1993]

Exercise and Bone Loss

CONCERNS about fragile bones have joined worries about being overweight and at risk for heart disease in prompting millions of women near or past menopause to start exercising. Having heard that exercise can help maintain and even increase bone mass, they are walking, running, swimming, cycling and even lifting weights to ward off the fractures caused by osteoporosis.

But many exercise enthusiasts are not getting the benefits they think they are, recent studies indicate. First, not all kinds of exercise are equally beneficial to bone strength and some types may do little good. And second, exercise is but one of three crucial factors in maintaining healthy bones. The other two, an adequate intake of calcium throughout life and, for women at or past menopause, estrogen replacement therapy, complement the effects of exercise and may even be essential to its potential bone-building benefits.

Thus, Dr. Morris Notelovitz, an osteoporosis specialist in Gainesville, Florida, warns that women who think they need not worry about calcium or estrogen because they exercise regularly could be sadly mistaken.

Osteoporosis is a debilitating and sometimes fatal disorder of fragile bones that is now epidemic among older Americans, causing 1.3 million bone fractures a year at an annual cost of $10 billion. The size of the problem is expected to grow dramatically as people continue to live longer and as baby boomers who grew up on soft drinks instead of milk pass the big 5-o.

After the age of 35 women lose bone mass at a rate of 1 percent a year, a rate that doubles or quadruples in the years right after menopause. In the decade after menopause, women typically lose 5 to 10 percent of the bone-sustaining minerals in the spine alone. As a result, according to the National Osteoporosis Foundation, one-third of American women over 65 suffer spinal fractures and 15 percent break their hips because of osteoporosis.

For men, significant bone loss usually starts 10 to 20 years later than in women. Men have denser bones to begin with, and the predominant kind of bone men lose is less crucial to overall bone strength. But men, too, are affected by osteoporosis; a quarter of hip fractures occur in men. And among men who reach their 80s, one in six will break a hip.

As with many other things in life, if you do not use bones, you lose them. Using bones means working the muscles that support them against a resistant force like gravity. Bone is built up in response to stress and breaks down almost as soon as the stress dissipates. Thus, astronauts outside the tug of gravity and people bedridden by illness or disability lose bone very rapidly.

Although the research findings are often conflicting, many studies, both large and small, have indicated that exercise can help to maintain and even increase the density of bones. For example, a study at the University of California in San Francisco found that men in their 20s who combined weight training with aerobic exercise for an average of six hours a week for at least two years had denser spinal bones than men who did only weight training or only aerobics. In turn, all those groups had denser bones than a comparable group of sedentary men.

Among women, a large study by researchers at Family Health International in Durham, North Carolina, found that women aged 40 and 54 who were physically active had significantly higher bone mineral density in the spine and arms than a comparable group of nonexercisers.

At the University of Missouri, a one-year study among previously sedentary women who had recently gone through menopause found that both low-impact and high-impact exercise done for three 20-minute periods a week helped maintain their spinal bone. Another study among women in their 50s found that both brisk walking and aerobic dancing resulted in increased bone size and strength. And Dr. Everett Smith at the University of Wisconsin has shown that even people in their 80s and 90s can increase bone mass in their legs and hips simply by marching in place while holding a support.

Bone is a "fluid" tissue, constantly being broken down and re-formed. To favor buildup over breakdown, the muscles attached to the bones must be contracted and strengthened. This produces piezoelectricity, a force that results in bone deposition at the stress points. Unless bones are repeatedly subjected to stress, the breakdown process outruns the buildup and bones gradually become porous and weaker. Activities like weight lifting that involve high loads and high stresses (and consequent muscle strengthening) are more effective at building bone than activities that involve many repetitive cycles, like running, walking or swimming.

Strength training like lifting weights or working out on resistance machines like Nautilus and Universal equipment has recently emerged as one of the best ways to strengthen bones in the spine and elsewhere, even in the elderly. Alternative activities include using a rowing machine or an exercise cycle with increased resistance on the flywheel.

The benefits of exercise to bone seem to be specific to the activity. Thus, runners and cyclists tend to have denser bones than sedentary people in the legs and hips, but not in the arms or spine. Tennis players have denser bones in their playing arm than in the arm that merely tosses serves. Swimmers who do a vigorous crawl would have denser bones in their arms and shoulders than in their legs. To strengthen bones bodywide, then, a variety of activities should be pursued that use different muscles against resistance, for example, cycling and swimming.

Exercise helps bones in another important way: by increasing a person's stability and reaction time and decreasing the likelihood of a bone-breaking fall.

Researchers at the Washington University School of Medicine in St. Louis showed that exercise sped the brain's ability to process information. Accordingly, they found that elderly people who were physically active were less likely to fall and when they did fall, they were less likely to fracture a hip. They may instead suffer a broken wrist, which is far less serious than breaking a hip, because they are quick enough to allow their hands to break their fall.

Although exercise is the only way known to increase bone mass after a person's 20s, it cannot work without the proper support. This means taking in an adequate amount of the bone-building mineral calcium, preferably from food and, if not, through supplements: 1,000 milligrams a day before menopause and 1,500 milligrams after.

Nor can exercise alone increase bone mass enough to offset the losses that result from estrogen depletion at menopause. Thus, experts in osteoporosis often recommend estrogen replacement therapy for all postmenopausal women who can use it safely.

Furthermore, they recommend adopting bone-building living

habits during the teenage and young-adult years to establish a larger "retirement fund" of bone.

[JEB, July 1993]

The Longevity of Long-Distance Runners

ACTIVE Americans do not wear out, but sedentary ones are likely to rust out, according to the findings of an eight-year study of nearly 800 people age 50 and over. As they age, the study showed, those who regularly engage in vigorous aerobic exercise like running are much less likely to develop life-inhibiting disabilities.

The study, conducted by a research team from Stanford University and published in a recent issue of *Annals of Internal Medicine,* followed the health of 451 members of a runners' club and 330 nonrunners living in the same community. All participants were 50 to 72 when the study began.

"Long-distance running, and presumably other regular aerobic exercise activity, is associated with preservation of good physical function in the later years of life, compared with persons with more sedentary lifestyles," the researchers concluded. They said their findings underscored the importance of promoting "regular lifetime physical exercise to improve the quality of life of the growing older population."

The study also showed, as have earlier ones, that the runners had a lower death rate than the nonrunners.

As one might suspect, at the time of enrollment the runners were in better shape than the nonrunners. When the study began, the runners, who had already been pursuing their chosen activity for an average of 12 years, were leaner, had fewer medical problems and fewer joint symptoms, took fewer medications and were less likely to have experienced previous disability than were the nonrunners.

The researchers, headed by Dr. James F. Fries, a specialist in arthritis, suggested that the initial health differences could be the result of the previous years of running or it could reflect the fact that people in good shape initially are more likely to choose to be vigorously active. Nonetheless, in following the fates of the two groups of men and women for eight years, the researchers showed that the health differential persisted and further increased, even after taking the participants' initial health status into account.

The nonrunners, both men and women, were several times more likely to develop some form of disability during the eight-year period. This health difference persisted even when the data were adjusted for potential health influences like smoking, body weight, history of arthritis, age, sex and disabilities present when the study began.

"There was but a slight increase in disability in the runners and a substantial increase in the nonrunners during this period," the team reported. By the end of the study, the nonrunners reported three and a half times more disabilities than did the runners. Disability measures included the participants' ability to walk, arise from a straight chair and grip objects.

"These findings underscore the fact that people who are physically active will remain physically fit despite the process of aging and the chronic diseases that can accompany aging," said Dr. Ralph Paffenbarger, a professor of epidemiology at the University of California at Berkeley. "They are another argument for undertaking activities to promote flexibility and strength and to reduce the risk of fatal coronary heart disease and stroke and the risk of developing hypertension, osteoporosis, obesity and non-insulin-dependent diabetes."

To eliminate a possible bias that would result if some people had once been runners but gave it up because of health problems, the researchers divided the participants into "ever runners" and "never runners," and here they found an even greater difference in disability between the runners' club members and the entire nonrunning group.

The runners reported less frequent joint pain and swelling than did the nonrunners. But when X rays of joints were taken of a smaller group of participants in the study, no differences in arthritic changes were found between the runners and nonrunners, suggesting that differences in disability rates were due to factors like improved conditioning and low rates of other health problems like heart disease, rather than a reduced incidence of arthritis.

[JEB, October 1994]

Experts Preach the Virtues of Moderate Exercise . . .

A N important health message was delivered recently to the many millions of Americans who have yet to make even moderate physical activity a regular feature of their lives. The message from a prestigious group of experts in preventive medicine and exercise physiology was this: you don't have to become a jock or a fitness nut, you don't have to exercise vigorously three times a week for 20 minutes at a time and you don't have to build muscles à la Arnold Schwarzenegger to reap major health benefits from regular physical activity.

All you have to do, these experts concluded, is to incorporate a total of about 30 minutes a day of moderate activity into your routines. That means actions like taking stairs instead of elevators and escalators, walking short distances instead of driving door to door, gardening, raking leaves, doing housework, dancing, playing actively with children or pets, riding a stationary bicycle while watching the evening news, playing golf without a cart or doing any other activities at the intensity of a brisk walk for however long you choose—as long as you log a total of 30 minutes a day.

To those who have assiduously pursued the fitness gospel of exercising three or more times a week for 20 or more minutes at a time at a level that gets the heart beating at a rate of 60 to 90 percent of its maximum, the new guidelines may sound like heresy or at least a capitulation to a basically sedentary society that has so far largely resisted the exhortations to work up a sweat.

But several basic facts and an accumulation of recent research findings prompted the nation's fitness leaders to rethink the message that they have been broadcasting to Americans for more than two decades. Probably the most important one is that despite widely publicized evidence for the physical and mental benefits of regular exercise and the public's apparent acceptance of the importance of physical activity, "millions of U.S. adults remain essentially sedentary," the experts wrote in *The Journal of the American Medical Association*.

The 20-member panel of experts was convened by the federal Centers for Disease Control and Prevention and the American College of Sports Medicine, which endorsed the panel's conclusions.

There are many reasons for the failure of Americans to put their stated beliefs about the benefits of exercise into practice. Common excuses include a lack of time; a lack of affordable, accessible or safe exercise areas; scheduling difficulties; injury or other physical limitations; bad weather; a dislike of vigorous activity; and a lack of confidence in one's physical abilities.

"Participation in regular physical activity gradually increased during the 1960s, 1970s and early 1980s, but seems to have plateaued in recent years," the experts said. The majority of American adults now get little or no physical activity of a kind that could promote their health. This lack of regular activity has been cited as responsible for as many as 250,000 deaths a year in this country, or 12 percent of total mortality.

Large, long-term studies by Dr. Ralph Paffenbarger, now at the University of California at Berkeley, and Dr. Steven N. Blair of the Cooper Institute for Aerobics Research in Dallas showed that habitual inactivity and low levels of physical fitness were associated with a marked increase in death rates from all causes and especially from heart disease.

Studies have shown that the risk of developing heart disease associated with a sedentary life is comparable to the hazards of high cholesterol, high blood pressure or cigarette smoking. Furthermore, Dr. Paffenbarger's research showed that people who increased their activity level in midlife reduced their chances of an early death.

Another major motivation for the new advice is an accumulation of study findings that all point to substantial protective health benefits that can be achieved through moderate activity pursued for varying intervals throughout the day. "Intermittent activity confers substantial benefits," the experts said.

In other words, it appears that many if not most of the benefits associated with physical fitness are really the result of physical activity. The distinction is not trivial. Fitness refers to a condition of being able to perform demanding activities—like climbing stairs, walking uphill or carrying heavy packages—without getting out of breath or becoming unduly fatigued.

Any amount of physical activity can increase a person's level of fitness, and if activity is pursued often and vigorously, a person can become optimally fit, which the experts say will almost certainly confer additional health benefits. But, they added, studies strongly indicate that activity itself, not necessarily optimal fitness, is the main protector in lowering the risk of developing a host of chronic health problems, including coronary heart disease, hypertension, diabetes, osteoporosis, colon cancer, anxiety and depression.

The panel pointed to mounting evidence indicating that "the health benefits of physical activity are linked principally to the total amount of activity performed" and that the amount of activity "is more important than the specific manner in which the activity is performed."

The panel concluded, "An active lifestyle does not require a regimented, vigorous exercise program. Instead, small changes that increase daily physical activity will enable individuals to reduce their risk of chronic disease and may contribute to enhanced quality of life."

You can increase your level of activity without having to adopt a regimented program or invest chunks of time or spend money. It takes but 10 minutes to walk half a mile and half that time to cover the same distance by bicycle. The possibilities are endless. Consider riding a bicycle all or part of the way to work or to run errands around the neighborhood. Do calisthenics, pedal a stationary cycle or work out on a ski machine while watching television.

Chop food and mix dough by hand instead of throwing everything into a food processor. Push a power mower instead of using a riding mower. Carry your clubs around the golf course. Use a hand saw to cut up wood for the fireplace. Shovel snow and rake leaves instead of blowing them off the walk with a machine. Do some or all of your own gardening and yard work. Play ball with the children. And walk: up stairs, to stores, to work, to social engagements, wherever and whenever it is possible and safe to walk.

[JEB, February 1995]

... But Others Say Only Strenuous Exercise Lengthens Life

MODERATE exercise may well be the route to a healthier life, but if living longer is your goal, you will have to sweat.

A new Harvard study that followed the fates of 17,300 middle-aged men for more than 20 years has found that only vigorous—not nonvigorous—activities reduced their risk of dying during the study period. The beneficial effects of vigorous exercise on longevity have long been assumed but were not firmly established.

Men who reported doing at least 1,500 calories' worth of vigorous activity each week had a 25 percent lower death rate during the study period than those who expended less than 150 calories a week. To achieve the level of exercise associated with longevity, a person would have to do the equivalent of jogging or walking briskly for about 15 miles a week.

In general, the more active the men were, the longer they were likely to live. This effect of vigorous exercise was seen even in men who smoked or were overweight, although those with neither of these health-robbing factors did better. However, no consistent beneficial effect on longevity was found among the men who pursued only nonvigorous activities like golf.

The enhanced longevity associated with vigorous exercise mainly resulted from a reduced number of deaths from cardiovascular disease, said Dr. I-Min Lee, an epidemiologist at the Harvard School of Public Health, who directed the study. She said the risk to longevity associated with a failure to exercise vigorously was comparable to the life-shortening effects of smoking a pack of cigarettes a day or weighing 20 percent more than one's ideal weight.

The finding, reported in a recent issue of *The Journal of the American Medical Association*, might seem to contradict a recent recommendation that 30 minutes a day of moderate activity, done all at once or in smaller increments, can produce significant health benefits. But that recommendation, by the Centers for Disease Control and Prevention and the American College of Sports Medicine, was described primarily as a route to better physical and emotional health, not necessarily to a longer life. It was intended to inspire the

60 percent of American adults who are now completely sedentary to become more active, even if all they do is walk rather than ride whenever possible and take the stairs instead of an elevator.

Consistent with that advice, the researchers emphasized that "even nonvigorous exercise is preferable to sedentariness," since any form of activity can enhance psychological health and reduce the risk of developing high blood pressure, diabetes and colon cancer.

The study defined as vigorous any activity that raised the metabolic rate to six or more times the rate at rest. Such activities include brisk walking, jogging, singles tennis, swimming laps, fast cycling and doing heavy chores at home or in the yard, Dr. Lee said in an interview.

"We're not asking people to run marathons," she said. "Until we have data that say otherwise, my belief is that moderation is best." She estimated that any of the following activities, or a mix of them, would achieve the level of caloric expenditure associated with the lowest death rate measured in the study:

- Walking at four to five miles an hour for 45 minutes five times a week
- Playing one hour of singles tennis three days a week
- Swimming laps for three hours a week
- Cycling for one hour four times a week
- Jogging at six to seven miles an hour for three hours a week
- Rollerblading for two and a half hours a week

Participants in the study, all graduates of Harvard University who had no known heart disease, cancer or lung disease when they entered the study in 1962 or 1966, completed questionnaires about their medical histories and health habits. Asked again in 1977 about their exercise and other health habits, many of the men were found to have increased their physical activity. This increase resulted in an even greater reduction in death rates than was associated with their 1960s activity levels.

Dr. Lee said most previous studies, including earlier analyses of the Harvard men, had looked only at the total amount of activity, not its intensity, in relation to heart disease and mortality risks. For example, Dr. Ralph S. Paffenbarger Jr. of the Stanford University School of Medicine had reported from the same study of Harvard men that those who expended 2,500 calories a week on any activities lived significantly longer than those who burned fewer calories through exercise.

Dr. Lee said only a study by Dr. Jeremy Morris of the London School of Hygiene and Tropical Medicine had examined different types of activities; it found that those who took part in vigorous sports, but not nonvigorous ones, suffered fewer heart attacks and a lower cardiovascular death rate.

Cardiologists have long recommended that to reduce heart attack risk, one should exercise at least 20 minutes at a time three times a week at a heart rate of about 70 percent of one's maximum. A vigorous activity, like jogging or brisk walking, is often necessary to achieve this level. Dr. Lee said the advice had been based on physiological studies showing that "this level of activity was most efficient at building up cardiorespiratory fitness."

She added, "It was assumed that this would help decrease the risk of heart attack and premature death, but at the time the advice was issued such a benefit had not been demonstrated in people." Finally, in the 1980s, Dr. Steven Blair of the Cooper Institute in Dallas found that people with greater cardiovascular fitness had lower death rates. Last week, Dr. Blair and colleagues reported that among 9,777 men, those who maintained or improved in fitness over a 10-year period were less likely to die from all causes. The new study is further evidence of the value of vigorous exercise for those who are able to pursue it, Dr. Lee said.

[JEB, April 1995]

Exercise and Health: A Science in Progress

THE new finding from a continuing study of 17,300 Harvard alumni suggesting that longevity is fostered by vigorous, but not nonvigorous, exercise has surprised leading researchers in the field. They are striving to reconcile it with many other studies that point to a lifesaving benefit from moderate exercise, and they are

perplexed that the Harvard study failed to find the expected benefit.

Science often advances by indirect steps, however, and an anom-
alous finding may overturn conventional wisdom, or be reconciled
with it, or turn out to be in error. Such moments are as fascinating
for specialists as they are troubling for the public, which wants clear,
dependable advice.

"Everyone is confused," said Dr. Ralph Paffenbarger, Jr., of Stanford University, a coauthor of the new study. "Even the scientists are
confused." Dr. Paffenbarger was also the author of an important
earlier study of the Harvard men, which concluded in 1986 that
moderate physical exercise in adult life can significantly increase
life expectancy. He found that men who participated in activities
like walking, climbing stairs and sports, in which they used 2,000 or
more calories a week, had death rates one-quarter to one-third
lower than those who were least active.

The purpose of the new study, led by his collaborator, Dr. I-Min
Lee of the Harvard School of Public Health, was to find out just
what kinds of activities actually led to a longer life among the Harvard men. Using the same subjects, but with 10 more years of data,
she found a significant increase in life expectancy only among those
who regularly engaged in vigorous exercise like jogging and fast
walking, but not those whose activities rarely caused them to break
into a sweat.

Dr. Lee, the lead author of the study published last week in *The
Journal of the American Medical Association,* defined "vigorous" as de-
voting at least three hours a week to activities like singles tennis or
running at six or seven miles an hour or walking at four to five miles
an hour.

Dr. Paffenbarger cosigned the article, having no question about
its validity. But he and other experts still have confidence in studies
finding that moderate exercise confers health benefits that can prolong life.

Such studies, in fact, formed the basis for advice recently issued
by the federal Centers for Disease Control and Prevention and the
American College of Sports Medicine. These organizations concluded that 30 minutes a day of moderate activity, even in 10-
minute spurts, would confer significant health benefits. Dr.
Paffenbarger was one of 20 exercise specialists who took part in for-
mulating this recommendation.

Dr. Paffenbarger, among many other researchers, maintains that a person does not have to become an athlete to reduce the risk of developing diseases that can shorten life. But in his earlier analysis of the Harvard men, while he indeed found that engaging in moderately vigorous sports extended life, he also found that the more vigorous the activities the men engaged in, the greater was the benefit.

"A little exercise is better than none, but more is better than a little," Dr. Paffenbarger said. "Even moderate exercise can reduce the risk of coronary heart disease, stroke, diabetes, colon cancer and clinical depression, and it stands to reason that if you reduce these risks you would automatically increase survival rates and longevity." On the basis of earlier findings, he had calculated that men could gain an average of two years of life by expending 2,000 calories a week on things like stair climbing and walking.

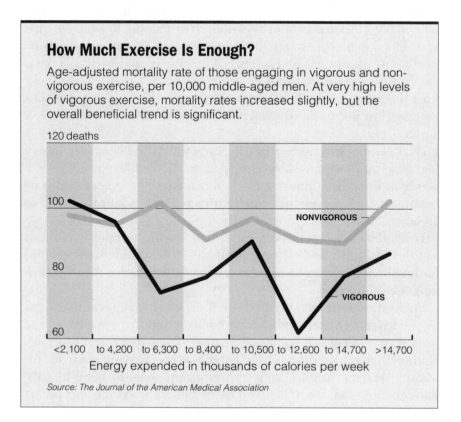

How Much Exercise Is Enough?

Age-adjusted mortality rate of those engaging in vigorous and non-vigorous exercise, per 10,000 middle-aged men. At very high levels of vigorous exercise, mortality rates increased slightly, but the overall beneficial trend is significant.

120 deaths

100

NONVIGOROUS

80

VIGOROUS

60

<2,100   to 4,200   to 6,300   to 8,400   to 10,500 to 12,600 to 14,700   >14,700

Energy expended in thousands of calories per week

Source: The Journal of the American Medical Association

Dr. Arthur Leon of the University of Minnesota has reported that even very moderate activities, like walking and working around the house and yard for three-quarters of an hour each day, reduced overall mortality rates by 20 percent and coronary death rates by 30 percent among men at high risk for developing heart disease.

The Centers for Disease Control and Prevention estimated that if every American who is sedentary would walk, work around the house, dance or do something comparable for 30 minutes a day, there would be an annual decline in deaths of about 250,000 a year. The centers' recommendation was intended to inspire the 60 percent of Americans who get little or no exercise to do at least some activities that can diminish their risk of disease and improve the quality of their lives.

Dr. Steven N. Blair of the Cooper Institute for Aerobics Research in Dallas said: "Our data support the belief that moderately intense activity does have mortality benefits. When men improved from being moderately fit to being highly fit, there was a 15 percent decline in mortality, but there was an even greater benefit—a 40 percent decline in deaths from all causes—among the men who improved from being unfit to being moderately fit." His finding, based on a five-year follow-up of 9,777 men, was published in *The Journal of the American Medical Association* a week before Dr. Lee's report appeared.

Why did the new study fail to find the same benefit from moderate exercise as found by these other studies? One possibility is that the other studies are wrong and there is no benefit. Another is that the benefit may have been masked because of the design of the new study, which put moderate and low exercisers into a single category to be compared with the vigorous exercisers.

"There still may be a benefit associated with moderate exercise that we could not measure in this study," said Dr. Lee. She added that in this kind of investigation, "each study is a piece in the puzzle."

Dr. Paffenbarger also noted the difficulty of classifying the Harvard men as vigorous and nonvigorous exercisers simply on the basis of their descriptions of their habits; "Studies like these are by nature imprecise. In the Harvard study the men were classified by self-reported activities. We know that singles tennis is apt to be played vigorously, but that doesn't mean every Harvard man played tennis at this level, or ran or swam vigorously."

Because of the difficulty in all exercise studies of measuring physical activity exactly, many important issues remain unresolved. "What we don't yet know is the minimal amount, the optimal amount or—if there is one—the hazardous amount of exercise or how these levels differ from one person to the next," Dr. Paffenbarger said.

Also, age and genetics undoubtedly play a role in the benefit gained from exercise. What is a desirable level of activity in a person of 30 is likely to be unachievable by that person at age 75, Dr. Leon said. "People differ in their ability to sustain a high level of activity," he said. "On average, men have a 10 percent greater aerobic capacity than women and there are genetic differences in aerobic capacity as well."

It is also unknown how closely the health benefits of exercise for men would apply to women. Few studies have examined the life-saving effects of exercise in women, especially in women past menopause.

Dr. Paul Williams of the Lawrence Berkeley Laboratory at the University of California at Berkeley has found that among runners, both men and women show such benefits as lower total cholesterol, higher levels of protective HDL cholesterol, lower body weights and less high blood pressure, all helpful in combating cardiovascular disease.

Dr. Williams is one who takes issue with the new advice that focuses on moderate exercise, however. "I think the centers made a mistake by deemphasizing the importance of vigorous exercise," he said. "We saw a continued improvement as people ran more miles, at least up to fifty miles a week. We estimate that, compared to men who run less than ten miles a week, those who run forty to forty-nine miles a week have a thirty percent lower risk of heart disease. The results in women are similar, showing continued improvement in those who exercise much beyond the current recommendation."

[JEB, April 1995]

Doing the Fitness Walk

I know, you have known how to walk since infancy. But when you walk for fitness two or three miles a day three or more times a week, your walking technique can make a big difference in the benefits you derive, how soon you tire and your chances of developing discouraging aches and pains. During my own daily fitness excursions in a local park, I have seen all kinds of walkers, many of whom could get a lot more from their activity with some minor adjustments in how they walk. Think of fitness walking as a sport: every participant can benefit from a little coaching. This is National Walk for Health and Fitness Month, so there is no better time than now to review your reasons for walking and your style.

Walking is the nation's most popular fitness activity, five times as popular as jogging. But if you are still among the sedentary millions, consider these advantages of fitness walking and the benefits you are likely to derive from making it a habit.

Almost everyone can do it safely, including pregnant women; the elderly and the obese; those with arthritis, diabetes or osteoporosis; and people recovering from heart attacks or bypass surgery.

It is highly adaptable. You can walk alone or with company (human or canine), and you can talk while walking. You can walk on the streets, on roads, on the beach, along wooded paths, in malls, on tracks (indoors or out), on a treadmill, even down the halls of a hotel, as I often do when traveling. You can walk at any time of the day or, in safe neighborhoods, night, but please wear reflective clothing if there is little daylight. You can walk in almost any kind of weather. You can sing (perhaps not like Gene Kelly) while walking in the rain; walking is not impeded by waterproof clothing. Trudging through snow is great exercise, and walking on a steamy summer day is a lot more pleasant than running.

You can lose weight walking. Dorine Watson of New York City, featured recently in *Walking Magazine*, lost 103 pounds, going from a size 24 to a size 7, by giving up fad diets and walking one and a half hours every day. Colleen Gifford, a 5-foot-3-inch working mother from Glenwood City, Wisconsin, reports that along with minor dietary changes, daily walking helped her drop 15 extra pounds in a year.

The faster you walk (and the more you weigh), the more calories you use. A 120-pound woman will burn 189 calories walking three miles in an hour, or 232 calories walking four miles in an hour. For a woman who weighs 180 pounds, the comparable caloric burn would be 282 and 348. Walking uphill (outdoors or on a treadmill) greatly increases your caloric burn. A 150-pound person walking up a 10 percent incline at three miles an hour will use 500 calories.

Walking's health benefits include an increase in HDL, the "good" cholesterol, enough to halve a previously sedentary woman's risk of suffering a heart attack; a reduced risk of bone loss and resulting fractures; a decrease in blood pressure; a diminished risk of the complications of diabetes; and an increase in mobility for people with arthritis.

Walking can have major emotional benefits: countering depression, relieving stress, freeing your mind to see, if not smell, the roses; and giving you an opportunity to talk over problems with a friend. Walking refreshes the spirit. I found when my children were small that just doubling the distance I had to walk home from the subway each stress-filled workday supplied the mental stamina I needed to enjoy the hours with my family.

Proper posture is primary. Poor walking posture increases fatigue and invites injuries. Stand up straight and walk with your ears, shoulders, hips, knees and ankles in a vertical line. Keep your head erect, chin pulled in toward your neck, back straight and buttocks and stomach tucked in. Leaning forward when you walk, which some people do when trying to walk faster, can cause back strain.

Look forward, with your eyes focused about 15 to 20 feet ahead. Try to avoid walking where obstacles force you to watch your feet.

Keep your shoulders relaxed and directly above your hips, not slumped forward or raised up toward your ears. Arms should be bent at the elbow at 90 degrees, with wrists straight and fingers gently curled into a loose fist. A straight-arm swing can result in swollen fingers and a slower pace. Your bent arms should swing in a straight line from front to back, close to your body, with the hand opposite the forward leg rising to chest level while the other hand moves back parallel to the hip.

Take a full natural stride, letting your legs be your locomotive. Stride with straight knees and with the forward leg directly in front of the body. Walk heel to toe, letting your foot roll gently forward through each step. Try to maintain a rhythmic cadence, stopping as little as possible. If you already have a proper stride and wish to increase your speed, step more frequently rather than trying to stretch your stride, which can injure your knees.

If you are walking up a significant hill, you have no choice but to lean into the hill, but you can still keep your back straight, eyes forward and chin in. Your stride will have to shorten, your knees will remain bent and, if the hill is quite steep, more of your weight will be on the balls of your feet.

Be sure to stretch before and after your walk. The American Physical Therapy Association recommends side bends and trunk rotations (turning the upper body while feet remain planted) as well as leg stretches for the inner thigh, calf muscles, quadriceps and hamstring.

Shoes for fitness walking should have flexible, nonsticky soles, good arch supports, cushioned insoles, heel cushions that are about one-half to three-quarters of an inch thick and roomy toe boxes. If your socks get holes in the toes, your shoes do not fit properly; either they are too short or your foot is sliding forward on each step. If your walking shoes wear unevenly or if you develop discomfort in your feet, knees or hips, orthotic inserts (over-the-counter or custom-made) in your shoes might help. If not, consider consulting a sports medicine specialist.

Most experts advise against adding weights to your walking. Ankle weights can strain the knees and increase the risk of tripping. Hand weights, although they increase the caloric burn and add a moderate upper-body workout to your walk, can also strain your elbows. Wearing a backpack weighing about five pounds would be less stressful, but be sure to maintain proper walking posture, standing straight with chin in and shoulders relaxed.

Advice on Walking

The popularity of walking has spawned magazines, newsletters and a host of helpful books, including the following:

Walking Magazine, 9–11 Harcourt Street, Boston, MA 02116, published six times a year for $14.95; phone (800) 829-3340.

The newsletter *Walk Off Weight,* published 10 times a year by *Walking Magazine* for $30; phone (800) 829-3340.

The 90-Day Fitness Walking Program by Mark Fenton and Seth Bauer, editors of *Walking Magazine*, a $10 Perigee paperback published in 1995 by the Berkley Publishing Group.

Aerobic Walking by Mort Malkin, a $14.95 paperback published in 1995 by John Wiley and Sons.

Dr. James M. Rippe's Complete Book of Fitness Walking by James M. Rippe, M.D., and Ann Ward, Ph.D., with Larry Rothstein, a $9.95 paperback published in 1990 by Prentice Hall.

Walking Medicine by Gary Yanker and Kathy Burton, prepared with 50 medical experts, published in 1990 by McGraw-Hill, $16.95.

Aerobic Walking by Casey Meyers, a $7.95 Vintage paperback published in 1988 by Random House.

[JEB, April 1996]

Runners and Swimmers: Which Burn More Energy?

DR. Howard Wainer, a swimmer and statistician at the Educational Testing Service in Princeton, New Jersey, first began wondering if runners spend energy as efficiently as swimmers when he was an undergraduate in the early 1960s, and used to argue with his runner friends over whose workout was harder.

Now he has put those two interests together in a study published in a recent issue of *Chance*, the journal of the American Statistical Association.

The human body, it seems, simply was not meant to move quickly through water. Dr. Wainer's study found that champion runners can go about three and a half times farther than champion swimmers in the same amount of time. But in that time, the less efficient swimmers burn 25 percent more calories.

Swimmers can take solace, however, in the finding that they appear to be better conditioned as athletes. Runners' performances peter out as their distances get longer, while swimmers maintain a much more consistent pace. And female swimmers are faster, compared with female runners, than male swimmers are compared with male runners.

If a person is running at top speed for a given length of time, say 20 minutes, and another person is swimming at top speed for that time, Dr. Wainer asked, how far will the runner go relative to the swimmer? To answer the question, he looked at world record times in running and swimming, so as to be sure he was comparing the very best performances in the two sports. He found that the theoretical maximum ratio is 3.75 to 1 for male athletes, which means that in 20 minutes a man can run 3.75 times as far as he can swim. The ratio was 3.5 for women in a 20-minute period. The ratio differs slightly for different times.

The study, said Dr. Sally Morton, a statistician at the Rand Corporation in Santa Monica, California, is "creating a buzz in the statistics community among the more athletic biathlete-triathlete types."

One immediate consequence of the results, said Dr. Al Loosli, a sports physiologist at the Center for Sports Medicine at St. Francis Memorial Hospital in San Francisco, is that it allows athletes to calculate whether they are more efficient runners or swimmers by looking at the ratio of their best times.

Some statisticians say they are already putting that idea into practice. Dr. Morton, who is a competitive long-distance ocean swimmer, said that she immediately calculated her relative speeds of running versus swimming to see if they came close to the theoretical maximum, which is 3.5 to 1 for female athletes. Her ratio, she said, was 2.6 to 1, indicating that she swims much better than she runs.

Dr. Richard De Veaux, a statistician at Princeton University who competes in triathlons, did the same thing. He said his ratio was exactly the same as the figure Dr. Wainer calculated for male athletes, 3.75 to 1. "The way I look at it, I'm equally bad at both sports," Dr. De Veaux said.

Dr. De Veaux said he was intrigued with Dr. Wainer's analysis. "I thought it was absolutely fascinating," he said.

Dr. Wainer said that when he analyzed the relative efficiencies of running and swimming, he deliberately rejected an approach that had been tried in the past: to assume that the efficiency of exercise depends on the number of calories that are required to move one gram of body mass a distance of one centimeter. In this sort of analysis, the time factor is ignored, since whether someone walks a mile or runs it, the total energy expended would be the same. This is the basis of advice often given by trainers in health clubs, who say that people wanting to lose weight are just as well off walking as running as long as they keep their distance constant.

"That idea seemed patently false," Dr. Wainer said. "It seemed to me that the distance traveled isn't the key thing. It's how hard it is to do it."

Dr. John Duncan, an exercise physiologist who is associate director of the Cooper Institute for Aerobics Research in Dallas, agreed with this approach. The idea that only distance matters in calculating efficiency "is an old myth," he said. Dr. Duncan said his group found substantial differences in calories expended when women strolled, walked quickly or racewalked for three miles.

Dr. Wainer theorized that the greater efficiency he found in female swimmers, as opposed to men, might be a result of women's having more body fat. He said the body fat might be an advantage for women in swimming, helping them to remain parallel to the surface of the water, but a hindrance in running.

Given the ratios he found for swimmers and runners, as well as measurements of oxygen consumption, Dr. Wainer deduced that champion swimmers burn 25 percent more calories than runners in a given time.

This finding, Dr. Duncan said, is somewhat surprising because swimmers in general tend to have lower heart rates when they exercise than runners. Also, many people who take up swimming to lose weight are disappointed when the sport does little to burn off extra fat, perhaps because they do not exercise at extremely high intensity levels, Dr. Duncan said.

[GK, April 1993]

The Pleasures of Cross-Training

MOST of us are not and will never be Olympic athletes. We are not obliged to train day after day to improve our performance in a particular activity. Yet many amateur players and ordinary fitness buffs act as if their chosen activity were the only one they could or would want to do. They are the Johnny One Notes of exercise.

Among my friends, for example, there is Arthur, who runs seven miles a day, every day, seven days a week; Kuchela, who plays singles tennis—and only tennis—four or five times a week; and Jane, who swims—and only swims—half a mile or more every day. To be sure, they are doing far more than most other Americans to stay in shape as the years tick on. But there is growing evidence that they would be much better off with a more varied activity program.

I learned the hard way that combining two or more complementary forms of exercise is the safest way to be physically active and the only way to achieve balanced fitness. This approach to exercise, called cross-training, is fast catching on with active Americans, including many elite athletes who were once single-sport devotees.

My foray into multiple activities is like an advertisement for cross-training. It began with a passion for singles tennis that I pursued for an hour or more a day, seven days a week. Initially, it was my only activity, other than walking and biking to the courts. Then, in my mid-30s, I found myself getting winded on the tennis court. Thinking I needed to increase my aerobic capacity, I started jogging three or more times a week, while continuing to play daily tennis. Suddenly, my back went out, and I had to abandon all activity, even walking, for six weeks. When I was finally able to resume exercising, I took up swimming to get back in shape without stressing my back. Cycling, too, proved to be an activity I could pursue without back pain.

Eventually, I got back to running and tennis, but I soon began to realize that seven days a week of singles was more than my body would take without complaint. Besides, my performance on the court seemed to become increasingly erratic. I could not help but notice that when I was forced to spend a day or two off the courts, I played all that much better the next time. My body seemed to be telling me that it needed a rest from tennis every few days if it was going to be at its best.

Fitness, it turns out, is far more than being able to run a mile or more without getting winded or having your muscles turn to jelly. In addition to developing aerobic endurance—the ability to sustain a demanding oxygen-using activity like running, cycling or brisk walking for prolonged periods—balanced fitness includes muscular strength and endurance, flexibility and having a healthy ratio of muscle to fat.

In her excellent book *Cross-Training* (Fireside/Simon & Schuster, 1992, $12), Gordon Bakoulis Bloch listed the above features of total-body, or balanced, fitness as one of the main benefits of mixing activities. Even if you are aerobically fit, you may not be strong enough to lift a heavy object, open a tightly closed jar or carry a heavy package a long distance. And you may not be flexible enough to bend without breaking or to survive a misstep without spraining a ligament or pulling a muscle.

Then there is the matter of overuse injuries, which come from overworking certain body parts by overdoing one activity. Among the more common problems are shinsplints, tennis elbow, plantar fasciitis and runner's knee.

By reducing the frequency with which any one activity is pursued, cross-training allows time for overly stressed parts of the body to rest and recover from the damaging effects of exercise before a chronically painful injury results.

In the meantime, you can stay in shape with your alternative activity. Or, if you should already be injured, cross-training allows time for the injured part to heal while you maintain the benefits of activity.

By introducing variety into your exercise program, cross-training counters boredom and burnout and increases the likelihood that you will remain physically active for as long as you live. It also permits flexibility in your workout. It may not be possible to swim or play tennis or jog every day or in every place you happen to be. Cross-training gives you choices, as many choices as you may want, regardless of weather or circumstances.

Your choice of activities should be determined not only by your interests, opportunities and abilities, but also by whether they contribute to balanced fitness. A given activity may improve more than one facet of fitness. These are some of the possibilities:

- *For aerobic conditioning:* The ability of your heart and lungs to function most efficiently can be enhanced by activities that sustain a raised heart rate for at least 20 consecutive minutes without making you become breathless. Depending upon your initial fitness level, these can include brisk walking; jogging; swimming laps; cycling; skating; cross-country skiing; water or step aerobics; jumping rope; playing vigorous tennis, squash or racquetball; or working out on a treadmill, ski machine, exercise bicycle or step machine.

- *For muscular strength and endurance:* Muscles must be stressed to get stronger. The activities listed above that promote aerobic fitness will also strengthen some muscles and increase their ability to sustain repeated contractions. But other opposing muscles will be relatively neglected, which increases the risk of injury. To achieve a balance, try lifting weights or working out on resistance machines to strengthen neglected muscles. For example, women naturally have weak upper-body muscles, and those who walk or jog are doing nothing to enhance upper-body strength. For them, lifting free weights, swimming the crawl or using a rowing machine would be ideal.

- *To foster flexibility:* Muscles and joints that can move freely through their full range of motion are least likely to become injured. Activities that promote endurance or strength also tighten certain muscles at the expense of others. In runners, for example, muscles in the back of the legs become stronger and tighter than those in the front, increasing their vulnerability to knee and ankle injuries. Flexibility is fostered by gentle, nonstressful activities like stretching, yoga and tai chi. Regardless of which activities you choose, stretching before and after exercise should always be part of your routine.

- *To reduce body fat:* Any activity that burns a significant number of calories will help you lose body fat and increase the ratio of muscle to fat. The biggest calorie burners are the activities that involve the sustained use of large muscle groups in the legs, arms and torso, like those listed under aerobic conditioning. Especially helpful are weight-bearing activities, which increase bone mass.

[JEB, July 1996]

For Exercisers,
Drink Before You're Thirsty

WHEN Alberto Salazar won the Boston Marathon in 1982, he fell into a coma right after crossing the finish line. Mr. Salazar sweats heavily, and he became so hot and dehydrated during the race that his organ systems were near collapse. Dr. William Castelli and a police officer saved his life by squeezing more than three quarts of replacement fluids into his veins.

Few recreational athletes push themselves to such limits. But even those who, say, play an hour and a half of singles tennis or run a 10-K or cycle 20 miles, especially on a hot day, often risk the detrimental effects of dehydration.

Recently a 15-year-old boy from Utah died from the heat after he and his friends ran out of water while hiking in the Grand Canyon. But even an ordinary fitness walker can lose large amounts of water in hot weather or on a challenging course.

Unfortunately, thirst is an imprecise signal that often fails to kick in until the body is approaching a danger point. You may have lost two quarts of water—four pounds—before thirst prompts you to start drinking.

Experts in exercise physiology say that few athletes, whether amateur, elite or professional, drink enough fluids before and during their activities to counter the ill effects on performance and well-being that can result from below-normal amounts of body water.

People who sweat heavily are especially at risk and are least likely to drink enough, said Dr. Michael N. Sawka, an expert in thermal physiology at the U.S. Army Research Institute for Environmental Medicine in Natick, Massachusetts. Older people who are physically active are also at greater-than-average risk because thirst sensation, sweat production and ability to concentrate urine decline with age. It is especially dangerous to exercise in clothing that does not breathe. Wearing plasticized garments to foster sweating does not increase the loss of body fat and can endanger health.

Dr. Sawka, who spoke at a recent National Institutes of Health workshop on dietary needs of physically active people, said water loss that resulted in as little as a 1 percent drop in body weight (a mere 1.5 pounds for a 150-pound person) could raise body temperature because dehydration causes the body's main cooling mechanisms—blood flow to the skin and sweating—to become less efficient.

As body temperature rises, the risk of heat exhaustion and heatstroke, which can be fatal, rises too. The heart beats faster (an indication of cardiovascular strain), muscles fatigue sooner and exercise performance declines by 20 to 50 percent. As the American College of Sports Medicine put it in a recent position statement on exercise and fluid replacement, "Inadequate water intake can lead to premature exhaustion."

Instead of feeling relaxed and invigorated after a workout, the dehydrated exerciser is likely to feel stressed out, unduly fatigued and lethargic, perhaps even headachy, dizzy and nauseated, and may not feel much better the next day either.

Dr. Edward F. Coyle, director of the Human Performance Laboratory at the University of Texas at Austin, said cyclists rarely drink enough while riding. Yet few realize the decline in performance that results. So he placed a group of cyclists in a heat chamber to dehydrate them and, before and after, had them peddle a bicycle ergometer that measured speed and heart rate. "When they saw how much dehydration caused their heart rates to rise and slowed them down, it turned them into true believers about drinking more," the professor of kinesiology said.

The college's statement put it this way: "During exercise, humans do not typically drink as much water as they sweat and, at best, voluntary drinking only replaces about two-thirds of the body water lost as sweat. It is common for individuals to dehydrate by 2 percent to 6 percent of their body weight during exercise in the heat despite the availability of adequate amounts of fluid."

Becoming acclimated to the heat does not help the body conserve water. In fact, Dr. Sawka said, because acclimatized individuals are better able to sweat, they actually need more water, not less, to avoid dehydration.

The smart athlete or exerciser will always start out well hydrated. Ideally, two hours before an activity, you should drink about 16 ounces (two 8-ounce cups or a half liter) of water. Any excess will be lost through urination before the event. But if you do not have to urinate within an hour, drink another 8 ounces. If you cannot drink water two hours in advance, drink 8 to 16 ounces before starting your activity. In either case, continue to drink water throughout the activity, consuming 6 to 12 ounces every 15 to 20 minutes, especially when exercising in the heat. To foster maximum consumption and rapid absorption into the blood, the water should be cool—from 40 to 50 degrees Fahrenheit—but not ice-cold.

To be sure you have consumed enough water, weigh yourself before and after the activity, preferably unclothed, since sweaty clothes weigh more than dry ones. For each one-pound deficit in body weight, you will need to drink a pint (two cups) of water to replace the water you lost as sweat. Remember, you cannot rely on thirst to tell you how dried out you are.

Of course, in addition to water, sweat contains essential minerals: sodium, chloride ion and potassium. But their concentration in sweat is much lower than in blood, so in sweating you lose proportionately more water than minerals. Ordinarily, these minerals are readily replenished through foods consumed as snacks and meals. Special sports drinks are not recommended unless you engage in intense exercise for more than an hour. The main advantage of such drinks for the average active person is that their flavor and sweetness encourage greater fluid consumption.

While a small amount of caffeine (the amount in a Diet Coke, for example) may foster muscle action, Dr. Sawka says that those who drink a lot of beverages containing caffeine before exercising could start out dehydrated, since caffeine is a diuretic. Alcohol too is dehydrating, and anyone who has more than one drink the night before a morning activity should drink two cups of water before bed and another two upon arising.

The statement from the college of sports medicine points out that small amounts of sugar can enhance the absorption of water and, for prolonged, intense activities, delay muscle fatigue by maintaining normal levels of glucose in the blood. But a drink with too much sugar—the amount, say, in an ordinary soft drink or juice—has the opposite effect. It draws water into the gut from the blood, which aggravates dehydration, and may cause bloating and cramps. Also, drinks that contain fructose as their main sugar are converted to glucose too slowly to be useful in delaying fatigue.

If you prefer a flavored drink, engage in prolonged, intense exercise or provide drinks for a team, you can save money and avoid lugging home heavy bottles by making your own sports drink.

Nancy Clark, sports nutritionist and author of the *New York City*

Marathon Cookbook (Rutledge Hill Press, 1994, $19.95), devised this simple, inexpensive and highly palatable recipe, which has considerably less sugar than a soft drink:

SPORTS DRINK

$^1/_4$ cup sugar
$^1/_2$ cup hot water
$^1/_4$ cup orange juice
$^1/_4$ teaspoon salt
$3^1/_4$ cups cold water

1. In a quart jar or pitcher, dissolve the sugar in the hot water.
2. Add the remaining ingredients and stir.

Yield: 4 cups

[JEB, June 1996]

The Science of Eating Right

NUTRITION:
THE NEVER-ENDING DEBATE

Japanese eat rice and fish and live longer than Americans. Their diet is almost certainly a reason. But what is it in the diet of Japan and certain Mediterranean countries that confers greater health?

The exact foods that make a diet healthful or unhealthful are a matter of continuing debate among experts. It is widely agreed that Americans eat too much fat. There is less consensus on more detailed issues, such as whether a low-fat diet reduces the risk of breast cancer or whether fish oils help avert heart attack.

Consumers often complain about the conflicting advice that emanates from diet experts—eat margarine, not butter; don't eat margarine; eat fish; forget fish oil. But the experts are in a difficult position. Their clients have to eat and want answers now. Yet the available data often support only guesses, not clear answers.

Given the circumstances, the experts tend to offer the best advice they can. That doesn't mean nutrition is a subject like astrology that lacks a rational basis, just that its experts sometimes guess wrong and get corrected by new facts.

The difficulty of giving dietary advice is evident in the various disputes that still rage about fat. For even the most basic concepts, the proof can be surprisingly hard to nail down. Since high cholesterol is firmly associated with greater risk of heart disease, lowering cholesterol should reduce the risk. Studies designed to prove this point by having people eat low-fat diets haven't, however, given unambiguous proof, perhaps because it's hard to make people stick to truly low-fat eating habits. Only recently, in studies that rely on the new cholesterol-lowering drugs, has the benefit of low cholesterol been put beyond doubt.

The standard advice is that people should derive no more than 30 percent of their calories from fat. But as with the recommendation that even moderate exercise is good for health, this prescription is strongly influenced by knowledge of a patient's limited appetite for self-denial. The benefit of a 30-percent-fat diet is hard to prove, as an article later in this section points out. This doesn't mean that the benefit isn't there, just that Americans and others probably need to eat an even leaner diet before clear health benefits will show up.

Will a low-fat diet help reduce the risk of breast cancer? Breast cancer rates are relatively high in countries with high-fat diets, so health experts have long felt it was reasonable to advise women at risk of breast cancer to eat less fat. Meanwhile, studies were launched to acquire evidence in support of this very plausible advice. Surprise: low-fat diets—at least in adulthood—do not seem to reduce the risk of breast cancer.

Given the uncertainties that still gnaw at the edges of the conventional wisdom about fat, it is not too amazing that controversies swirl around many lesser aspects of diet. Nutrition is a science that advances in the style of two steps forward, one step back. That latest food story you hear may belong to either category. But don't tune out: the correction process is what makes better understanding possible.

Common Sense When
Health Studies Conflict

MANY health-conscious Americans are understandably confused. Medical researchers cannot seem to make up their
minds about what people should do to preserve their health for as
long as possible.

After years of advice to reduce fat intake to 30 percent of daily
calories and to limit cholesterol consumption to less than 300 milligrams a day, the public learns that a British scientist has concluded
after reviewing the best available studies that such a diet has a minimal—if any—effect on the incidence of heart disease and coronary
death rates.

After being told that any amount of exercise is bound to be beneficial, the public learns that a Harvard researcher has found that
only vigorous exercise prolonged the lives of Harvard alumni.

After being told to eat more seafood to prevent heart disease, the
public learns of a study of thousands of male doctors that found no
such protection.

Whom are people to believe?

The time has come to start applying logic and good sense to these
questions: to decide exactly what individuals hope to achieve and
then adopt living habits commensurate with those goals.

By now, it should be obvious to all concerned that no one activity,
food or attitude can guarantee untarnished golden years and that
the surest path to a long and healthy life comes from a combination
of factors including diet, exercise and stress management along
with avoidance of health-robbing habits like smoking and excessive
drinking. To make a real dent in disease, disability and premature
death, people need to accept the whole package, not just one small
part.

Some of the best clues to longevity come from studies of long-
lived populations that have, at least in the past, largely avoided the

costly chronic and life-threatening diseases that afflict Americans in epidemic proportions. Further clues come from an increased understanding of the biochemical machine that is the human body, a machine that has not changed in any substantive way since it first evolved.

Finally, while more research is clearly needed, especially on the factors that most influence longevity in women, there have been quite a few reliable studies from which sound guidance can be gleaned.

Homo sapiens evolved as gatherers and sometime hunters. As best as anthropologists and anatomists can determine, humans were designed to be primarily vegetarians with occasional feasts of meat and other animal foods. The early human diet was necessarily very low in fat, rich in fruits and vegetables and sparing in low-fat animal protein from lean and sinewy wild animals, not cattle, hogs and chickens raised on corn and grain and confined to pens where they put on lots of fat. And early humans were an active bunch, working hard physically every day to obtain food and shelter.

Until this century, life expectancy rarely exceeded the reproductive years, with most people dying of infectious diseases. The advent of modern sanitation, immunizations and antibiotics brought most lethal infections under control, and the industrial revolution eliminated the need for all that activity just to stay alive. As American affluence increased, people lived not only longer but also higher on the hog. They ate more animal protein and more fat, they became increasingly sedentary, they got fatter and fatter, and they took up cigarette smoking as a major means of stress control.

Japan has served as a living laboratory. Until recently the Japanese, who were largely free of heart disease and breast and lung cancer and who still live longer than Americans do, consumed a diet that closely resembled the early human diet and contained less than half the fat Americans now eat. With rising affluence, the Japanese began eating more meat and fat, and Japanese men took up smoking with a vengeance. As expected, the Japanese rate of heart disease began rising, and lung cancer and other smoking-related cancers are likely to follow.

In a carefully designed study, Dr. Dean Ornish of the Preventive Medicine Research Institute in Sausalito, California, proved the value of a diet very low in fat and rich in vegetable foods in patients already seriously afflicted with heart disease.

His plan, a rather strict vegetarian one that includes nonfat dairy products and egg whites but excludes all oils, calls for 10 percent of calories from fat and only five milligrams of cholesterol a day. Along with a daily regimen of moderate exercise and meditation and other techniques to reduce stress, the approach not only vastly improved participants' coronary risk factors but also significantly reversed arterial clogging and increased coronary blood flow.

The average still-healthy American is unlikely to need a diet as strict as Dr. Ornish's to remain healthy, but the message from his studies is clear: for most people who hope to live healthfully into their 80s, their diets need serious fat (and calorie) stripping. Without question, cigarettes and other forms of tobacco must go, and if alcohol is consumed, it should be only in moderation: no more than one drink a day for women or two drinks for men.

And, last but hardly least, the human body needs regular physical activity. How vigorous must that activity be? That depends on the individual and what he or she hopes to achieve. Experts agree that any kind and amount of exercise are better than none. Regular physical activity—even just walking or working around the house or garden for an hour a day for a person who was formerly sedentary—can help one reduce harmful blood fats, cut blood pressure, normalize blood sugar, relieve stress, shed extra pounds and preserve bone mass.

But the experts also agree that while some exercise is good, more is better. Up to what point, they have not yet determined. Although studies have shown that the people who exercise the longest and hardest are likely to remain alive and healthy the longest as well, they have also shown that moderate exercise has undeniable health and longevity benefits. The new study of Harvard men did not examine longevity in moderate exercisers separately from that in men who did little or no exercise and for this reason may have failed to show a longevity increase from moderate exercise.

As for a failure in the latest study to find a benefit from eating fish or taking fish oils, this does not mean that eating seafood often cannot help to lower the risk of developing heart disease or cancer or obesity. There are several potential pitfalls in that study (including the possibility that most of the fish the men ate was low in the oils believed to be protective) that could account for its negative finding when several other studies have suggested otherwise.

The best lesson to learn from the new finding on fish is not to change one's living habits on the basis of one study. For a finding to become a fact, it must be replicated by independent scientists in different groups of people and it should have a demonstrable biological explanation.

Meanwhile, for a currently healthy person, moderation appears to be the wisest course. Follow a diet low in fat (15 to 20 percent of calories from fat seems reasonable and likely to be beneficial) and rich in grains and other starches, fruits and vegetables, and get regular, preferably daily, exercise, switching among two or three moderate to vigorous activities like brisk walking, cycling, swimming laps and strength training.

[JEB, May 1995]

The Rights and Wrongs
of Dietary Fat

ADMONISHED for decades to cut back on saturated fats to lower their cholesterol, millions of Americans made sensible dietary changes that they thought would protect their hearts. They switched from butter to margarine, looked for "made with pure vegetable shortening" on packages of baked and fried products and sought fast foods that were not fried in beef fat, and many even gave up eating meat.

And after recent reports that walnuts and olive oil may promote cardiovascular health, many have begun chomping on nuts and sprinkling olive oil on foods as if it were a magical elixir.

But now they are hearing disturbing news that margarine may not be so good for the heart after all, that vegetable shortening is even less advantageous than margarine, that at least some of the saturated fat in red meat does not raise cholesterol but that overdoing the nuts and olive oil can put on pounds that in turn may send cholesterol levels soaring.

It is enough to make a health-conscious person wonder whether to return to the eggs-butter-cream-and-steak diet of yore and let the old ticker fend for itself until scientists make up their minds about what is and what is not healthful for the heart.

But wait. The dietary fat picture is not as confusing as it may seem. And once you understand the science behind recent findings, you will have a rather clear picture of how to put together a diet that helps to prevent not just heart disease but many cancers and obesity (and its attendant risks of hypertension and diabetes) as well.

There are three main types of fatty acids—saturated, monounsaturated and polyunsaturated—and the various fats in foods are classified by which type of fatty acid predominates. The more saturated fatty acids in a fat, the harder it is at room temperature and, in general, the more damaging it is to serum cholesterol.

Thus, butter, meat fat and the tropical "oils" (coconut, palm and palm kernel) are considered saturated fats because most of their fatty acids are saturated and they are solid at room temperature. Olive oil, canola oil and most of the nut oils, like peanut, walnut and avocado, are monounsaturated. Soybean, corn, safflower, sunflower and cottonseed oils are polyunsaturated.

An unsaturated fat can be made more saturated, and thus firmer, by a process called hydrogenation. This is how margarine and Crisco-type vegetable shortenings are made from liquid vegetable oils. Stick margarines are more fully hydrogenated than soft tub or squeezable margarines.

The method of hydrogenation used by commercial producers of edible fats in this country creates a chemical form called *trans* fatty acids, which have been shown to raise blood levels of harmful low-density-lipoprotein, or LDL, cholesterol both in young healthy people with normal cholesterol levels and in middle-aged people who start out with moderately high cholesterol levels.

In a recent report from the continuing Nurses' Health Study at the Harvard School of Public Health, frequent consumption of margarine and vegetable shortening was linked to a 50 percent higher rate of coronary deaths, though the study could not distinguish between the harm that might be caused by *trans* fatty acids and the damage attributable to the saturated fatty acids in these fats.

But even with unnaturally introduced *trans* fatty acids, scientists who study fat metabolism have shown that margarine and vegetable shortening are considerably less damaging to cholesterol levels than butter and other natural fats that are highly saturated. Most saturated fats raise blood levels of cholesterol overall and especially those of artery-clogging LDL cholesterol.

An exception is stearic acid, one of the saturated fats in beef fat and the primary fat in cocoa butter, from which chocolate is made. Stearic acid, according to well-designed studies at the University of Texas Southwestern Medical School in Dallas, does not raise or lower cholesterol.

Polyunsaturated oils have been promoted for years as more healthful for the heart because they lower the total cholesterol level in the blood. Unfortunately, they reduce not only harmful LDL cholesterol but also beneficial HDL, or high-density-lipoprotein, cholesterol, a fact that has prompted a recent reexamination of recommendations for a heart-healthy diet.

Monounsaturated fats like olive oil, which had long been thought to have a neutral effect on blood cholesterol, are now known to lower LDL cholesterol while leaving untouched or slightly raising protective HDL cholesterol, which helps to clear fatty deposits from artery walls. This finding fits with the observation that heart disease is relatively uncommon among people living along the Mediterranean, where olive oil is the main cooking and table fat.

But regardless of which fat is studied, the more total fat consumed, the higher the coronary risk is, in part because high-fat diets are associated with overweight and in part because most such diets are filled with artery-damaging saturated fats.

First and foremost, your goal should be to reduce the amount of fat you consume overall. For average Americans this means eating about a third less fat. This is accomplished by choosing mainly low-fat foods, cooking with little or no fat and adding as little fat as possible to prepared foods. Certain sources of saturated fats, like lean meat and chocolate in circumspect amounts, can remain part of a heart-healthy diet, but others, like butterfat, lard, suet, tropical oils and chicken fat, are best avoided whenever possible.

Experts say that even with its *trans* fatty acids, margarine is still preferable to butter as a table spread. But the ideal choice is to quit smearing your bread with fat (tasty whole-grain breads need no embellishment); second best is to adopt the Italian custom and use olive oil; third best is to use the reduced-fat tub or squeezable margarines, which are less saturated and have fewer *trans* fatty acids than stick margarine.

Also watch out for hydrogenated vegetable oils. Check ingredient lists on packaged foods for the words "partially hydrogenated" or "hydrogenated" vegetable oil. Unfortunately, the same kind of information is not available to consumers of commercially prepared foods that are sold without an ingredients list, like fast foods and restaurant foods that are fried or sautéed and bakery goods (cookies, cakes, muffins, pies, Danish pastries) that are made with fat. All such products can contain substantial amounts of hydrogenated fats and suspect *trans* fatty acids.

Remember that body weight is a major contributor to high cholesterol and coronary risk. If you fail to lose weight when shifting to a low-fat diet, you cannot expect much change in your cholesterol level. As Dr. Scott Grundy of the Southwestern Medical School puts it, "It's not just a question of what you eat but of how much you eat."

[JEB, March 1993]

Proof That a Cholesterol-Lowering Drug Saves Lives

FOR the first time, a study has found that lowering cholesterol not only reduces the risk of heart attack but also saves lives.

Until now, large studies of cholesterol-lowering drugs have shown that they can reduce deaths from heart attacks but not the overall death rate. People who lowered their cholesterol levels with drugs died at higher rates of other causes, like cancer or violence or suicide. The connection was a mystery, but the numbers sparked a bitter debate over whether lowering cholesterol was worthwhile.

A new study in Scandinavia, scientists say, emphatically answers that question. The study involved 4,444 men and women age 35 to 70 with heart disease who had moderate to high cholesterol levels. Half took a potent cholesterol-lowering drug, simvastatin, that cut their cholesterol levels by an average of 35 percent. The others took a dummy pill. After following the participants for a median of 5.4 years, the researchers discovered that the death rate in the simvastatin group was 30 percent lower than that in the control group.

These results, coming after 20 years of futile efforts to show that lowering cholesterol could save lives, is expected to resolve the contentious debate over lowering cholesterol that has divided scientists and confused the public. And it is expected to herald a new emphasis on the aggressive treatment of high cholesterol levels in people at risk for heart attacks. Although most doctors do not now prescribe cholesterol-lowering drugs even to those who have already had a heart attack, researchers agreed that will now change. "This study will change medical practice," said Dr. Michael Brown, a Nobel laureate and a heart disease researcher at the University of Texas Southwestern Medical Center in Dallas.

The findings are "dynamite," said Dr. Suzanne Oparil, the president of the American Heart Association and a cardiologist at the University of Alabama at Birmingham. She added that she had been a skeptic on lowering cholesterol, but that the new results "changed my mind."

The investigators said that for every 100 people who took simvastatin, 9 would have been expected to die of heart disease, but only 4 did. Similarly, 21 would have been expected to have a nonfatal heart attack, but only 7 did. And of the 19 who would have been expected to have bypass surgery or balloon angioplasty, only 6 required these procedures. And most important, the simvastatin group had no increase in deaths from other causes, like cancer.

The drug had very few side effects. Six percent of the simvastatin group dropped out of the study, as did the same percentage of the placebo group.

"There is an alleged claim that lowering cholesterol in general would increase the risk of cancer and also depression, making people more likely to die of suicide or violence," said Dr. John Kjekshus, the director of the study and head of the cardiology section at the National Hospital at the University of Oslo. "We refute that claim. There is nothing to it."

The results are "absolutely astonishing," Dr. Brown said. He added that the study was "pivotal," since "the public has been confused about cholesterol and it's very understandable why."

"Part of the reason is that the scientific community has been unable to supply definitive data that cholesterol lowering actually prolongs life," he said. "This study answers that question and does it in an extremely definitive way."

The study, called the Scandinavian Simvastatin Survival Study, was sponsored by Merck & Company, the maker of simvastatin, and carried out independently at 94 clinical centers in Denmark, Finland, Iceland, Norway and Sweden. Dr. Kjekshus and his colleagues presented the results to a handful of senior managers at Merck in late September, but others in the company did not learn about them until recently. The investigators plan to announce their findings to cardiologists tomorrow at a plenary session of the American Heart Association meeting in Dallas. The findings will be published on Saturday in *The Lancet,* the British medical journal.

For more than 50 years, scientists have pointed to high cholesterol levels as a risk factor for heart disease. And starting in the 1960s, they began conducting large studies in an attempt to show that people who had a high cholesterol level would live longer if they reduced it. It was not hard to show this for other risk factors for heart disease, like smoking, high blood pressure and diabetes. But cholesterol-lowering studies were disappointing, in part, researchers said, because reducing cholesterol levels was very difficult. Standard cholesterol-lowering diets have very little effect on most people's blood cholesterol levels. Until recently, cholesterol-lowering drugs were not tremendously effective and were plagued by side effects.

In 1987, the first of a new class of drugs, called statins, was approved for marketing, and the picture changed dramatically. These drugs were designed to do one thing—to block an enzyme that is needed to manufacture cholesterol. When cholesterol production is blocked, the liver takes up more cholesterol from the bloodstream, meaning that less cholesterol is carried to coronary arteries. There are now four statins on the market, including simvastatin, which was introduced in 1992 and is the most powerful of the statins in lowering cholesterol.

The drugs are expensive—simvastatin costs between $650 and $1,000 a year, depending on the dose.

Dr. Kjekshus and his colleagues suggested that if it was correct that lower cholesterol levels meant longer life, they should be able to prove it by using simvastatin to markedly reduce cholesterol levels and by giving it to people who already had heart disease and so were at high risk of dying. They predicted they would see a 30 percent reduction in death rates if they enrolled about 4,500 people in the study and followed them for about five years. And that is exactly what happened.

"The whole thing is like Babe Ruth pointing to the stands and saying, 'This is where I'm going to hit it next,' " Dr. Brown said. "That's what they did."

The next question, however, is, What about people with moderate to high cholesterol levels who do not have symptoms of heart disease? Should they take a statin drug?

The problem, Dr. Brown said, is that only 40 percent of people with high cholesterol levels die of heart disease, and no one knows how to identify those people in advance. "If we could pick out those 40 percent, we could be really aggressive with them and the rest could eat steak to their heart's content," he said.

For now, doctors have to guess who is most at risk and make recommendations based on family history and factors like smoking and high blood pressure that boost cholesterol's potentially dangerous effects. The new study, Dr. Brown said, "gives us more support for being very aggressive with people at high risk."

A recent study suggested that people over age 70 may not fall into that high-risk category, since for them high cholesterol levels do not seem to translate into a high likelihood of dying from heart disease.

Dr. Oparil of the American Heart Association said that the study certainly suggested that lowering cholesterol will also save lives and prevent heart disease in people who have no symptoms of heart disease. But, she said, no clinical scientist would say its results prove that people without obvious heart disease should take a cholesterol-lowering drug.

However, Dr. Oparil added, "as an individual, particularly if I were male and had a strongly positive family history and a high cholesterol level, I would take it."

[GK, November 1994]

Good Eggs and Bad Cholesterol

IN recent decades the egg, like Humpty-Dumpty, has had a great fall. Since the mid-1940s, concern about cholesterol and heart disease has sent per capita consumption plummeting from more than 400 eggs a year to only 235 in 1992, according to the latest figures available.

But after a half century of hard knocks, 1995 may be the year that the egg, unlike Humpty, gets put together again. After three decades of blanket dietary advice to keep daily cholesterol intake below 300 milligrams and to limit egg consumption to four yolks a week, some experts on diet and heart disease are considering a more individualized approach that would allow a large portion of the population to eat more eggs, as well as other foods, like shrimp, that are relatively high in cholesterol but low in fat.

The interest in eggs stems from several incontrovertible facts. Eggs are inexpensive, readily available, easy to chew and digest, simple to prepare, relatively low in calories, and rich in protein, iron and many other essential nutrients. Unfortunately, eggs are also rich in cholesterol. The yolk of one large egg (the whites are free of both fat and cholesterol) has 213 milligrams of cholesterol and 5 grams of fat; 2 of them are saturated fat, which can raise blood levels of cholesterol.

Cholesterol in the diet became a health issue after studies of thousands of people in a dozen countries showed a direct link between the amount of cholesterol in the blood and the risk of developing and dying of coronary heart disease. However, subsequent research revealed two main influences on blood cholesterol: the amount of saturated fat in the diet and heredity. Dietary cholesterol is only weakly associated with coronary risk. For the average American, eating an additional 200 milligrams of cholesterol a day (about the amount in one egg) raises blood cholesterol about 3 milligrams, which in turn raises the risk of coronary disease by 6 percent.

But people are not averages. There are several ways in which the body can compensate for an increase in dietary cholesterol. In most people, cholesterol production in the liver is reduced in direct proportion to the amount consumed. In addition, excretion of cholesterol through the production of bile acids often rises as more cholesterol is eaten. And when a lot of cholesterol is consumed at once, the percentage absorbed through the digestive tract commonly drops.

Genetically, people fall into three groups: those who are very sensitive to dietary cholesterol and whose blood levels rise significantly when they eat more cholesterol; those who are insensitive and whose blood levels remain the same or even fall when more cholesterol is consumed; and those in between. Researchers at Bowman Gray School of Medicine in Winston-Salem, North Carolina, recently identified a common genetic mutation that makes people resistant to dietary cholesterol, allowing them to eat 1,000 milligrams a day without raising their blood levels.

To add to the confusion, in healthy adults, daily egg consumption has been shown to raise blood levels of the so-called good cholesterol—high-density-lipoprotein, or HDL, cholesterol—which helps to keep blood vessels free of cholesterol deposits.

Experts estimate that about one-third of Americans fall into the high-response group, the ones who should be most concerned about limiting dietary cholesterol to 300 milligrams or less each day.

"We're now at a point where we can be a little more targeted in making dietary recommendations," said Dr. Wayne Callaway, a specialist in metabolism and nutrition at George Washington University in Washington, D.C. "Those with a family history of early heart disease or high cholesterol are the ones who most need preventive dietary advice."

Dr. Neil J. Stone of Northwestern University School of Medicine in Chicago, who heads the American Heart Association's nutrition committee, generally endorses the association's dietary advice to all Americans to adopt the so-called Step 1 diet, which consists of no more than 30 percent of calories from fat and 10 percent from saturated fat, 300 milligrams of cholesterol a day and four egg yolks a week. He points out that since the 1960s, such advice has helped to reduce the average American's blood cholesterol "from the 240s to about 213, saturated fat intake from 17 or 18 percent of calories to 13 percent and total calories from fat from 42 percent to 36 percent." This shift has accounted for much of the decline in coronary heart disease in middle-aged Americans, he said. "If you can push most heart attacks from the fourth, fifth and sixth decades of life into the seventh and eighth decades by changing the diet, this is a major accomplishment," he said.

Still, he said, "It doesn't make a lot of sense to restrict eggs in most premenopausal women or in people over the age of 75 who do not have coronary heart disease." He added, "I'd rather they not smoke cigarettes than not eat eggs. Those with no risk factors whose parents lived to 95 should keep going with whatever they are now doing."

As for people with a family history of heart disease or high cholesterol, he said, "If the cards are stacked against you healthwise, it makes sense to adopt the Step 1 diet." For people with several major risk factors and those who already have heart disease, the recommended diet consists of less than 30 percent total fat, less than 7 percent saturated fat and no more than 200 milligrams of cholesterol a day.

The Egg: A Nutrition Profile

One large egg contains the following:

Protein........................6.3 grams   Saturated fat......1.6 grams
Total fat......................5 grams   Cholesterol.........213 milligrams
Monounsaturated fat...2 grams   Carbohydrates....0.6 grams
Polyunsaturated fat.....0.7 gram   Sodium...............63 milligrams

Percentage of U.S. Recommended Dietary Allowances

Protein	15	Vitamin B6	4
Vitamin A	6	Folacin	8
Vitamin C	*	Vitamin B12	8
Thiamin	4	Phosphorus	10
Riboflavin	10	Iodine	15
Niacin	*	Zinc	4
Calcium	2	Biotin	4
Iron	6	Pantothenic acid	8
Vitamin D	6	Copper	2**
Vitamin E	2	Magnesium	2

* Less than 2 percent of the U.S. R.D.A.
** Percentage of estimated safe and adequate daily intake

Sources: U.S. Food and Drug Administration; U.S. Department of Agriculture.

Ideally, a decision about one's diet would be based on individual tests of susceptibility to dietary cholesterol. This would mean, for example, taking blood cholesterol measurements before and about 10 weeks after an increase in egg consumption to determine if a person is sensitive to dietary cholesterol. In the future a simple blood test may be used to find out who has the genetic mutation that permits risk-free consumption of cholesterol.

One concern about eggs involves their ability, when eaten raw or minimally cooked, to transmit the food-poisoning bacterium *Salmonella,* which can be fatal to people who are very old or very ill. According to the U.S. Department of Agriculture, eggs that are soft-boiled can be eaten safely, as long as the egg is cooked at 140 degrees Fahrenheit for three and a half minutes. This kills the bacteria, yet leaves the egg soft enough to use in dressings like mayonnaise and sauces.

[JEB, January 1995]

Low-Fat Diet May Not Help Avert Breast Cancer

A new study has failed to find any relationship between the amount of fat a woman eats and her chances of developing breast cancer.

The study found that even extremely-low-fat diets, with fat providing less than 20 percent of total calories, failed to reduce breast cancer risk. A diet that low in fat includes less animal foods than most Americans eat.

The researchers also found no evidence that the predominant type of fat in the diet—whether saturated, monounsaturated or polyunsaturated—affected a woman's risk of breast cancer.

Although there may be a widespread belief or hope that low-fat diets protect against breast cancer, many leading researchers say that they have been skeptical for years about such a link. Study after study, they said, has failed to find any association, leaving proponents of the fat hypothesis to postulate that perhaps the fat content of the diet needed to be very low, below 20 percent of total calories, or perhaps women had to start eating low-fat diets when they were children.

The new study, published in a recent issue of the *New England Journal of Medicine,* analyzed data pooled from seven studies in four countries. An international team of epidemiologists, including those who had the most experience investigating the diet–breast cancer hypothesis, reasoned that by combining data from all the studies, which included more than 335,000 women, they would have enough to answer this lingering question about dietary fat in adulthood and breast cancer.

In each of the seven studies, women's diets were ascertained and then the women were followed for up to seven years. Some women developed breast cancer in that period, and so the investigators could determine whether these women had eaten more fat than those who did not develop breast cancer.

The answer, said Dr. David J. Hunter, the study's lead author, was that fat made no difference in breast cancer rates. "I feel that it is fairly definite that even at less than 20 percent fat, there is no protection against breast cancer," said Dr. Hunter, the executive director of the Harvard Center for Cancer Prevention.

"There is no doubt that a diet that is low in red meats and high-fat dairy products and high in fruits and vegetables is beneficial with respect to other diseases," Dr. Hunter said. But, he added, the fat hypothesis "has been a dead end and ultimately a distraction" from studies that might explain what predisposes women to breast cancer.

The dietary fat hypothesis was based in large part on studies with laboratory animals and on epidemiological studies that compared breast cancer rates in countries where the diet was high in fat with the rates in countries where dietary fat was low. For example, said Dr. Regina Ziegler, a nutritional epidemiologist at the National Cancer Institute, the incidence of breast cancer in the United States and other Western countries is about five times higher than it is in Asian countries.

"Fifteen years ago, everyone would have said that dietary fat explains the differential breast cancer rates between countries," Dr. Ziegler said.

But when researchers started studying the hypothesis in depth, with studies like the seven analyzed by Dr. Hunter and his colleagues, as well as studies that compared the diets of women who developed breast cancer with those of others who did not, they found "nothing of the magnitude to explain the international differences," Dr. Ziegler said.

But Dr. Ziegler said she was reluctant to say that diet in general is unimportant to breast cancer risk. "To say that this nails it, that this disproves a role for diet, is too strong," she said.

Dr. Ziegler said, for example, that the studies to date have not addressed the question of diet in childhood and adolescence. And, she said, the studies have involved women in Western countries eating Western diets, leaving open the question of whether some as-yet-undetermined aspect of Asian diets is protective against breast cancer.

[GK, February 1996]

The Puzzle of
Diet and Breast Cancer

MANY health-conscious Americans are beginning to feel as if they are being tossed around like yo-yos by conflicting research findings. One day beta-carotene is hailed as a lifesaving antioxidant and the next it is stripped of its health-promoting glory and even tainted by a brush of potential harm. Margarine, long hailed as a heart-saving alternative to butter, is suddenly found to contain a type of fat that could damage the heart.

Now, after women have heard countless suggestions that a low-fat diet may reduce their breast cancer risk, Harvard researchers who analyzed data pooled from seven studies in four countries report that this advice may be based more on wishful thinking than on fact.

The researchers, whose review was published recently in the *New England Journal of Medicine,* found no evidence among a number of studies of more than 335,000 women that a diet with less than 20 percent of calories from fat reduced a woman's risk of developing breast cancer. Nor was risk related to the types of fats the women ate, the study reported.

Is this the final word on the subject, and does it mean that diet is not an important factor in breast cancer? Not at all. There are several possibilities still to be explored. One is the relationship between breast cancer risk and fats consumed in childhood, adolescence and early adulthood. The current studies considered fat intake in mid–adult life. But evidence from other breast cancer studies, like those involving exercise and hormones, suggests that exposure to fats early in life plays a stronger role in determining risk.

Another factor to consider is the accuracy of women's dietary reports. People are notoriously poor at remembering what and how much they consume, especially if they are consuming foods that they think they should avoid, like fat-rich ice cream or cream cheese. A third factor is whether a diet share of less than 20 percent of calories from fat is low enough to be protective, and a fourth concerns the possibility that the kind of fat, not the amount, is the issue.

For example, in animal studies, monounsaturated fats like olive and canola oils do not promote tumor growth the way polyunsaturated fats do. And in Spain and Greece, women with breast cancer were found to consume less olive oil than did healthy women. But until recently monounsaturated oils were not commonplace in American diets, and they may not have been well enough represented in the Harvard study to show up as protective.

Finally, and perhaps most important, is the possibility that fat consumption may simply be an indicator of other dietary and lifestyle factors that play a more direct role in protecting against breast cancer.

The suggestion that dietary fat may influence the risk of breast cancer originally arose from international comparisons. Breast cancer is much less common in Asia and in poor countries that habitually consume a low-fat diet. Until recently, about 42 percent of the calories in the diets of American women came from fat (it is now at about 34 percent), whereas among Japanese women fat provided only about 10 to 15 percent of calories. But when Asian women move to the United States, their breast cancer risk begins to climb, and in a generation or two it reaches the high level of American women, who face a 1-in-8 lifetime risk of developing the disease.

Now the equivocal findings about the role of fats are prompting a closer look at other elements in the diets and lives of women that may account for international differences in breast cancer risk. In a review of breast cancer and diet in the January–February issue of

Nutrition Action Health Letter, nutritionist Bonnie Liebman points out that when Asian women move to this country, they and their descendants gradually adopt Western eating habits.

For example, they start eating less soy and more meat. Soy foods like tofu, miso and soy milk contain substances called isoflavonoids, which act in the body like weak estrogens and may interfere with the action of estrogens the body produces. Since natural estrogens are known to promote the growth of breast tumors, anything that interferes with their activity should lower the risk of breast cancer. But this too may be a red herring; in two recent studies, Japanese women with breast cancer consumed no less soy than their healthy counterparts.

Another possibility is that in countries with low breast cancer rates, women mainly subsist on plant-based foods: grains, vegetables, fruits and beans. Evidence is growing that plant foods, especially beans and vegetables, are rich in substances, including weak estrogens, that protect against cancers in general and specifically against cancers influenced by hormones. Supporting this possibility is the observation that in countries where women rarely get breast cancer, men rarely develop prostate cancer, which is also influenced by hormones.

Alcohol, too, may be an important factor. Although one drink a day helps to prevent heart disease, the leading killer of American women, it may raise the risk of breast cancer anywhere from 10 percent to 40 percent, and the risk may be even higher among women who consume two drinks a day.

In every country that has a low rate of breast cancer, women traditionally get far more exercise than American women, most of whom have been rendered inactive by motor vehicles and labor-saving devices. Among Americans, Dr. Leslie Bernstein of the University of Southern California found that premenopausal women who exercised for one to three hours a week had a 30 percent lower risk of developing breast cancer than inactive women, and those who exercised for four or more hours a week had less than half the risk. An earlier study had linked exercise in adolescence and early adulthood to a reduced risk of breast cancer in midlife.

Physical activity and a low-fat, plant-based diet are also related to yet another factor associated with breast cancer: body weight and especially distribution of body fat. Asian women are much leaner on average than American women. Among Americans, being overweight (by American standards) is associated with a slight increase in the risk of breast cancer, perhaps because body fat is a source of estrogen. But when fat gathers around the waist—the so-called apple shape—the relationship to breast cancer, as well as heart disease, is much stronger. Abdominal fat raises insulin levels in the blood and, at least in laboratory studies, insulin promotes the growth of breast cancer cells.

Height may also play a role. Tall women have a breast cancer risk 30 to 40 percent higher than that of short women. What makes women tall? In part, it is a childhood diet high in protein, which is common among Americans and, until recently at least, rare among the Japanese and other peoples with a low risk of breast cancer.

A possibly protective factor, at least for premenopausal women, is prolonged breast-feeding—for 4 to 12 months—which until recently has been rare among "modern" American women.

[JEB, February 1996]

Critic Doubts Benefit of Standard Low-Fat Diet

ANOTHER given in the health field came under scrutiny recently as an expert challenged the notion that a diet consisting of 30 percent fat, a widely promoted goal, would reduce the incidence of heart disease. The notion has only the flimsiest scientific grounding, the expert, a British cardiologist, said after reviewing the world's medical literature.

His analysis follows on the heels of studies raising questions about the cardiac protective value of fish, the life-prolonging effects of moderate exercise, the benefits of vitamin supplements and margarine, and various other nutritional issues.

Groups ranging from the National Academy of Sciences to the American Heart Association to the National Heart, Lung and Blood Institute have recommended that Americans reduce their consumption of fat so that it makes up no more than 30 percent of their diets. And as national surveys of dietary habits are published periodically, public health officials compare the percentage of fat in the diet—now 34 percent—with that goal.

But Dr. Michael F. Oliver, emeritus professor at the National Heart and Lung Institute in London, begs to differ with the value of that goal. In an analysis presented recently at the First International Conference on Fats and Oils and Human Disease, held at Rockefeller University in New York, he concluded that studies of people whose diets achieve the 30 percent goal show that the diets had virtually no effect on cholesterol levels. More restrictive diets are effective, but few healthy people comply with them for very long, Dr. Oliver, a heart disease researcher, said.

In addition, Dr. Oliver said, large clinical trials conducted over the last two decades have failed to demonstrate that the national goal of a 30-percent-fat diet has any effect on heart disease rates.

Dr. Oliver said he was not suggesting that cholesterol is irrelevant in heart disease. Studies have repeatedly shown that high cholesterol levels increase the risk of heart disease. And a recent large study showed decisively that powerful cholesterol-lowering drugs not only reduce cholesterol levels but prevent heart attacks and save lives in people who had heart disease and high cholesterol levels. But, Dr. Oliver said, he is taking issue with the standard advice that a 30-percent-fat diet, the so-called Step 1 diet of the American Heart Association, is some sort of potion for the general population.

"Studies of this low-fat, low-cholesterol diet are completely negative," Dr. Oliver said. "We should face up to the fact that the Step 1 diet doesn't work." But, Dr. Oliver said, "vast sums of money are being spent on nutritional programs, dietitian advice, and nurse counseling in pursuance of diets which may be completely ineffectual."

Other leading researchers said that Dr. Oliver was correct, although some argued that indirect evidence still strongly indicates that a low-fat diet will prevent heart disease.

"Oliver's point is well taken," said Dr. Walter Willett, a professor of epidemiology and nutrition at the Harvard School of Public Health. He added that public health specialists have been "very dogmatic" in their recommendations without the proof that most people assume lies behind the recommendations.

Dr. David Gordon, a researcher at the National Heart, Lung and

Blood Institute who studies diet and heart disease, agreed that "the evidence isn't as good as we'd like it to be." Although small studies in carefully controlled circumstances found that people who followed low-fat diets "could achieve pretty good cholesterol lowering," larger studies involving low-fat diets "essentially didn't change cholesterol levels or heart disease rates very much."

Dr. Neil J. Stone, who is chairman of the American Heart Association's nutrition committee, said of Dr. Oliver's conclusions that "many of us share his concerns that the so-called population diet may not be strict enough to make a difference for high-risk people or it may be too strict for healthy people." He added that "the sticking part of the issue is that the diet, when used in high-risk populations, is not a very effective diet," and people who are not at risk because their cholesterol is already low also will not see much benefit.

On the other hand, Dr. Stone said, the diet "is our best approximation" to prod the population toward eating less fat, which is generally thought to be a laudatory goal.

Dr. Basil Rifkind, a senior scientific adviser at the heart institute, said that although the diet's effects "in the real world have been disappointing," that does not mean the message is wrong. "The greater the cholesterol reduction, the greater the reduction in risk," he said. "If you're eating a 45-percent-fat diet, a 30-percent-fat diet is a bit better, 20 percent is better and 15 percent is much better." He added that the advice to Americans to aim for a diet that is 30 percent fat "was a compromise between what is ideal and what is practical and we didn't go further because we felt that Americans were not likely to switch to a Japanese-type diet of 14 or 15 percent fat." He said it "would be a great mistake" if Americans conclude from Dr. Oliver's remarks that they can slip back into eating fatty foods.

In his analysis, Dr. Oliver cited six large studies of people at high risk for heart disease. All the studies included low-fat diets along with other interventions, including smoking cessation, control of blood pressure and increasing exercise. Only two found a reduction in heart disease rates or in death rates from heart disease or in deaths from all causes. And one actually found that the group following a low-fat diet had more deaths, including more deaths from heart disease.

One of the studies finding a correlation involved patients confined to a mental hospital in Finland, where diet could be completely controlled. Yet even in this study, Dr. Oliver noted, the major effect was in heart disease rates, not death rates.

The second study was a Norwegian study of high-risk men. Those in the intervention group lost weight and stopped smoking in addition to changing the amount of fat in their diet, so it is difficult to know how much of an independent effect the low-fat diet had.

Moreover, Dr. Oliver reported, other studies show that 30-percent-fat diets are not highly effective in lowering cholesterol. One recent study involving 309 people with high cholesterol levels found that, after six months, the subjects' cholesterol levels had fallen by less than 2 percent.

One argument of those who support the guidelines is that they are a realistic goal people should aim toward, and the more the guidelines can motivate people to reduce the fat in their diets, the better. A 30-percent-fat level is preferable, and one lower than 20 percent is better still.

But, said Dr. Jules Hirsch, who is physician in chief at Rockefeller University, people may reach a point of diminishing returns. In his studies with Dr. Lisa Hudgins, he found that when the fat content in people's diets got below 20 percent, they started making fat out of the carbohydrates they ate. Moreover, he said, when that happens, "the fat you make is saturated," the worst kind for the heart. Dr. Hirsch said it would be premature to conclude that particular low-fat diets were dangerous. But, he said, the finding "brings up very serious questions; it's a real worry."

Dr. Willett also asks if physicians know enough to advise that all healthy people try to get their dietary fat down to 30 percent. He said that the effects of dietary fat reduction can depend on which fats are reduced. If people preferentially cut saturated fats, they lower the proportion of high-density lipoproteins in their blood, which protect against heart disease. If they substitute carbohydrates for fats, they can once again proportionately reduce their HDL levels and also increase their triglyceride levels, which increases heart disease risk. "No one know what all this means, but it could easily be deleterious," Dr. Willett said.

Of course, all agree that more research is needed. But, some say, it is better to tell the truth about the uncertainties of current knowledge than to insist that the dietary advice is beyond question.

"The most important thing is that where there is uncertainty we have to pay more attention and try to get better data," Dr. Willett said.

[GK, April 1995]

How to Control Cholesterol Levels

RICHARD Erde of Brooklyn smoked his last cigarette on the way to the hospital during a heart attack at age 53. In a matter of weeks, Richard was back on the tennis court, his pack-and-a-half-a-day habit behind him and his diet changing rapidly from meat, potatoes and gravy to rice, beans and salad. On the days he does not play singles tennis, and some days when he does, he cycles or jogs. He is now lean and fit and has his cholesterol checked regularly to be sure that the level of damaging LDL cholesterol stays low and the protective HDL cholesterol remains in a normal range without drugs. He has taken many steps to improve his cholesterol level and thereby lower his risk of a second, and possibly fatal, heart attack.

By quitting smoking and increasing his exercise, he raised his blood level of beneficial HDL cholesterol. By losing weight and cutting way back on—indeed, almost eliminating—saturated fats, both animal and vegetable, he lowered his total cholesterol, especially the harmful LDL cholesterol. And by adding beans to his diet, he further improved his cholesterol readings.

But for the average person trying to control an elevated cholesterol level through the dietary changes suggested by the American Heart Association, the reduction is almost always a modest one of about 5 or 10 percent.

The association recommends initially limiting cholesterol intake to 300 milligrams a day and fat consumption to 30 percent of calories, with no more than 10 percent of calories derived from saturated fats, meaning those that are firm at room temperature. For those who need it, the next level of the association's cholesterol-lowering diet calls for a daily limit of 200 milligrams of cholesterol, 28 percent fat calories and 8 percent saturated fats. The third level cuts intake to 100 milligrams of cholesterol, 22 percent fat calories and 6 percent saturated fats.

Still, such diets are rarely enough to reduce a cholesterol reading of, say, 270 or 300 milligrams per deciliter of blood serum to a level associated with a low risk of developing heart disease. This "safe" level is said to be below 200 milligrams, though it can inch up above 200 if the contribution of protective HDL cholesterol is very high. The average American man has an HDL level of about 42 and consequently a relatively high risk of heart disease; a level of 60 or more is considered low-risk.

Dr. Dean Ornish and the late Nathan Pritikin both demonstrated that adhering to a far more austere diet—one that is nearly or completely vegetarian and contains very little fat of any kind—can often dramatically lower serum cholesterol. And Dr. Ornish showed that along with daily exercise and stress management, the strict diet can actually reverse some of the damage done to coronary arteries by years of sedentary living too high on the hog.

It is unlikely that the Ornish regimen would ever gain a wide following among currently healthy Americans whose cholesterol levels are too high. Dietary habits die hard, and the temptations to stray from a low-fat, vegetarian diet are just too prevalent.

But cholesterol-conscious Americans could benefit from a less extreme approach, like the "real" Mediterranean diet, which, though high in fat because it is rich in olive oil, consists primarily of grains, beans, vegetables and fruits, with small amounts of yogurt and cheese daily, fish, eggs and poultry only a few times a week and red meat only a few times a month, or more often when used in tiny amounts as a flavoring.

There are still other cholesterol-improving measures that are promising, though less firmly established than a strict diet, regular exercise and stopping smoking. One is eating many small meals a day, instead of two or three big ones. Another is having an alcoholic drink or two each day. Those who consume moderate amounts of alcohol tend to have higher HDL levels, fewer heart attacks and a longer life expectancy. Wine, especially red wine, is believed to be most helpful, particularly when consumed with meals. But moderation is the key to health; beyond two drinks a day (eight ounces of wine), the risks of cirrhosis of the liver and other adverse effects rise.

Also potentially protective is a daily capsule containing 400 international units of vitamin E, which can help prevent damaging LDL cholesterol from being oxidized into a form that readily adheres to artery walls.

Consuming half a clove or more of garlic each day can produce a modest drop in total cholesterol and especially LDL cholesterol. Fish oils—the so-called omega-3 fatty acids, which are prominent in fatty fish like salmon, sardines and mackerel—may lower blood levels of triglycerides, which, like cholesterol, can increase coronary risk.

The monounsaturated fats found in olive and canola oils and nuts may help to lower LDL cholesterol and raise HDL cholesterol, especially if they replace sources of saturated fats. But oils and nuts are very high in calories, and if they result in weight gain, the effect may be counterproductive.

Oat bran and other soluble fibers, which were all the rage less than a decade ago, have faded in popularity among consumers, but are still effective in helping reduce high cholesterol levels. Good sources include oats, beans and peas, barley, apples, carrots, citrus fruits, rice bran and corn, processed foods containing guar gum and pectin, and the supplement psyllium.

But there may be more than cholesterol in blood to worry about. Recent studies have linked high blood levels of an amino acid called homocysteine with an increased risk of developing coronary disease as serious as that associated with high cholesterol. Just a small decline in homocysteine levels could save 35,000 lives a year in this country, experts say.

To lower homocysteine levels, all one need do is consume more foods rich in the B vitamin folic acid, primarily dark green, leafy vegetables like spinach, kale, broccoli, collards, chard and brussels sprouts, and fruits like apples and oranges. An alternative approach is to go back to the pills: a folic acid supplement of 400 micrograms a day.

[JEB, January 1996]

Fish Stories and
the Hoopla over Fish Oils

THE words are big—eicosapentaenoic acid and docosahexaenoic acid—but the sales are even bigger, exceeding $45 million a year. These are the scientific names of two prominent fatty acids in fish oils, better known as omega-3s, supplements of which have become hot items among the health-conscious.

Despite the popularity of fish oil capsules, most researchers in the field say this pill popping is scientifically unjustifiable and may even be dangerous to some people. Furthermore, some of the early claims for benefits attributed to fish oils have not yet been borne out, despite well-designed studies.

The enthusiasm for fish oils began with the observation that Greenland Eskimos, whose diet is rich in marine oils, rarely suffer heart attacks or strokes caused by blood clots. Several effects of fish oils have been cited as the probable explanation for this association. First, the oils lower blood levels of artery-damaging fats called triglycerides. Elevated levels of these fats can increase the risk of a heart attack. Some preliminary research also indicates that fish oils may help to prevent a potentially fatal disruption in heart rhythm called ventricular fibrillation.

But most important, fish oils were found to have two potent anti-clotting effects. They reduce the stickiness of platelets, the blood cells that initiate clots, and inhibit the formation of four coagulation proteins, one of which, fibrinogen, is considered a risk factor for heart disease. Since most heart attacks and strokes are caused by clots trying to squeeze through arteries narrowed by fatty deposits, anything that inhibits clotting would logically lower the risk.

The claims for fish oils then went hog-wild, with hints of benefits being turned into established facts long before proper studies had explored them. One was the suggestion that fish oils lower blood pressure. And indeed they do, in relatively large doses in people who have both high blood pressure and high blood cholesterol levels or atherosclerosis. But, according to a recent review of 31 studies involving 1,300 patients, in the majority of people with hypertension, fish oils at practical doses have at best a very modest effect on blood pressure.

More promising has been the association between fish oils and the prevention or treatment of autoimmune diseases like lupus, kidney disease and rheumatoid arthritis. The Greenland Eskimos are reported to have a relatively low incidence of certain disorders that involve the immune system, including multiple sclerosis, asthma and psoriasis. Most of the studies to date have been done in laboratory animals that are prone to autoimmune diseases. But studies of patients with rheumatoid arthritis found that fish oil supplements (about 6 grams a day) can diminish morning stiffness and joint tenderness, a benefit that can persist for four weeks after the supplements are stopped.

Although this may seem unrelated, studies of chronic migraine sufferers who did not respond to other remedies showed significant relief associated with very large (20-gram) doses of fish oil supplements given every day. Researchers believe that fish oils change the balance of substances called prostaglandins and leukotrienes, which are potent mediators of inflammation and immune responses.

The anti-inflammatory effects of fish oils are believed to be responsible for the new finding that frequent consumption of fish helps to protect smokers from chronic obstructive pulmonary diseases like chronic bronchitis and emphysema. According to a study of 8,960 current and former smokers, published recently in the *New England Journal of Medicine*, those who ate two and a half or more servings of fish each week halved their odds of developing these lung diseases.

There is also some preliminary evidence to suggest that fish oils may inhibit the spread of some cancers, particularly breast cancer. The omega-3 fatty acids are thought to inhibit proliferation of tumors by preventing the formation of tumor-stimulating prostaglandins. In a study in mice published recently in the *Journal of the National Cancer Institute*, the spread of human breast cancer to the lungs was inhibited in animals fed a diet rich in fish oils, but no such benefit was observed in mice fed primarily corn oil, which is rich in the omega-6 fatty acid linoleic acid.

Despite the suggested benefits of fish oils to the heart, no major health organization, including the American Heart Association, recommends taking fish oil supplements outside a well-designed research study. There are good reasons for this reluctance.

The clot-inhibiting properties of fish oils have an unfortunate downside: they increase bleeding tendencies. In the Greenland Eskimos, the fish oil–rich diet appears to raise their risk of suffering usually fatal hemorrhagic strokes. In a person susceptible to other bleeding problems, like a bleeding ulcer, or for someone undergoing surgery or injured in an accident, fish oils could make matters worse.

There is also concern about the inhibiting effects of fish oils on the immune system. Whereas suppressing excessive immune reactions may be beneficial to those with autoimmune disorders, it may also reduce the ability of certain white blood cells to fight off infections. And unless taken with vitamin E, large doses of fish oils can deplete the body's supply of this critical antioxidant nutrient.

There is some evidence that fish oils can actually raise low-density-lipoprotein, or LDL, cholesterol, the so-called bad cholesterol. There is a possibility of toxic effects from contaminants like pesticide residues in fish oil capsules that are produced with less-than-stringent care. And there are some some distressing side effects, including excessive belching, diarrhea and a fishy odor among those who take high doses.

No one questions the health value of eating fish, a food rich in top-quality protein, B vitamins and minerals like iron, magnesium, zinc and potassium and very low in artery-damaging saturated fats. Most of the benefits of fish oils are associated with studies of people who eat fish regularly. Just two fish meals a week have been shown to reduce the risk of coronary death. A person who takes supplements might continue eating a diet high in damaging saturated fats, but those who eat fish are likely to substitute it for fattier meats.

The fish richest in omega-3 fatty acids include salmon, sardines, mackerel, herring, bluefish, whitefish and halibut, with more modest amounts in rainbow trout, striped bass, shark, swordfish and squid.

[JEB, August 1994]

A Fish-Heavy Diet Offers
No Protection to the Heart

A large study has failed to confirm a cherished nutritional belief: that the more fish you eat, the better you will be protected against heart disease.

The study, by Dr. Alberto Ascherio of the Harvard School of Public Health and his colleagues, followed 44,895 men for six years to determine whether those who ate the most fish would have the lowest incidence of heart disease. To the researchers' surprise, they found that it did not matter whether the men ate fish once a month or six times a week—the rate of heart disease was unaffected.

Given the results of the study, some people who do not particularly like fish but eat it three or four times a week in the expectation that it will forestall coronary disease may now feel tempted to abandon it.

"I hate fish," said one such person, Dr. Arnold Levine, a Princeton University professor, "but I've been eating it several times a week for years."

But experts cautioned against now dropping fish from the diet. One study does not necessarily prove that fish has no beneficial effects on the heart, they said, and in any case fish remains a wholesome food for a variety of reasons.

Dr. Ascherio said his study could not answer whether it was better to eat some fish than none. The reason is that so few of the men studied, just 2,042, ate no fish at all that comparison of their heart disease rate with that of the others was not statistically significant. For example, although the men who did not eat fish had a 26 percent greater risk of dying of heart disease than those who did, that number could have occurred by chance, Dr. Ascherio said. In any case, he said, "the belief that eating fish helps your heart is not supported by this or other studies. Some things," he said, "are more complex than we believed them to be."

In an editorial accompanying Dr. Ascherio's study, which was published in a recent issue of the *New England Journal of Medicine*, Dr. Martijn B. Katan of Wageningen Agricultural University in the Netherlands said the results "should somewhat dampen enthusiasm for fish and fish oil as a panacea against coronary heart disease."

But he and others said the study did not firmly rule out any benefits that fish might have on the heart.

"It is premature to close the books on fish oil based on one study," said Dr. Neil J. Stone, chairman of the American Heart Association's nutrition committee and associate professor of medicine at the Northwestern University School of Medicine. But, he added, "it certainly means we have to reexamine what the benefits of fish are."

Others suggested that eating fish might have indirect benefits.

"I think it's probably not the fish but the dietary habits associated with eating fish," said Dr. Margo Denke, a member of the heart association's nutrition committee and associate professor of medicine at the University of Texas Southwestern Medical Center in Dallas. "Look at fish as a substitute for fattier meats. If you eat fish, and let's say you substituted it for barbecue or spareribs or brisket, that's probably an improvement."

The idea that fish helps protect the heart has become entrenched in public perception even though it has never been firmly proved. Fish oil capsules are a staple at health food stores, where they are promoted as protection from heart disease, and fish itself has taken on a magical aura. "I've had people tell me they eat fish every single day," Dr. Denke said.

The fish hypothesis began a decade ago with the observation that Eskimos in Greenland had fewer heart attacks than residents of Denmark, even though the Eskimo diet was very high in fats. Perhaps, a number of researchers proposed, it was a special class of fats—the omega-3 fatty acids, found in fish oils and seafoods—that were protective. Cold-water fish like salmon, bluefish and mackerel, which are high in the omega-3 fatty acids, were considered more healthful than low-fat fish like flounder and orange roughy. "This was a very hot story indeed," Dr. Stone said.

The study on Eskimos was followed by several others indicating that the death rate from heart disease was lower among men who ate fish than among those who did not. These were population studies, Dr. Ascherio said, and they were not completely consistent. For example, he said, "we also have populations who eat lots of fish and have high rates of heart disease." In eastern Finland, for example, "they have the highest rate of heart disease in the world, and they eat lots of fish."

But the hypothesis gained credibility when a mechanism for the supposed effects was discovered. Taken in large quantities, fish oils inhibit the formation of blood clots, a weak variation of the effect that aspirin has on blood clots. And they lower triglycerides, fats in the blood that are linked to an increased risk of heart disease.

But the fish oils also had deleterious effects, Dr. Stone said. For example, they raised blood sugar levels in obese diabetics, who are most likely to have high triglyceride levels.

In addition, it was not clear whether the fish oil studies were predictive of effects that might occur from eating fish rather than taking supplements. In the studies, people consumed 3 grams of fish oil a day. In contrast, Dr. Ascherio said, a serving of even fatty fish, like salmon, provides only about 1.4 grams of fish oil.

In the end, Dr. Stone said, "we didn't have good, hard data—just these intriguing snippets of information."

The new study involved healthy men who were health professionals from 40 to 75 years of age, mostly dentists. During the six years these 44,895 men were studied, from 1986 to 1992, 264 died of heart disease, 547 had nonfatal heart attacks, and 732 had bypass surgery or angioplasties.

The investigators tried to rule out circumstances that could have obscured a finding that fish protects against heart disease. For example, some of the men in the study had high cholesterol levels. The researchers figured that men in this group might have been eating fish regularly in the hope that it would be beneficial. So they reanalyzed their data without these men. They still found no effect of fish consumption on heart disease risk.

[GK, April 1995]

Chemists Learn Why Vegetables Are Good for You

CACHED away in the soul of every red-blooded American who fondly recalls when carnivory was a virtue, and supper wasn't supper without a centerpiece of pork chops or prime rib, lies the frail hope that all the recent emphasis on fruits, grains and vegetables, vegetables, vegetables, will somehow turn out to be a terrible mistake.

Well, abandon that hope, ye who harbor it. The truth is that the more researchers understand about the ingredients found in fruits, vegetables, beans and herbs, the more impressed they are with the power of those compounds to retard the bodily breakdown that results in cancer and other chronic diseases. Nutritionists and epidemiologists have long observed that people who eat a plant-rich diet suffer lower rates of cancer than do meat loyalists, and now scientists are beginning to figure out why.

Beyond the well-known benefits of vitamins and fiber, plant foods are plush with chemicals that have no nutritional value and are not necessary for immediate survival yet may impede cancer at a variety of stages in its slow, savage evolution.

Most of the experiments performed so far have been done on animals or isolated cells, and no specific ingredient from fruits or vegetables has been proved in long-term human trials to prevent or retard cancer. But biologists are encouraged because many laboratory results are in harmony with the empirical studies of long-lived populations.

And just when researchers thought they had a reasonable grasp of the basic anticancer compounds that might be found in a healthy diet, they have discovered a novel pathway through which ingredients in plants may help foil disease.

In a recent issue of the *Proceedings of the National Academy of Sciences,* scientists from Children's University Hospital in Heidelberg, Germany, report that they have isolated a compound called genistein from the urine of people who eat a traditional Japanese diet, heavy on soybeans and vegetables. Through test-tube experiments with a synthetic version of the chemical, Dr. Lothar Schweigerer, his student Theodore Fotsis and their colleagues have discovered that genistein blocks an event called angiogenesis, the growth of new blood vessels.

That talent could have significant implications for both the prevention and the treatment of many types of solid tumors, including malignancies of the breast, prostate and brain. Scientists had previously determined that if a tumor is to expand beyond a millimeter or two in size, or four-hundredths to eight-hundredths of an inch, it must first foster the growth of new capillaries around it. Once it is fully vascularized, the malignancy then receives the oxygen and nourishment it needs to keep swelling, eventually invading the blood and lymph system and seeding fatal metastatic colonies elsewhere in the body. By inhibiting capillary growth, genistein just may keep nascent tumors from growing beyond harmless dimensions.

Genistein is found in high concentrations in soybeans and to a somewhat lesser degree in cruciferous vegetables like cabbage. In those on a traditional Japanese diet, the scientists found, the urine level of the compound is at least 30 times that of Westerners. Dr. Schweigerer also speculated that such a diet could explain why, when Japanese men leave their country for several years to work in the United States or Europe, their rate of invasive prostate cancer rises sharply. He proposed that any tiny prostate tumors that had been kept in check by daily intake of, say, miso soup would finally be free to grow once the Japanese men had assumed a more Western, genistein-poor culinary style. But he stressed that this was merely a theory, unsupported by data.

Nevertheless, if genistein proves its mettle through testing in animals, the compound may be useful not only as a dietary measure to prevent cancer but in a concentrated form to treat tumors already in progress.

"This is a fascinating report," said Dr. Judah Folkmann of Harvard Medical School, who has worked out many of the details of how tumors become vascularized as they grow. "It's a novel finding. Nobody has ever suggested before that you could find in the urine certain dietary factors that inhibit the proliferation of blood vessels, and I think this work will get wide attention."

Dr. Folkmann and others view blocking angiogenesis as an ideal sort of therapy, one that would attack the malignancy while leaving normal tissue intact. Apart from the sinister demands of tumors, new blood vessels grow in the adult body only after fairly rare events like extreme injury, heart attack or the implantation of an embryo in the uterus, and thus any compound that blocked angiogenesis would have few side effects. Four such blockers are now being tested against conditions like Kaposi's sarcoma, a highly vascularized tumor common in AIDS patients. Genistein would be the first compound isolated from food to be added to the list.

Encouraged as they are by the findings of anticarcinogens in foods, researchers admit that the field of food analysis is in its infancy. Food is chemically daunting, with every stalk of broccoli or slice of melon composed of hundreds or thousands of individual yet interacting chemicals. Some plant products may contain chemicals that promote cancer along with compounds that inhibit the disease, and it can be difficult to sort out which class of chemicals predominates in a given food.

Beyond its inherent difficulties, nutrition has been viewed as an area prone to faddishness and charlatanism, another reason traditional researchers have tended to avoid it.

"Serious scientists have stayed away from the field because it gets tied up with all the supplementation people and the antiaging crowd," said Dr. Barry Halliwell of the University of California at Davis, who studies antioxidant chemistry. "All the hype has made good scientists wary."

Nor has there been much encouragement for studies aimed at the prevention of cancer rather than its treatment. On average, only about 5 percent of the approximately $1.8 billion annual budget of the National Cancer Institute has been earmarked for disease prevention, with far more going toward expensive and high-profile studies like those on gene therapy, which, if it works, will take years before it is of use to many cancer patients.

"It's predicted that we'll end up spending a billion dollars on taxol, a drug that on average adds about five months to the life of an ovarian cancer patient," said Dr. James Duke, an economic botanist at the Department of Agriculture. "I think the country would be a lot better off if we spent a billion dollars on cancer prevention." And that sort of investment demands greater knowledge of the things people put into their mouths.

To be sure, some of the benefits of a herbivorous diet are what it helps one avoid: by taking in lots of fruits and vegetables, a person is less likely to fill up on fatty foods. "There are not a whole lot of good things you can say about eating animal fat," said Dr. Daniel Nixon of the American Cancer Society in Atlanta. What is more, vegetables have fewer calories than do meats and cheeses, and restricting calorie intake has been shown in animal studies to sharply reduce the incidence of cancer.

Suppressing Cancer Growth

The positive benefits of vegetables are many. In the course of metabolizing energy and using oxygen, the body's cells constantly generate hazardous molecules called free radicals, which can mutate genes and set the foundation for cancer. Most of the radicals are sopped up by the body's native antioxidant enzymes, but yellow and green vegetables, as well as melons and citrus fruits, contain a wealth of antioxidant compounds, including vitamins C and E and beta-carotene, the precursor of vitamin A.

Dr. Allan H. Conney, director of the Laboratory for Cancer Research at Rutgers University, has also found in animal experiments that rosemary, green tea and curcumin, the chemical responsible for curry's yellow pigment, all suppress cancer growth, and he says he has evidence that they do so by acting as antioxidants, neutralizing free radicals before they reach the cell's kingpin, DNA.

Dr. H. Leon Bradlow of the Strang-Cornell Cancer Research Laboratory in New York has explored how plant chemicals influence estrogen metabolism and thus how diet might inhibit breast cancer. Scientists know that estradiol, the precursor of estrogen, can take one of two metabolic pathways, turning into either a 16-hydroxylated or a 2-hydroxylated form of estrogen. The 16 form is stimulatory and more dangerously reactive: women with a high risk of breast cancer show elevated levels of the 16 type in their blood, and researchers have determined that tissue from breast tumors contains more of the 16-hydroxylated form than does surrounding, noncancerous breast tissue.

By contrast, the 2-hydroxylated form is relatively inert and has been found to be elevated in women who are vigorous athletes—exercise is believed to reduce the risk of breast cancer—and in those who eat many cruciferous vegetables like broccoli, brussels sprouts and cabbage.

Isolating ingredients from these leafy green vegetables, Dr. Bradlow and his colleagues have shown that one chemical in particular, indole-3-carbinol, will induce estradiol to follow the harmless metabolic route toward 2-hydroxylation. A study is now under way in which 60 women are taking daily capsules of 400 milligrams of indole carbinol, equivalent to the amount in half a head of cabbage. Within several weeks, their levels of the harmless 2-hydroxylated estrogen had risen to concentrations seen in marathon runners, and the levels have stayed elevated throughout the months of the ongoing trial.

The researchers will now be testing lower doses of the compound on larger groups of women, but whether or not the difference in estrogen metabolism affects breast cancer rates will take years to sort out.

Protective Enzymes

Dr. Paul Talalay and his coworkers at the Johns Hopkins School of Medicine, who recently reported on the detection in broccoli of a robust anticancer ingredient called sulforaphane, continue to focus on this class of protective compounds. Sulforaphane and other so-called isocyothionates, found in cruciferous vegetables, mustard, horseradish and many other plants, seem to guard against cancer by stimulating the production of protective enzymes in the body. Such enzymes, also called phase 2 enzymes, detoxify carcinogens and swiftly flush them out of the body.

The scientists have been able to identify other enzyme inducers in foods through a simple system that relies on cultured mouse liver cells and scans for a spike in phase 2 enzyme activity. Applying the screening method not only to different vegetables but to diverse varieties of the same vegetable, they have found that the amount of inducer ingredients varies tremendously from one sample to the next, either because of natural genetic variations among strains or because of differences in how the vegetables were cultivated.

"It's all well and good to say eat more vegetables, but the data are extraordinarily soft on what we mean by that," Dr. Talalay said. "We're trying to survey all these vegetables grown in all these different natural conditions, and it's extremely slow going to get this straightened out."

Nothing in food analysis is proving to be simple. Vitamin C, beyond its antioxidant muscle, also inhibits the creation in the stomach of nitrosamine, a potentially dangerous carcinogen. Beyond its suppression of blood vessel growth, genistein deters the proliferation of cancer cells in test-tube experiments. And fiber, which has resuscitated the breakfast cereal industry (but also is at the heart of fruits and vegetables), exerts an assortment of positive effects on the body: among other things, it dilutes the concentration of carcinogenic compounds in the colon, so the toxins have less of a chance of harming the delicate mucosal tissue there, and it moves everything through the system faster.

Studying fiber on a microscopic level, Dr. Banderu S. Reddy, chief of nutritional carcinogenesis at the American Health Foundation in Valhalla, New York, has determined that it also alters the environment of the gut and colon. Through a poorly understood mechanism, it discourages the growth of harmful bacteria that release enzymes believed to promote cancer, probably by transforming precarcinogenic chemicals in food into active agents of cancer. At the same time, fiber bolsters the growth of benign bacteria, which themselves crowd out the unsavory strains.

Other scientists propose that fiber also encourages the creation of the healthier form of estrogen and thus may also impede breast cancer. Considered together, the intricacy and synchronicity of the chemicals in plants argue firmly against an undue reliance on vitamins and supplements to compensate for a rotten diet of snacks and french fries. If scientists have yet to understand all the subtleties of a brussels sprout, how can anybody hope to recapitulate it in a pill?

[NA, April 1993]

Potential Cancer Fighters in Foods

Although no food or food combination has yet been clinically proven to prevent or retard cancer in people, animal and test-tube research strongly suggests that many components have specific biological actions that may prove helpful. Scientists suspect that to treat tumors, compounds would have to be extracted or synthesized and given in larger doses than those found naturally; on the other hand, extracts or synthesis might overlook protective compounds in a healthful varied diet.

Component	Possible Disease-fighting Properties	Food Sources
Allylic sulfides	May protect against carcinogens by stimulating production of a detoxification enzyme, glutathione-S-transferase	Garlic, onion
Carotenoids (vitamin A precursors)	Acts as antioxidants and cell differentiation agents (cancer cells are nondifferentiated)	Parsley, carrots, winter squash, sweet potatoes, yams, cantaloupe, apricots, spinach, kale, turnip greens, citrus fruits
Catechins (tannins)	Acts as antioxidants, linked to lower rates of gastrointestinal cancer; mechanisms not understood	Green tea, berries
Flavonoids	Block receptor sites for certain hormones that promote cancers	Most fruits and vegetables, including parsley, carrots, citrus fruits, broccoli, cabbage, cucumbers, squash, yams, tomatoes, eggplant, peppers, soy products, berries
Fiber	Dilutes carcinogenic compounds in colon and speeds them through digestive system; discourages growth of harmful bacteria while bolstering healthful ones; may encourage production of healthier form of estrogen	Whole grains and many vegetables

Genistein	In test tubes, blocks angiogenesis (growth of new blood vessels), essential for some tumors to grow and spread, and deters proliferation of cancer cells	Found in urine of people with diets rich in soybeans and, to a lesser extent, cabbage-family vegetables
Indoles	Induce protective enzymes	Cabbage, brussels sprouts, kale
Isothiocyanates	Induce protective enzymes	Mustard, horseradish, radishes
Limonoids	Induce protective enzymes	Citrus fruits
Linolenic acid	Regulates prostaglandin production	Many leafy vegetables and seeds, especially flaxseed
Lycopene	Acts as antioxidant	Tomatoes, red grapefruit
Monoterpenes	Have some antioxidant properties; inhibit cholesterol production in tumors; aid protective enzyme activity	Parsley, carrots, broccoli, cabbage, cucumbers, squash, yams, tomatoes, eggplant, peppers, mint, basil, citrus fruits
Phenolic acids (tannins)	Have some antioxidant properties; inhibit formation of nitrosamine, a carcinogen, and affect enzyme activity	Parsley, carrots, broccoli, cabbage, tomatoes, eggplant, peppers, citrus fruits, whole grains, berries
Plant sterols (vitamin D precursors)	Act as differentiation agents	Broccoli, cabbage, cucumbers, squash, yams, tomatoes, eggplant, peppers, soy products, whole grains
Vitamin C	Acts as antioxidant; inhibits creation of nitrosamine, a potentially dangerous carcinogen, in the stomach	Citrus fruits, tomatoes, green leafy vegetables, potatoes
Vitamin E	Antioxidant	Wheat germ, oatmeal, peanuts, nuts, brown rice

Sources: Dr. Christopher W. W. Beecher; *Eating Well* magazine.

Other Carotenoids Are
Outshining Beta

AS doubts increase about the wisdom of taking supplements of beta-carotene, the Cinderella nutrient of the 1990s, some of its relatives are threatening to walk away with the glass slipper and the prince's heart. Researchers who study the carotenoids, the family of nutrients to which beta-carotene belongs, are now thinking that beta-carotene may be only partly responsible for the health benefits that have been attributed to it, and that one or more of the hundreds of other carotenoids should be sharing, if not stealing, the limelight.

Using modern laboratory methods, chemists have recently identified more than 600 carotenoids in plants, including about 40 that are prominent in common fruits and vegetables. Beta-carotene has long been the focus of attention for three main reasons: it makes up about one-quarter of edible carotenoids, it is the one that is most efficiently converted in the body into vitamin A and it is a powerful antioxidant that may block free-radical damage to cell membranes and body chemicals.

Until recently, chemists at the U.S. Department of Agriculture analyzed foods only for the carotenoids, including beta-carotene, that the body converts to vitamin A. Now a growing body of evidence indicates that these nutrients may not be the most important ones in preventing such common problems as heart attacks, strokes and cancer.

An editorial, "All That Glitters Is Not Beta-Carotene," published recently in *The Journal of the American Medical Association,* pointed out that "beta-carotene is but one, albeit the best known, of a large group of carotenoids with antioxidant activity." The ability to prevent oxidation has been touted as the weapon beta-carotene wields in its presumed ability to ward off life-threatening illnesses.

But now researchers, many of whom met at a recent conference on carotenoids in Ventura, California, are questioning both the mechanism and the absolute value of beta-carotene, especially when it is taken separately from its carotenoid companions. Rather, recent evidence from both laboratory and human studies strongly suggests that carotenoids may be most powerful as a team, working perhaps in combination with a large group of substances in plants called phytochemicals—among them, indoles and flavonoids—that appear to have value as disease preventives.

In light of this uncertainty and faced with an unsettling recent report linking beta-carotene supplements to an increase in deaths from lung cancer and heart disease in Finnish men who had been lifelong smokers, most experts have returned to the advice traditionally given by mothers: "Eat your fruits and vegetables"—especially dark green, yellow-orange and red ones like spinach, chard, collards, kale, carrots, sweet potatoes, winter squash, apricots, cantaloupes, tomatoes and red peppers.

"Beta-carotene may just be an indicator nutrient for other substances in fruits and vegetables that are beneficial in warding off disease," said Dr. Dexter Morris, a heart researcher at the University of North Carolina School of Medicine in Chapel Hill. "Though most studies have looked at beta-carotene, other carotenoids may be just as important or more important. Or it may not be carotenoids at all that are important, but something else in vegetables and fruits that happen to have carotenoids."

Dr. Morris and his colleagues examined the carotenoid levels in the blood serum of thousands of middle-aged men at risk of heart disease. Over 13 years, those with the highest blood levels of carotenoids were one-third less likely to suffer a heart attack than the men with the lowest levels, the researchers reported recently in *The Journal of the American Medical Association*. Nonsmokers appeared to benefit most from carotenoids in this first large, long-term study of the relationship between serum carotenoids and heart disease. For nonsmokers with the highest carotenoid levels, the risk of heart attack was only 20 percent that of nonsmokers with the lowest levels.

Previously, another researcher at the university, Dr. Lenore Kohlmeier, a professor of nutrition and epidemiology, reported that in 683 men who had just suffered a heart attack, the level of beta-carotene in their body fat was significantly lower than the amount in the fat of 727 comparable men who were still healthy. Here, too, nonsmokers showed the strongest effects of high beta-carotene levels. The importance of this study, part of an international investigation of antioxidants, heart disease and cancer called the Euramic Study, is that carotene levels in body fat reflected the men's long-standing diets as opposed to their most recently consumed foods or their less accurate reports of what they normally ate.

Dr. Kohlmeier said that beta-carotene levels were measured because this was the nutrient other researchers had focused on as protective against heart disease and stroke. For example, in an ongoing study of 87,000 nurses, Dr. JoAnn Manson and colleagues at Brigham and Women's Hospital and Harvard Medical School in Boston found that the women who said they ate five or more servings of carrots a week had a stroke rate 68 percent lower than those who ate no more than one serving a month. Carrots are one of the richest sources of beta-carotene.

But Dr. Kohlmeier said in an interview that based on unpublished evidence another carotenoid, lycopene, "a very potent antioxidant, might be the most protective against cardiovascular disease." Lycopene is prominent in tomatoes, which contain relatively little beta-carotene. Dr. Kohlmeier advised against taking supplements of beta-carotene because there is some evidence that "flooding the system with beta-carotene may reduce the body's ability to absorb lycopene."

Dr. Regina Ziegler, who studies the relationship between carotenoids and cancer at the National Cancer Institute in Bethesda, Maryland, said, "Lycopene, not beta-carotene, happens to be the most common carotenoid in human blood." Dietary studies of cancer patients have suggested that lycopene may protect against cancers of the colon and bladder. In the laboratory, it inhibits the growth of cancer cells in mice.

Lycopene is responsible for the red color of tomatoes and is found at especially high levels in concentrated tomato products like ketchup and tomato sauce. Dr. Paul LaChance, a food scientist at Rutgers University in New Brunswick, New Jersey, who called lycopene "a very effective scavenger of free radicals," mused, "What shape would we be in without pizza?"

In anticipation of good news about lycopene, companies in Israel and Australia are already working on methods of extracting this carotenoid from foods so that it can be used as a food coloring and perhaps as a supplement, Dr. LaChance said.

Still other carotenoids, lutein and zeaxantin, found in green leafy vegetables like spinach, collards and kale, may be the leading protectors against age-related macular degeneration, a deterioration of the retina that is a common cause of blindness in older adults. Dr. Johanna M. Seddon, an ophthalmologist at the Massachusetts Eye and Ear Infirmary of Harvard Medical School, and her colleagues evaluated the diets of 356 patients with macular degeneration and compared them with the diets of 520 similar people without this disorder.

The researchers concluded that the people with the highest intake of carotenoids had a 43 percent lower risk of developing macular degeneration than those with the lowest carotenoid intake. Especially protective was the consumption of dark green leafy vegetables, the researchers reported in November in *The Journal of the American Medical Association.*

The interest in carotenoids in preventing cancer dates back to the 1960s, when studies first suggested that vitamin A may offer some protection against lung cancer in men who smoked cigarettes. For the next decade or so, cancer researchers focused on retinoids—cousins of vitamin A—as possible cancer preventives. But the results were disappointing. While retinoids are still being studied for anticancer activity, it now appears that the precursors of vitamin A, beta-carotene and its relatives, as well as other carotenoids that the body does not convert into vitamin A, are the more likely agents against cancer, said Dr. Ziegler of the National Cancer Institute.

"In the 1980s, tens and tens of studies were published that were consistent with the idea that carotenoids are associated with a decreased risk of many but not all cancers, particularly cancers of the respiratory and digestive tracts: lung, oral cavity, throat, stomach, colon and rectum, pancreas and bladder," Dr. Ziegler said. Unfortunately, she added, the researchers failed to ask the "crucial question: Was beta-carotene more important than other carotenoids or than fruit and vegetable intake?"

In the late 1980s, she added, several studies showed that "fruit and vegetable intake was, in fact, more predictive of a decreased cancer risk than the estimated intake of beta-carotene and other precursors of vitamin A." While people with the highest blood levels of beta-carotene had the lowest incidence of certain cancers, Dr. Ziegler said, "serum beta-carotene levels may simply be the single best marker of fruit and vegetable intake."

When beta-carotene supplements were studied as possible protectors against cancer, they came up short, and in the best-designed study yet undertaken, the one of Finnish men who smoked heavily, researchers were shocked to find an 18 percent higher incidence of lung cancer and an 8 percent higher death rate among those who took beta-carotene supplements than among the men who got a dummy pill.

"This was a sobering result, and although we don't yet have an explanation for the increased cancer risk among beta-carotene takers, it certainly put an end to the strong interest in placing health claims on packages of beta-carotene," Dr. Ziegler said. Two possible reasons for the finding, she suggested, are that at the very high blood levels of beta-carotene reached in the study, "beta-carotene may interfere with the utilization of other beneficial nutrients in fruits and vegetables and it could also be acting as a pro-oxidant rather than as an antioxidant."

In the face of such evidence, Dr. LaChance of Rutgers cautioned against taking supplements of individual carotenoids. "In nature we get a mix of carotenoids, and we don't yet know how important it is to get this mix," he said. "If you take a pill, you have no choice. You're only getting one—beta-carotene—and it may not be the most important one."

Dr. Ziegler added: "Until we identify the protective entities in fruits and vegetables, we can't encapsulate them into a pill. At this point, the best advice to the public is to increase their intake of fruits and vegetables. It helps to remember that it has been observational studies showing that people with high intakes of fruits and vegetables have a lower risk of cancer that have driven the research in this area."

[JEB, February 1995]

The Virtues of Soy Protein

PREPARE for the onslaught: soy cookies, soy bread, soy muffins, soy milk shakes, soy pretzels, soy soups and a new, surely improved version of that old unfavorite, the soy burger.

Researchers reported in a recent issue of the *New England Journal of Medicine* that soy protein significantly lowers cholesterol levels in people with moderately high to high cholesterol. In fact, the addition of soy protein to either a low-fat or even the ordinary American diet appears to be among the most potent cholesterol-lowering dietary factors yet discovered. Because elevated cholesterol levels sharply increase the risk of heart attacks and stroke, soy protein may prove a safe, relatively painless and in some cases even tasty weapon in the battle against cardiovascular disease, America's number one killer.

People are already familiar with soy protein in products like tofu and soy milk and even as an additive in sloppy joes. Now researchers are getting a handle on how much soy protein one would have to eat to bring down elevated cholesterol levels.

The higher a person's cholesterol level, the greater is the power of soy protein to reduce it, the scientists said. In the new report, they determined that a diet of 47 grams of soy protein a day cuts cholesterol levels in a month by an average of 9.3 percent. But for those people who began with extremely elevated cholesterol levels, measuring over 300 milligrams per deciliter of blood, the concentration plunged by 20 percent. Equally promising, the protein specifically cuts just the type of cholesterol one wants to minimize, lowering low-density-lipoprotein levels without affecting high-density lipoproteins, the so-called good cholesterol. Many other approaches to taming cholesterol, including some low-fat diets and anticholesterol medications, have the undesirable effect of decreasing HDL as well as LDL concentrations. Soy protein also inhibits levels of undesirable triglycerides, the researchers reported.

"Even a ten to fifteen percent reduction in blood cholesterol levels results in a twenty to thirty percent reduction in the risk of coronary heart disease," said Dr. James W. Anderson of the University of Kentucky and chief of the endocrine-metabolic section at the Veterans Affairs Medical Center in Lexington. "This has the potential of making a huge impact on American public health."

Dr. Anderson and his coworkers, Dr. Bryan M. Johnstone and Margaret E. Cook-Newell, were supported in part by Protein Technologies International of St. Louis, which manufactures and markets soy protein products and soy fiber ingredients. Dr. Anderson is in the company's Health and Nutrition Advisory Group. However, the paper was put through the usual independent scientific review mill at the *New England Journal of Medicine* before being accepted, and Dr. Anderson is considered by his peers to be a reputable scientist who would not allow the soybean industry to bias his judgment or results. "The only vested interest I have is in healthy food," said Dr. Anderson. "Some people think I can wax evangelical and they would like to see me be more cautious. But my interest is in helping people develop healthier diets and lowering risk of disease."

Doctors generally recommend that people do what they can to keep cholesterol levels below 200 milligrams per deciliter, and under 180 when possible.

"It's great news that something as simple as soy protein is effective in lowering serum cholesterol," said Dr. John W. Erdman Jr. of the University of Illinois in Urbana-Champaign. Dr. Erdman wrote an editorial that accompanies the new report, and he has worked on using soy protein to lower cholesterol levels in patients.

The new study is not an original clinical exploration of soy protein's effects on cholesterol but instead is a "meta-analysis," a review of all the studies done to date on the subject. After eliminating what they considered to be poorly designed or inappropriate studies, the researchers focused on 38 trials that included 730 subjects of both sexes, children and adults alike. Meta-analyses are sometimes criticized for being subjective in what they include and what they discount, but Dr. Erdman said, "I think this study was very well done."

The results appear to contradict a statement in 1993 from the nutrition committee of the American Heart Association that concluded that while soy protein clearly lowers cholesterol in rabbits and other laboratory animals, it does not do so in humans.

Responding to the new meta-analysis, Dr. Ronald Krauss, chairman of the committee, said that the "use of soy protein in moderation is entirely consistent with AHA dietary guidelines" but that "no single report can be conclusive."

"We cannot use this 'averaged' information to make specific dietary recommendations," he said, until his committee has looked more closely at the recent data.

Dr. Charles H. Hennekens, a professor of medicine at Harvard Medical School and chief of preventive medicine at Brigham and Women's Hospital in Boston, also sounded a note of caution. "It adds to the wealth of evidence that the substitution of soy protein for animal protein will lower blood cholesterol," he said. "But I don't think we should instigate public policy based on a meta-analysis. I certainly would not want people to continue eating a high-calorie, high-fat diet and think it's all right if they just substitute soy for animal protein."

Other researchers praised the new analysis and pointed out that beyond its salubrious effects on cholesterol, soybeans also have shown potential in studies for helping to prevent cancer, osteoporosis and other chronic illnesses.

"Soy protein is pretty potent stuff," said Dr. Susan M. Potter at the University of Illinois, who has done considerable work on the benefits of the bean.

Yet soy has no apparent downside and is eaten in great quantities by many Asian cultures, which could partly explain their comparatively low rates of heart disease and cancer.

The scientists said that benefits can be seen with as little as 25 grams of soy protein daily, though 50 grams worked better still. Already there are many ways of incorporating soy protein into one's diet, Ms. Cook-Newell said. Among the most familiar are soy milk, tofu and tempeh, but soy protein is also found in some cheeses, as an extender and stabilizer in processed foods, in meat substitutes like "Notdogs" and fake sausages, in flour form in baked goods, and in nondairy frozen desserts.

"There are twelve thousand soy products on the market," Ms. Cook-Newell said, "and many more will be coming soon." Soybeans are the second biggest cash crop in the United States after corn, though most of them are made into animal feed.

Despite the ubiquitousness of soy products on the shelves, most of it is used in small quantities. Even a glass of soy milk has only about 8 grams of soy protein in it; a similar amount is found in a half-cup serving of tofu. A soy burger might have 18 grams of soy protein; and, sorry, but soy sauce is a negligible source of the protein. In the clinical studies considered in the meta-analysis, participants were given isolated soy protein or textured soy protein, mixed into liquids or solids in a palatable form. However, what can be done in a clinical trial may be hard to recapitulate nationally. Dr. Erdman said the food industry will need to be creative to broaden soy's appeal. "Americans are going to have to give soy foods a second chance," he said. "We all remember the first generation of soy foods that had a beany, bitter aftertaste and poor texture, but some of the newer food products are much, much better."

[NA, August 1995]

Fiber, Fat and Heart Disease

F findings on dietary fat are confusing to many Americans, conflicting findings on dietary fiber may make them want to throw away their diet plans in disgust. Are oat bran muffins good or not? Is it the fiber that matters or the fat?

The latest research suggests that increasing dietary fiber does help fight heart disease, though probably not as much as cutting back on fats. A six-year study of nearly 44,000 male health professionals from 40 to 75 years old showed that those who consumed the most fiber suffered 35 percent fewer heart attacks than those whose fiber intake was lowest. The findings suggest that simply switching to fat-free but low-fiber foods may not be enough to protect middle-aged men from heart attacks.

The findings also indicate that while the fiber in oats can lower cholesterol, as advertisers can now proclaim, it takes more than oatmeal to prevent heart disease. Leading the list of fiber-containing foods in the men's diets were cold breakfast cereals, followed by apples, bananas, oranges, peas, cooked carrots and tomato sauce.

Neither dried beans nor soy-based foods, which are known to lower cholesterol, were important items in the men's diets. Nor was most of their dietary fiber the soluble kind found in oats and beans that can lower cholesterol levels in the blood. Rather, the men, like most Americans, mainly consumed insoluble fiber.

Those with the highest fiber intake consumed 25 or more grams a day, as against half that amount for the group with the lowest intake. The average American adult now consumes about 15 grams of fiber from grain, fruit and vegetable sources, while the recommended daily intake for fiber is 20 to 25 grams. The researchers estimated from their findings that each 10-gram increase in fiber consumption could result in a 20 percent decrease in coronary risk. In other words, a person with a 50 percent chance of having a heart attack might be able to reduce that to 40 percent by eating 10 more grams of fiber, and then to 32 percent by eating 10 more grams.

The findings support the latest government recommendation to "choose a diet with plenty of grain products, vegetables and fruit." The advice was issued recently in the new "Dietary Guidelines for Americans."

Although people often think "bran" when they hear fiber, many cereals besides bran are high in fiber. For example, one cup of Shredded Wheat supplies 5 grams of dietary fiber, a cup of Wheaties has 3 grams and a serving of oatmeal (made from half a cup of oats) supplies 4 grams. There are 6 grams of fiber in half a medium-size grapefruit, 1.77 grams in a half cup of cooked green peas and 0.91 grams in a half cup of cooked sliced carrots.

The researchers, led by Dr. Eric Rimm, a professor of epidemiology and nutrition at the Harvard School of Public Health, found that even among men whose fat intake was high, consuming lots of fiber was protective, suggesting that fiber lowered coronary risk independently of its effects on the amount of fat and cholesterol the men ate. In other words, the reduction in coronary risk did not result solely because fiber-rich foods replaced fats in the men's diets.

Still, in an editorial accompanying the new report published in a recent issue of *The Journal of the American Medical Association,* Dr. Ernst Wynder and colleagues at the American Health Foundation disputed the Harvard conclusion, suggesting instead that the men who consumed the most fiber generally led healthier lives overall. They exercised more, smoked less and ate less fat, less saturated fat and less cholesterol and were more likely to take vitamin E supplements, all of which are associated with a reduced coronary risk. Dr. Wynder said this "healthy lifestyle effect" among high fiber consumers might account for most or all of the coronary protection found in this group.

But Dr. Rimm pointed out in an interview that his analysis took into account these and other risk factors for heart disease and showed that with all other things being equal, fiber remained protective. He said that if Americans followed the guidelines in the eating pyramid promulgated by the U.S. Department of Agriculture, they would automatically consume the amount of fiber he found most protective, 25 or more grams a day. The pyramid calls for daily consumption of 6 to 11 servings of cereals and other grain-based foods, 3 to 5 servings of vegetables and 2 to 4 servings of fruit.

"We shouldn't be focusing on only one aspect of diet, whether it's fat or fiber," Dr. Rimm said. "Nor can we abandon attention to other coronary risk factors and think that if we eat a lot of fiber we can continue to smoke, be sedentary and eat all the fat we want." He expressed concern about the current focus on nonfat and low-fat foods because many of those foods are rich in sugars and refined starches, which contain little or no dietary fiber.

As to how fiber might help the heart, Dr. Rimm reiterated mechanisms first outlined by the late Dr. Denis Burkitt in the 1970s. In his book *Don't Forget Fiber in Your Diet* (Arco, 1984), Dr. Burkitt cited studies showing that bran, a cereal fiber, reduced the risk of blood clots, which can cause heart attacks by blocking blood flow through coronary arteries. Dr. Burkitt also pointed out that dietary fiber "reduces absorption of cholesterol in the diet, may decrease its manufacture in the liver and increases elimination" of cholesterol in the stools.

As Dr. Rimm put it, fiber seems to "push more fat through the system so that it is not absorbed." Another possibility he suggested is the tendency of fiber to "blunt" the rise in blood sugar that typically follows a meal. This rise, and the insulin the body puts out to cope with it, has been linked to an increased risk of heart disease. He said he and his colleagues would be examining the effect of blood glucose and insulin on heart disease in a forthcoming study.

There are other benefits of a diet high in fiber, Dr. Rimm said, in particular its ability to reduce the risk of polyps in the colon and colon cancer.

But Dr. Wynder cautioned against jumping to a premature conclusion about the relative importance of fiber and fat in the diet. "While we do not agree that fiber alone protects against heart disease, we join Rimm and his associates in recommending fiber as a 'component for the prevention of heart disease,' provided that dietary fat is also considered," he wrote. He said his organization, which does research on preventing cancer and heart disease, suggests a "25/25" diet plan: 25 grams (about nine-tenths of an ounce) of fiber daily in a diet that derives no more than 25 percent of its calories from fat.

Dr. Wynder also pointed out that the Harvard study of health professionals was an "observational" study and rife with the possibility of distortions. For example, because they are very aware of what is and what is not good for health, the men may have underreported their consumption of fats and overreported their intake of fiber-rich foods. Dr. Wynder said he would favor a clinical trial of fiber in which the men's diets are carefully controlled, instead of having to rely on what they say they eat.

[JEB, February 1996]

A Revisionist View of
Salt and Health

IT is an article of prevailing dietary faith that when it comes to salt, less is better. The federal government recommends that Americans reduce their average salt consumption by a third, to six grams a day, about one and a quarter teaspoons.

But articles in recent issues of two leading medical journals suggest that scientists beg to differ—with each other. One report, in the *British Medical Journal,* says the American dietary guidelines are warranted; the other, in *The Journal of the American Medical Association,* says they are not.

The director of the National Heart, Lung and Blood Institute supports the federal guidelines. The president of the American Society of Hypertension does not.

"This will confuse a lot of people, for sure," said Dr. Walter Willett, a professor of epidemiology and nutrition at the Harvard School of Public Health, who is not involved in the controversy.

The problem facing researchers is that there has never been a study showing that people who reduce their salt consumption are healthier or live longer, which is, scientists agree, the bottom line. Instead, the arguments over salt are indirect.

Richard L. Hanneman, president of the Salt Institute, said that although most Americans were convinced salt was bad for them, there had been no decrease in the consumption of salt since the federal guidelines were published in 1980. In fact, he said, salt consumption in this country has remained constant for the last hundred years.

The article in the British journal concluding that the dietary guidelines are warranted is by Dr. Paul Elliott, a professor of epidemiology and public health at the Imperial College School of Medicine at St. Mary's in London, and colleagues from Belgium and the United States.

The group reanalyzed data from a 1988 study called Intersalt, involving 10,074 adults in 32 countries. The participants had had their blood pressure measured and they had provided urine samples, which show how much sodium is excreted. The more salt a person consumes, the more sodium is excreted in the urine.

The investigators conclude that there is a relationship between salt intake and blood pressure at all ages, but that the link is stronger in the middle-aged than in young adults. At the extreme, middle-aged people who consumed an extra six grams of salt a day had systolic blood pressures that averaged five to seven points higher than those who forswore that extra salt.

Systolic pressure, the higher of the two blood pressure numbers, is the force blood exerts on vessels when the heart contracts. A normal systolic blood pressure is about 120 millimeters of mercury.

Dr. Elliott said the message was clear. "To my mind, there is a strong consensus," he said. "There is too much salt in the diet and it ought to be removed. We ought to work with the industry to get the salt out of the diet."

The paper in the American journal asked a different question: If people do go on low-salt diets, does their blood pressure drop?

The authors of this paper, headed by Dr. Alexander Gordon Logan, an epidemiologist and high blood pressure specialist at the University of Toronto, grouped together data from 56 studies involving 3,505 volunteers.

They concluded that low-salt diets had virtually no effect on people with normal blood pressure, a vast majority of the population, and, at best, resulted in only a small drop in the systolic pressure of people with high blood pressure, averaging 3.7 points.

The group wrote that their analysis "questions the wisdom of universal sodium restriction."

Of course, said Dr. David DeMets, a clinical trials specialist at the University of Wisconsin, the two studies are very different, and each has its limitations.

Dr. DeMets said the paper by Dr. Elliott "is fine as far as it goes, but it doesn't mean that changing sodium consumption would result in reduced blood pressure." And the paper by Dr. Logan, he said, "has all the weaknesses" of a study based on a literature search that must decide what to include and what to exclude in an analysis.

If there is an effect of a low-salt diet on a population's blood pressure, it is not very large, Dr. DeMets said. "We wouldn't be going through all this if it wasn't subtle," he said. "And because it is subtle, confounding biases and other factors can sneak in and confuse interpretations."

But Dr. Claude J. Lenfant, director of the National Heart, Lung and Blood Institute, said he remained convinced by the weight of evidence going back for decades that salt did play a crucial role in driving up blood pressure and that everyone would be better off if salt consumption were reduced. "What's unfortunate is that the salt industry is taking this personally," he added.

And with good reason, said Mr. Hanneman of the Salt Institute. "The public has been told by the government years ago that this was a settled question, that it's all signed, sealed and delivered and we know what the answer is," he said. But, he said, although "our opponents" may disagree, "we think it's an ongoing debate."

One participant in that debate is Dr. Michael Alderman, president of the American Society of Hypertension and chairman of the Department of Epidemiology and Social Medicine at the Albert Einstein College of Medicine in the Bronx. Yes, Dr. Alderman said, there does seem to be a relationship between salt consumption and blood pressure. But, he added, "that's not the public health issue."

"To know whether a population's blood pressure increases by a millimeter or so is interesting to scientists," Dr. Alderman said. But, he added, the real public health question is, Does a change in blood pressure by these techniques translate into a health benefit? And when the question is phrased in that way, he said, "I would argue that the evidence simply is not available."

Although it might seem obvious that a low-salt diet would be, at worst, harmless, scientists have seen before that seemingly harmless interventions can have unforeseen effects. And, Dr. Alderman said, low-salt diets are not the same as diets higher in salt; they contain few dairy products, for example, because dairy products, while high in calcium, are also high in salt.

There are no data to support the safety or value of a low-salt diet, Dr. Alderman said. Moreover, he said, there are not even any data pointing to an optimum salt consumption. "There is not a single study saying that 2,400 milligrams are better than 2,000 or 3,000 or 4,000," he said, referring to the dietary recommendation that Americans consume 2,400 milligrams of sodium a day, the equivalent of six grams of salt. "Somebody made up that number," Dr. Alderman said. Whenever people have free access to salt, he added, they eat the same amount, about the amount that Americans consume.

"A lot of people have a career in this," Dr. Alderman said. "Once you've said that the whole country should stop eating salt, if someone comes along and says, 'Where's the data?' you get your back up."

But, Dr. Alderman added, "In the absence of data, why are we so prepared to be so dogmatic?" After all, he said, "there are people asking all Americans to change their diet for a lifetime in a very dramatic way." And so, he said, "at least we have an obligation to make sure it's safe."

Both studies were financed, in part, by grants from industry or government groups with particular interest in the outcome. The study in the British journal was financed by a variety of government groups, including the National Heart, Lung and Blood Institute in Bethesda, Maryland. The study in the American journal was financed by an unrestricted grant from the Campbell's Institute for Research and Technology in Camden, New Jersey, and the Medical Research Council of Canada.

[GK, May 1996]

The Moderate Benefits of Moderate Alcohol Consumption

ALCOHOL consumption rises precipitously in this holiday season, but before you raise yet another glass to everyone's health, take heed of these new findings based on data from 21 affluent countries: while wine and other forms of alcohol may protect your heart, when consumed in large amounts alcohol does nothing to prolong your life.

The analysis, by Dr. Michael H. Criqui and Brenda L. Ringel of the University of California, San Diego, School of Medicine in La Jolla, indicated that although heavy alcohol consumption was associated with a very low risk of death from coronary heart disease, it raised overall death rates and the rates of death from other causes, especially cirrhosis of the liver.

The researchers were seeking a clearer understanding of the so-called French paradox. The paradox refers to the fact that the French have long had low rates of heart disease (Japan is the only developed country with a lower rate), despite a diet relatively rich in saturated animal fats. The French propensity to drink wine the way some Americans guzzle soft drinks has been cited as a likely explanation of the paradox, since numerous studies have indicated that alcohol consumed in moderation helps to prevent atherosclerosis, or accumulation of fatty deposits in arteries, which is the underlying cause of most heart attacks.

People who drink alcohol regularly tend to have higher blood levels of protective HDLs, or high-density lipoproteins, which carry cholesterol out of the body and presumably help to keep coronary arteries unclogged. Red wine, by far the most popular alcoholic beverage in France, is believed to be most beneficial, since, in addition to the effects of the alcohol on HDL, substances in red grapes appear to inhibit the formation of blood clots.

But the new findings, reported in a recent issue of *The Lancet,* an international medical journal published in Britain, indicate that for the population as a whole, the protective effects of alcohol for the heart come at the cost of life-shortening alcohol abuse by large numbers of people. Alcohol abuse increases the chances of an early death from cirrhosis of the liver, accidents and several forms of cancer, as well as from other forms of heart disease. The net effect on the population at large is to obliterate any beneficial effect alcohol may have in slowing the development of atherosclerosis.

This finding prompted the California researchers to caution against recommending alcohol consumption to the general public as a means of curbing heart disease.

Explaining his opposition to a public health policy that advocates drinking wine or other forms of alcohol, Dr. Criqui said: "If everybody could drink a glass of wine a day, period, that would be fine. But everybody can't drink a glass of wine a day. It would be okay for physicians to recommend a drink a day to patients they know won't abuse alcohol, but I think a general recommendation is dangerous."

In their paper, the researchers noted that "countries in which wine is the predominant alcoholic beverage have the largest overall alcohol consumption." They added that while the benefits of alcohol in preventing coronary heart disease might persist at intakes as high as four or five drinks a day, consuming more than two drinks a day was associated with higher risks of other forms of heart disease and other causes of death.

"The benefit for total mortality is maximized at one or two drinks per day," they wrote. Calling their data "sobering," the researchers added that when the per capita consumption of alcohol in a country was high enough to reduce that nation's coronary death rate significantly, there was also a very high level of alcohol abuse.

Nonetheless, other experts believe it is irresponsible for doctors not to inform the public that moderate alcohol consumption can help the heart, especially since atherosclerosis is by far the leading underlying cause of death in this country.

Dr. R. Curtis Ellison of the Boston University School of Medicine said: "The best recommendation should be: if you choose to drink alcohol, it will reduce your risk of heart disease. I think it would be irresponsible not to let patients know that." He added that he had seen no data to support the belief that "if you say anything favorable about drinking alcohol, you increase the chances for abuse."

In their study, the California researchers compiled data on alcohol consumption, diet and death rates among people 35 to 74 years old in 21 developed countries, including the United States, Australia, Finland, Ireland and Japan, for the years 1965, 1970, 1980 and 1988.

In addition to finding a relationship between alcohol consumption and death rates, the researchers found that the more animal fat and the fewer vegetables and fruits consumed, the higher the coronary death rate was in the countries studied.

The researchers also cited evidence to indicate that the French drink much more alcohol than might be needed to get the most benefit for the heart. They pointed out that in France there has been a decline in per capita alcohol consumption—from 18.3 liters of pure alcohol a year in 1965 to 13.1 liters in 1988. Alcohol consumed as wine has also dropped, to 9.1 liters of pure alcohol from 13.3. At the same time, however, coronary death rates have fallen, to 71.3 per 100,000 in 1988 from 94.9 per 100,000 in 1965, and deaths from cirrhosis have fallen even more sharply, to 37.9 per 100,000 in 1988 from 68.5 per 100,000 in 1975.

"Thus," the researchers noted, "the French on average consumed far more alcohol than necessary for maximal cardioprotection." Taken together, the data from their study and many others prompted the researchers to conclude that "there is a protective effect on total mortality only for light to moderate drinking."

[JEB, December 1994]

Alcohol:
Heart Benefits Versus Cancer Risk

THE Janus faces of alcohol have emerged once more, this time throwing health-conscious women into what could be a life-and-death quandary. Should they drink, to protect their hearts; or not drink, to reduce their risk of breast cancer?

As evidence mounts for the protective effect of moderate drinking against heart disease in both men and women, it is also accumulating for the potential hazards to the breasts of even one drink a day. To decide how to reconcile these opposing effects, it helps to understand the nature of the evidence and the relative risks of the two diseases.

The Heart

More than half a dozen very large long-term studies have linked moderate alcohol consumption to a reduced risk of suffering a heart attack and dying of coronary heart disease. While most of the studies involved men or mostly men, a recent report from the continuing Nurses' Health Study of 89,000 middle-aged women at the Harvard School of Public Health found that women who typically consumed three to nine drinks a week were 40 percent less likely to develop heart disease than nondrinkers.

A report from a 10-year study of nearly 130,000 men and women by researchers at the Kaiser Permanente Medical Center in Oakland, California, found that people who typically consumed one or two drinks a day were 30 percent less likely to die from coronary heart disease than people who abstained from alcohol.

And then came the so-called French paradox: the apparent fact that despite a diet rich in animal fats, the French seem to be spared Americans' epidemic rates of heart disease. The French penchant for wine, particularly red wine, was singled out as the likely protector against saturated fats and cholesterol.

Researchers at Cornell University and the University of California at Davis quickly isolated from red wine substances called phenolic flavonoids, which they say act as antioxidants, preventing LDL cholesterol from clogging coronary arteries.

Another Kaiser Permanente researcher, Dr. Arthur Klatsky, reported that white wine appeared to be equally beneficial, on the basis of coronary rates among the 82,000 people in the study who drank various alcoholic beverages. In fact, Dr. Klatsky said in reviewing the various large studies, benefits to the heart have been seen not just from wine but also from beer and hard liquor.

In addition, the Framingham Heart Study, among others, has linked alcohol consumption to an increase in the protective HDL cholesterol, which acts like arterial Drāno, cleaning out accumulated fatty deposits. Alcohol also seems to have an anticlotting effect, accounting for a related benefit in moderate drinkers: a reduced risk of stroke.

Breast Cancer

Unfortunately, the adverse effects of alcohol on the breast occur at the same levels of drinking that protect the heart. In the Nurses' Health Study, for example, women who typically consumed three to nine drinks a week were 30 percent more likely than nondrinkers to develop breast cancer. Other studies have indicated that one drink a day is associated with an increased breast cancer risk of from 18 to 40 percent.

Dr. Matthew Longnecker of the University of California at Los Angeles analyzed 38 studies on alcohol and breast cancer. He concluded that one drink a day increased breast cancer risk by about 10 percent and two drinks increased it by 25 percent.

This spring, Dr. Marsha E. Reichman at the National Cancer Institute showed that premenopausal women given the equivalent of two drinks a day had a shift in estrogen hormones that could be the mechanism behind the rise in breast cancer associated with alcohol. Breast tissue is acutely sensitive to estrogen, and certain types of estrogen are known to stimulate the growth of breast cancer cells.

Benefit and Risk

Dr. Longnecker has pointed out that fewer than 3 percent of American women have two or more drinks a day. Indeed, more than half of women report that they average zero drinks a day. Those who do drink typically have one or fewer a day.

Furthermore, Dr. Meir Stampfer, a Harvard epidemiologist who is a coinvestigator on the Nurses' Health Study, points out that heart disease is by far the more important cause of death in American women, at least for women over 50. Whereas 4 percent of women die of breast cancer, about 40 percent die of heart disease. And while heart disease is most likely to be fatal late in life, from the ages of 50 to 70 the coronary death rate in women is still two to four times the death rate from breast cancer.

Even for women with a family history of breast cancer, Dr. Stampfer believes that "a drink a day is not too much" and "there's little health reason to stop."

He has also noted that how much women drink in midlife may not be the critical factor in breast cancer risk. He cited one study suggesting that drinking before the age of 30 accounted for the entire association between alcohol and breast cancer.

Even if a cause-and-effect relationship is established between alcohol and breast cancer, he said, "differences in alcohol intake would explain only a small fraction of breast cancer rates." In other words, alcohol at worst would account for only a small percentage of the breast cancers that afflict American women.

For women, one drink a day is the definition of moderate. That means one 4-ounce or 5-ounce glass of wine, one 12-ounce beer or a single 1½-ounce shot of 80 proof hard liquor. This amount has a biological effect similar to that of two drinks a day in men, who tend to weigh more and have less body fat and who metabolize alcohol more efficiently than women do. Heavier drinking—more than two drinks a day—actually harms the heart, erasing the benefits of alcohol.

Nutrition Action, a consumer newsletter published by the Center for Science in the Public Interest in Washington, D.C., further cautions pregnant women and those trying to become pregnant to abstain from alcohol entirely, because of the risk of damaging the developing fetus, a position taken by many doctors' groups.

Similarly, the newsletter warns, alcohol should be avoided by people taking antihistamines or prescription drugs that interact with alcohol, by those who expect to be driving or operating machinery within two hours and by those who are addicted to alcohol and cannot stick to moderate levels.

Finally, women with a family history of alcoholism might think twice about drinking at all.

[JEB, September 1993]

The Addictiveness of Coffee

GIVEN how easily I got hooked on caffeine, it is a good thing I never tried cigarettes or cocaine. Not that I had ever been a heavy consumer of caffeine. Maybe three or four cups of coffee a day, but no tea or soft drinks or No-Doz and only an occasional indulgence in chocolate. Through the years, I had gradually cut down to just two cups of coffee a day, usually instant coffee, one upon awakening and the other in midafternoon.

But when I recently tried to give up caffeine altogether, my body rebelled. I developed a headache so intense that if I had not known better I would have sworn I had a brain tumor or had suffered a stroke. Neither aspirin nor acetaminophen made a dent in the pain. My headache was so overwhelming that I never noticed whether I suffered any of the other common effects associated with caffeine withdrawal: fatigue, depression, difficulty concentrating, stiffness and flulike symptoms.

I kept telling myself that the pain would soon pass. But all it did was get worse. By the third day I got desperate enough to plow frantically through the painkillers in my medicine chest. Where was Excedrin when I needed it? Finally, I turned up an antique bottle of Anacin—aspirin plus caffeine, 32 milligrams in each tablet, the amount in about two ounces of instant coffee. Just 15 minutes after I swallowed two tablets, my headache began to dissipate, then disappear. Obviously, it was not the aspirin that worked. It was the caffeine.

That did it. No caffeine-free life for me. A headache like that, even for a day, was not worth it. It was not that I had to stop drinking coffee. I was perfectly healthy, not pregnant or trying to be, and I had no particular adverse reaction to caffeine. I had been trying to quit on principle. I did not like the idea of being dependent upon a mind-altering drug, however socially acceptable that drug might be. And while I thoroughly enjoyed a good cup of coffee, especially after dinner with company, I happily drank decaf since, when brewed from high-quality beans, it tasted as good as coffee with caffeine.

Then I faced an impending day of reckoning: a scheduled bicycle tour of the Yucatán. Where, I wondered, would I get my afternoon coffee while biking through the back roads of Mexico? Since I did not consume soft drinks, Coke was not a suitable substitute. And the amount of chocolate I would have to eat to reach the caffeine level of one cup of coffee would have more than made up for all the calories I used cycling. I did not want to rely on Anacin, Excedrin, No-Doz or any other drugs that contain caffeine.

So back to the caffeine countdown. This time I was smarter. Instead of going cold turkey from two cups to none, I first cut back to one cup, then to half a cup of coffee with caffeine a day, divided between morning and afternoon. (Experts recommend reducing one's intake by about 20 percent a week over a period of four to five weeks to minimize withdrawal symptoms.) By the time I left for Mexico, my caffeine intake for the previous week was about 40 milligrams a day, the amount in half a teaspoon of instant coffee.

Still, midafternoon on the first cycling day, a headache reminded me that I was overdue for a dose of caffeine. With only soft drinks available as caffeine sources, I begged to share a companion's Coke. That did the trick. The next day, no caffeine, and no headache. It was a miracle, I thought. I was finally free of that monkey, and I was determined not to get hooked ever again.

Not that I am completely abstinent. I now use caffeine judiciously, when I really need it. As one who has twice fallen asleep driving, I dose myself with caffeine as a safety measure before driving any distance. I also use it to avoid wasting $75 theater tickets and to be sure I will hear all the movements of a concerto or symphony. When I was a daily caffeine consumer, the drug did little or nothing to keep me awake when I really had to stay awake. Now all it takes is the caffeine in about two ounces, or less than half a cup, of coffee to keep me alert for three or more hours.

I now appreciate an attribute of stimulants that researchers have long understood: their ability to induce tolerance. When a person regularly consumes caffeine, a tolerance for its stimulant effects commonly develops. Those who claim they can drink coffee at night and still fall asleep easily are not kidding. Even people with high blood pressure, whose blood pressure normally moves higher after a dose of caffeine, no longer experience this effect once they develop a tolerance for the substance.

I also appreciate the fact that caffeine meets the psychiatric profession's current criteria for a drug that can induce dependency, as Dr. Eric C. Strain and colleagues at the Johns Hopkins University School of Medicine in Baltimore pointed out recently in *The Journal of the American Medical Association*. In addition to developing a tolerance for a given dose and suffering withdrawal symptoms when the drug is abruptly discontinued, some people find themselves unable to give up caffeine despite pressing health or social reasons for doing so, and some people will go to remarkable extremes to get their next dose, the researchers noted. It is not uncommon for caffeine addicts to get into arguments with family members and friends over their caffeine use.

Dr. Strain's team found (as I discovered so dramatically) that a diagnosis of caffeine dependency does not necessarily depend on the dose consumed. In their study of 11 caffeine addicts, the researchers said that "three subjects with a diagnosis of caffeine dependence had a daily consumption less than the average daily consumption of caffeine in the United States," which is 280 milligrams a day for each adult who consumes caffeine, the amount in about 14 ounces, or just under three cups, of ordinary coffee.

"The recognition of syndromes of intoxication, withdrawal and dependence suggests that caffeine is like other psychoactive drugs," the researchers concluded.

Caffeine addicts may be encouraged to learn that the drug's positive effects—increased feelings of well-being, alertness, energy and endurance—are associated with low doses, ranging from 20 to 200 milligrams, or from the amount of caffeine in an 8-ounce soft drink to the amount in 10 ounces of ordinary coffee.

However, at higher doses, up to 800 milligrams or more, caffeine can produce negative effects like nervousness, anxiety, panic attacks and palpitations, especially in people who usually abstain from caffeine. It can also double the adverse effects of stress, aggravate stomach ulcers, interfere with sleep and increase the side effects of certain medications.

[JEB, September 1995]

Coffee's Impressive Safety Record

WITH coffee bars proliferating from Seattle to Boston, and the specialty coffees they feature promising to turn around a decades-long decline in American coffee consumption, the news about coffee's effects on health is surprisingly good.

A substantial amount of research, including several large studies done in the last few years, has turned up very little solid scientific evidence to indict a moderate intake of coffee or caffeine as a serious or even minor health threat.

"Some of the most serious hazards that were linked to caffeine in the past have not panned out," said Dr. James L. Mills, who studies caffeine's effects on pregnancy at the National Institute of Child Health and Human Development in Bethesda, Maryland.

After peaking in 1962 at 3.12 cups per person a day, coffee consumption endured a 30-year slide in popularity, finally stabilizing in the mid-1990s at around 1.7 cups, according to a survey conducted recently by the National Coffee Association.

Of course, caffeine is also present in black and green teas and in soft drinks. Eighty percent of Americans consume at least one beverage containing caffeine every day, and among Americans over 18, the per capita consumption of caffeine is about 200 milligrams a day.

Dr. Mills noted that heavy caffeine consumers—those who drink eight or more five-ounce cups of coffee a day—tend to be "very overworked, driven people who are generally not the best health risks."

For the average healthy person, about the most serious charge science can levy against caffeine is that it may be addictive. After 18 to 24 hours, its absence, even in those who consume it moderately, sometimes results in withdrawal symptoms, including severe headaches, fatigue, depression and poor concentration.

Concerns about the effects of caffeine on pregnancy and fetal development also persist. Despite a score of studies on the relationship between caffeine and a woman's ability to conceive and deliver a full-term, full-size, healthy infant, researchers are still arguing about the reproductive risks of even relatively high doses of caffeine before or during pregnancy. All relevant studies have suffered from one or more methodological limitations that might invalidate their findings, scientists say.

And while moderate consumption—usually defined as two to four five-ounce cups of coffee daily—has thus far received a relatively clean bill of health even in people at high risk for developing heart disease or cancer, new studies have linked heavier daily intakes to heart attacks and bone loss in women. And in men with mild high blood pressure, several recent studies have shown that a significant rise in blood pressure can occur after just two or three cups of coffee, especially if caffeine is consumed before exercising.

Along with these cautionary findings has come encouraging news about caffeine's potential role in weight control. Caffeine raises the rate at which the body burns calories for three or more hours after it is consumed, according to studies of healthy volunteers of normal weight in Denmark. Just 100 milligrams of caffeine—the amount in one cup of coffee or two cans of cola—can raise the metabolic rate by 3 to 4 percent, and larger intakes raise it even higher. If the consumer also exercises, the caloric burn stimulated by caffeine is greater still. But caffeine is no free lunch for dieters because it also effects the release of insulin, causing blood sugar to fall, which induces hunger pangs.

Caffeine's ability to bolster physical performance is well known among professional athletes. A recent study by Dr. Terry Graham and Dr. Lawrence L. Spriet at the University of Guelph in Ontario indicated that even a moderate amount of caffeine—1.5 milligrams per pound of body weight—had a potent exercise-enhancing effect.

Caffeine helps to mobilize body fat and make it available as fuel for exercising muscles, allowing them to work longer before they fatigue.

Caffeine, known chemically as 1,3,7-trimethylxanthine, is one of a class of methylxanthine compounds found in 63 plant products, including tea leaves, cocoa beans and coffee beans. Similar to amphetamines but milder in its effects, caffeine stimulates the sympathetic nervous system, which regulates the body's automatic functions. As a central nervous system stimulant, it makes people feel more alert, temporarily relieves fatigue and promotes quick thinking. Its contrary effects on blood vessels often render it medically useful: it dilates arteries feeding the heart, increasing blood flow, and constricts arteries in the head, helping to counter migraine headaches.

But caffeine is only one, albeit the best known, of some 500 chemicals in coffee. Indeed, caffeine was recently absolved of at least one of coffee's reputed ill effects—the ability to raise serum cholesterol levels. That drawback, researchers in the Netherlands say, stems not from caffeine but from the oils in coffee beans that are extracted when the grounds are boiled. Those oils are not a problem when coffee is brewed through a paper filter, because the oils are left behind, but they are in coffee prepared with a press.

Decaffeinated coffee has lately captured a growing body of devotees who spurn caffeine's stimulating effect but still covet coffee's flavor and social attributes. Yet research sponsored by the National Institutes of Health and directed by Dr. H. Robert Superko while he was at Stanford University has suggested that decaffeinated coffee is more likely than its caffeine-rich counterpart to raise levels of artery-damaging LDL cholesterol. He says this condition may occur because stronger-flavored coffee beans, known as robusta, are typically used to prepare decaffeinated coffee to compensate for the flavor lost in the decaffeinating process. These same beans are used to prepare instant coffees with and without caffeine. But most brewed coffee containing caffeine is prepared from milder arabica beans. This finding has not yet been confirmed by other studies.

Sorting out the health effects of drinking coffee, with or without caffeine, is complicated by the fact that coffee drinkers are, on the whole, a different breed from drinkers of other beverages, including caffeine-containing tea. At least three large studies conducted here and in Europe have shown that coffee drinking, especially at high levels, is associated with behavior that is linked to serious illnesses, like cigarette smoking.

Furthermore, decaf drinkers are different from those who drink coffee with caffeine. In a recent study of 2,677 adults by Alan Leviton and Elizabeth N. Allred of Harvard Medical School and Boston Children's Hospital, women who drank only decaffeinated coffee behaved more like women who drank no coffee at all than like women who consumed coffee with caffeine. Decaf drinkers in the study were more likely than other women to take vitamin supplements, eat vegetables in the cabbage family, use seat belts routinely and exercise regularly. The men who drank decaf exclusively typically weighed less and were more likely to consume a low-fat diet and to eat such vegetables.

To determine whether drinking coffee increases the risk of disease, researchers must take into account many lifestyle factors, since these factors and not coffee or caffeine could be responsible.

Heart Disease

In studies that have taken other risk factors into account, people who consume fewer than four or five cups of coffee a day seem to incur no added cardiac risk, even if they already have clogged coronary arteries or irregular heart rhythms. Several studies found no drop in blood cholesterol levels when people with or without high cholesterol switched to decaf. But cardiac trouble begins to accrue at five or more five-ounce cups of coffee a day among both smokers and nonsmokers and especially in people with high blood pressure.

Cancer

In 1981, coffee aficionados were momentarily dismayed by a report from Harvard researchers linking coffee (with and without caffeine) to pancreatic cancer, a disease with a very poor prognosis. But at least seven major studies, including one conducted recently in a large retirement community, have failed to find such a link, and five years after the initial scare, the Harvard researchers, after further analysis of their data, retracted their findings.

Likewise for breast cancer and benign fibrocystic breast disease. Despite widespread publicity given to anecdotal findings that linked caffeine and other methylxanthines to symptoms of fibrocystic breast disease, no well-designed studies have confirmed a clear-cut relationship. And in several large studies, including a continuing Harvard-based study of 121,700 nurses, no risk of breast cancer associated with coffee drinking has been found. In fact, among the nurses, coffee drinkers have developed fewer breast cancers than abstainers so far.

A similar inverse relationship was found between heavy coffee consumption and cancers of the colon and rectum in a study of 1,255 cancer cases and 3,883 matched patients with unrelated conditions. Those who consumed five or more cups of coffee a day had a 40 percent lower risk of developing colon cancer, according to a research team headed by Dr. Lynn Rosenberg of the Boston University School of Public Health.

The first link reported between coffee and cancer concerned the bladder. But cigarette smoking, a known cause of bladder cancer, apparently accounted for the relationship (smokers drink more than twice the amount of coffee that nonsmokers do). After analyzing 35 studies of the coffee–bladder cancer relationship, Yale University researchers concluded in 1993 that regular coffee consumption was not a "clinically important" risk factor for bladder cancer in men or women. Soon after, however, another study linked heavy coffee consumption to bladder cancer in nonsmokers. And so the debate continues.

Bone Disease

Caffeine has an undisputed negative effect on calcium metabolism. When exercise levels and smoking are taken into account, women who consume caffeine lose more calcium in their urine and have less dense bones than do nonconsumers, and thus may be more prone to fractures. Indeed, the nurses' study linked caffeine intake to an increased risk of hip fractures, though not wrist fractures, in postmenopausal women. Among those who consumed the most caffeine (more than 817 milligrams a day), the risk of suffering a hip fracture was nearly three times higher than for those who did not consume caffeine.

But among more moderate coffee consumers, drinking just one glass of milk a day can offset the calcium loss induced by the caffeine in two cups of coffee, a recent study of nearly 1,000 postmenopausal women in southern California showed.

Pregnancy

In 1980, following a study in which pregnant rats that were force-fed the human equivalent of 56 to 87 cups of strong coffee gave birth to pups with missing toes, the Food and Drug Administration warned pregnant women to avoid or at least moderate their consumption of caffeine. Two years later, the agency's concerns were reinforced by a study of 12,000 pregnant women that linked drinking four or more cups of coffee daily to premature birth and low birth weight. But while smoking turned out to be the chief culprit, the agency has yet to ease its warning.

Studies of caffeine and pregnancy continue to produce conflicting results. One study of 2,800 fertile women found no effect of caffeine on their chances of conceiving, while another study of 1,900 women linked drinking more than 300 milligrams of caffeine daily to a delay in conception. A study of more than 7,000 Canadian women linked increasing doses of caffeine to a rising risk of fetal growth retardation, but there was no rise in premature births or low birth weight. And the newest study, published recently by researchers at the University of North Carolina, also failed to document a link between caffeine consumption during pregnancy and preterm births.

Still, enough research has suggested that caffeine may delay conception, increase the risk of miscarriage and slow fetal growth to prompt many public health specialists to advise women planning pregnancy, as well as those who are already pregnant, to eliminate caffeine or restrict its consumption to the amount in one or two cups of brewed coffee a day. "Based on the better studies, I don't think caffeine is a problem," said Dr. Mills of the child health institute. "But during pregnancy, you should be cautious about any substance that has metabolic effects."

[JEB, September 1995]

The Hazards of Food-Borne Illness

RECENT outbreaks of severe illness and deaths from contaminated food have shaken American confidence in what has long been considered the safest food supply in the world and have drawn attention to the antiquated methods used to inspect foods like meats and poultry.

People who dismissed earlier warnings about the growing hazards of eating raw and undercooked eggs could hardly ignore the nearly 500 cases of illness and four deaths (three of them children) that were traced recently to undercooked hamburgers at fast-food restaurants in the Northwest.

Health experts estimate that 33 million Americans, and perhaps as many as 81 million, develop food-borne illnesses each year at a cost of as much as $23 billion in health care and lost productivity.

Three experts writing in *Patient Care* magazine recently pointed out that "food-borne infections are not what they used to be" in terms of the organisms and foodstuffs responsible for food poisoning and the types and numbers of actual and potential victims.

A Growing Problem

In years past, relatively few pathogens were believed to be trouble-makers in foods, causing all-too-familiar but usually short-lived bouts of diarrhea, nausea, vomiting and abdominal pain. But in the last few decades, partly as a result of changing food production methods, new and sometimes deadly culprits have emerged. These include antibiotic-resistant bacteria believed to have evolved through the nearly universal practice of giving food animals low doses of antibiotics to enhance their growth.

Foods not previously considered a problem, like some cheeses, fruits and vegetables, are cropping up as causes of food poisoning.

In addition, entirely new organisms not previously associated with food poisoning have been incriminated, and some food-borne organisms have been linked to life-threatening conditions. For example, the three children who died after eating undercooked

hamburgers had developed a deadly kidney disorder called hemo-
lytic-uremic syndrome.

There are also now many more people at risk of suffering severe
and even fatal effects of food poisoning, including people with debilitating chronic ailments and those with poorly functioning immune systems due to AIDS, diabetes, old age, cancer therapy and
medications taken to control autoimmune diseases.

In a recent report, the Institute for Science in Society, a nonprofit
educational organization in Kensington, Maryland, called for a
major overhaul of food safety and inspection systems used by industry and the federal Department of Agriculture to ensure that
meats and poultry will not cause illness.

Inspectors now rely on 80-year-old methods—what they can see,
touch and feel—rather than actual tests for microbial contamination when approving animals for the marketplace. Yet, the report
said, "the vast majority of illnesses caused by food are now the result of microorganisms that cannot be detected by visual or other
sensory means." Many, in fact, come from animals that appear to be
perfectly healthy.

The organization, known as ISIS, also recommended the use of
irradiation to reduce or eliminate microbial contamination, especially in high-risk foods like ground meats and poultry products. It
called for a national education program to inform the public about
the wisdom and safety of food irradiation.

The Department of Agriculture has proposed legislation to improve safety standards for packing plants that handle raw meat and
poultry. And it recently announced plans to start using a rapid test
for bacterial contamination of beef and poultry carcasses. But this
test detects relatively high levels of bacteria, while in some cases a
low level of contamination can cause illness.

This is especially so for *Escherichia coli* 0157:H7, the toxin-pro-
ducing bacterium, relatively new to food poisoning, that caused the
hamburger episode and is now one of the leading causes of food
poisoning. Although the main source is raw and undercooked
ground beef, disease-causing levels of the bacteria are easily transferred to other foods, including fresh produce, and may even contaminate drinking water and swimming pools.

Until there is an improved food safety program, as promised by
Michael R. Taylor, the department's new administrator of the Food
Safety and Inspection Service, it is up to consumers to be alert to

possible problems and to practice sanitary habits and safe preparation methods in handling all types of foods, including fresh produce.

Most cooks know that they must be wary of salmonella poisoning from cracked eggs and raw poultry. But this organism has recently flourished because it can now be transmitted from hens to the yolks of intact eggs. It may also contaminate beef, poultry, unpasteurized milk or cheese, chocolate, fruits and vegetables. Tomatoes and cantaloupes, for example, have been linked to large multistate outbreaks of salmonella poisoning caused by a failure to wash their contaminated skins.

Experts recommend these precautions:

- Minimize microbial growth by keeping foods refrigerated or frozen. If there will be a significant time lag between purchase and taking the food home, take along a cooler to keep cold foods cold. Refrigerate or freeze leftovers without delay. Thaw frozen food in the refrigerator or microwave oven, not on the kitchen counter.

- Check the temperature of your refrigerator and freezer. The refrigerator should be at least 40 degrees Fahrenheit or colder, and the freezer should be zero degrees or colder. Store raw meats, poultry and seafood in the coldest parts.

- Buy only clean, uncracked eggs, keep them refrigerated, use them within five weeks of purchase and avoid eating raw or undercooked egg yolks in any form. Do not taste batters containing raw eggs. Use only pasteurized eggs or an egg substitute (both sold in labeled cartons) when preparing Caesar salad dressing and other foods calling for raw eggs that will not be cooked before they are consumed. Before ordering such foods in a restaurant, ask if the chef uses raw eggs.

- Place uncooked meats, poultry and fish in leakproof containers or store them on the bottom shelf of the refrigerator. Never put cooked meats, poultry, fish or any other food in the same container or on the same unwashed work surface that held raw animal products. Wash cutting boards and knives with hot water and soap immediately after processing the raw foods.

- Wash all vegetables and fruits thoroughly, including those that will be peeled and the edible leaves of leafy vegetables. If possible, use a separate cutting board to prepare foods that are to be eaten uncooked.

- Do not taste or eat raw, rare or even pink ground meat or poultry in any form. Hamburgers, meat loaf, ground turkey and ground chicken should be cooked all the way through until the juices run clear. There should be no pink meat or juice. When dining out, order ground meats thoroughly cooked.

- Do not eat raw oysters or clams, no matter how expensive the restaurant, and avoid eating raw fish, like sashimi and some sushi, unless you can be certain it was first frozen at minus 4 degrees Fahrenheit for at least three days.

- Be compulsive about washing your hands before preparing food and after using the bathroom, blowing your nose or touching your pet.

- It is also important to keep milk, even pasteurized milk, and soft cheeses refrigerated and to use them promptly. It is, however, safe to eat cheese that has become moldy.

[JEB, October 1994]

Chemical Residues in Food
Are an Overrated Danger

AMERICANS trying to avoid cancer-causing substances in foods would benefit most from eating fewer calories and fats and more fruits and vegetables, a prestigious scientific panel concluded in a recent report. The panel suggested that people should worry far less about the risk of cancer from pesticide residues and food additives.

In a finding that is sure to appeal to anyone tired of washing vegetables in detergent to remove pesticides, a 20-member panel of the National Research Council, an arm of the National Academy of Sciences, confirmed that there were many natural and synthetic cancer-causing chemicals in foods, but it said their importance as cancer-causing agents was minimal compared with the overconsumption of calories and fat.

The report, "Carcinogens and Anticarcinogens in the Human Diet," based on an exhaustive review of scientific reports and other relevant information, said that about one-third of the 1.35 million new cancer cases in the nation each year could be traced to diet but probably not to natural or synthetic chemicals in significant numbers.

"The great majority of individual naturally occurring and synthetic food chemicals are present in the human diet at levels so low," the report said, "that they are unlikely to pose an appreciable cancer risk."

Food scientists and food industry representatives applauded the report. Dr. Joyce A. Nettleton of the Institute of Food Technologists, most of whose members work in industry, said: "No responsible scientist in the food system would deny there are substances in the food supply that in theory could be nasty if consumed in excessive amounts, but bodies aren't piling up because of lethal substances in food. Diet-related health conditions are related to our overall habits, not to specific food chemicals present in minuscule amounts."

And Timothy Willard, a spokesman for the National Food Processors Association in Washington, D.C., said that the report was "in harmony with what the industry and scientists have said for years about food and health: that consumer and public health attention should focus on the real risks, rather than trivial and mostly hypothetical risks posed by synthetic or natural carcinogens."

In another segment of the food industry, Robert Scowcroft, executive director of the Organic Farming Research Foundation in Santa Cruz, California, said he did not expect the report to have much of an impact on organic foods, which are grown without pesticides. Mr. Scowcroft said, "What motivates people to buy organic are not just food safety issues but a desire for fresh foods and taste and to protect the environment and farmworkers" from pesticides.

Al Meyerhoff, senior lawyer for the Natural Resources Defense Council, which has long championed a cleaner, safer environment, said that even though chemical carcinogens in foods were much less important than tobacco, alcohol and obesity as causes of cancer, "they can still cause thousands of cancers in consumers, and they should be avoided wherever possible."

The research council committee not only assessed the importance of the overall diet and carcinogenic chemicals but also concluded that if any chemicals were important to human cancers, the naturally occurring carcinogens, which far outnumber the synthetic ones, probably made a greater contribution to the cancer risk.

Mr. Meyerhoff, reacting to this finding, said that little could be done about natural carcinogens but that "the more than 100 known man-made carcinogens in foods are avoidable and involuntary exposures."

About 6,000 chemicals, both synthetic and natural, are deliberately or inadvertently added to foods, whereas hundreds of thousands of chemicals—perhaps a million—are naturally present in foods. Coffee aroma alone consists of about 1,000 different chemicals.

Relatively few chemicals that occur naturally in foods have been tested for their cancer-causing potential, the committee noted, adding that natural food substances are not tested and regulated as are chemicals like pesticides and preservatives that are applied or added to foods.

Still, the committee, led by Dr. Ronald Estabrook, a biochemist at the University of Texas Southwestern Medical Center in Dallas, cited examples of several well-established natural carcinogens that are widely consumed in ordinary foods.

One is caffeic acid, most prominent by far in coffee but also found in notable amounts in apples, lettuce, peaches, pears, potatoes, tomatoes and citrus fruits. Caffeic acid causes cancer in laboratory animals, but its role, if any, in human cancer is unknown. Despite many studies exploring the relationship of coffee drinking to cancer in people, no link has been established.

"While some chemicals in the diet do have the ability to cause cancer, they appear to be a threat only when they are present in foods that form an unusually large part of the diet," Dr. Estabrook said. "The varied and balanced diet needed for good nutrition—including fruits and vegetables—seems to provide significant protection from the natural toxicants in our foods."

Might cancer result from eating vegetables and fruits containing caffeic acid or those contaminated by residues of possibly carcinogenic pesticides? The committee expressed strong doubts, noting that plant foods are major sources of substances that protect against cancer, including the antioxidant vitamins A, C and E and other natural chemicals, including isoflavonoids, phenolic acids and isothiocyanates.

The committee pointed out that little was known about the interaction of carcinogens and anticarcinogens in foods. Many foods have both. For example, broccoli contains arsenic, a carcinogen, and chlorogenic acid, which is converted in the body to caffeic acid, but it also has anticarcinogens: vitamin C, sulforaphane, indole and other isothiocyanates. And cooked beefsteak contains carcinogens like benzanthracene, heterocyclic amines and traces of arsenic and a fungal toxin, ochratoxin A. But it also has anticarcinogenic substances like linoleic acid and selenium.

Studies of different groups of people with different diets have strongly suggested that in a diet rich in fruits and vegetables, anticarcinogens are far more influential than natural and synthetic carcinogens. In the case of beef, natural and synthetic carcinogens and cancer promoters like fat appear to play a greater role. Several recent studies have found a strong link between the consumption of red meat and cancers of the prostate and colon.

Though nearly all that is known about the cancer risk of chemicals in foods comes from studies of laboratory animals exposed to very high doses of each suspect chemical, the committee urged caution in drawing conclusions from animal studies about cancer risks in humans. Animal studies have limitations, the report pointed out, because the bodies of animals and people might handle a chemical differently, and the effects of ingesting a single substance in isolation might differ from the effects of consuming it as part of a varied diet. Also, an animal study uses very large doses of a chemical that people are exposed to in only minute amounts.

Without studies more relevant to human exposures to back up laboratory findings, the committee said, few conclusions can be drawn about the risk to people of consuming chemicals that cause cancer in animals. The report stressed the need for better studies of synthetic chemicals and more studies of natural food chemicals that might be suspect carcinogens.

The committee said that to use laboratory studies to estimate the cancer risk to humans, better information was needed on human exposure to the chemicals—what, how much and how often various sources of those chemicals are consumed.

The report also called for more research on natural anticarcinogens. Some of those might be added to foods to help protect people against cancer, the panel suggested.

Meanwhile, the committee said, "it is of utmost importance to continue recommending that the public consume diets rich in fruits and vegetables but low in fat and calories. The consumption of vitamins and minerals in a moderate, varied and balanced diet—not as dietary supplements—continues to be one of our best strategies for cancer prevention in people."

[JEB, February 1996]

Some Old Wives' Tales Withstand Scrutiny

EAT your carrots; you'll see better in the dark. Don't go swimming until an hour after you eat. Fish is brain food.

It's my mother's voice exhorting me. It could be your mother's voice, too. Or maybe she made you wear garlic around your neck to ward off colds or insisted that you have chicken soup if the cold arrived.

Old wives' tales are still being told, but they are also being subjected to scientific scrutiny. And it turns out that some of the things old wives intuited, perhaps through observation, have now been proven by scientists.

Years ago, for instance, manufacturers of cranberry juice were frustrated because they could not claim the juice helped prevent urinary tract infections, even though thousands of people swore by its efficacy. In 1991, a group of Israeli scientists found that cranberry juice, as well as blueberry juice, keeps a bacterium that commonly causes infections from clinging to the walls of the bladder. And a recent study at the Harvard Medical School offers additional backup of that claim.

Another study does not prove that carrots prevent night blindness but does show that they may prevent macular degeneration, an eye disease that can eventually cause blindness. The protective aspect comes from carotenoids, which are present in lots of other fruits and vegetables. A study of 3,000 older Americans done by the University of Chicago in 1988 showed that eating just one carrot a day, or some other food rich in carotenoids, reduced the chances of macular degeneration by 40 percent.

Is fish a brain food? It depends on whether there is a zinc deficiency in the diet, according to *Food—Your Miracle Medicine* by Jean Carper (HarperCollins, 1993). The book mentions a study done at the University of Texas Medical Branch in Galveston that found that a marginal lack of zinc "can mildly impair mental functioning, including memory." The study said that when women with a slight zinc deficiency ate adequate amounts of zinc, their recall of words jumped 12 percent and their recall of visual design jumped 17 percent.

Ms. Carper quotes A. E. Bender, a professor emeritus at the University of London, who said there was a theory "that man evolved in areas bordering seas and lakes because fish provided material for brain development, which other species lacked. So the folklore that said fish is food for the brain may be vindicated."

Mama would be pleased to know that eating chicken soup really works. In 1978, the Mount Sinai Medical Center in Miami Beach published a study that proved that "Jewish penicillin" worked better than hot or cold water in fighting the congestion that accompanies a cold. Further proof of its effectiveness came more recently when Dr. Irwin Ziment of the University of California at Los Angeles found that because chicken is a protein food it contains an amino acid called cysteine, which is chemically similar to a drug called acetylcysteine. Acetylcysteine is prescribed for people with respiratory infections because it thins the mucus in the lungs.

Wearing cloves of garlic may keep people at a distance in the winter, when close contact in an enclosed space over a long period leads to shared infections. But eating garlic is a more surefire way to stay well, scientists have found. In her book, Ms. Carper quotes James North, chief of microbiology at Brigham Young University in Provo, Utah, who confirmed that "garlic extract killed nearly 100 percent" of both a human rhinovirus that causes colds and parainfluenza 3, a flu and respiratory virus. Eating garlic cloves or onion is just the ticket when a sore throat signals the beginning of a cold, Dr. North said.

Other old wives' tales have been conclusively disproved or are hanging by a thread. You can, after all, go swimming right after eating. When I think of all the hours I wasted hanging out in the sand, waiting to go into the water, while my tuna-fish sandwich digested . . . Normal meals should not cause problems for swimmers, according to the August 1992 issue of the *Berkeley Wellness Letter.* Dr. Ernest Maglischo, the swimming coach at California State University at Bakersfield, said in the newsletter that marathon swimmers often eat high-carbohydrate meals before swimming.

And chocolate doesn't cause acne. Numerous studies have failed to show that any amount of chocolate causes an outbreak of acne. In fact, there appears to be little evidence that diet affects acne at all.

As for candy and tooth rot, it depends on the candy. Jelly beans and caramels won't do it, but peanut butter crackers, potato chips and salted crackers are just a few of the foods that are most likely to cause tooth decay. Here's how it works. Simple carbohydrates—sugars—are easily washed out of the mouth by saliva, while complex carbohydrates, found in crackers and potato chips, stick between the teeth for several hours, encouraging the growth of the bacteria that cause tooth decay. In addition to potato chips and crackers, other offenders include oatmeal cookies, cereal flakes coated with sugar, puffed-oat cereal and cream-filled cookies. The least sticky foods, and therefore the least likely to cause tooth decay, are apples, bananas, hot fudge sundaes and milk chocolate bars.

One old wives' tale was suggested for years in advertisements in Britain: that nursing mothers should drink a pint of beer a day because it was good for the baby. The ads are no longer allowed to make the claim, but the idea that a little beer is good for both mother and baby, which dates back to the first century after Christ, lingers, presumably because it relaxes Mom and increases the infants' milk consumption.

The February 1992 issue of the Tufts University *Diet & Nutrition Letter* reports that "Scientists at the Monell Chemical Senses Center in Philadelphia found that breast-fed infants drank an average of 22 percent less milk after their mothers consumed orange juice mixed with the amount of alcohol in a can of beer than when the

women drank the same amount of juice straight on a different day."
The newsletter acknowledges that the study was brief, but one of
the researchers said: "If someone tells a woman that drinking alcohol will help her nurse the baby, she should be aware that the advice is not based on scientific fact."

[MB, February 1994]

SECTION FIVE

Vitamins and
Other Supplements

THE BAD NEWS ABOUT VITAMIN MEGADOSES

There is news about vitamins, and it is not good. The vitamin industry can be counted on to fight it tooth and nail. Consumers will be loath to believe it. Even the scientists who produced it were extremely surprised and disappointed.

The news is this: with the possible exception of vitamin E, massive doses of vitamins do nothing to prevent heart disease or cancer and may even promote some forms of cancer.

The vitamin industry sells $3.5 billion worth of pills every year. Some 30 to 40 percent of Americans take vitamin C. The basis of this vast enterprise is a plausible idea based on the observation that people who eat lots of fruits and vegetables tend to suffer slightly less heart disease and cancer.

Since fruits and vegetables are rich in vitamin C and beta-carotene, the precursor of vitamin A, it seemed reasonable to suppose that the essence of vegetable goodness could be captured in a little pill without the bother of eating piles of broccoli.

There is a plausible rationale for this theory. Vitamins A, C and E are so-called antioxidants, meaning that they protect the body's tissues from a class of chemicals called free radicals. Free radicals damage DNA, the genetic material, and the damaged genes can interfere with the cell's ability to suppress cancerous changes. Free radicals also oxidize cholesterol-carrying blood proteins, hastening their buildup as plaque on arterial walls. So what could be better than to load the bloodstream with vitamins that suppress free radicals?

The theory requires hefty doses of vitamins, far larger than the minute amounts present in most people's ordinary diet that are required to prevent nutrient deficiency diseases such as scurvy. In the megadoses thought to prevent heart disease and cancer, vitamins are being used as a drug, not a nutritional supplement.

The enticing theory has persuaded many people to take large doses of vitamins, on the calculation that it can't hurt and may even do some good. For all who regard jogging and fibrous vegetables with equal disfavor, the little daily pill is such a painless alternative. And something that everyone agrees is vital in minute doses must surely be even better in megadoses.

The vitamin megadose theory, though, has been involved in a collision with the facts. Doctors who generally believed in the theory set up the large-scale, multiyear clinical trials needed to measure just how large the beneficial effect might be. The results of the first of these trials, on vitamins A and C, have now become available: their beneficial effect is zero. (The jury is still out on vitamin E.) "The biggest disappointment of my career" is how one researcher described the outcome.

For most scientists, schooled in the necessity of abandoning favorite theories when experiment so dictates, the vitamin megadose theory is dead. It will probably take a lot longer for others to be convinced.

A Surprising Setback for Megadoses of Vitamins A and C

A large and careful study to see if vitamins can protect against cancer and heart disease has found no evidence of any such benefit and even hints at actual harm. The finding is surprising because many earlier studies had suggested a benefit from these supplements, vitamin E and beta-carotene.

Experts involved in the study say it is possible a benefit may emerge as the study continues. They also say that the advice to eat a lot of fresh fruit and vegetables still stands, since the benefit seen in earlier studies may have come from something other than the vitamins. But the experts acknowledge that the case for vitamin supplements should be considered unproved for now.

The study, published in a recent issue of the *New England Journal of Medicine*, was sponsored by the National Cancer Institute in Bethesda, Maryland, and the National Public Health Institute in Finland. It was designed to show if vitamins A and E reduce the incidence of heart disease and lung and other cancers.

Its subjects were 29,000 Finnish men aged 50 and up, all of them long-term smokers. The study purposely used long-term smokers, who were more likely to develop lung cancer or heart disease, because that enhanced the chance that researchers would see the effect of the vitamins if there was one.

One group took vitamin E alone; a second group took beta-carotene, which the body converts to vitamin A; a third group took both vitamins; and a fourth took a dummy pill, or placebo. After five to eight years, the investigators reported, they could find no evidence that the supplements had helped.

Instead, they saw a confusing pattern of mostly adverse effects, raising the possibility, they say, "that these supplements may actually have harmful as well as beneficial effects."

The men in the beta-carotene group were somewhat more likely to die from lung cancer and heart disease. The vitamin E group suffered slightly more strokes from bleeding in the brain and slightly less prostate cancer, but both effects could be due to chance, the researchers said.

Public health experts expressed surprise at the new results. For years they have been gathering indirect evidence that certain vitamins, particularly vitamins E and C and beta-carotene, might protect against cancer and heart disease. The hypothesis was that these vitamins, which belong to a class of chemicals known as antioxidants, can mop up free radicals. Free radicals are reactive molecules that can injure genes, leading to cancer, and also initiate the buildup of plaque in arteries.

Many studies have shown that people who ate a lot of fruits and vegetables, which are high in these antioxidant vitamins, had slightly lower incidences of cancer and heart disease. Another set of studies showed that people who take vitamin supplements had less disease. But the question remained: Did the protective effect lie in the vitamins or in some other aspect of the people's behavior? For example, those who ate lots of fruits and vegetables or took vitamin supplements might also have better health habits in general. Or there could be something other than the vitamins in the fruits and vegetables that protected people against cancer and heart disease.

The new study, experts said, was the first using the best available scientific design to address the vitamin question in a well-fed Western population. The results, they say, do not prove that vitamin supplements cannot help prevent cancer or heart disease but do show that the case for supplements is far from proved.

The participants took 20 milligrams of beta-carotene daily, which an accompanying editorial in the medical journal said was as much as is practical. The doses raised blood levels 10-fold, and a quarter of the participants turned yellow. The dosage of vitamin E was 50 milligrams a day, which raised blood levels by a third. The dosage is far less than in supplements, which often contain a few hundred milligrams.

"This study raises a big yellow caution flag," said Dr. Gilbert S. Omenn, who is the dean of the School of Public Health at the University of Washington in Seattle. "It's quite important."

Dr. Omenn said it made sense to look at smokers because they were more likely to develop cancer and heart disease, so an effect in preventing disease might be more easily discerned. "Smokers get the same diseases as the rest of us," he said. "If you want to do a study with 29,000 people rather than 100,000 people, you have to look at high-risk people."

Dr. Charles Hennekens, a professor of medicine at the Brigham and Women's Hospital in Boston, said, "The results are surprising and unexpected." And, he added, "when something is unexpected, that means you shouldn't discount it." With the new results, Dr. Hennekens said, people can no longer say that they might as well take vitamins because vitamins cannot hurt and might help. Now, he said, "it's a whole new ball game."

Dr. David Harrison, a researcher on aging at the Jackson Laboratory in Bar Harbor, Maine, said he too was surprised by the finding but questioned whether the results would apply to nonsmokers. He said he took vitamins C and E and beta-carotene and, as a nonsmoker, hoped they might do some good. "I personally have thought that modest amounts of vitamin E and beta-carotene are more likely to be helpful than harmful," he said. "For those of us who like to believe that antioxidants are helpful, this study is a significant blow."

Experts said they were puzzled by the hints from the study that beta-carotene might be harmful. Dr. Hennekens said these results might be due simply to the play of chance when so many variables are examined in so large a study.

If vitamin E really encourages strokes, Dr. Omenn and Dr. Greenwald said, it could be because the vitamin discourages platelets in the blood from clumping, making bleeding more likely. Dr. Greenwald added that people who have high blood pressure and bleeding tendencies should be cautioned against taking vitamin E until more is known.

Dr. Hennekens is directing two large studies of the vitamin hypothesis. Both involve smokers and nonsmokers and include more than a decade of treatment and follow-up, which Dr. Hennekens said could be required to see a positive result. He said that it might be that when the smokers took vitamins for five to eight years, it was too little, too late to protect them.

Dr. Omenn is also directing a large study involving smokers, former smokers and people exposed to asbestos who will be followed for an average of six and a half years. In Dr. Omenn's study, participants are taking vitamin A as well as beta-carotene. That, he hopes, will make a difference.

But in the meantime these experts say they stand by their previous advice. Do not take vitamin supplements, they say, unless their health claims are proved. Instead, Dr. Greenwald said, people should eat plenty of fruits and vegetables.

And, Dr. Hennekens noted, if the smokers in the Finnish study had stopped smoking, they would have done far more to protect themselves from lung cancer and heart disease than even the most wildly optimistic projections of what vitamins might have done for them.

[GK, April 1994]

Interpreting the Finnish Vitamin Study

THOSE who are looking for quick fixes for their bad health habits, or who simply want an inexpensive insurance policy, received disappointing news recently when a large study of lifelong smokers in Finland revealed no apparent protection against lung cancer or cardiovascular disease from daily supplements of the antioxidant nutrients vitamin E or beta-carotene or both.

As if that were not distressing enough, the study also suggested that some harm might result from daily supplements of beta-carotene, which was previously considered harmless in megadoses many times higher than those needed to prevent nutritional deficiencies. Smokers who took 20 milligrams of beta-carotene each day developed 18 percent more lung cancers than those who were given vitamin E or a dummy pill, and those who took 50 milligrams a day of vitamin E had a slightly higher rate (which was not statistically significant) of hemorrhagic stroke.

The study was conducted among 29,000 men initially aged 50 to 69 who were randomly assigned to take different vitamin regimens. It has been widely hailed as the most carefully designed investigation in people into the presumed protective role of supplements of antioxidant nutrients. It was especially welcomed by the Food and Drug Administration, which is now trying to stop an effort by the vitamin industry to make health claims on supplement labels and to distribute studies that support the claims to consumers even if other research contradicts the studies.

But did the study prove that such supplements were useless or harmful either for smokers or, more important, for the vast majority of people who do not smoke but who are otherwise exposed to countless substances that can cause oxidative damage to their genes or cells?

A new finding should never be accepted at its face value without an attempt to evaluate it in the context of other studies. When this is done for the Finnish study, it becomes apparent that no definite conclusion can be reached at this time as to the benefit or harm of the supplements studied for smokers or for anyone. Several factors are worth considering.

First, does the finding make biological sense? Antioxidants—specifically vitamins E and C and beta-carotene—have been found in numerous studies to slow, block or reverse harmful oxidative changes in body substances and cells. For example, vitamin E helps to block oxidation, which converts LDL cholesterol from a form that stays in the blood to a form that can stick to and clog arteries. And beta-carotene has been shown to reverse precancerous changes in cells that line the mouth and cervix.

Neither in animal studies nor in human studies has a toxic effect of either nutrient been noted, and the Finnish researchers were unable to explain the higher lung cancer rate among those who took beta-carotene. But some laboratory evidence suggests that when antioxidants like beta-carotene reach very high levels in blood and tissues, they can cause oxidation instead of preventing it. Such levels are reached when people take a high-dose supplement but not when they eat ordinary carotene-rich foods.

Second, does the finding mesh with research observations among large groups of people? These so-called epidemiological studies can never prove cause and effect; they can only show an association between two factors that may indeed result from a direct link between them or that may, on the other hand, simply suggest that another associated factor is the real cause of the observed result.

Two major epidemiological studies involving 120,000 people, smokers and nonsmokers, found a significant reduction in heart disease among men and women who took large daily supplements of vitamin E, and one study of 333 male doctors with a history of heart disease showed a similar benefit from taking 50 milligrams of beta-carotene every other day for 10 years.

As for anticancer effects, at least 17 studies in people have found that those whose diets are richest in carotenoids have the lowest risk of developing lung cancer. Beta-carotene is the most prominent, but hardly the only, carotenoid in the American diet. Another group of studies links diets rich in carotenoids to protection against stroke and heart attack.

As with all epidemiological studies, these do not prove that vitamin E, beta-carotene or carotenoids in general are protective. The findings may mean that people who choose to take such supplements or eat a carotenoid-rich diet also have other characteristics that are the real source of protection. Or the failure of the Finnish study to find a benefit from taking supplements of beta-carotene could mean that something else in carotene-rich foods—other carotenoids, dietary fiber, various cancer-blocking chemicals like sulforaphane, recently isolated from broccoli, or something not yet discovered—confers the observed benefit.

Third, was the new study designed in a way that would give a meaningful answer to the research question? If the question was whether taking a beta-carotene supplement or a small dose of vitamin E for six years can block the lung damage caused by 36 years of smoking an average of a pack of cigarettes a day, then, yes, the study answers this: the supplements were not effective. But if you want to know whether, as a smoker or nonsmoker, you might benefit from or be harmed by taking beta-carotene or a large dose of vitamin E for decades, the study cannot help you.

With regard to vitamin E, the dosage used in the study may account for its failure to find a benefit. Study participants were given a daily dose of only 50 milligrams (international units) of a synthetic form of vitamin E that is not well absorbed and that raises blood levels of the vitamin by only one-third. The vitamin E dose used in studies that showed a beneficial effect, by comparison, is hundreds of milligrams, which doubles the blood levels of the vitamin.

As for beta-carotene, if this nutrient confers its anticancer effect early in the cancer process, then taking it for a short time after decades of heavy smoking would be useless against a disease like lung cancer, which may take 20 years or more to develop. Only a much longer study begun early in people's smoking careers could conceivably reveal a benefit.

In an editorial accompanying the Finnish report in the *New England Journal of Medicine,* researchers from Boston and Oxford, England, said the results "do not disprove the potential benefits of antioxidant vitamins, but they do provide timely support for skepticism and for a moratorium on unsubstantiated health claims." In other words, further careful research is needed before any conclusions can be drawn about the benefits and risks of antioxidant supplements for smokers and others.

Other studies are already under way in women as well as in men, using higher doses taken for a longer time. Until they are completed, people have three options: They can change harmful habits like cigarette smoking, sedentary living and careless eating. They can eat more foods rich in carotenoids and other protective substances, like carrots, cantaloupe, broccoli and other cabbage-family vegetables, spinach, collard greens, winter squash, apricots and sweet potatoes. Or they can hedge their bets and, in addition to the first two options, also take supplements, particularly supplements of vitamin E, which is not readily available in a low-fat diet and cannot be obtained in any diet in the doses that are believed to protect the heart.

[JEB, April 1994]

The Rationale for Antioxidant Supplements

IN the last few years, the word "antioxidant" has moved rapidly from the domain of chemists and biochemists into common use, at least among health-conscious Americans. Millions of people concerned about preventing heart disease and cancer and staving off the ravages of age have turned to antioxidant nutrients like vitamins C and E, beta-carotene and selenium as if they provided a protective cloak against both self-inflicted and environmental insults.

Medical researchers, too, have jumped on the antioxidant bandwagon, undertaking huge studies to see whether and how well antioxidants might guard against the damage wrought by such noxious influences as cigarette smoke, fatty diets, air pollution and a host of inescapable carcinogens.

The idea behind antioxidants is to block the action of omnipresent free radicals, highly reactive oxidizing substances that form in the body during normal metabolism and that enter the body from the external environment. Cigarette smoke and polluted air, for example, contain many of these oxidizing substances. Oxidation, the chemical process that makes iron rust, can wreak havoc in the body as well.

For example, oxidation reactions caused by free radicals can damage cell membranes that protect tissues against noxious agents like toxins and carcinogens. Free radicals can change some substances that are potential carcinogens into a form that can initiate the cancer process.

Free-radical damage is thought to be an important contributor to the bodywide deterioration that accompanies aging. And recent studies have shown that LDL cholesterol, the so-called bad cholesterol, is changed through oxidation from a form that circulates freely in the blood to a form that can latch onto artery walls, narrowing their passageway and thus increasing the risk of heart attack and stroke.

Considerable circumstantial and laboratory evidence suggests that nutrients with antioxidant properties can at least partly protect against such damage. For example, studies done in university laboratories in Texas and California showed that vitamins C and E can prevent the oxidation of LDL cholesterol, therefore presumably reducing the risk of cardiovascular disease.

Two very large studies, one involving 40,000 men followed for four years and the other 80,000 women who were followed for eight years, revealed that those who took daily supplements of vitamin E averaging 200 to 400 international units were 40 percent less likely than those who did not take the supplements to develop heart disease during the study period.

A British study among 110 patients with angina (chest pain caused by insufficient oxygen to the heart muscle) and 394 men free of angina found that in those with low blood levels of vitamin E, the risk of developing angina was nearly three times as high.

And a continuing study among 22,000 American male doctors yielded a surprising interim finding: those taking a supplement of beta-carotene to test the nutrient's anticancer potential suffered only half the expected number of serious cardiovascular events, like heart attacks and strokes.

The possibility of an anticancer effect of foods rich in beta-carotene has been suggested by a number of long-term studies. For example, in a study begun in 1958 in Chicago among 2,100 men, those with a low intake of foods containing carotene were more likely to have died of lung cancer 19 years later.

In a Swiss study of nearly 3,000 men begun in 1971, cancer deaths were significantly higher among those with low levels of carotene and vitamin C in their blood. Low levels of carotene were especially associated with a greater risk of lung cancer, and low levels of vitamin C were linked to an increased risk of cancers of the stomach and intestines. In studies of women with precancerous changes in the cervix, abnormal tissues were far more commonly found in those with low blood levels of beta-carotene and vitamin C.

But in all these cancer studies the possible beneficial effects observed were associated with the consumption of foods rich in antioxidants, not supplements. Such foods contain many potentially beneficial substances in addition to beta-carotene and vitamin C, and it is not possible to say whether the apparent protection against cancer is attributable to any one substance or even to these foods per se. Rather, it is possible—in fact, likely—that people who eat lots of wholesome foods like fruits and vegetables rich in beta-carotene and vitamin C also practice other good health habits that lower their cancer risk.

To control for this possibility, long-term studies must be conducted among large numbers of people who are randomly assigned to take either the nutrient in question or a look-alike dummy pill. Such a study has yet to be completed, particularly among people who do not smoke.

[JEB, April 1994]

Another Thumbs-Down for Vitamin Megadoses

A new study of people at high risk for colon cancer has failed to find evidence that vitamin supplements protect against the development of precancerous growths in the colon. People who took vitamin C or vitamin E or beta-carotene or all three over four years were no freer of disease than people who took dummy pills.

The findings came as a surprise to some researchers. It is well established that people whose diets are rich in fruits and vegetables have lower rates of colon cancer than do those who eat less of these foods. Some researchers had thought that the vitamins in fruits and vegetables might have been the source of their benefits. The study was an effort to test this thesis.

The study, published recently in the *New England Journal of Medicine*, involved 864 people who had previously had colorectal adenomas, or polyps that precede cancer. It follows another carefully designed study of vitamin supplements, involving heavy smokers, that failed to find any protective effect of vitamin E and beta-carotene against lung cancer.

But, experts say, the final answer to the question of whether vitamin supplements can protect against cancer is not yet in. It may be necessary to conduct longer studies or studies with different designs to see an effect. Or it may be that something else about fruits and vegetables, the fiber perhaps, confers benefits. Another possibility is that people who eat a lot of fruits and vegetables eat less meat and fat, and that the meat and fat elicit colon cancer.

The colon cancer study is "very important," said Dr. Peter Greenwald, director of cancer prevention and control at the National Cancer Institute. Both it and the previous study on lung cancer were "very well designed," Dr. Greenwald said. But, he added: "It's still early on. We're going to have to continue the clinical trials program."

The food supplement industry, represented by its trade organization, the Council for Responsible Nutrition, said the new study did nothing to change its recommendation that people take vitamins. "We still feel that the bulk of the evidence supports the hypothesis that generous intakes of antioxidants will help prevent a number of chronic diseases, including some cancers," said Dr. Annette Dickinson, the council's director of scientific and regulatory affairs.

In the study, patients were randomly assigned to four groups. One group took daily doses of beta-carotene. A second took vitamin C and vitamin E. A third took all three vitamins each day. The fourth took a pill with inert ingredients. The participants were examined regularly to see if they were developing polyps in the colon.

After four years, the researchers reported, there was no difference among the groups. Those taking the vitamins had virtually the same rates of new polyp formation in the colon as those taking the dummy pills.

Dr. E. Robert Greenberg of the Dartmouth-Hitchcock Medical Center in Hanover, New Hampshire, who directed the study, said in an interview on Tuesday that he found the results "disappointing." He said that many studies had found that people who eat large amounts of fruits and vegetables had lower colon cancer rates and that fruits and vegetables are known for providing vitamins C and E.

There is a biochemical theory of how these vitamins might work. They mop up highly damaging molecules formed in cells, known as free radicals, which can injure a cell's genetic material, leading it down the path to malignancy.

In addition, Dr. Greenberg and his colleagues wrote in their paper, two previous studies had indicated that vitamin supplements might reduce the rate of polyp formation among people who had had colon cancer. Two other studies had failed to find effects, but all four studies were too small to be definitive.

Still another study showed that it took just a short time for vitamin A and C supplements to reduce abnormal cell proliferation in the colons of people who had had cancer. All in all, Dr. Greenberg said, the positive results were encouraging.

In retrospect, Dr. Greenberg said, he feels researchers have been "somewhat naïve" to think that the vitamins in fruits and vegetables were sufficient to prevent cancer. He said that fruits and vegetables contain hundreds of other compounds that seem to prevent cancer, on the basis of laboratory and animal studies. "My hunch is, it's a lot of things" in fruits and vegetables that make them so effective in cancer prevention, he said.

But others are not so quick to disregard vitamins. Dr. Charles Hennekens, a professor of medicine at Brigham and Women's Hospital in Boston, said that the colon cancer study did not continue long enough to show an effect if there was one. He is directing a study of beta-carotene's anticancer effects in more than 22,000 healthy doctors.

And, Dr. Hennekens said, he is waiting 12 years from the start of the study before drawing conclusions. He said that his study would end in late 1995 and that the results would be analyzed and published in 1996.

Dr. Bruce Ames, a professor of biochemistry and molecular biology at the University of California at Berkeley, also said that more time might be needed to see an effect. "I think there's going to be a fair amount of ups and downs in this field," Dr. Ames said.

In an editorial accompanying the colon cancer article, two editors of the *New England Journal of Medicine,* Dr. Marcia Angell and Dr. Jerome P. Kassirer, addressed the question of what the public is to believe. They concluded that studies were essentially hypotheses in progress and added that people should reserve judgment while evidence accumulated.

"People who felt betrayed when they learned of a new study showing that vitamin E and carotene do not protect against cancer should ask themselves why they so readily believed that antioxidants had this effect in the first place and why they now believe that there is no effect," they wrote.

[GK, July 1994]

Beta-Carotene and Vegetables

A S more and more questions are raised about beta-carotene, until recently considered a wonder nutrient that all on its own could protect against the scourges of disease like cancer and heart disease, another shortcut to good health is falling on hard times.

Like many another easy alternative, the lesson with beta-carotene seems to be that popping a pill is not enough. You have to eat those carrots and broccoli and dark leafy greens, just as you have to exercise to lose weight and make yourself relax to reduce stress.

Although a number of studies have suggested that beta-carotene could have a protective effect against cancer and heart disease, nearly all involved people whose diets were otherwise exemplary. They ate fruits and vegetables and other foods rich in carotenoids, the large family of nutrients that includes beta-carotene. After a well-designed Finnish study suggested recently that beta-carotene supplements might be harmful, many researchers began to revise their thinking about using supplements alone to reap the purported benefits of the nutrient. Even if beta-carotene turns out to be of primary importance, it might have to be consumed with other carotenoids to be effective.

For decades, the main interest in beta-carotene had been in its role as a parent compound for vitamin A. Several other carotenoids can also become vitamin A, but none are as good a source or as prominent in foods as beta-carotene. Once in the body, beta-carotene can be split into two parts, each of which becomes a molecule of vitamin A, an essential fat-soluble vitamin. Vitamin A assists in the formation and maintenance of healthy skin, hair and mucous membranes; it aids in the ability to see in dim light; and it is needed for proper bone growth, tooth development and reproduction.

Preformed vitamin A is found in animal foods like liver, eggs, cheese and butter; all are high in cholesterol, saturated fats or both and are therefore not featured in a heart-healthy diet. If consumed in excessive amounts, preformed vitamin A can be highly toxic, causing blurred vision, loss of appetite, headaches, rashes, digestive and menstrual irregularities, abnormal bone growth, brain and nerve injury, joint pain and liver damage.

But when vitamin A is obtained from beta-carotene, the body makes only enough to meet its needs. The conversion is not very efficient; six milligrams of beta-carotene are considered to be the nutritional equivalent of one milligram of vitamin A. Excess beta-carotene, a yellow-orange pigment, enters the circulation unchanged, and when consumed in very large amounts (for example, by drinking lots of carrot juice), it may give the skin a jaundiced look. But it is not known to be toxic, and it cannot cause vitamin A poisoning.

The modern-day enthusiasm for beta-carotene stems from the

many observational studies that have linked high dietary or blood levels of this nutrient to a reduced risk of suffering a heart attack or developing a number of lethal cancers, especially cancers of the respiratory and digestive tracts. Beta-carotene is known to be an antioxidant, a substance that can sop up cell-damaging free radicals and block harmful changes in normal body constituents and in potential carcinogens that enter the body through food, air or water. Beta-carotene may further protect the body by enhancing the immune function.

But in three studies that have been completed thus far, taking supplements of beta-carotene did not prevent cancers of the lung or skin or precancerous lesions of the colon. As for preventing heart attacks, only one small and as-yet-unpublished study, a part of the Physicians' Health Trial being conducted by Harvard Medical School, suggested that beta-carotene supplements might reduce the risk of heart attack in men with serious atherosclerosis. Thus far, however, vitamin E seems to be far more effective as a heart-protecting supplement.

But keep in mind that beta-carotene is only one of about 40 carotenoids that are prominent in common foods. Until recently, little was known about which and how much of the other carotenoids were present in typical American diets. However, Dr. Gary R. Beecher and his colleagues at the U.S. Department of Agriculture have spent almost a decade analyzing the various carotenoids in fruits and vegetables.

Values for five major carotenoids—lutein, lycopene, alpha-carotene, beta-cryptoxanthin and beta-carotene—are now available for 150 fruits and vegetables and more than 2,000 combination foods. Scientists may now be able to sort out more precisely the relationship between carotenoid consumption and the risk of various cancers and other potentially lethal or crippling disorders.

In addition, fruits and vegetables contain other substances like indoles, phenols and flavonoids that may interact with carotenoids to protect against cancer.

The best way to get all the possible benefits that the various carotenoids may bestow is to eat at least five servings a day of a variety of fruits and vegetables, especially those that are dark green, deep yellow, orange and red. Currently, however, Americans fall short even on beta-carotene, the easiest carotenoid to obtain because it makes up one-fourth of dietary carotenoids. While nutrition experts recommend that adults consume at least 6 milligrams of beta-carotene a day, the average adult consumes only 1.5 milligrams. Among the foods that are Americans' top 10 sources of pre-vitamin-A carotenoids are vegetable soups, beef stew and orange juice, none of which is a concentrated source of these nutrients.

Nutritionists are also concerned about the current penchant for stripping fat from the diet. Without fat, carotenoids are not absorbed, and if a low-fat diet is carried to an extreme, it could deprive the body of potentially protective carotenoids. Thus, eating a carrot between meals or consuming a salad with a fat-free dressing without simultaneously eating a food that contains some fat may not be a useful source of carotenoids.

[JEB, February 1995]

Beta-Carotene: The Limited Value of Megadoses

TWO large studies have found that, contrary to the beliefs or hopes of the millions of Americans who take it, beta-carotene, a vigorously promoted vitamin supplement, is completely ineffective in preventing cancer or heart disease. One of the studies found that it might even be harmful to some people.

Federal health officials said they hoped that this would spell the end of the beta-carotene fad. The idea that a simple supplement capsule might fend off cancer and other diseases, they said, has simply proved too good to be true.

Dr. Richard Klausner, director of the National Cancer Institute, which financed both studies, said, "With clearly no benefit and even a hint of possible harm, I can see no reason that an individual should take beta-carotene."

Beta-carotene is a naturally occurring substance in fruits and vegetables that is converted to vitamin A in the body. The cancer institute recommends that rather than rely on supplements, people eat low-fat diets abundant in fruits and vegetables, whose hundreds of substances combined might be fostering the disease protection that has been sought in beta-carotene.

Americans spend $3.5 billion a year on vitamin and mineral supplements, said Dr. Annette Dickinson, the director of science and regulatory affairs at the Council for Responsible Nutrition, a trade association of supplement manufacturers.

But the health claims for many of these supplements have not been verified by rigorous scientific investigation, and the Food and Drug Administration is not empowered to regulate claims that vitamin manufacturers make in advertising and promotional brochures except for those that accompany the supplements themselves on retailers' shelves.

One of the beta-carotene studies, the Physicians' Health Study, involved 22,071 doctors who were randomly assigned to take 50 milligrams of beta-carotene or a dummy pill every other day. The study ended on December 31, 1995, after 12 years, with the conclusion that beta-carotene supplements did not protect against cancer or heart disease.

The other study, the Beta-Carotene and Retinol Efficacy Trial, or CARET, tested both beta-carotene, in a dose of 30 milligrams a day, and vitamin A, in a daily dose of 25,000 international units. The 18,314 participants in this study took beta-carotene, vitamin A, both, or a placebo. Preliminary studies had hinted that beta-carotene might be especially effective in preventing lung cancer, and all the subjects in the CARET study were at high risk for lung cancer because they smoked or had worked with asbestos.

The study was halted on January 10, 1996—21 months ahead of schedule—when investigators concluded not only that the vitamins were not helpful but also that they might be harmful: the rate of death from lung cancer was 28 percent higher among the participants who had taken the supplements than among those who had taken the placebo, and the rate of death from heart disease was 17 percent higher. The reason for these increases is unclear, and they were too small to be considered statistically significant. But they were nonetheless worrisome.

These two studies were preceded by a Finnish study of 29,133 men who were smokers. That study, published in 1994, found a slight increase in the death rate among those who had taken beta-carotene. But some critics of the research said the beta-carotene dose, 20 milligrams a day, had been too low to find the benefit that they had expected. Others said the men had been studied for too short a time, five to eight years. And still others said that even if beta-carotene did not help smokers, it would help healthy people.

Dr. Klausner said that as a consequence of the results, researchers would immediately remove beta-carotene from another study, involving 40,000 female health professionals who have been taking beta-carotene, vitamin E and aspirin.

The CARET study's director, Dr. Gilbert S. Omenn, dean of public health at the University of Washington in Seattle, said its results were not definite proof that beta-carotene is harmful. But the reason it was halted, he said, is that its findings were reminiscent of those in the Finnish study.

"These vitamins were providing no benefit," Dr. Omenn said, "and may—with the emphasis on *may*—have adverse effects."

But Dr. Dickinson, of the supplement manufacturers' trade association, said the new results were not enough to indicate that Americans should stop taking beta-carotene, especially in lower doses or in multivitamins. Although she acknowledged that heavy smokers "ought to be aware of the CARET trial and take it into consideration," she said that "there is still a strong suggestion" that beta-carotene might be beneficial among the population as a whole.

The study researchers disagree. "There is absolutely no benefit" in beta-carotene supplements, said Dr. Charles Hennekens of the Brigham and Women's Hospital in Boston, who was the director of the Physicians' Health Study. And that finding, Dr. Hennekens added, is "the biggest disappointment of my career."

The two studies began in the early 1980s, when researchers had high hopes that beta-carotene or vitamin A might protect against cancer and heart disease. The hypothesis was that these substances served as antioxidants, mopping up dangerous chemicals known as free radicals, which, although a normal product of body function, can damage DNA, leading to cancer, and can convert cholesterol, which is normally inert, into a substance that can lead to heart disease.

In support of the hypothesis were epidemiological studies showing that people whose diets were rich in fruits and vegetables, the sources of beta-carotene, had less cancer and heart disease than people whose diets were not. And studies found that the more beta-carotene in people's serum, the lower their risk of cancer.

Some scientists urged caution at the time, saying that beta-carotene in the serum might simply be a marker for fruit and vegetable consumption and that the complex mixture of chemicals involved in this consumption might be what promotes health. Or it might be that people who ate fruits and vegetables were healthier to begin with: more likely to exercise, less likely to smoke and leaner than those whose idea of a vegetable is a dollop of ketchup.

One of those cautious experts, Dr. Victor Herbert, a professor of medicine at the Mount Sinai School of Medicine in New York, warned that the vitamin supplements could actually be harmful, because beta-carotene acts as a pro-oxidant in some circumstances.

But the antioxidant craze took on a life of its own. "The enthusiasm ran ahead of the evidence," said Dr. Daniel Steinberg, a professor of medicine at the University of California at San Diego, who studies antioxidants and heart disease.

Now, given the new studies' finding that beta-carotene supplements are useless or worse, some experts are saying that at least the scientific process was brought to fruition. "The reality is that science has worked here," said Dr. Hennekens, the director of the Physicians' Health Study. Despite people's willingness to accept less-than-definitive evidence, he said, scientists pushed ahead with carefully designed clinical trials.

"The major message," Dr. Klausner said, "is that no matter how compelling and exciting a hypothesis is, we don't know whether it works without clinical trials."

Others criticize the dietary supplement industry for promoting beta-carotene so vigorously without an adequate scientific basis. "The health food industry is selling America a bill of goods," said Dr. Herbert, who added that he had long been "a leading voice against this quackery."

Dr. Peter Greenwald, director of the Division of Cancer Prevention and Control at the cancer institute, said: "We ought to give this some real thought. Someone's promoting supplements. Where does the responsibility lie to show efficacy?"

[GK, January 1996]

The Case for Vitamin E

IN a nation hungry for simple nutritional solutions to complex health problems, vitamin E might seem to be a panacea. Various studies have singled it out as the most promising and possibly the safest antidote to the nation's leading killers, heart disease and cancer. And while it is protecting coronary arteries against atherosclerosis and DNA against attacks by chemical carcinogens, it may also be keeping normal cells throughout the body from aging prematurely.

But vitamin E, chemically named alpha-tocopherol, does all this and more at levels well above those needed to prevent a nutritional deficiency, levels that render it a drug, not a nutrient. As a vitamin, it aids in the formation of red blood cells, muscles and other tissues and prevents oxidation of vitamin A and essential fatty acids. At high levels not attainable through diet—40 times or more the nutritionally needed amount—vitamin E functions as a potent antioxidant.

Well, then, shouldn't everybody take vitamin E supplements? Certainly, most if not all researchers who study it are taking it, but most are not yet willing to tell the general public to do the same. Are these scientists being hypocritical, telling us one thing and doing another?

The answer lies in the difference between advice to an individual and a public health recommendation. When considering an individual, like a smoker or someone with high cholesterol, who is known to face an unusually high risk of developing heart disease or cancer, it seems safe to assume that the potential benefits of taking vitamin E would easily outweigh any possible risks. But before advising the public to do the same, public health specialists first insist on proof that the expected benefits for the general population far exceed any possible hazards. And such proof for vitamin E, as for any other nutrient that has lately been touted as a promising preventive or remedy, is still lacking.

What researchers need in order to establish proof is a double-blind, controlled clinical trial. This is a study, preferably involving large numbers of people followed for several years, in which the participants are randomly assigned to take either the substance under study or a look-alike placebo and in which the scientists evaluating their effects do not know who is taking what until the study is completed. Otherwise, it cannot be known whether those who choose to take, say, vitamin E are perhaps different in ways important to health from those who do not. Nor can it be known whether the researchers' evaluations of the results are influenced by their beliefs about the nutrient's benefits or risks.

In the absence of such a study it is impossible to interpret the most recent vitamin E finding: evidence in men with existing heart disease that taking it daily for two years slowed the progress of atherosclerosis.

Another reason for hesitancy is that while vitamin E in large doses appears to be very safe for most people, no drug lacks side effects. Vitamin E in large doses interferes with blood clotting and can result in bleeding problems in some people. It may also raise blood pressure.

Cardiovascular Disease

The strongest evidence for the value of vitamin E supplements concerns the heart. At high levels, vitamin E prevents oxidation of LDL, or low-density-lipoprotein, cholesterol, the so-called bad cholesterol, and as a result curbs its ability to latch onto artery walls and form the artery-clogging plaque of atherosclerosis. A recent study in healthy men by Dr. Ishwarlal Jialal and colleagues at the University of Texas Southwestern Medical Center in Dallas found that a minimum dose of 400 international units of vitamin E a day is needed to counter LDL oxidation. (The Recommended Dietary Allowance—or RDA—is only 8 to 10 international units, and even at this low dose, more than 40 percent of elderly Americans fall dangerously below it.)

Among patients with poor circulation in their legs due to atherosclerosis, those who took a 300-milligram supplement of vitamin E and started an exercise program had a much greater improvement in walking ability than the people who did not get the supplement. After 12 to 18 months of treatment, the researchers measured improved blood flow in those taking vitamin E.

Vitamin E also inhibits clotting and, in one small but well-controlled study of people with vascular disease, vitamin E plus daily aspirin was more effective than aspirin alone in countering heart attacks and strokes.

Cancer

The evidence for vitamin E as an anticancer agent is less compelling. Most of the studies have been conducted in laboratory dishes and animals, and while most have suggested that vitamin E can protect against the initiation and development of cancer, not all have shown a benefit. In studies of animals exposed to cancer-causing substances, vitamin E supplements (sometimes in conjunction with other antioxidants like selenium) inhibited the development of breast cancers in rats, colon and esophageal cancers in mice and oral cancers in hamsters.

Among the studies involving people, several have suggested a potential benefit. For example, patients with cancers of the lung, breast, cervix, mouth and throat, colon or stomach had significantly lower levels of vitamin E in their blood than comparable people free of cancer.

Aging and Immunity

Damage to body cells by ubiquitous substances called free radicals, which are powerful oxidizing agents, is thought to be a major factor in aging and the decline in immunity with age. By inhibiting the oxidation of fats, vitamin E helps to protect cell membranes against damage from oxidizing agents in the environment and those produced in normal metabolism. Studies in both animals and people—and especially elderly people—have shown that supplements of vitamin E can improve immunological responses. In animal studies vitamin E has stopped the development of cataracts, many of which may be caused by sunlight-induced oxidation of fats in the lens.

People's habits may increase their need for vitamin E supplements, notes Dr. Mohsen Meydani, an expert in antioxidants at the U.S. Department of Agriculture's Human Nutrition Research Center on Aging at Tufts University near Boston. For example, vigorous exercise generates free radicals that cause muscle damage, and a study in men by Dr. William J. Evans at Pennsylvania State University found that vitamin E supplements helped protect against such damage. Cigarette smoking exposes the body to many oxidizing substances in tobacco smoke and tar. Air pollution exposes the lungs to oxidizing free radicals. Taking fish oil supplements or consuming a high-fish diet can use up the body's supply of vitamin E. And most vegetable oils and margarine supply the wrong kind of tocopherol and increase the body's need for vitamin E. (Olive oil, in contrast, is rich in the form of tocopherol that is biologically most effective.) Finally, those consuming a very low-fat diet may not come close to meeting the RDA for vitamin E.

Vitamin E is soluble in fat and is sold in gel caps dissolved in oil. It is usually measured and sold in international units, which are equivalent regardless of the source of vitamin E. While natural vitamin E is, gram for gram, 50 percent more active than synthetic vitamin E, 100 international units of natural vitamin E will offer the same activity as 100 international units of the synthesized version.

Vitamin E is commonly available in doses ranging from 100 to 1,000 international units. Most evidence suggests that 400 international units daily are likely to be the most beneficial supplementary dose. Doses of 3,200 international units have been taken safely by some people, but there is at this time no obvious benefit at this high level that would warrant risking a chance of adverse effects.

[JEB, July 1995]

The Recommended Doses of Vitamin C May Be Too Low

HOW much vitamin C is enough? Is it the 60 milligrams a day—the amount in half a cup of fresh orange juice—that is the current Recommended Dietary Allowance (RDA), the 30 to 40 milligrams that some nutritional biochemists think it should be, the hundreds of milligrams that millions of Americans now take as a daily supplement or the thousands of milligrams that Dr. Linus Pauling believed would protect against serious illnesses, including cancer?

A detailed new federally sponsored study, by far the most comprehensive done to date, says none of the above. The study, directed by Dr. Mark Levine and published recently in the *Proceedings of the National Academy of Sciences*, found that the "optimal" daily intake of vitamin C was more like 200 milligrams, although only about 10 milligrams are needed to prevent vitamin C deficiency.

The researchers, at the National Institutes of Health, also concluded that daily doses above 400 milligrams "have no evident value" and that amounts of 1,000 milligrams (1 gram) or more, which many people now take as daily supplements or on occasion to prevent or treat illness, could be hazardous. Beyond a dose of about 400 milligrams, the study showed, the body's ability to absorb vitamin C sharply declines and excess vitamin is excreted.

Unlike previous studies used to establish recommended amounts, this one looked beyond the levels needed to prevent scurvy.

"This means Linus Pauling was all wrong, at least with respect to healthy people," Dr. Levine remarked in an interview. "He had the best of intentions, but he did not have the science to support his hypothesis." Dr. Levine said that "in healthy people, megadoses are doing nothing and may do harm, and in sick people, I don't think they will be helpful either."

Industry sources estimate that 30 to 40 percent of Americans now take vitamin C supplements, and that about 1 in 5 supplement users takes more than 1,000 milligrams a day.

Although the 200-milligram level is more than three times the currently recommended amount, it is a level that can still be readily obtained from foods, especially if one follows the latest federal advice to eat five or more servings a day of fruits and vegetables. For example, one would exceed the 200-milligram level by consuming four ounces of orange juice, half a cup of cooked broccoli, one baked potato and one kiwifruit.

But the most recent national survey indicated that fewer than a third of Americans consumed five or more servings of fruits and vegetables a day. This suggests that unless significant improvements are made in people's eating habits, it would be necessary to take supplements or fortify commonly eaten foods with vitamin C for most of the population to consume 200 milligrams each day.

Dr. Adrianne Bendich, assistant director of human nutrition research at Hoffmann–La Roche, a major manufacturer of bulk vitamin C, said a recent review she had conducted of dozens of well-designed studies of vitamin C showed that even at daily doses of 1,000 milligrams or more, no adverse effects had been reported in otherwise healthy people. Dr. Bendich said she saw "no problem with raising the current RDA." The RDAs are established by the academy's Food and Nutrition Board as safe and desirable levels of intake by healthy people to prevent nutritional deficiencies.

Martin Hirsch, public policy director for Hoffmann–La Roche, said the company "welcomes publication of new data that support a shift from thinking about the RDAs as a means of preventing nutritional deficiency to viewing them as a way to promote optimal health."

But other nutrition scientists who served on the last RDA committee challenged the study's conclusions that 200 milligrams of vitamin C, also known as ascorbic acid or ascorbate, were necessary or desirable. Dr. Victor Herbert, a nutrition researcher at the Bronx Veterans Affairs Medical Center who generally disputes the need for supplements, called the study's conclusions "fraudulent." He noted that the study had excluded people with health conditions, like a family history of kidney stones or a tendency to accumulate iron, which could be worsened by taking amounts of vitamin C beyond the current RDA. He said that even consuming 200 milligrams a day could be harmful to as many as one-third of Americans. For example, he said, 12 percent of Americans have iron overload and could be made worse by this amount of vitamin C.

Dr. Levine said he had excluded people with various illnesses because he did not want to risk harming anyone with the high doses used in part of the study. He also said that the findings strictly applied "only to young, healthy men," and he noted, "We don't know what will happen to sick people, women, the elderly or children." A similar study is under way in young, healthy women.

Dr. John N. Hathcock, director for nutritional and regulatory science at the Council for Responsible Nutrition, a organization supported by the supplement industry, agreed that "you can't say from this study that 200 milligrams of vitamin C [are] safe or harmful for people with conditions that were excluded." But, he added, "If a person has such a condition, that person should be under the care of a physician and should take his or her advice regarding vitamin C intake."

Dr. James Allen Olson, a biochemist at Iowa State University in Ames who, like Dr. Herbert, served on the committee that established the current RDAs, questioned the study's assumption that because the 200-milligram dose was best absorbed and utilized by body tissues, this would mean it was the most desirable amount.

But Dr. John Erdman Jr., a nutritional scientist at the University of Illinois who is a member of the academy's Food and Nutrition Board, said the group was already considering a change in the basic concept of the RDA "to consider outcomes that would go beyond just the prevention of deficiency diseases." For vitamin C, for example, such outcomes might include "enhancing the immune response," he said. He added that the new study provided "the kind of data the RDA committee would look at very strongly." He said the committee "would have to decide whether saturation of cells with vitamin C was a necessary and a desirable goal."

The study, sponsored by the National Institute of Diabetes and Digestive and Kidney Diseases in Bethesda, Maryland, analyzed the biochemical effects of various amounts of vitamin C administered to seven healthy young men who lived in a hospital ward for four to six months. Nutrient requirement studies, which are very costly and time-consuming, are typically done on small numbers of participants. Although most researchers would prefer larger studies, these small studies are exacting in nature and thus can yield meaningful results, unlike clinical and epidemiological studies, which require many participants to achieve statistical significance.

The men's blood levels of vitamin C were first depleted by placing the men on a daily diet that contained less than 5 milligrams of this essential nutrient. Then, while continuing their vitamin C–deficient diet, the men were given seven different doses of the vitamin to determine which level was best absorbed and would result in peak amounts in the blood and tissues. The doses studied, which were administered sequentially, were 30, 60, 100, 200, 400, 1,000 and 2,500 milligrams a day.

The team of 11 researchers determined which doses were fully absorbed, which produced "saturation levels" in blood plasma, white blood cells and other tissues and which resulted in excretion of vitamin C or its metabolic products in the stool and urine. The white blood cells, a vital component of the immune system, were saturated at a dose of 100 milligrams a day. That is, beyond this dose no more vitamin C was absorbed by the cells. The blood plasma was nearly saturated by a dose of 200 milligrams and fully saturated at 1,000 milligrams, the researchers found.

But beyond 100 milligrams, the volunteers began to excrete some vitamin C in their urine, indicating that the body was not using all that it absorbed. Absorption levels through the gut also declined as dosages were increased beyond 200 milligrams. At 500 milligrams, less than three-fourths of the vitamin C administered to the volunteers was absorbed, and at 1,250 milligrams, less than half was absorbed, Dr. Levine said.

At 1,000 milligrams or more, the urine was found to contain oxalate, a breakdown product of vitamin C that in some people can result in the formation of kidney stones. A second substance, urate, which results from the breakdown of nucleic acids, the building blocks of genes, also accumulated in urine at these high doses, Dr. Levine reported. An endocrinologist by training, Dr. Levine is chief of the Molecular and Clinical Nutrition Section at the federal institute.

"It looks as if the body is very tightly regulated with respect to vitamin C," Dr. Levine said. "It seems to be saying 'enough is enough.' Beyond two hundred milligrams, the cells don't fill up anymore, plasma fills up very little, absorption goes down and excretion goes up."

Dr. Levine said there was no "absolute proof" that it was best to be saturated with vitamin C. "Our study doesn't prove that two hundred milligrams a day will prevent heart disease, cancer or infectious illnesses," he said. But he added that he and his colleagues were impressed by the fact that many pieces of evidence "converge on two hundred milligrams as the right dose," including the amount that people get from diets rich in fruits and vegetables, how much is absorbed by the body, the dose that results in saturation of cells and blood, the amount that may be toxic and the amount that is consumed by people who are relatively well protected against various serious diseases.

Dr. Levine said: "The current RDA for vitamin C is based on flawed studies, and its very concept—to prevent scurvy—is outmoded. We should be basing our recommendation on what is best for the population, not just to prevent a deficiency disease."

[JEB, April 1996]

Searching for the Secrets of Garlic

WHILE the producers of garlic supplements battle over whether consumers are likely to benefit more from a powder or an extract of the "stinking bulb," scientists are zeroing in on exactly what components of garlic might be medically helpful and how the substances work.

The good news is that whatever good garlic does, the effects do not seem to depend upon its culinarily prized but socially scorned scent.

Allicin, the odoriferous chemical formed when a garlic clove is cut or bruised, "is not important at all," said Dr. Herbert Pierson, formerly of the National Cancer Institute who now heads Preventive Nutrition Consultants Inc., an international consulting company in Woodinville, Washington.

"Allicin is highly unstable and degrades instantly in processing when exposed to heat, oxygen, light, proteins or changes in acidity," he explained. "It is not crucial to any of garlic's biological activities." That is a good thing, because allicin is a toxic substance that can kill cells indiscriminately.

You do not have to purchase supplements to derive garlic's benefits; just eating it in any form or using garlic powder sold as a condiment in grocery stores should do as much good. Furthermore, garlic is not the only member of the allium family that is likely to confer medicinal benefits: onions, scallions, shallots and chives contain many of the same substances and may be equally helpful.

At a recent meeting on so-called designer foods in Washington, D.C., organized by Dr. Pierson and Dr. Paul A. Lachance of Rutgers University in New Brunswick, New Jersey, scientists from research centers around the world used many eight-syllable words and described elaborate laboratory experiments to define scientifically what the Chinese have believed for more than 4,000 years: that garlic seems to have preventive and therapeutic actions on many fronts, from battling infections and neurological deterioration to helping prevent and treat heart disease and cancer.

But the researchers emphasized that garlic is no panacea, nor should it be relied upon as a primary treatment. No one questions that modern antibiotics, a heart-friendly diet and exercise regimen and established treatments for cancer are far more effective than any amount of garlic. Rather, garlic may serve as an adjunct that helps to enhance the immune response, curb coronary risk factors, block the action of carcinogens and perhaps even contain the spread of cancer.

Garlic and its relatives are rich sources of sulfur-containing compounds that have a variety of pharmacological activities. Many of these compounds are formed when allicin breaks down. But just as the amounts of these substances can vary from one garlic bulb to another, depending on the variety or on growing conditions and storage after harvest, the composition of garlic supplements also varies depending upon the processing procedure used. Thus, an oil extract of garlic will contain only those compounds that are fat-soluble and a water extract will contain only those that are water-soluble. Nonetheless, all forms of garlic—raw, cooked, dried and powdered; and extracted in oil or water—contain some sulfur compounds that tests indicate are beneficial to health.

"All garlic products have some efficacy, at least in animal systems," said Dr. John Milner, a nutrition researcher at Pennsylvania State University. "There's not ten cents' worth of difference between any of them."

The product that has undergone the most extensive testing is an odor-free, aged water-and-alcohol extract sold commercially in both liquid and dried forms as Kyolic, manufactured by the Wakunaga Pharmaceutical Company in Hiroshima, Japan. The product's main virtue is that it has been standardized to contain a specific amount of one of the pharmacologically active compounds in garlic, S-allylcysteine.

Some of garlic's constituents act on substances in the blood or directly on blood vessels to reduce the risk of a heart attack. For example, saponins, which are steroidlike compounds, inhibit an enzyme in the muscle cells of arteries, resulting in arterial dilation and a reduction in blood pressure. Other sulfur-containing compounds that act like the antihypertensive drugs known as ACE inhibitors also help to lower blood pressure "without causing side effects like impotence and headaches," Dr. Pierson said.

Various garlic compounds with antioxidant properties help to lower cholesterol levels in the blood. In people with elevated cholesterol, garlic supplements taken daily for months, including the tablets sold as Kwai that are widely used in Europe, lowered cholesterol levels by an average of from 9 to 14 percent, which should translate into an 18 to 28 percent reduction in heart attack risk. Garlic can also lower levels of potentially harmful blood fats called triglycerides.

Probably more important is the ability of garlic components to reduce the blood's clotting tendency by lessening the stickiness of blood platelets and by promoting anticlotting activity. Scientists at the Washington meeting said garlic is much more potent than aspirin in this regard.

Following leads like the findings that garlic eaters in Iowa have a reduced risk of colon cancer and those in China have a lower rate of stomach cancer, Dr. Milner and others have identified several compounds in garlic that block the formation of potent carcinogens called nitrosamines as well as the gene-damaging effects of other carcinogens.

In animal studies, those treated with garlic and exposed to cancer-causing agents developed fewer cancers than animals that did not get any garlic. Dr. Milner has also studied five human tumors in laboratory cultures and has shown that one garlic compound, diallyl disulfide, is very effective in inhibiting tumor growth. Other studies suggest that garlic can help prevent metastasis, the spread of cancer from its original site to other parts of the body.

Dr. Pierson said that in healthy people both the liquid and the dried forms of aged garlic extract resulted in a rise of natural killer cells. These immune system cells help to block the spread of cancers.

French researchers at the Washington meeting described experiments in laboratory rats with a brain syndrome resembling Alzheimer's disease. They reported that aged garlic extract's antioxidant properties slowed the deterioration of the brain. Other neurological effects included a normalization of the brain's serotonin system, which can cause depression when it malfunctions.

Garlic as Food Versus Garlic Pills

Sales of garlic supplements in the United States are estimated at $100 million a year. Fresh garlic, even at $2 a pound, is much less expensive than supplements, and garlic powder seasoning is even cheaper, selling for about $2 for four grams, as against $10 to $14 for a quarter-teaspoon of active ingredients in a garlic powder supplement, says Dr. Herbert Pierson of Preventive Nutrition Consultants Inc.

Dr. John Milner of Pennsylvania State University reminds consumers that "eating is one of the pleasures of life, and people should be encouraged to eat garlic."

Garlic is least irritating to the body when cooked; when used in dressings, whole unpeeled cloves can be parboiled for a few minutes. For those concerned about garlic breath, Dr. Milner said, "a deodorized form is a viable option."

Anyone who has a bleeding disorder or ulcers or who is taking anticoagulants would be wise to avoid garlic supplement products, since they can promote bleeding. Those who take them should do so only with food or at regular meals and should not exceed the manufacturer's recommended dosage.

[JEB, July 1994]

The Virtues of Folic Acid

FOLIC acid, long unheralded even by health food enthusiasts, has suddenly been thrust into the nutritional limelight. A series of recent studies suggest that this B vitamin may be a major player in warding off heart attacks, strokes and certain common cancers. Even in people not now considered deficient in the vitamin, a less-than-optimal intake can double or triple the risk of developing one or more of these killer diseases.

Often called folacin or folate (its biologically active form), folic acid is already well established as critically important in preventing spina bifida and anencephaly, both devastating birth defects of the neural tube. A nationwide effort is under way urging women to take supplements containing folic acid and to increase their intake of folate-rich foods, like dark green leafy vegetables, before becoming pregnant as well as during the first months of pregnancy. This is especially important for women who have been taking oral contraceptives, which interfere with the body's use of folic acid.

The latest available national nutritional data, completed in 1988, revealed that half the women of peak childbearing age consume less than the recommended dietary allowance of folic acid, which is 180 micrograms a day. Even this level is now considered by most experts to be dangerously low.

Various studies have shown that a relatively small supplement of folic acid—400 micrograms a day added to these women's regular diet—can reduce by 60 to 70 percent the risk of infants' being born with neural tube defects. These crippling or fatal defects occur in the first six weeks of gestation, often before a woman has consulted a physician about her pregnancy.

But now folic acid has begun to attract a much wider audience, an audience that expects it to join nutrients like vitamins E and C as a star in the emerging "nutraceutical" era, as the medicinal use of nutrients is being called.

Folic acid, discovered in 1941 in green leafy vegetables, derives its name from the Latin word for leaf, *folium*. Serious deficiencies of folic acid can result in an uncommon blood disorder, megaloblastic anemia, which mainly afflicts people with chronic intestinal disorders, alcoholics and those taking certain drugs for epilepsy.

"For decades, people only thought of folate in terms of anemia," said Dr. Joel Mason, a specialist in nutrition and gastroenterology at Tufts University School of Medicine in Boston. "But in the last two years, there's been an explosion of observations indicating that a mild deficiency—not severe enough to cause anemia—may be enough of a deficiency to cause all kinds of problems, including heart disease, cancer and neural tube defects."

Coincidentally, the new findings indicating a far broader role for folate in health and disease than even its staunchest supporters had initially guessed come as consumption of folate-rich foods appears to be at an all-time low. Folate is especially prominent in liver, certain fortified cereals, dark green leafy vegetables, asparagus, some nuts and seeds, dried beans and, to a lesser extent, various fruits and fruit juices. Yet the average intake of the foods richest in folate is so low that orange juice, which provides 75 to 109 micrograms of folic acid per cup, is the leading source of this nutrient in the American diet.

Commercial white bread, which provides about 8 to 10 micrograms of folate a slice, is the second leading source, according to an analysis by Dr. Amy Subar of the National Cancer Institute and Dr. Gladys Block of the University of California, Berkeley. (Whole-wheat bread provides about three times that amount.)

To help reduce the incidence of neural tube defects, which affect 2,500 to 3,000 babies born in the United States each year (and result in an unknown number of miscarriages), the Food and Drug Administration plans to require that flour, breads and other grain products be fortified with folic acid. Critics say the proposed level of fortification—350 micrograms of folic acid per 100 grams of flour—is too low to have a major impact on the problem. But the drug agency, which expects to issue a final regulation in a few months, prefers to err on the side of safety rather than risk the possibility that some people, like the elderly, might consume enough folic acid to cause health problems.

Folic acid is one of the safest nutrients when taken in large doses. But because it can correct pernicious anemia, the primary symptom of vitamin B-12 deficiency, folic acid can mask a lack of B-12, which in turn can result in nerve damage. And so the Food and Drug Administration restricts the amount of folic acid that can be used in vitamin supplements and is moving cautiously toward fortification of foods with the vitamin.

In what some experts now call a grave misjudgment, the Food and Nutrition Board of the National Research Council/National Academy of Sciences in 1989 cut in half the Recommended Dietary Allowance, or RDA, for folic acid. This prestigious advisory group lowered the RDA from 400 micrograms a day for all adults to 200 micrograms for men and 180 micrograms for women (but 400 micrograms during pregnancy and 280 when breast-feeding).

At the behest of Congress, however, the FDA has shelved a proposal to lower its recommended daily amount, the USRDA, to match the new RDA. The USRDA serves as a consumer guide to the percentages of required nutrients found in packaged foods and vitamin supplements, and for folic acid this still stands at 400 micrograms.

Researchers who have been examining folate's role in preventing cancers and cardiovascular diseases have found several strong links between low levels of folate and these diseases. For example, a collaborative study of nearly 15,000 male physicians by researchers in Massachusetts and Oregon revealed that the risk of suffering a heart attack was elevated more than threefold by a common metabolic abnormality that is correctable by consuming more folate. While none of the study participants who suffered heart attacks would be considered folate-deficient in a nutritional sense, their intake of this vitamin, among others, was clearly less than optimal for preventing cardiovascular diseases, the findings indicated.

The researchers matched the risk of heart attack to levels in the participants' blood of an amino acid called homocysteine. Folate is involved in breaking down homocysteine, and when intake of the vitamin is low, homocysteine tends to build up in the blood. In a study of 1,160 elderly residents of Framingham, Massachusetts, published in December 1993 by Dr. Jacob Selhub and colleagues at Tufts University, 21 percent of participants had homocysteine levels that more than tripled their risk of a heart attack, and those with the highest homocysteine levels had the lowest blood levels of folate.

Dr. Selhub said that "homocysteine concentrations were elevated among individuals with folate intakes up to 280 micrograms per day, which is higher than the current Recommended Dietary Allowances for adult men and women." He added that blood levels of folate now considered normal may be too low to ward off heart attacks.

The findings are similar for tumors called adenomas, which are the forerunners of cancers of the colon. A research team at Brigham and Women's Hospital in Boston has linked diets low in folate to a change in DNA that may allow cancer-causing genes to be expressed. In the study, which was of nearly 26,000 men and women and which was published recently, those with adenomas of the colon or rectum generally had the lowest intake of folate.

Dr. Edward Giovannucci, who directed the study, said higher intakes of folate were especially protective in people who regularly consume alcoholic beverages, which interfere with the body's use of folate.

Folate appears to protect against cancer by aiding in the production of chemical units called methyl groups. These, in turn, enable DNA to resist the action of cancer-causing genes. Dr. Giovannucci said that in a study of people with ulcerative colitis, who face an abnormally high risk of developing colon cancer, precancerous changes in the colon were less often found in those who took folate supplements.

"We're not talking about megadoses here," he said. "At a supplementary level of 400 micrograms of folate a day, there's a very low probability of side effects." He added that the apparent ability of a diet rich in fruits and vegetables to protect against colon and rectal cancer may be due at least in part to the high levels of folate naturally present in these foods.

At Tufts, Dr. Mason and his colleagues are now studying whether folate supplements at a level 20 times the current recommended amount can prevent colon cancer in people with precancerous polyps. He said that in animals prone to colon cancer, a mild folate deficiency doubles the risk of malignancy.

Low levels of folate have also been linked to the development of cellular abnormalities that precede cancer of the cervix in women infected with a cancer-causing strain of human papillomavirus. In women with adequate folate intake, the virus appeared to be harmless, the study indicated.

Still other studies have suggested that low levels of folate may increase the risk of cancers of the lung, esophagus and breast, perhaps by impairing the ability of DNA to repair itself when it is assaulted by carcinogens, such as those in tobacco smoke. Folic acid is a crucial part of enzymes involved in synthesizing the building blocks of the genetic material DNA and RNA. Thus, it is most needed by tissues that are frequently replaced or that grow

Changing Recommendations on Doses

Experts are now recommending a return to the old, higher recommended dietary allowance of folic acid, and the change from current levels is under official consideration. Women contemplating pregnancy should start the higher pregnancy dose three months beforehand.

ALLOWANCES OF FOLATE PER DAY (in Micrograms):		
	Current Recommended Dietary Allowance	Suggested New Allowance
ADULT MEN	200	400
ADULT WOMEN	180	400
PREGNANT WOMEN	400	800
LACTATING WOMEN		
First 6 months	280	500
Second 6 months	260	500

rapidly, like the lining of the intestines, or the tissues of fetuses and infants.

Where to Turn for a Vital Nutrient

Because of a change in calculation methods, these figures generally understate the amount of folic acid in foods. Foods that are especially rich in folic acid include the following:

FOOD	AMOUNT (micrograms)
FRUITS	
1 cup orange juice from concentrate	109
1 cup frozen raspberries	65
1 cup canned pineapple juice	58
1 cup orange sections	55
1 cup papaya	49
VEGETABLES AND LEGUMES	
½ cup cooked lentils	179
½ cup cooked spinach	131
½ cup cooked black beans	128
½ cup cooked white beans	123
½ cup cooked asparagus	121
1 cup raw, chopped spinach	108
½ cup cooked turnip greens	86
½ cup cooked collard greens	65
GRAINS AND CEREALS	
1 cup Total	466
1 cup Grape-Nuts	402
1 cup All-Bran	301
1 cup Ralston Bran Flakes	173
⅓ cup wheat germ	108
1 cup Wheaties	102
NUTS	
⅓ cup peanuts	117
⅓ cup sunflower seeds	109
½ cup trail mix	54
MEAT AND POULTRY	
4 ounces cooked beef liver	162
¼ cup braised chicken liver	269

Source: U.S. Department of Agriculture.

Nursing mothers must consume extra amounts of the nutrient because breast milk is rich in folate. A high-folate diet or supplements may be necessary to maintain an adequate supply for themselves and their babies. "The current RDA underestimates the folic acid burden of lactation by 100 percent," said Dr. Mary Frances, a professor of nutrition at Pennsylvania State University.

Foods naturally rich in folic acid are somewhat less reliable sources of folic acid than are fortified foods and supplements. The nutrient can be destroyed during cooking and processing. Its absorption can be blocked by alcohol and intestinal ailments. And to be used by the body, folic acid in foods must first be stripped of molecules of glutamic acid and then converted to folate, its active form. Supplements and fortified foods contain the stripped-down version of folic acid, which is more readily absorbed than the natural forms of the nutrient.

[JEB, March 1994]

The Elusive Search for the True Aphrodisiac

JUST as we fertilize gardens to give nature a boost, throughout human history people have used a host of tricks to enhance sexual desire.

Be they tantalizing scents, soothing lights, sensuous music, stimulating drugs, herbs, foods or drinks or even exercise, these tricks of the sexual trade are known as aphrodisiacs. The name comes from Aphrodite, the Greek goddess of physical love. With low sexual desire now a leading psychiatric complaint, millions of Americans are seeking ways to excite their sex drives.

Many of the reputed aphrodisiacs, like ginseng and yohimbine, have been used for centuries by primitive—and not so primitive— cultures to enhance sexual interest and performance. Yet few have been put through a true scientific test. Even if a researcher were intent on properly exploring a substance's stimulatory potential, it would be quite a challenge to come up with accurate and reproducible data on its effects on people. Sex therapists, among others, maintain that the mind is the primary source of sexual arousal, so any test of a suspected aphrodisiac would also have to measure the placebo effect, the stimulation that results from just thinking one is being exposed to something that ignites desire.

Reviewing reputed aphrodisiacs sold as nonprescription drugs, an advisory panel for the Food and Drug Administration found in 1982 that only two studies had made a scientific attempt to demonstrate specific aphrodisiac action. One focused on a product combining methyltestosterone, yohimbine hydrochloride and nux vomica, the other on an extract of a plant called the pega palo plant. Both studies were said to have serious deficiencies; the panel concluded that all drugs alleged to be aphrodisiacs when taken internally should be categorized as "not recognized as safe or effective."

Given a lack of research, not much has changed since. Currently, the evidence in support of most aphrodisiacs is anecdotal, so the placebo effect cannot be ruled out. A person tries something reputed to be a turn-on, feels turned on and declares it an aphrodisiac.

However, some substances and other less tangible things, like exercise, have biological effects that could conceivably help the sex drive. For example, some herbs and drugs contain substances that have a mild testosteronelike effect. Although testosterone is classified as a male sex hormone, women produce it as well, and it serves as the primary fuel for libido in both sexes.

Dr. Helen Singer Kaplan, director of the human sexuality program at New York Hospital–Cornell Medical Center, said, "Certain drugs are now known to increase sexual desire by acting on the brain's 'sex center' in the hypothalamus." The emerging understanding of the biochemistry of the brain has shown that drugs that are thought to interact primarily with receptors for dopamine, a neurotransmitter that helps brain cells communicate with one another, can stimulate the sex drive, although in most cases this is an undesirable side effect. Among those drugs are an antidepressant called Wellbutrin (bupropion) and an anti-Parkinson's drug called Eldepryl (selegiline), whereas those that act primarily on serotonin receptors—most notably the antidepressant Prozac—appear to depress the sex drive severely.

Most drug companies are reluctant to test potential aphrodisiacs, Dr. Kaplan said, "because they don't want to be accused of selling chemical sex." Also, she said, "the drug would have to be selective—able to increase flagging desire but not make normal people hypersexual."

In a recently published book, *Love Potions: A Guide to Aphrodisiacs and Sexual Pleasures* (Jeremy P. Tarcher/Perigree, $10.95), Dr. Cynthia Mervis Watson, a family practitioner in Santa Monica, evaluates most of the popular measures said to lift the libido. Some of Dr. Watson's assessments are as follows: Ancient peoples believed that foods with the shape or qualities of sex organs were stimulatory. In various cultures, avocados, carrots, cucumbers, figs, oysters, pomegranates and tomatoes were assumed to have aphrodisiac properties. Other reputed aphrodisiac edibles include honey, royal jelly (from bees), bird's nest soup (from the nests of sea swallows), fertilized duck eggs, cacao beans, caviar, lobsters, bear meat and "prairie oysters," the testicles of bulls and rams. If only it were that simple!

More likely to be effective, Dr. Watson maintains, is a well-balanced diet replete with fresh vegetables and fruits and lean sources of protein to supply essential nutrients but keep calories low enough.

Many widely used drugs—including various remedies for high blood pressure, high cholesterol and depression and some contraceptive drugs—can suppress libido, potency or orgasmic ability. But a few medications have the reverse effect, though they are not prescribed for this purpose. Besides Wellbutrin and Eldepryl, they include L-dopa, used to treat Parkinson's disease; oxytocin, the hormone used to stimulate labor; and Estratest, a hormonal combination used for menopausal women. Recreational drugs, including alcohol and marijuana, are counterproductive. While some loosen inhibitions, all can impair performance.

Ginseng, for all its popularity, has no specific effects on sexuality. Yohimbine does stimulate blood flow to the genitals but has serious toxic side effects. Dr. Watson discusses the effectiveness of the olive-like berries of saw palmetto and infusions made from damiana, a shrubby plant that grows in the deserts of Texas and Mexico. She also endorses wild yams and licorice as well as the herb gotu kola, a kind of cola nut.

Several large studies of men and women have attested to the libido-enhancing effects of regular exercise. As a relaxant, body toner, energy booster, antidepressant and confidence builder, it may well be the most accessible, safest and most effective aphrodisiac available, and it has lots of other benefits.

Well-worn but often successful measures include dim lighting or candlelight, a walk in starlight, the subtle use of scents, romantic music, titillating garments, wine (in moderation) and a light but wonderful meal.

The most potent aphrodisiacs, according to Dr. Stephen B. Levine, a Case Western Reserve University professor of psychiatry who studies aphrodisiacs, are "psychological intimacy and voyeurism—looking at pictures or movies of people engaged in genital or romantic interplay."

And, finally, novelty—in personal appearance or physical location—is a well-known stimulant that helps to keep clothing manufacturers, hairdressers and motels in business.

[JEB, August 1993]

Protecting the Heart

THE HEART'S WORST ENEMY: AFFLUENCE

Through most of human history, infectious diseases have probably been the leading cause of death. Their cruel constraint on the human life span was loosened with the advent first of public health measures and then of antibiotics. The leading killers are now the degenerative diseases of old age—heart disease and cancer. Heart disease is a particular danger in developed countries, since it is fostered by a sedentary lifestyle and rich, fat-laden foods that clog the arteries.

A population cannot avoid heart disease altogether, but there is much that can be done to postpone it, especially now that long-term surveys like the Framingham study have exposed many of the factors that damage the heart. But these lessons are hard to implement. The present generation of Americans, the Framingham study suggests, is more overweight than its parents. Death rates from heart disease are lower, but more because of expensive medical interventions than because vulnerability to heart disease has been averted.

Some 30 million to 50 million adults have high blood pressure, a risk factor for heart disease. Even borderline high blood pressure is unhealthy, since if untreated it can lead to heart-damaging high blood pressure.

Heart disease does have a genetic component. Not much can be done about that. But paying attention to diet and exercise, and if necessary taking medications that lower cholesterol and high blood pressure, are means that give people control over the other components of this common killer.

A Generation Later,
Heart Disease Is Still Rampant

NO anatomical or surgical study has revealed more about the health of the American heart than the four-decade-long project involving the people of Framingham, Massachusetts. Beginning in 1949, more than 5,200 Framingham residents have participated in a unique study that has shown how living habits like smoking and inactivity, and health factors like obesity and high blood pressure, influence a person's chances of developing and dying of cardiovascular diseases, the nation's leading killers.

For the last two decades, 5,100 of the children of the original participants have also been studied, carrying the Framingham work into an era when deaths from heart attacks and strokes have fallen sharply while the costs of cardiovascular care continue to soar.

The Framingham offspring, now middle-aged, are in many respects significantly healthier than their parents were when they entered the federally financed study 44 years ago. Blood pressure and cholesterol levels are considerably lower, and far fewer participants smoke cigarettes. But the men are heavier and less active, and both the men and the women have much higher rates of diabetes than their parents did at comparable ages.

In most ways, the children of Framingham mirror the health trends in the nation as a whole, which suggests that falling cardiovascular death rates have sparked a false sense of optimism. "Since the early 1970s, when the offspring study began, there has been nearly a forty percent drop in the death rate from heart attacks and a fifty-eight percent decline in the death rate from strokes in the United States," observed Dr. William Castelli, director of the Framingham Heart Study. "But the rate at which people suffer heart attacks and strokes has not fallen to a comparable degree."

He continued: "Most people who get heart attacks and strokes don't die. They live. This is how our country is going broke, paying for the bypass operations, angioplasties and truckloads of medicines needed to keep people with cardiovascular diseases alive. Hospitalizations for coronary disease may have actually increased, not declined."

Dr. Castelli said: "We have to look at the whole picture, not just pat ourselves on the back because death rates have fallen. We have a long way to go in preventing these diseases."

Dr. William B. Kannel, who has been monitoring changes among the Framingham offspring, said, "So far, there is no evidence that the underlying prevalence of hypertension has changed in the Framingham population." The main difference between the offspring and their parents is the rate of detection and drug treatment of high blood pressure, a major risk factor for both heart attacks and strokes, he said.

"Currently," Dr. Kannel noted, "twenty percent of the fifty-year-olds, forty percent of the sixty-year-olds and fifty percent of the seventy-year-olds in Framingham are taking drugs to lower their blood pressure. When you get to numbers like these, you might as well put the drugs in the reservoir."

Nor are the Framingham offspring doing very well in controlling their weight, which increases their risk of both hypertension and diabetes, another leading risk factor for heart disease. "The women in Framingham are on the whole somewhat thinner than their parents were, but they are still too fat," Dr. Kannel said. "Older women especially seem to have a tough time battling the bulge. And at every age, the men of Framingham are fatter than the previous generation."

Dr. Kannel attributes this deleterious weight trend to inadequate exercise and increasing opportunities to dine on fattening foods. "Many spouses eat out often because both are working," he noted. "The husband comes home from work and calls out, 'Hi, honey, what's for dinner?' and the wife answers, 'Reservations.' Families with two working parents go out often for fast-food meals, and many more people today eat out a lot just for entertainment."

A study by researchers from the National Heart, Lung and Blood Institute among Framingham participants revealed that men with highly educated wives who work outside the home faced a greater risk of suffering and dying of a heart attack than did men with less educated wives. Dr. Kannel suggested that this reflected frequent dining out and perhaps "a lack of nurturing." He speculated that instead of getting sympathy from his wife when he complained about a hard day at work, a husband might hear "*You've* had a hard day? Let me tell you about *my* day."

Then there is the lack of exercise as part of one's daily routine. "We've engineered physical activity out of daily living," Dr. Kannel said. "Men used to have to use muscles to get food and to work. Technology has removed the need to use muscles. Even laborers nowadays have only to turn a valve and a machine, not a shovel, does the digging."

Nor do many people exercise in their free time. Those with less education, in particular, tend to spend their leisure hours in front of a television set, sitting and eating. On the other hand, Dr. Kannel reported, "women with doctoral degrees get five times more exercise than women who are just high school graduates."

But perhaps most distressing to the Framingham researchers is their finding that the rate of adult-onset diabetes is soaring. Dr. Kannel noted that the prevalence of diabetes in Framingham had risen nearly threefold over the last three decades and was continuing to climb. The phenomenon seems to be nationwide.

"We don't really know why this is happening," Dr. Kannel said. "Among the men, increasing weight may be a factor, but the diabetes rate in women, who are not heavier overall, is rising comparably. And it's not just due to the side effects of drugs to lower blood pressure, since the rise in diabetes also applies to people with normal blood pressures who are not on medication."

Dr. Kannel is particularly concerned because the cardiovascular risk for women with diabetes is about twice as high as for men. "Diabetes in women is a very powerful risk factor that virtually wipes out women's cardiovascular disease advantage over men." Even an abnormality in the ability to process blood sugar—below the level at which diabetes would be diagnosed—carries an increased coronary risk, he said.

A major benefit of the Framingham Offspring Study is as a tool for studying trends over time in the rates of disease and risk factors in the population. "Since the Framingham offspring come from the same genetic stock as their parents, any differences we find must be largely environmental," Dr. Kannel observed. "We can determine directly whether established risk factors are as important today as they were a generation ago and what benefits there are to reversing those risks." This could help preventive-medicine specialists decide what to emphasize most in trying to conquer cardiovascular diseases.

"Right now," Dr. Kannel said, underlining Dr. Castelli's warning, "we're salvaging more and more people with coronary disease who, instead of dying, are living to develop heart failure. Heart failure rates are not going down. Rather, they are leading to numerous costly hospitalizations and nursing home care. Only if we prevent this disease entirely will the nation's health care costs decline."

[JEB, January 1994]

Women's Different Pattern of Heart Disease

FOR many years, American women thought they were relatively immune to heart disease, long the leading killer of American men. But now a tide of information intended to dispel this myth has many thinking that heart disease is the newest epidemic to afflict women.

Both ideas are wrong. Women were never immune; they just lag 10 years behind men in developing heart disease. After the age of 65, a woman's risk of suffering a heart attack is almost as high as a man's. Nearly half the 500,000 Americans who will die of heart attacks each year will be women, most past menopause.

Heart disease has been the leading killer of American women since 1908. But the long-standing epidemic is now on the wane. Since the late 1960s, coronary death rates and the chances of developing coronary heart disease before old age have been declining for women and men.

Still, heart disease remains the leading killer of women, striking from 1 in 3 to 1 in 2 women. Breast cancer, the disease women fear most, is a far less common cause of illness and death. Over an 85-year life span, one woman in eight will develop breast cancer, mostly in the later years. Half or more will be cured of the disease.

But when women develop heart disease, they often do not fare well. Women are twice as likely as men to die after a heart attack.

Women are also less likely to survive coronary bypass surgery and angioplasty, procedures to improve blood flow to the heart. No one knows why survival statistics are poorer for women with heart disease than for men.

Given these grim facts, women would be wise to do what they can to prevent heart disease. While genes most definitely play a role in determining who will and who will not develop the arterial clogging that is the prelude to most heart attacks, genes are by no means the whole story. The harmful genes need an environment conducive to carrying out their dirty work. By failing to give the genes an opportunity to perform, it is usually possible to delay damage to the coronary arteries or ward it off entirely.

Part of the reason it seemed that heart disease was only a man's problem is that most of the studies to define coronary risk involved only men. Because many men suffered heart attacks and died in midlife, often leaving young families without a breadwinner, the pressure was on medical researchers to quell this epidemic of premature death and disability.

They did indeed find some strong and potentially controllable predictors of the high rates of heart disease in American men: smoking, high blood pressure and elevated blood cholesterol as the leading determinants, with obesity, sedentary lifestyle, diabetes and overreaction to stress among the other important factors.

At long last, however, researchers have begun to study women to see which coronary risk factors are most influential and what might be done about them. Much of what has been known about coronary disease in women was learned through the Framingham Heart Study in Massachusetts, where thousands of initially healthy middle-aged men and women and their offspring have been followed for decades.

But now women are being singled out for more intensive studies. For example, newly published research among women who already had heart disease, conducted by Dr. Anita Zeiler Arnold and colleagues at the Cleveland Clinic, corroborates and extends the Framingham findings.

It has come as no surprise to any of these researchers that cigarette smoking stands out as a powerful risk factor in women as well as in men. Even women who smoke as little as one to four cigarettes a day face an increased risk of developing and dying of heart disease, a study of thousands of nurses has shown.

In one Cleveland Clinic study of women 18 to 30 years old with symptomatic heart disease, 72 percent had been smokers. In another study in Cleveland among 653 women, 36 percent of the 494 who proved to have coronary artery disease were smokers, as against only 14 percent of the 159 women without the disease.

Cholesterol levels also figure prominently in a woman's risk. But while total cholesterol levels above, say, 250 milligrams per deciliter of blood serum significantly increase a woman's risk, the amount of artery-cleansing HDL cholesterol in her blood is far more predictive. The higher her HDLs (high-density lipoproteins), the better. Less important to a woman is her blood level of artery-damaging LDL cholesterol, the strongest predictor of coronary disease in men. At greatest risk are women with low HDL levels but high levels of another blood fat, triglycerides.

The findings about HDL may largely explain why women are relatively protected against heart disease before menopause, with their risk rising sharply when their bodies stop producing estrogen. Estrogen helps to keep HDL levels high, and available evidence strongly indicates that women who take estrogen replacement hormones after menopause see a 50 percent reduction in their risk of dying from a heart attack or stroke. Estrogen also seems to help maintain flexibility in artery walls, which otherwise become more rigid with age.

Most women who now take estrogen after menopause also take progesterone to protect the uterine lining from cancer. It is not yet known for sure whether the benefits of estrogen to the heart persist when this second hormone is taken. Of course, women who have undergone a hysterectomy have no need for progesterone.

Other ways to raise HDL levels include exercising regularly and vigorously, the equivalent of a brisk one-hour walk five or six times a week, and drinking moderate amounts of alcohol; for a woman, "moderate" means one drink a day. In both women and men, complete abstinence and excessive drinking are both associated with an increase in coronary risk compared with moderate drinkers'.

Then there is the matter of overall diet. Diets with very little fat (only 10 to 15 percent of a day's calories from fat) are associated with very low coronary disease rates. Although both men and women consume less fat than they used to, women still derive on average 34 to 36 percent of their daily calories from fat, more than twice the protective amount. And far too much of that fat is artery-damaging saturated fat, prominent in foods from land animals.

Those who rely mainly on fish and vegetable foods for protein tend to have much healthier hearts. And women who eat lots of fruits and vegetables rich in antioxidants like beta-carotene and vitamin C can reduce their risk of heart attack by one-third.

Reducing dietary fat and exercising regularly also help control still another heart hazard, excess weight around the abdomen, which can raise coronary risk as much as threefold in women as well as in men.

A pamphlet, "Silent Epidemic: The Truth About Women and Heart Disease" is available from local chapters of the American Heart Association or by telephoning (800) AHA-USA1 (242-8721). Risk reduction guidelines, including a diet and exercise program, are offered in *The Woman's Heart Book* by Dr. Frederic J. Pashkow and Charlotte Libov (Dutton, $22).

[JEB, November 1993]

Learning to Take High Blood Pressure Seriously

WITH good evidence that an ounce of prevention is worth a pound of cure, the National Heart, Lung and Blood Institute has begun a major effort to prevent high blood pressure, rather than just detect and treat it. The effort, if successful, could result in Americans who are thinner, more active and less saturated with salt and alcohol, as well as being less susceptible to heart attacks, strokes, congestive heart failure, circulatory disorders and kidney disease.

The problem is daunting. Thirty million to 50 million adults in the nation have high blood pressure, and each year another 2 million join their ranks. This makes high blood pressure, or hypertension, the most common risk factor for diseases of the heart, blood vessels and kidneys.

Because high blood pressure is so common, lacks warning signs and seems so innocuous for so many years, many people are far too casual about it. They typically fail on one or more of three counts: having their blood pressure checked regularly, adopting living habits that could lower it and, once hypertension is diagnosed, taking the medication that can control it. The result is tens of thousands of avoidable deaths and billions of dollars spent on medical care each year for preventable illnesses.

Even more lackadaisical are those whose blood pressure is on the high side of normal, just below the 140/90 reading that doctors have arbitrarily designated as the cutoff where "normal" ends and hypertension begins. Being high-normal is not a risk-free status. As blood pressure rises, so does the risk of developing any of its complications. People with high-normal pressure account for more than a third of preventable deaths related to blood pressure.

When the millions of Americans with high-normal blood pressures are added to those with outright hypertension, the total comes to about three-fourths of Americans aged 35 and above having potentially life-threatening blood pressures.

Doctors consider an optimal blood pressure to be below 120/80. The numbers refer to pressure measured in millimeters of mercury, with the higher number, or systolic pressure, representing blood pressure when the heart beats and the lower number, or diastolic pressure, representing blood pressure when the heart rests between beats. Both numbers are important; if either is elevated, the risk rises, and if both are elevated, it rises even more.

Careful studies have proved that lowering blood pressure in people with hypertension is lifesaving. But according to the latest national health survey, in 1991 only 49 percent of those with hypertension were being treated with medications to lower blood pressure and only 1 in 5 of those under treatment had pressures below 140/90. Clearly, despite two decades of an intensive national effort to detect and treat people with hypertension, many continue to be at very high risk because of uncontrolled high blood pressure.

Even when high blood pressure is reduced to the normal range, the risk of illness and premature death is higher than if the person never had hypertension. Hence the current campaign to prevent this scourge.

That hypertension is preventable in the vast majority of people is obvious from one universal fact: only in industrialized countries does blood pressure rise with age. In less developed countries, where few people are overweight, where the diet does not promote clogged arteries, where daily physical activity is routine, where heavily salted processed foods do not overload the body with sodium and where heavy drinking of alcoholic beverages is uncommon, blood pressure does not creep up and up as people get older, and hypertension is not a national epidemic.

In a new report on primary prevention of hypertension prepared by 15 experts, the institute pointed out that even a small reduction in blood pressure in the population can save a significant number of lives. Lowering systolic blood pressure by a mere two millimeters of mercury can reduce deaths from stroke by 6 percent, heart disease by 4 percent and all causes by 3 percent. And as little as a one-to-three-millimeter drop in diastolic pressure can reduce the incidence of hypertension in the population by 20 to 50 percent, the report said.

The experts listed these strategies as most likely to be effective:

- *Watch your weight.* An estimated 20 to 30 percent of hypertension is the direct result of excess body weight. Those who are overweight are two to six times as likely to develop hypertension as people of normal weight, and losing excess weight results in a commensurate drop in blood pressure.

- *Consume less salt and other sources of sodium.* Americans consume many times more sodium than the body needs and substantially more than their ancestors did. A 52-center study of 10,000 men and women in 32 countries showed that in those centers where body weight was low but sodium intake was high, hypertension was seven times more common than in centers where both body weight and sodium intake were low. Reducing sodium in the diet can lower blood pressure in people with normal blood pressure as well as in those with high blood pressure. This is particularly true for blacks and the elderly, who are more likely than others to develop hypertension. In addition to using less salt in cooking and at the table, check the labels of packaged foods for sodium content.

- *Become physically active.* Hypertension is less common among people who are physically active or physically fit, and such people are less likely to experience a rise in blood pressure with increasing age. Introducing regular physical activity to sedentary people results in an average drop in blood pressure of six to seven millimeters, even if no weight is lost. Daily activity is more effective than exercise done on a less frequent schedule, and exercise of low to moderate intensity is as effective as higher-intensity activities.

• *Drink less alcohol.* Although consumption of one to two drinks a day is associated with a diminished risk of heart disease, a larger intake of alcohol raises the risk of various diseases, including hypertension. From 5 to 7 percent of hypertension cases can be attributed to excessive alcohol consumption. Cutting back to a maximum of two drinks a day can lower blood pressure independently of any weight loss.

• *Consume more potassium.* A low intake of potassium-rich foods has been suggested as one reason why American blacks are more likely than whites to develop hypertension, and consuming more potassium in foods and perhaps as a supplement may help prevent this disorder. Potassium-rich foods include bananas, oranges and cantaloupes.

For more information, there is a toll-free information line—(800) 575-WELL (575-9355)—operated by the National Heart, Lung and Blood Institute. Consumers can learn more about controlling high blood pressure from a 20-page brochure, "Empower Yourself: Control the Pressure . . . and Feel Good!," produced by the Coalition for Hypertension Education and Control. Designed to help those with high blood pressure obtain satisfactory treatment, the brochure includes a self-assessment test to help patients discuss with their physicians measures they might take to control their blood pressure. The brochure is available free to consumers who call (800) 664-4447.

[JEB, May 1994]

Sudden Exertion Plus Long
Inactivity Equals Heart Risk

TWO large new studies have provided the strongest evidence yet that a sudden burst of physical activity can set off a heart attack. But even more important, the studies showed a strong protective effect of regular physical activity.

Overall, the risk of a heart attack during or just after heavy physical exertion is two to six times greater than the risk during less strenuous activities or no activity, the studies showed. But regular physical activity diminished the added risk to practically none at all.

Normally sedentary people who try something strenuous like shoveling snow, sprinting to catch a bus, playing tennis or pushing a car out of a snowdrift are especially at risk.

The findings, published in a recent issue of the *New England Journal of Medicine,* suggest that sedentary people, particularly those with other risk factors for heart disease like smoking, high blood pressure or diabetes, might be wise to hire a young neighbor to shovel the walk or have the driveway plowed.

"Better yet," said Dr. Gregory Curfman, an associate editor of the journal, who wrote an editorial about the two reports, "would be for people who are sedentary to gradually get themselves into shape." For, he said, another important finding of the two studies was that regular physical activity strongly protected people against an exertion-related heart attack.

While many people have believed that intense activity can precipitate a heart attack, this had never been clearly established because early studies were smaller and less statistically certain. The new findings "really settle the question that intense activity can trigger a heart attack," Dr. Curfman said in an interview.

Among the cardiovascular benefits of regular exercise, he said, are a diminished tendency of the blood to form clots, an improved cholesterol profile, more efficient use of oxygen by the muscles, a larger volume of blood pumped with each heartbeat and, during periods of exertion, greater dilation of the arteries, lower heart rate and lower blood pressure.

Dr. Ralph Paffenbarger of Stanford University, who has been

studying the relationship of exercise to heart disease for more than three decades, said, "Even more important than confirming the increased risk of a heart attack during or shortly after intense activity is the finding that physically active, physically fit people have a lower risk overall than people who are not active."

In one of the studies, directed by Dr. Murray A. Mittleman of Deaconess Hospital and Harvard Medical School in Boston, a sedentary person's chance of suffering a heart attack during or just after heavy exertion was nearly 50 times that faced by people who usually exercise five or more times a week. In fact, exercising just one or two times a week cut a person's risk by more than 80 percent. Overall, in the study a sedentary person was more than 100 times as likely to suffer a heart attack during or soon after heavy exertion than during rest.

One study involved 1,228 heart attack patients in the United States and the other involved 1,194 patients in Germany.

Earlier studies that were smaller and less statistically certain had shown that intense bursts of activity could result in sudden death even in people without previous symptoms of heart disease. In fact, in the German study, directed by Dr. Stefan N. Willich of the Free University of Berlin, patients with known coronary heart disease, including those who had previously had a heart attack, did not appear to be at greater risk from heavy exertion than presumably healthy people, many of whom actually had hidden coronary disease.

Dr. Curfman noted that only about 5 percent of heart attacks occurred in association with heavy physical exertion; the rest occurred while the person was resting or performing moderate activities like driving a car, shopping, golfing with a cart or raking leaves. But he added, "So many heart attacks occur each year that even five percent is quite a large number." For example, the authors of the American study calculated that in this country at least 75,000 heart attacks a year, leading to 25,000 deaths, are related to exertion.

Lest the new findings cause panic among those who must change a tire or rush to catch a plane, the Boston team noted that while the relative risk of suffering an activity-related heart attack could be very high, especially for habitually sedentary people, the absolute risk for any given hour of intense activity was actually very low. In other words, even a sedentary person is not very likely to have a

What Is Heavy Exertion?

Physical exertion can be measured in multiples of a unit called MET (for metabolic equivalent), the energy expended in a minute by somebody lying quietly. In the heart risk study, "heavy exertion" was an activity involving six MET or more.

Estimated Number of MET	Description	Examples
1	Sleeping, reclining	Sunbathing, lying on a couch watching television
2	Sitting	Eating, reading, desk work, sitting watching television, highway driving
3	Very light exertion	Office work, driving in the city, personal care, standing in line, strolling in a park
4	Light exertion, with normal breathing	Mopping, slow walking, sweeping, golfing with a cart
5	Moderate exertion, with deep breathing	Normal walking, golfing on foot, slow biking, raking leaves, cleaning windows, interior painting, hunting, fishing, slow dancing, light restaurant work
6	Vigorous exertion, with panting; overheating	Slow jogging, speed-walking, tennis, swimming, cross-country skiing, shoveling snow, fast biking, mowing with a push mower, pruning, heavy gardening, softball, picking up garbage, hurried, heavy restaurant work
7	Heavy exertion, with gasping; much sweating	Running, fast jogging, nonstop racquetball, pushing a car stuck in snow, moving boulders, shoveling heavy or deep snow
8	Extreme or peak exertion	Sprinting, fast running, jogging uphill, aggressive sports with frequent sprinting and no rest, pushing or pulling with all one's might

Source: New England Journal of Medicine.

heart attack within an hour of doing something strenuous like shoveling snow or digging up a garden.

For example, previous research has shown that a 50-year-old man who does not smoke or have diabetes has a one-in-a-million chance of suffering a heart attack during a given one-hour period. "If this man was habitually sedentary but engaged in heavy physical exertion during that hour, his risk would increase 100 times over the base-line value, but his absolute risk during that hour would still be only one in 10,000," the Boston researchers wrote.

Dr. Mittleman said sexual activity was considerably less strenuous than the types of exertion that precipitated heart attacks in the study.

As other studies of the timing of heart attacks have shown, the German study found that a large proportion of heart attacks occur during the morning hours. In this study, the risk of a heart attack during the first three hours after people awoke was nearly triple that of an attack occurring during the rest of the day. The authors said, "This suggests that both physical exertion at any time during the day and routine activities after awakening and arising may be triggers" of a heart attack.

To determine the relationship of exertion to heart attacks, both research teams interviewed patients, asking them what they were doing at the time of their attack or during the hour before it as well as during the same hour the day before.

This new research technique enabled the patients to act as their own controls. As a further check on their findings, the researchers also interviewed nonpatients of the same age and sex as the patients to determine what they were doing during the hours in question.

[JEB, December 1993]

Even Slightly High Blood Pressure Should Not Be Ignored

PEOPLE with slightly elevated systolic blood pressure, the higher of the two blood pressure readings, are at increased risk of developing full-fledged hypertension and heart disease compared with those with normal blood pressure, a new study has found.

People with the condition, borderline systolic hypertension, have generally not been classified as having high blood pressure because the slight elevations were not known to be potentially harmful.

The findings concern systolic blood pressures of 140 to 159 millimeters of mercury and a diastolic reading (the lower number) of below 90. The findings come from the landmark Framingham Heart Study, which has been following initially healthy adults in Massachusetts for more than 40 years to determine which factors most strongly influence a person's risk of developing heart disease. The findings were published in a recent issue of the *New England Journal of Medicine*.

The authors said such borderline hypertension was the most common form of untreated high blood pressure among those over 60 years old and the least thoroughly studied type of high blood pressure.

The nomenclature for systolic readings varies among medical groups. The Framingham study used the World Health Organization's definition of borderline isolated systolic hypertension for readings of 140 to 159. ("Isolated" means the hypertension definition is based on the systolic pressure independent of the diastolic reading.)

The federally sponsored National High Blood Pressure Education Program defines a systolic pressure of 140 to 160 and a diastolic of less than 90 as Stage 1 systolic hypertension.

The authors of the new Framingham study urged doctors to inform people if they have borderline systolic high blood pressure and to advise them to have it checked frequently. But the authors said further research was needed to determine whether treatment with measures like diet, exercise and drugs would prevent heart ailments and extend the lives of people with borderline systolic hypertension. The reason is that studies have not been done to determine the benefits of such treatment among people with borderline systolic hypertension.

Two independent experts underscored the need to tailor therapy to each patient and urged caution in first treating borderline systolic hypertension with drugs. Dr. Marvin Moser of White Plains, a consultant to national high blood pressure programs, said it would be prudent to first try to reduce borderline systolic blood pressure by diet and weight loss. But, he added, it might be difficult to do so in many people.

Dr. Michael H. Alderman, an expert in high blood pressure who heads the department of preventive medicine at Albert Einstein Medical School in the Bronx, said further research on drugs to treat borderline systolic hypertension was needed because the adverse effects of standard anti–high blood pressure drugs might be greater than the benefits.

Dr. Alderman said the new study added "weight to the notion that at any level of blood pressure, you are better off if your blood pressure is lower."

The study also adds to what the authors said was "compelling evidence" that the systolic reading was at least as important as the diastolic reading as a contributor to heart disease. For decades, doctors emphasized that the greatest risk of hypertension was from high readings of the diastolic pressure. But in 1991, a federally financed study showed that treatment of definite systolic hypertension in elderly people substantially decreased the incidence of stroke, heart attacks and other heart disease. Such problems are long-term complications of untreated high blood pressure.

The authors of the Framingham study said it was not clear whether the risk of borderline systolic hypertension on the heart was indirect or direct by progression to definite hypertension. The authors were headed by Dr. Daniel Levy and included Dr. Martin G. Larson and Dr. Alex Sagie. The study was financed by the National Heart, Lung and Blood Institute, a federal agency in Bethesda, Maryland.

The study's findings were based on 2,767 of the original participants in the Framingham study. The participants, who ranged in age from 28 to 62 at entry, were monitored with checkups every 2 years for up to 34 years. Fifty-nine percent of the participants were women.

After 34 years, 1,132 participants had died. A total of 1,010 had developed heart and circulatory disease, and 228 had developed heart failure.

After 20 years of follow-up, 80 percent of those who early on had borderline systolic hypertension progressed to full-fledged high blood pressure, compared with 45 percent of the participants with normal blood pressure. Those with borderline systolic hypertension had a significantly greater risk of developing heart attacks, heart failure and strokes than those with normal blood pressure.

The risk of heart disease was also increased among those with borderline systolic hypertension who did not later develop full-fledged high blood pressure.

[LKA, December 1993]

The Protective Power of Testosterone

A surprising new finding by researchers in New York City challenges the long-held belief that the male sex hormone, testosterone, is important in causing heart attacks in men.

Rather, the researchers conclude, testosterone may actually help protect men against heart attacks, which are the leading cause of death in the United States and many other countries.

The study found a very strong correlation between a low level of testosterone and a higher degree of coronary artery disease, which underlies most heart attacks. When coronary arteries become clogged with fatty material, less blood can flow through them to nourish the heart, and chest pains from angina often develop. If a blood clot forms, it can suddenly shut off blood flow, producing a heart attack and killing vital heart muscle.

Although it has been known that as men age the amount of testosterone declines and the incidence of heart attacks increases, the study is the first to correlate testosterone with the degree of coronary artery disease, the researchers reported recently in *Arteriosclerosis and Thrombosis,* a scientific journal published by the American Heart Association.

Dr. Gerald S. Phillips of St. Luke's–Roosevelt Hospital in Manhattan, the chief author, said his team did not know precisely how low levels of testosterone might lead to a heart attack or normal amounts might protect against one.

Two other small studies have found that administration of testosterone has decreased risk factors for heart attacks.

But in an interview Dr. Phillips cited two reasons why it would be premature to recommend testosterone therapy to prevent heart attacks. First, the findings of his own study need to be confirmed. Second, the safety and effectiveness of testosterone therapy in preventing heart attacks have not been determined in large studies.

In Dr. Phillips's study, the amounts of testosterone correlated with those of high-density lipoprotein, the so-called good form of cholesterol, suggesting that the hormone might protect against atherosclerosis through an effect on lipoproteins.

But the study did not find a correlation between low amounts of testosterone and other known risk factors for heart attacks, like high blood pressure, smoking and the amounts of cholesterol, glucose, insulin and factor 7 (which is involved in the formation of blood clots) in the blood.

Other scientists have found a correlation between abdominal fat and heart attacks. Dr. Phillips's team did not measure the distribution of body fat in the participants.

The New York City team measured the amount of testosterone and other hormones in 55 men who had angina and who were undergoing coronary arteriograms to determine the degree of their coronary artery disease. No symptoms could be attributed to the low testosterone, Dr. Phillips said. Men who had had a heart attack were excluded to eliminate the possibility that some unknown factor resulting from a heart attack might affect the amount of testosterone in the blood.

The correlation of low testosterone and high degree of coronary artery disease was highly significant in statistical terms. As an independent check on the findings, Dr. Phillips eliminated 21 men who had conditions like diabetes that put them at greater risk for heart attacks. Even so, the very strong correlation of low testosterone with the degree of coronary artery disease persisted.

Although the study did not prove that low testosterone led to coronary artery disease, the researchers wrote that "because the correlation is so strong, it suggests that is a possibility."

[LKA, May 1994]

Aspirin:
An Ally Against Heart Disease

"CHEAP 100-Year-Old Household Drug Found to Fight Heart Attacks, Strokes, Cancer, Etc." sounds like a too-good-to-be-true headline. But dozens of studies involving more than a million people have hailed such a drug. It is none other than ordinary aspirin, the standby for reducing pain, fever and inflammation.

The findings of recent studies strongly suggest that an aspirin a day—or at least every other day—may be better than an apple at keeping the doctor away. Aspirin, these studies indicate, can reduce a person's chances of suffering a heart attack or stroke and of developing cancers of the colon and other digestive organs. It may also improve brain function in people with dementia who have suffered little strokes, ward off or reduce the severity of migraine headaches and help prevent hazardous high blood pressure in pregnant women. Also being studied are aspirin's possible roles in preventing cataracts and averting recurrences of gallstones.

And, in general, these benefits accrue from very low doses of the drug, known chemically as acetylsalicylic acid, derived from a substance in the bark of the willow tree that was used medicinally by the Greek physician Hippocrates in the fifth century B.C. But aspirin did not officially enter the medical armamentarium until the 1890s, when a chemist who worked for the Bayer division of a German pharmaceutical company developed it partly out of a desire to relieve his father's painful, crippling arthritis.

Hailed as the closest thing to a pain-relieving panacea, aspirin soon became one of the world's most widely used drugs. Despite heavy competition from other nonprescription painkillers in recent decades, aspirin still leads the pack; Americans take about 30 billion aspirin tablets a year.

When scientists in the 1960s and 1970s finally unraveled how aspirin works chemically in the body, the drug assumed a whole new life. Aspirin was found to block the production of substances called prostaglandins. Among many other actions, prostaglandins promote the clumping of blood cells called platelets, a crucial step in the formation of blood clots that could precipitate heart attacks and strokes. The finding supported the unheeded claim of a California doctor who had observed in the 1950s that regular doses of aspirin seemed to prevent heart attacks and strokes.

In a well-designed five-year study of 22,000 middle-aged doctors, those who took one ordinary aspirin tablet every other day suffered 40 percent fewer heart attacks than those given a look-alike dummy medication. A similar placebo-controlled study is now under way in women. It has already been noted in a six-year study of nearly 90,000 nurses that those who said they took one to six aspirins a week suffered 25 percent fewer heart attacks than non–aspirin users.

Aspirin had previously been found to be effective in treating heart attacks; when given within hours of an attack (the sooner the better), it was shown to reduce deaths by 25 percent. And when taken regularly by heart attack patients, it reduced cardiovascular deaths by 23 percent and reduced the risk of a second nonfatal attack as well as nonfatal strokes by nearly 50 percent. On the basis of these findings, experts have urged that a supply of aspirin be kept wherever a heart attack victim might not be able to receive immediate medical attention. Such places include planes and ships; in backpacks, purses and cars; at health clubs and tennis courts; and, of course, in homes.

The latest excitement surrounds the observation that regular users of aspirin have reduced rates of cancers of the colon, rectum, stomach and esophagus. These cancers combined cause about 81,000 deaths a year in this country. Colorectal cancer alone is the nation's second leading cause of cancer deaths and the leading cancer killer among nonsmokers.

The most telling study to date, conducted by the American Cancer Society, involved more than 660,000 men and women whose health status has been monitored for a decade. It suggested that as aspirin use rose, the risk of cancer death fell; those who used aspirin 16 or more times a month were about half as likely to die of colon cancer as nonusers.

Looking at all four digestive system cancers together, cancer society researchers found a 40 percent lower death rate among men and women who used aspirin 16 or more times a month for at least one year. And the longer aspirin had been used, the lower the risk, they reported.

Other studies have supported the cancer society's findings, although proof of aspirin's benefit in the form of a placebo-controlled study has yet to be obtained. But one controlled study of an aspirinlike drug, sulindac, showed that it could inhibit the growth of polyps in people genetically prone to developing polyps that ultimately become cancerous.

Aspirin may also be useful in fighting cancer. It stimulates production of two cancer-fighting components of the immune system: gamma-interferon and interleukin-2. Researchers are now studying its effect as an adjunct to conventional treatment.

Despite its long history and popularity, aspirin does have side effects that can become serious in some people. It increases bleeding tendencies and in some people causes bleeding in the stomach, an effect that can often be countered by using enteric-coated aspirin. The larger the dose, the more likely this problem will occur. It is therefore fortunate that most of the benefits newly attributed to aspirin, especially the cardiovascular effects, involve very low doses: one ordinary aspirin tablet (325 milligrams, or 5 grains) every other day or one baby aspirin (80 milligrams) daily.

Preventive aspirin therapy is most often recommended for men over 40 and women over 50 who have one or more major risk factors for heart disease, including smoking, a family history of heart attack before 55, high blood pressure, unfavorable cholesterol levels, obesity or diabetes.

Most researchers say it is too soon to recommend aspirin as a cancer preventive, except perhaps for those with a family history of colon cancer. Here again, low doses seem effective: one adult or one baby aspirin each day.

Some people should not take aspirin on a regular basis: those who have had any sort of bleeding disorder (including hemorrhagic stroke), stomach ulcers, uncontrolled high blood pressure, eye problems related to diabetes, kidney or liver disease or a personal or family history of cerebral aneurysms. Aspirin also should not be used by people already taking an anticoagulant or some other nonsteroidal anti-inflammatory drug like ibuprofen.

[JEB, February 1994]

A Simple New Way of Diagnosing Heart Disease

A cheap and painless set of tests developed in leading medical centers around the country promises to predict heart disease and stroke, and pinpoint the patients who really need aggressive therapy, far more accurately than do the traditional risk factors.

The new method includes a simple measurement of the difference in blood pressure between arms and ankles and a noninvasive acoustic test that measures narrowing of the carotid arteries, which carry blood to the brain.

Many people with high cholesterol levels do not in fact develop heart disease. Conversely, there are also many who develop silent heart disease without having any of the known risk factors like high cholesterol, smoking or diabetes. The scientists who developed the new test hope that it will focus attention on those in both categories who are most at risk.

"You don't necessarily have to apply aggressive treatment to everyone with bad risk factors," said Dr. Lewis Kuller, an epidemiologist at the University of Pittsburgh. Dr. Kuller helped develop the new method as part of an ongoing study of the emergence of cardiovascular disease in people 65 and older.

He predicted that the technique would prove most useful for people over 60, especially those with high cholesterol, and for people of any age whose doctors think they may need drugs to help lower blood cholesterol or triglycerides, another fatty component of the blood. He also said the screening technique could be useful for people with moderately elevated systolic blood pressure (measured by the larger of the two blood pressure numbers) and for children and young adults with a strong family history of cardiovascular disease.

Without so much as a needle prick, the method indirectly measures the extent of hidden atherosclerosis, or clogging of the arteries, in people who have no outward symptoms of cardiovascular disease, such as chest pains. In a soon-to-be-published study of 5,200 older adults from four communities across the country, the researchers showed that people with significant clogging of their arteries, as determined by the new method, were two to three times as likely to die within a few years as were those without evidence of hidden, or so-called subclinical, arterial disease.

The risk of developing fatal and nonfatal coronary heart disease within the next three years was doubled for men and two and a half times greater for women who had evidence of subclinical disease. Consideration of traditional risk factors did little to change these results, the researchers concluded.

Dr. Michael Criqui, a specialist in preventive cardiology at the University of California at San Diego, described the work as "an area of major importance." He said the tests "provide a measure of an individual's propensity for developing atherosclerosis, and that outweighs all other risk factors" in predicting who will suffer a heart attack or stroke.

Dr. Criqui added, however: "In a medical care system with finite resources, before recommending that something be done, we have to know what benefit would be achieved and at what cost. So far, there is limited data to show that intervention in people with subclinical disease is helpful, though logically it should be. Then, if it is beneficial, we have to find out how much it costs and what benefit is achieved for that cost."

The tests involve no dyes or injections and no pain or risk of injury. They can be performed by trained technicians with instruments that cost a few hundred dollars and a computer to calculate the results. Two of the tests involve the use of high-frequency sound waves to assess potential blockages in the arteries that feed the brain. One of the most revealing tests, which measures the difference in blood pressure in the arms and the legs, could be put into widespread use almost immediately, Dr. Kuller said.

The study involved 2,239 men and 2,962 women aged 65 and older in Forsyth, North Carolina; Sacramento County, California; Washington County, Maryland; and Pittsburgh, Pennsylvania. Participants were followed for an average of two and a half years, some as long as three years. The findings, which will soon be published in the journal *Circulation*, showed that men with subclinical, or hidden, atherosclerosis face a higher risk of developing or dying of cardiovascular disease than do women with the same condition.

Dr. Kuller said in an interview that the new method "could save a lot of money by identifying those people who are most likely to benefit from aggressive treatment to control cardiovascular risk factors." He pointed out that many older people with "high levels of risk factors" do not have subclinical disease and therefore might get no benefit from aggressive therapies, some of which are costly or have serious side effects.

He explained that this method of diagnosing subclinical atherosclerosis "converts risk factors, which are applicable to a population, into a measure of pathology in individuals."

"Do they have damage from their risk factors?" he continued. "For those who do, can we tailor risk factor reduction more aggressively?"

For example, while patients with elevated cholesterol levels would still be advised to reduce their cholesterol by modifying their diets, only those found to have significantly clogged arteries might have to take drugs for the rest of their lives.

"When people know that they have significant arterial disease, they are more motivated to stick with a preventive program," Dr. Kuller added. He said that people shown to have subclinical disease would be treated as if they had clinical arterial disease. A person with clinical disease has already suffered a heart attack or stroke or has outward signs of disease such as angina pectoris (chest pains that indicate the heart cannot get enough oxygen-rich blood) or transient ischemic attacks (ministrokes caused by momentary interruptions of blood flow to the brain).

Currently, people known to have serious atherosclerosis in the arteries feeding the heart or brain are advised to take daily medication and adopt risk-reducing habits, like eating a low-fat diet, losing excess weight, getting regular aerobic exercise and not smoking, to cut the risk of a heart attack or stroke. When atherosclerosis is severe, bypass surgery or angioplasty to improve circulation is often recommended.

The new method could also be used to identify patients with otherwise hidden abrupt narrowing, or stenosis, in the carotid arteries in the neck that carry oxygen-rich blood to the brain. An artery with such a narrowing, which resembles the indentation in a long balloon that is squeezed in the middle, can easily become completely blocked by a small clot, shutting off the blood supply to much of the brain and possibly leading to a stroke. To prevent a stroke, carotid artery stenosis is usually repaired surgically.

Narrowing in the carotid arteries can be detected with an instrument called a duplex scanner. High-frequency sound waves are aimed at the artery from outside the body to measure the speed of blood flow. A high speed indicates that the artery is narrowed, since blood entering a narrowed channel speeds up, just as a river does when the water's path suddenly narrows.

This same instrument can be used, again from outside the body, to "see" inside the arteries. Using echoes from the high-frequency sound, a computer constructs an image of the artery's interior, measuring the thickness of the artery walls and identifying areas of cholesterol-rich, artery-clogging plaque. The thickness of carotid artery walls and the degree of narrowing are a strong predictor of a future heart attack, research has shown.

The simplest and possibly the most accurate predictive test in the new scheme involves comparing a blood pressure reading in the ankle with the more traditional blood pressure reading in the arm. The lower the resulting ratio (that is, the lower the pressure in the ankle), the more extensive the atherosclerosis in the peripheral arteries to the legs is likely to be.

In a report published two years ago in *The Journal of the American Medical Association*, Dr. Anne B. Newman of the Medical College of Pennsylvania in Pittsburgh and her colleagues at the University of Pittsburgh reported that the ankle/arm blood pressure index was a strong predictor of cardiovascular disease and death in older people with high systolic blood pressure. Systolic pressure is a measure of pressure in the arteries when the heart pumps.

In a study of 1,537 men and women over 60 who had systolic hypertension, Dr. Newman's group found that those with a low ankle/arm blood pressure index were four times as likely to die within the next two years, a risk that was not altered when preexisting cardiovascular disease and traditional risk factors were considered.

In a subsequent study of 129 elderly men and women with systolic hypertension, Dr. Kim Sutton-Tyrrell of the University of Pittsburgh's Graduate School of Public Health and Dr. Sidney K. Wolfson Jr. of the University of Pittsburgh Medical School demonstrated that treatment to reduce systolic blood pressure appeared to slow the progress of carotid artery stenosis as measured by the duplex scanner. In some patients, in fact, treatment resulted in a regression of stenosis.

The researchers in the four-community study found other measures, including electrocardiograms, echocardiograms and questionnaires about symptoms, to be less helpful in determining the presence of serious atherosclerosis and predicting clinical disease. However, Dr. Kuller believes a resting electrocardiogram should be part of an assessment of subclinical disease.

Dr. Kuller is quick to point out that the new method, while a significant improvement over making treatment decisions based on a person's risk factors, "is not a perfect predictor" of who will get into trouble as a result of atherosclerosis.

"There are people without subclinical disease by our measures who suffer heart attacks, just as there are people who don't smoke and get lung cancer," Dr. Kuller said. Thus, he added, a finding that a person does not have subclinical disease is not a license to maintain unhealthful habits or ignore elevated risk factors.

[JEB, June 1995]

Averting Cancer Risks

THE BODY'S SUPERB DEFENSES
AGAINST CANCER

Cancer, like heart disease, comes with age. Aging cannot be avoided, but many kinds of cancers can be averted or at least made less likely.

The human body is a consortium of some 30 trillion cells, a sort of democracy in a way, since though the cells do not vote, they rule one another by an intricate system of exchanged signals. The signals allow cells to divide and multiply only when more are needed, as when new skin is built or the stomach is given a new lining.

Cancer arises when one of the cells breaks loose from these constraints and starts to divide and proliferate to its own tune. Biologists have only recently begun to understand the elaborate control system and how errant cells escape its restraints.

One reason is hereditary; some people are born with genes that make inefficient versions of the proteins that block runaway growth of cells. In other cases the genes that operate the control system suffer physical damage during an individual's lifetime. Chemicals such as those in tobacco smoke can disrupt the genes. So can sunlight. So does ionizing radiation like that from X-ray machines.

Against all these insults the cells have elaborate defenses. There are suites of enzymes that scan the DNA of the genes, cutting out and replacing damaged sections. There are suppressor proteins that sense when a cell is not responding properly to control signals and order it to self-destruct. There is a senescence system that counts how many the times a cell has divided during its lifetime and arranges for its death once it has had its day. The body's immune system probably senses and destroys most collections of errant cells while they are still minuscule tumors.

Because of this array of checkpoints, the body is able to maintain firm control over its 30 trillion cells, each one of which has the capacity at any time to foment a cancer that would destroy the whole organism.

Nevertheless, as the body ages it becomes more prone to cancer. A plausible theory is that year by year the cells accumulate genetic damage of various kinds and the control system becomes less efficient at suppressing errant cells. The odds start to turn unfavorable, and eventually a damaged cell manages to sneak through every one of the many cancer-suppressing checkpoints.

There are several ways of helping the body in its ceaseless vigilance against cancer. One is to avoid being routinely exposed to cancer-causing agents in the first place. The most significant possible step in this category is not smoking. And avoiding sunburn will lessen the hazard from excessive sunlight.

A diet rich in fruit and vegetables is protective against cancer. Fruit and vegetables contain antioxidants and other substances that suppress chemicals that damage the genes.

Being seriously overweight is a risk factor for cancer. Diet and exercise, as discussed in Chapters 3 and 4, can help reduce this source of risk.

Diagnostic tests that catch tumors early should improve the chances of a favorable outcome. This is certainly the case with breast cancer, where regular mammograms starting at age 50, and maybe even earlier, have been shown to enhance survival. But a new generation of diagnostic tests for other kinds of cancer, based on identifying errant genes or proteins, is harder to assess. The exquisitively sensitive tests may pick up minuscule tumors that are already destined to be destroyed or neutralized by the body's immune system and would never become a life-threatening cancer. Physicians have yet to learn how to interpret the data of the new genetic tests so they can take appropriate action. These tests are the first fruits of the new understanding of the genetic basis of human cancers.

Age-Related Cancer Cases Are Up, but There's No Epidemic

THE news about cancer is both bad and good, a new analysis shows: more of it is being diagnosed, but death rates are holding steady and in some cases are even declining, especially among younger Americans. And despite a widespread belief to the contrary, there is no evidence of a cancer epidemic.

The analysis, published in a recent issue of the *Journal of the National Cancer Institute,* is the most detailed and comprehensive look yet at recent trends in cancer incidence and mortality in the United States. The trends for 28 cancers in men and 30 cancers in women suggest that even as more cancers are being diagnosed, people treated for cancer are living longer. The latest data also reveal that in the first two years of this decade, death rates from cancer in the United States declined for the first time since records have been kept.

The analysis was prepared by Dr. Susan S. Devesa, an epidemiologist and biostatistician, and her colleagues at the National Cancer Institute in Bethesda, Maryland. These were among the major reasons they found for the rise in the incidence of cancer:

- Improvements in cancer screening and early diagnosis, which have contributed heavily to increases in the numbers of cancers of the breast, prostate and brain that are diagnosed.
- Smoking, which has resulted in a rise in related cancers, especially lung cancer in women and bladder cancer in men.
- Increased exposure to the sun, with an accompanying increase in melanomas.
- The AIDS epidemic, which has led to a rise in cancers like non-Hodgkin's lymphoma and Kaposi's sarcoma.

While the researchers found there was no reason to suspect that increases in common cancers like those of the breast and prostate are in any significant way the result of exposure to cancer-causing substances in the environment, they noted that for other cancers, "some trends remain unexplained and might reflect changing exposures to carcinogens yet to be identified and clarified."

One of Dr. Devesa's coauthors, Dr. William J. Blot, an epidemiologist now working for the International Epidemiology Institute Inc., a research and consulting firm in Rockville, Maryland, said the rise in non-Hodgkin's lymphoma, the cancer that killed Jacqueline Kennedy Onassis, while partly explained by its association with AIDS, was also possibly influenced by environmental exposures. But, he added in an interview, "lymphomas are relatively minor types of cancer."

Another coauthor, Dr. Joseph F. Fraumeni Jr., an epidemiologist at the cancer institute, said it was possible that environmental factors might be involved in increases in cancers of the brain, liver, testicles and kidneys, but he added that what these might be was not known.

As for breast cancer, the rise in tumors that are stimulated by estrogen, but not in those that do not respond to estrogen, "suggests that some hormonal factor may be involved," Dr. Fraumeni said. He listed as possible external influences the use of contraceptive and menopausal hormones and exposure to estrogenlike compounds in plants and to chlorinated hydrocarbons that act like estrogens.

Still, the research team concluded, "Increasing exposure to general environmental hazards seems unlikely to have had a major impact on the overall trends in cancer rates." But the team added, "Rising rates for certain tumors have been clearly influenced by changing exposures to tobacco smoking, HIV infection and sunlight."

The researchers' analysis compared the number of cancer cases and deaths per 100,000 people in different age groups during two periods: 1975 through 1979 and 1987 through 1991. Although the data represent only those cancers that occurred among whites in this country, the researchers did examine rates in other groups and said, acknowledging some exceptions, that "patterns among blacks generally resembled those among whites."

During the time span studied, cancer incidence, adjusted for age, rose by 18.6 percent among men and by 12.4 percent among women. Prostate cancer contributed most heavily to the increase in cancers among men. The researchers attributed all or nearly all of this rise to wider detection of early cancers through the treatment of benign prostate disease and the use of a highly sensitive blood test for prostate-specific antigen, or PSA.

Other major contributors to the rise in cancers in men were non-Hodgkin's lymphoma and Kaposi's sarcoma in men with AIDS, and melanoma. Among young men, there was a rise in cancers of the oral cavity and throat, which might be related to their increased use of smokeless tobacco and alcohol.

Among women, increased rates of breast and lung cancers accounted for the overwhelming majority of the rise in the incidence of cancer. The researchers said the ever-widening use of routine screening mammography was mainly responsible for the 30.1 percent rise in breast cancer incidence. Mammography is picking up many early cancers that might not have become clinically apparent for several years.

Dr. Philip Cole, an epidemiologist at the University of Alabama School of Public Health who commented on the study in an editorial in the same issue of the journal, added that changes in reproductive habits, specifically a tendency to delay childbearing and to have fewer children, were also likely factors in the rise in breast cancer. As for lung cancer, the researchers cited cigarette smoking as the main cause of the 65.3 percent increase in incidence in women. By contrast, lung cancer rose by only 2.5 percent in men, many more of whom have quit smoking in recent decades.

As for cancers on the decline, the analysis showed that the largest decrease occurred for cancer of the uterus, a decline that the researchers related to the now-standard practice of adding progesterone to the estrogen used by millions of postmenopausal women. Stomach cancer, which has been declining for decades, continued to fall; this is "most likely related to improvements in diet, including availability of fresh fruits and vegetables [and] better methods of food preservation," including refrigeration. They also cited a lowered prevalence of infection by *Helicobacter pylori,* the bacterium that is now known to cause ulcers and to play a role in stomach cancer.

On the basis of this detailed look at the changing rates of individual cancers, Dr. Cole predicted that the new findings belied the prospect of a cancer epidemic, which he said had been predicted for more than 20 years. Dr. Devesa's findings "suggest that it will not occur," he wrote.

During the time span studied, overall cancer mortality rates rose by 3 percent for men and by 6 percent for women. However, except for lung cancer, which is still a highly lethal disease that kills more than twice as many Americans as does any other cancer and thus has an inordinately large effect on overall rates, mortality rates for the majority of cancers remained steady or declined during the study period. In fact, among men and women under 55, overall cancer mortality has declined. Only among older people have cancer death rates risen.

And in the two years following 1990, which represent the latest available data, "there was actually a significant drop in cancer mortality for the first time in history," Dr. Cole said in an interview. The overall rise in cancer mortality is "a relative one due to the fact that deaths from cardiovascular diseases are dropping much faster than deaths from cancer."

Heart disease is still the nation's leading cause of death, but from 1979 to 1992, the death rate from heart disease declined by 27.7 percent, and Dr. Cole predicted that by the turn of the century cancer would surpass it as the leading killer of Americans, "even as its overall mortality rate declines." But it will take the lead only temporarily. Dr. Cole predicted that cancer's supremacy as a killer would fade early in the next century as progress continues to be made in cancer prevention and early detection and in treatments that can cure cancer or keep it at bay for many years.

In his editorial, Dr. Cole noted that "many of the advances made in cancer therapy during the last 30 years have been effective but not necessarily curative." He added that "such therapies would postpone death and thereby produce the pattern described" of declining cancer mortality among young and middle-aged adults but increased mortality among the elderly.

But he concluded that "in the long term, prevention will play the major role in controlling cancer, as it has for many of mankind's plagues."

[JEB, February 1995]

How to Quit Smoking

SMOKERS are finding it harder and harder to pursue their habit in socially acceptable ways. Smoking has been banned in most public buildings, at work sites and on public transportation and is becoming increasingly unacceptable in restaurants, private homes and cars. Smokers, no longer welcome to light up with cocktails or coffee, or while reading the paper or doing their work, are being forced to go outside when they can no longer resist the urge.

Yet 46 million American adults continue to smoke, mainly because nicotine, like heroin and crack cocaine, is an addictive drug. For smokers who have become dependent on nicotine, each dose—each cigarette—sets up a craving for the next one. If that craving is not satisfied, the smoker begins to experience withdrawal symptoms: anxiety, irritability, restlessness, difficulty concentrating, drowsiness, disturbed sleep, hunger and a strong urge for nicotine.

Yet half of all living Americans who have ever smoked have managed to break free of the tyranny of cigarettes. To be sure, many were light smokers who were not highly dependent on the stimulating and relaxing effects of nicotine and were able to quit rather easily without outside assistance. But many other former smokers were true nicotine addicts, and most quit cold turkey and endured the extreme discomforts of withdrawal for weeks, months or even a year.

It may now be easier to become a former smoker, thanks to a variety of new products to ease nicotine cravings while breaking the habit. Like the gum and patches that have been around for some time, the products supply low doses of nicotine in a way that allows smokers to taper off gradually, without the usual agony, over a period of months. Nicotine replacement therapy, as it is called, is available over the counter in the form of gum and slow-release skin patches.

It may seem odd to give doses of the very drug a person is trying to stop using, but studies have shown that, at least in a research setting, nicotine replacement does help smokers quit for good. In fact, it is the only treatment for nicotine addiction that has been proved beneficial. Although methods like hypnosis and acupuncture have helped some smokers quit, these techniques have not been shown to be more effective than dummy therapy.

When measured against a look-alike placebo, nicotine replacement therapy in the form of gum or patch has typically doubled the initial quitting rate and doubled the number who remain abstinent six months or one year later.

Still, even with a nicotine substitute, only about one smoker in four stops smoking and only about half the quitters remain abstinent over the long term. A recent analysis of 28 studies of gum or patch showed that, overall, nicotine replacement "could enable about 15 percent of smokers who seek help in stopping smoking to give up the habit."

Furthermore, the studies have shown, this approach is not suitable for everyone. Those most likely to benefit are smokers with a strong dependence on nicotine—for example, those who crave a cigarette as soon as they awake. Smokers with a low dependence on nicotine—those whose smoking is not mainly driven by an addictive urge—do no better with nicotine replacement therapy than without it. For them, the secret to quitting may simply be deciding that they will no longer smoke.

Nicotine replacement works by curbing the discomforts of withdrawal without providing the rapid, higher doses of nicotine that produce the stimulation and euphoria associated with smoking a cigarette. Cigarettes deliver repeated, brief, high blood levels of nicotine that directly affect the brain, whereas the gum or patch delivers smaller amounts more slowly, with only gradual rises and drops in blood concentrations.

Chewing nicotine gum or using the patch does not provide the satisfaction of smoking a cigarette, nor does nicotine replacement therapy necessarily reduce cigarette cravings (as opposed to nicotine cravings).

Chewing nicotine gum or using a patch is much safer than smoking because these products are free of the cancer-causing and lung-damaging substances in tobacco smoke. Also, because replacement products deliver nicotine more slowly, they produce a less intense effect on the heart and blood vessels. After reviewing various studies, the Food and Drug Administration concluded that nicotine replacement therapy is safe and effective.

In an analysis of 17 studies using the nicotine patch published recently in *The Journal of the American Medical Association,* Dr. Michael

C. Fiore, director of the Center for Tobacco Research and Intervention at the University of Wisconsin, raised many unanswered questions about nicotine replacement therapy. Among them is the most effective duration of treatment.

Most studies involved using the patch for eight weeks; longer did not seem to result in any further benefit. The gum is generally used for three or four months, although 10 to 20 percent of former smokers continue for more than a year, more or less as maintenance therapy when they feel they might relapse.

Another crucial question is the value of behavioral counseling as an adjunct to nicotine replacement. Dr. Fiore noted that studies had shown nicotine gum to be twice as successful when combined with intensive counseling. Counseling can teach smokers how to break

More Help for Quitters

The American Lung Association provides information booklets about quitting smoking. To get any of these aids or to find a smoking cessation clinic, call (800) LUNG-USA (586-4872) to reach your local lung association chapter.

"Freedom from Smoking," catalog No. 0055, a self-help manual geared to smokers at different stages of the quitting process that combines cessation and maintenance programs, including a quitting calendar.

"A Lifetime of Freedom from Smoking," No. 0026, a maintenance manual for the new ex-smoker.

"Freedom from Smoking Audiotape," No. 6182, provides strategies for quitting smoking and handling slips or relapse.

"Alive and Kicking Audiotape," No. 6177, combines behavior change information for smokers trying to quit with tips to help them through the difficult times.

"Helping Smokers Get Ready to Quit," No. 0390C, presents suggestions on how to talk to smokers about quitting.

"How to Help a Friend Quit Smoking," a booklet, helps friends and relatives deal effectively with someone trying to quit.

The **Freedom from Smoking Cessation Clinic** is an eight-session group program that teaches smokers how to quit, how to find safer substitutes for cigarettes and how to control weight when stopping smoking.

their associations with cigarettes and how to find effective substitutes for the benefits they derived from smoking, including relaxation, mental stimulation and weight control.

Also unknown is how well nicotine replacement works outside a research setting, which tends to attract those most committed to quitting. Most cigarette smokers shy away from organized programs to halt smoking, and more than 90 percent of patch users receive no counseling or advice from a doctor.

At a recent conference on stopping smoking, experts emphasized that nicotine replacement therapy was helpful but not a panacea. They also advised smokers who are trying to quit not to be discouraged by relapse. The average smoker relapses three or four times before ultimately quitting. As Karen Monaco of the American Lung Association put it, "Those who relapse have not failed—they are simply practicing quitting."

[JEB, April 1995]

The Ravages of Too Much Sunlight

ALTHOUGH most Americans work indoors, they spend much of their leisure time outdoors—running, walking, cycling, swimming, skating, skiing, playing golf and tennis, going to ball games and, of course, sunbathing. In the process many expose their skin and eyes to a heavy dose of harmful ultraviolet radiation.

If any other environmental agent caused 1 million cases of cancer a year, there would be an unprecedented hue and cry to get rid of it immediately. But it has been very hard to convince Americans that sunshine can be unhealthy. Just as people are admired for being thin even when they are too thin, those who sport a tan are congratulated for looking "healthy," even though tanning results from injury to the skin. Some sun worshipers may wonder how anything that feels as good as sunshine can be harmful. Others may decide they simply do not care, opting to enjoy the sun now and take their chances on the consequences. Unfortunately, some of those consequences are unpleasant and unattractive and do not occur until decades later.

Overexposure to the sun has caused a dramatic rise in all kinds of skin cancer. One in six Americans will develop skin cancer. The superficial skin cancers—basal and squamous cell carcinomas—are the most common of all cancers, with more than 1 million new cases a year, according to new data from the American Academy of Dermatology. And the more serious and potentially deadly form of skin cancer, melanoma, is now the fastest-growing cancer in the United States. The academy recently reported a 500 percent increase in the incidence of malignant melanoma in the 35 years from 1950 to 1985. However, in a newly published survey, dermatologists estimated that 80,000 new cases of melanoma were diagnosed in 1992 and that the incidence has been increasing by 4.2 percent a year.

While many melanomas cannot be attributed to sun exposure and arise in areas not unduly exposed to sun, the greatest increase has occurred in light-skinned people and on sun-exposed parts of the body, such as shoulders, upper back and legs. Melanoma has also been linked to blistering sunburns suffered in childhood. It usually occurs in or near an existing mole or some other dark spot on the skin. The mole may suddenly change—get scaly, ooze or bleed, itch, become tender or painful, or spread its pigment over a wider area. Though highly curable in its early stages, melanoma can spread and become deadly.

More often, sun causes superficial skin cancers, the most common type being basal cell carcinoma, which usually appears as a small, fleshy bump or nodule on the head, neck or hand and occasionally as a flat growth on the trunk of the body. These cancers do not spread quickly and may take many months or years to grow to half an inch in diameter. Although basal cell carcinomas rarely metastasize, they can extend to the underlying bone and cause considerable local damage.

Squamous cell carcinomas typically appear as red, scaly patches or nodules, usually on the face, ears and mouth. They can grow quite large and spread to other parts of the body. They cause about 2,300 deaths a year.

Actinic keratosis, a precancerous condition that usually appears as a raised, scaly, reddish patch, is a warning of things to come and should be treated by a dermatologist. You should also see a dermatologist if you notice any change in an existing mole or if you find skin changes symptomatic of cancer.

People whose eyes are exposed to the sun for hours every day without protection are three times as likely to develop cataracts as are people who wear sunglasses with UV protection or hats with brims. About 20 percent of cataracts, which are a clouding of the lens of the eye, are now attributed to repeated sun damage. Another serious eye condition related to chronic sun damage is pterygium, pronounced "ter-RIDGE-e-um," a thickening of the tissue on the cornea, or white of the eye, that can interfere with vision. Macular degeneration, a deterioration of retinal cells that causes a loss of the central field of vision, has recently been linked to chronic sun exposure.

Cataracts cannot be corrected with glasses. Surgery is required to replace the damaged lens with an implant. Millions of dollars are spent each year on eye surgery to treat sun-induced cataracts. For macular degeneration, however, there is currently no way to treat or correct the lost visual acuity, which eventually results in legal blindness.

Chronic sun exposure causes a degeneration of the skin that dermatologists call "premature aging." Eventually, sun-exposed skin can resemble elephant hide. And while surgeons may be able to take nips and tucks to smooth wrinkles on the face (at a cost of about $15,000 out of pocket), little can be done for leathery arms and legs.

The sun can also cause the appearance of large freckles, or "age spots," and fishnet-like clusters of damaged blood vessels. Freckling is a sign of sun damage, and anyone who freckles after being in the sun is particularly vulnerable to other harmful effects, including cancer.

To assess the extent of sun damage to your skin, compare sun-exposed areas to the much smoother skin on your buttocks. Unless you routinely sunbathe in the nude, you will probably be shocked at the difference.

Some people develop allergic reactions after even a short time in the sun. Common signs of sun allergy include bumps, hives, blisters or red blotches. These most often represent an interaction between sun exposure and cosmetics, perfumes, topical medications and even sunscreens, particularly those that contain PABA (para-aminobenzoic acid). In addition, people who take certain drugs, like birth control pills and some medications to treat high blood pressure, arthritis and depression, can develop skin rashes after being out in the sun.

While sun exposure helps to alleviate psoriasis, a skin disease, other medical conditions are made worse by the sun, including cold sores (herpes simplex infections), chicken pox and lupus erythematosus. In addition, people with a defect in pigmentation that prevents their skin from darkening in the sun and those with psoriasis who are receiving ultraviolet radiation treatments are at exceptionally high risk for skin cancer. It is important for people who fall into any of these categories to protect themselves routinely from even minimal sun exposure.

A sunscreen with an SPF (sun protection factor) of at least 15 should be used routinely; a higher SPF is called for on very bright days. For a comprehensive summary of other ways to prevent sun damage and to reverse some of its effects, consult *Safe in the Sun* by Mary-Ellen Siegel, a paperback book released recently in a revised edition published by Walker & Company ($8.95).

[JEB, June 1995]

Breast Cancer: Understanding the Numbers

THROUGHOUT the 1980s the incidence of breast cancer appeared to rise dramatically, increasing by nearly a third from 1980 until 1987. Doctors, advocates for women with breast cancer and frightened women talked about an epidemic. But recently the American Cancer Society and the National Cancer Institute have cast a cold eye on those upward curves and have come to what should be a reassuring conclusion. Both assert that there is not now nor was there ever an epidemic of breast cancer in this country. The increase was more of a statistical illusion, they say, resulting from an increased use of X-ray screening that caught cancers early.

There is also no rise in breast cancer rates among young women in their 20s and 30s, according to the cancer society. More young women are getting breast cancer, but there are more of them in the population.

"It's inappropriate to say there's an epidemic," said Dr. Larry Kessler, chief of the applied research branch at the cancer institute.

Recent studies showed that women under age 50 do not necessarily benefit from mammograms. The women most terrified by the idea of a breast cancer epidemic, researchers say, have been those in their 40s, who are actually at lower risk than older women. Those in their 40s who had mammograms had the same death rate from breast cancer as those who were not screened. However, the news that there was no epidemic should be reassuring.

Yet "epidemic" is a hard word to let go of.

Dr. Sarah Fox, an associate professor of family medicine at the University of California in Los Angeles, said that although "the scare is somewhat over as far as increased incidence" is concerned, the advantage of a word like "epidemic" is that "it certainly gets the attention of politicians and laypeople."

"It still seems to be that since we are a crisis-oriented society, the people who make the most noise get the most publicity," Dr. Fox said. "Interest groups do count as opposed to data and rationality."

Some advocates for women with breast cancer have learned from the success of advocates for people with AIDS, she added. "AIDS gets a lot of attention because it is an epidemic," she said. "It's getting a lot of the money. God knows they need it, but we all need it."

But Dr. William M. Landau, a neurologist at Washington University School of Medicine, deplored what he sees as the overpromotion of disease threats. "It's an epidemic of false publicity," said Dr. Landau, who has been examining statistics for a variety of diseases, including breast cancer.

Scientists define an epidemic as a disease that occurs more often than would be expected, Dr. Kessler noted. If the number of new cases remains essentially flat, the disease is endemic rather than epidemic.

Breast cancer is endemic, Dr. Kessler said; "As populations grow and women live to old age, it is just around." He is concerned about the intransigence of the disease, he said but added: "We don't need new hype. We don't need to make women afraid."

In the 1980s the sharp rise in breast cancer cases corresponded to a surge in women's getting mammograms, the X-ray screening tests that can detect tumors too tiny to feel. The cancer groups said the high number of new cases reported in the last decade was actually cancers that were detected early, not "new" cancers.

During the 1980s, the reported incidence of breast cancer in this country rose from 85 per 100,000 women in 1980 to 112 per

100,000 in 1987. But in the past two years the number of cases has been dropping, which would be the case if the increase was attributable to mammography and the surge in early diagnoses. Lawrence Garfinkel, a statistical consultant to the cancer society, said he suspects the incidence figures will continue to drop until they are at about the 1980 levels.

There also is no increase in breast cancer among young women in their 20s and 30s, Mr. Garfinkel said. Although mammography is not recommended for these age groups, doctors say they are detecting more instances of breast cancer among them. This clinical impression is probably correct, he said, but the reason for the rise is the increased number of young women in the population.

In fact, according to the cancer society, the underlying incidence of breast cancer has remained almost constant for decades, along with the death rate from the disease. Despite the recent attention given to this deadly disease, its statistics have remained virtually the same.

But some advocates for women with breast cancer are unwilling to abandon the idea of an epidemic. Frances Visco, president of the National Breast Cancer Coalition, said: "If you already have one in eight women getting breast cancer in their lifetime and you already have 2.5 million who have the disease and fifty percent of those diagnosed are dead in ten years, those are pretty horrible statistics. I certainly believe they rise to epidemic proportions."

Dr. Susan Love, a surgeon who is director of the Comprehensive Breast Cancer Center at the University of California in Los Angeles, agreed. "To me, an epidemic is an inordinate number of women getting breast cancer," Dr. Love said. "Whether we're picking them up a little early because of screening doesn't change the fact that there are huge numbers. There are too many women dying of breast cancer, and we have to do something about it."

[GK, February 1993]

The Riddle of Breast Cancer and Locality

IT may be something in her diet, or the air and water of her new home, or the vigilance of her doctor, or stress or exhilaration or none of the above. Whatever the cause, when a woman moves to a new country, her risk of dying from breast cancer will either rise or fall to match that of women native to her adopted land, researchers have found.

The new study, an examination of changes in the patterns of breast cancer deaths among a broad array of immigrant groups in Australia and Canada, suggests that environmental factors continue to influence a woman's chances of developing breast cancer throughout adulthood and that the effect can occur over relatively short spans of time.

The work thus contradicts the current notion that most of a woman's risk of breast cancer is set by puberty or early adulthood. It also suggests that by comparing migrant populations, scientists may get a handle on how women can modify their lives to avoid this hated malignancy.

Most of the women in the study moved to Australia or Canada as adults, and yet within 30 years or less their rate of breast cancer deaths often was indistinguishable from that of local residents. For those women who migrated from a country where the breast tumor rate was lower than in their new home, the risk of the cancer rose; but for those coming from nations where breast cancer is even more prevalent than in Australia and Canada, the risk of cancer dropped.

The new report, by Dr. Erich V. Kliewer of Australian National University in Canberra and Dr. Ken R. Smith of the University of Utah in Salt Lake City, was published in a recent issue of the *Journal of the National Cancer Institute*. In it, the researchers compiled data on nearly 60 groups of immigrants from all parts of the world, calculating what their breast cancer mortality rate would have been in their homelands, what it proved to be in Australia or Canada and how that compared with the prevailing rate among the native-born population.

Previous studies of cancer patterns among migrants have focused on people moving from countries with low cancer rates, like Japan, to those with high cancer rates, like the United States, showing that as a rule the rate of cancer among the migrants eventually mounted to Western dimensions.

The new study takes the compelling twist of seeing whether the opposite is true as well, and whether moving from a high-risk environment can have an incidental benefit in lowered cancer rates. The answer in many cases appears to be yes.

For example, the researchers calculated that among the English, the rate of breast cancer deaths in women 35 to 74 years old—the range of the women considered in this study—is 68 per 100,000. By comparison, among Englishwomen who moved to Australia, the figure dropped to 57 deaths per 100,000 women, more in keeping with the death rate of 50 per 100,000 for the Australian natives.

"The importance of this study is that it reinforces our notion that your risk of breast cancer isn't something you're born with," said Dr. Noel S. Weiss, professor of epidemiology at the University of Washington School of Public Health in Seattle, "but rather something that can be influenced by your experiences. They show us that the rates are capable of going down as well as up."

But the scientists embroidered their work with abundant caveats. Most important, they do not know why the cancer rates change from one place to another. They have no idea what it is about the Australian or Canadian way of life that either encourages or inhibits breast cancer in any particular group.

Like the United States, these nations tend to have a relatively high-fat, low-vegetable diet, though all this is changing as people limp toward healthier habits. By the same token, Australia and Canada, like the United States, have comparatively good health care systems, which emphasize mammography and other methods of detecting breast cancer in its early stages, before it becomes fatal.

The current report looks only at breast cancer deaths, not at overall incidence. Thus, if women moving to Australia or Canada end up with more vigilant medical care, their rate of cancer deaths may drop with no alteration in their habits, exposure to environmental toxins, or other risk factors.

Moreover, not all migrant groups show a shift in cancer death rates in their assumed land. Instead, the figures overall indicate a marked trend toward matching those of their new homeland. In Australia, 83 percent of the immigrant groups converged in their breast cancer death rates over a 30-year period toward that of the natives. In Canada, the rates were somewhat less than that.

"Our final conclusion is that there's a convergence," Dr. Smith said, "a tendency toward the prevailing mortality rate. But we tried not to make too much of any one group or population."

Dr. Susan Love, director of the Revlon-UCLA Breast Center in Los Angeles, praised the study and said it was the sort of large-scale epidemiological work needed to disentangle environmental factors from underlying genetic predisposition.

She said that women might be born with risky mutations in any number of genes, including such widely trumpeted players as the BRCA1 gene, p53, the AT gene and so forth; yet the environment can serve to either stimulate or quell such innate predispositions, she said. "Things that cause progression of tumors, rather than their initiation," she said, "may continue throughout adulthood."

Because many of the migrant groups being studied are relatively genetically homogeneous, she said, they may allow researchers to zero in on environmental risk factors.

Dr. Love argued that, in seeking risk factors, too much emphasis had been placed on fat and not enough on other things in the diet, like possibly protective compounds in plant foods; she also believes that the possible impact of exercise in reducing risk has yet to be fully explored. Evidence also implicates pesticides, delayed child-bearing and the use of birth control pills and hormone replacement therapy in the onset of breast cancer.

[NA, August 1995]

The Puzzling New Genetics of Breast Cancer

SIX years ago, when researchers first reported the existence of a gene that could predispose a woman to breast cancer, the hope among the public and perhaps even some scientists was that the discovery would provide answers that would be black and white. A woman would be able to take a test and find out that either she had the bad gene or she didn't. She would get cancer or she wouldn't. Granted, there would not be much she could do about it, but surely some new means of prevention or treatment could not be far behind the discovery of the gene.

So far, the hoped-for answers have instead come in many shades of gray. The breast cancer gene turned out to be two genes, BRCA1, identified in 1994, and BRCA2. As genes go, they are huge, and BRCA1, the better known of the two, has more than 125 mutant forms, which makes testing most people for it difficult and expensive. BRCA2 might have even more mutations. And researchers now suspect that two or more other breast cancer genes will be found.

BRCA1 and BRCA2 can indeed be bad genes: women with family histories of breast cancer who inherit a defective version of either one are estimated to have an 80 percent to 90 percent risk of developing the disease. But how the genes work is only partly understood. Scientists think that in their healthy form, the genes direct the production of proteins that keep cell division in check, and that if either gene is defective, rampant cell growth can turn to cancer.

First thought to cause only inherited breast cancer, which accounts for just 5 percent to 10 percent of all cases, the BRCA genes are now suspected of playing a role in some of the far more common "sporadic" cases, those in women with no family history of the disease. Both genes have been linked to inherited breast and ovarian cancer that comes on before the age of 50, though the ovarian link is stronger for BRCA1. And BRCA2 has a role in male breast cancer, which, though rare, is as serious as the disease in women.

Two papers on BRCA2 that are among several being published in a recent issue of the journal *Nature Genetics* provide new pieces of the puzzle, while simultaneously revealing the puzzle to be far more complicated than was previously thought. The articles reveal that specific BRCA2 mutations are found in different ethnic groups.

The articles suggest that BRCA2 may cause prostate, pancreatic and colon cancer as well as a variety of other tumors besides breast cancer, and the finding that a particular mutation causes a certain type of cancer in some families but not others strongly indicates that the gene is not acting alone.

"These articles are wake-up calls," said Dr. Stephen Friend, director of molecular pharmacology at the Fred Hutchinson Cancer Research Center in Seattle. "We're coming out of dreamland and looking at the realities. There will be clues about the genetics of breast cancer, but not black-and-white determinants."

In the first study, conducted at the Memorial Sloan-Kettering Cancer Center in New York, researchers found that one particular mutation of BRCA2 turned up unusually often in breast cancer patients of Ashkenazi, or eastern European, Jewish descent, a group that includes more than 90 percent of the 6 million Jews living in the United States. The mutation, called 6174delT, turned up about 8 percent of the time in Ashkenazi women with breast cancer, but not at all in other, non-Jewish breast cancer patients.

That finding comes just seven months after the same researchers identified another, completely different mutation, one affecting BRCA1, in 20 percent of Ashkenazi women who developed breast cancer before age 50. The authors of the article calculated that mutations in BRCA1 or BRCA2 may account for a quarter of all early-onset cases of breast cancer in Ashkenazi women.

Given that there is no cure or sure means of preventing breast or ovarian cancer, the notion of a predictive test has generated controversy. Women who test positive may opt for more frequent checkups or for experimental drug programs to prevent cancer. Or they may take the drastic step of having their breasts and ovaries removed, which reduces but does not eliminate the risk.

Ashkenazi women with personal or family histories of breast cancer early in life are being offered testing at Sloan-Kettering, and many of them want it, said Dr. Kenneth Offit, who directed the study. "But from our perspective, that testing is a very big deal," he said. It is performed as part of a research program, and only after hours of counseling. Although one commercial laboratory does offer the testing without insisting on counseling, Dr. Offit said, "I don't think one can address all the issues in a quick-blood-test environment."

One of his greatest concerns is making sure that women understand that a negative test result does not guarantee that they will never get breast cancer. Because the known genes account for only a fraction of all the cases, women without the genes are not in the clear.

The discovery of mutations in Ashkenazi Jews raises interesting questions about evolution, Dr. Offit said. "It's not surprising to find a single mutation in an ethnic group, but how do you explain two mutations for the same disease in one group?" he said.

One of his patients, well versed in Jewish history, helped provide a possible answer by reminding him that at various periods, the Jewish population dwindled in the face of wars, famines, epidemics and pogroms. When any population shrinks, particularly to the level of tens of thousands, a phenomenon called genetic drift may become important.

Genetic mutations that would normally be diluted in a large population may become unexpectedly common in succeeding generations in a small one. Drift is a random process, an example of the strange statistics that emerge from small numbers. It is analogous to tossing a coin 10 times instead of 100 or 1,000; 7 tails might come up. Only as the number of tosses increases does one approach the true 50-50 probability.

Genetic drift might have contributed to the unexpectedly high frequency of certain BRCA mutations among the Ashkenazi Jews, Dr. Offit speculated. Then, if groups split off, another genetic event, called a founder effect, might have occurred: the frequency of a particular gene might have increased, particularly in a population isolated by geography or customs and started by a small number of individuals.

A second study also pointed to the influence of a founder effect in the occurrence of a particular BRCA2 mutation in Iceland. Birth registries enabled researchers to trace six families they were studying back 11 or 12 generations, to a common sixteenth-century ancestor, and they suggested that a BRCA2 mutation may have emerged in Iceland at that time.

The discovery of the so-called Jewish mutations and Icelandic mutations for breast cancer does not mean that breast cancer is a Jewish or Icelandic disease. The frequency of breast cancer in Iceland is no higher than in other Western cultures, and although some studies have suggested a slight excess of breast cancer among Ashkenazi Jews, others have found no excess.

Finding a specific mutation that is unusually common in one ethnic group does provide a tool for studying the genetic origins of cancer. By studying the same defect in many people, scientists can find out how its effects vary from one person or family to the next. And that information may help explain how the gene works and provide ideas on blocking its cancer-causing effects.

"Knowing someone has a particular molecular defect will become the major determinant of therapy," Dr. Friend said. Future treatment, he said, will involve drugs that selectively kill cells with a particular defect in a breast cancer gene.

"This knowledge that has such an abstract, diffuse feel to it now," he said, "in five to ten years will be precisely what we need to give the correct treatment."

[DGr, April 1996]

Reducing the Risks
of Breast Cancer

I N the current "take charge of your health" climate, growing numbers of women are making adjustments in how they live in hope of keeping breast cancer at bay. Motivated by reports in the news media, many have changed to a low-fat diet and begun exercising, practices that are generally health-enhancing. But others who avoid alcohol and postmenopausal hormones in the belief that they are doing the healthful thing may in some cases be putting themselves at a disadvantage.

Despite hundreds of studies, researchers still do not have much definitive information about the causes of breast cancer and what women might do to prevent it. The most solid evidence involves factors that are either impossible or impractical for many women to do anything about. These include being born into families that have no history of the disease and having babies, preferably before 20 and certainly by 30, and the more babies the better.

Far less certain is the value of various steps that women can readily take. The evidence is at best suggestive and at worst contradictory.

Women worry far more about breast cancer than about any other health threat, and a recent survey showed that this concern makes most women greatly overestimate their chances of developing breast cancer within the next 10 years. Too often, they avoid practices that might protect against far worse threats. Anxiety also prompts many women to overreact to poorly documented reports about things like breast cancer risks from exposure to pesticides or hormones in meat.

Women would do far better to focus on the factors that are within their control. At the very least, making adjustments in diet and exercise habits can do no harm and will almost certainly reduce the risk of a threat to women's health that is statistically far greater: heart disease. In any case, though, the wise woman will start by considering her own chances of developing either heart disease or cancer before deciding what to do.

Since it may never be proved in one's lifetime that certain measures like regular exercise reduce the risk of breast cancer or that other practices like taking postmenopausal hormones promote breast cancer, in many cases decisions about preventive practices must be made on the basis of the best available evidence.

Some population studies have suggested that a diet high in fat, and particularly in highly saturated animal fats, can raise the risk of breast cancer. But evidence from the Mediterranean countries, where consumption of olive oil, a monounsaturated fat, is high but breast cancer rates are low indicates that dietary fat in general is not a factor. While it is true that the risk of breast cancer is very low in Japan, where fat intake is well below what it is in this country, and that it rises to American levels when Japanese women immigrate to this country, many other factors could account for the change.

Probably much more important is the amount of fruits and vegetables in the diet. Several studies point to the protective value of eating lots of fruits and vegetables, which are rich sources of nutrients and plant chemicals that in laboratory studies impede the development of cancer. Soybeans, products made from soybeans, and green tea have been cited as especially rich in substances called phytoestrogens that may block the tumor-promoting effects of natural estrogens.

Perhaps the most exciting recent news about preventing breast cancer was a study by Dr. Leslie Bernstein of more than 1,000 California women. She found that moderate but regular exercise appeared to reduce the risk in premenopausal women by as much as 60 percent. The greatest benefit was associated with four hours a week of an activity like jogging, tennis or swimming laps, but women who exercised for only two or three hours a week also had a significantly reduced risk.

This was one of several studies suggesting that exercise, particularly if pursued from adolescence through adulthood, protects against breast cancer. Dr. Bernstein, of the University of Southern California at Los Angeles, suggested that exercise might counter breast cancer by occasionally blocking ovulation and therefore reducing the output of cancer-stimulating ovarian hormones. Exercise may also curb the amount of body fat, which is a supplemental source of these hormones.

Alcohol is the focus of a heated dispute. While several studies have pointed to an increase in breast cancer among women who drink any amount of alcohol, when it comes to heart disease, which kills far more women over 55 than breast cancer does, others have shown a protective effect of moderate drinking.

The newest study, published in a recent issue of the *New England Journal of Medicine,* showed that among nearly 86,000 nurses, overall death rates were lowest among women who had only one to three alcoholic drinks a week. Those who consumed up to two drinks a day also had a lower mortality rate than abstainers, even though this amount of alcohol has been shown to raise estrogen levels (and therefore, presumably, breast cancer risk) in premenopausal women. Women with various risk factors for heart disease, including being over 50, showed the most benefit from a modest intake of alcohol.

Even more controversial than alcohol is the role, if any, that taking estrogens during or after menopause plays in breast cancer. Contradictory studies have left millions of women confused and concerned.

Prevailing evidence strongly indicates that replacement hormones not only reduce symptoms of menopause but also significantly lower the risk of heart disease and osteoporosis in older women. The amount of estrogen taken is far less than that produced naturally by women before menopause, so the stimulatory effects of replacement therapy on the breast are not nearly as great.

A new study at the University of Buffalo has for the first time indicated that smoking can be carcinogenic to the breast. Dr. Christine Ambrosone and colleagues showed that women who smoke and have a slow-acting version of an enzyme that detoxifies carcinogens in tobacco smoke were up to eight times as likely to develop breast cancer as women who smoked but had a fast-acting version of this enzyme. The risk was highest among women who had started smoking in their teenage years and those who smoked more than a pack a day.

Dr. John Gofman, an emeritus professor at the University of California at Berkeley and an expert on the effects of radiation, predicts that breast cancer cases will begin to decline now that physicians are far more circumspect in their use of X rays. On the basis of an analysis of the sometimes flagrant past uses of X rays and the much larger doses delivered by old X-ray equipment, Dr. Gofman has estimated that at least two-thirds of current breast cancer cases are the result of radiation exposure received up to 60 years ago.

While other experts dispute the extent of radiation-induced cancers, few deny the hazards of such former practices as using radiation to shrink enlarged thymus glands, to monitor treatment of tuberculosis and to treat various dermatological conditions, including severe acne. Whole-body fluoroscopic examinations were commonly done to check growth in children. Even mammograms, used to detect breast cancer, formerly involved more than 100 times the maximum dose allowed at present, as Dr. Gofman noted in his new book, *Preventing Breast Cancer: The Story of a Major, Proven, Preventable Cause of this Disease,* published by the Committee for Nuclear Responsibility Inc.

[JEB, May 1995]

Clues to the Development of Prostate Cancer

AMERICAN men whose diets are rich in animal fats, and particularly fats from red meat, face nearly an 80 percent greater risk of developing potentially fatal prostate cancer than do men with the lowest intake of such foods, a major new study has found.

The study, which has been following the medical fates of more than 51,000 male health professionals since 1986, provides the strongest evidence yet linking dietary fat to the chance of dying of prostate cancer, which is the second leading cause of cancer deaths in American men, after lung cancer.

The finding strengthens the credibility of earlier observations derived from studies of cancer–diet relationships in laboratory animals, international comparisons of prostate cancer rates, studies of cancer rates among immigrants from countries where prostate cancer is rarely fatal and examinations of the diets of men with advanced prostate cancer.

As in the laboratory studies, the new research suggests that fats derived from animal foods promote rather than initiate the development of prostate cancer and may be the crucial factor determining in which men prostate cancers change from a dormant, symptomless condition to a spreading and possibly lethal malignancy. The study, published in a recent issue of the *Journal of the National Cancer Institute,* was conducted by Dr. Edward Giovannucci and colleagues at Harvard's Medical School and School of Public Health.

Cancer researchers have long been puzzled by the fact that when men from different countries are examined at autopsy, 15 to 30 percent are found to have had latent prostate cancer that caused no symptoms. Yet there is as much as a 120-fold difference in prostate cancer death rates, with the rate for American men among the highest in the world.

The American Cancer Society estimates that the disease kills some 35,000 men a year and will be diagnosed in another 165,000. In the last three decades, the prostate cancer death rate among American men has risen more than 17 percent.

Studies have also shown that when men move here from Japan, where prostate cancer is a rare cause of death, their chances of developing the disease increase with the length of their stay, eventually equaling those of native Americans. Such evidence strongly suggests that environmental factors, rather than genetic differences, account for Americans' high rate of fatal prostate cancer.

In an editorial in the same issue, Dr. Kenneth J. Pienta of the Michigan Cancer Center and Peggy S. Esper of Harper Hospital in Detroit said, "Dietary fat currently seems to be the most likely environmental culprit."

Dr. David Rose, who conducts diet-cancer studies at the American Health Foundation in Valhalla, New York, said: "A number of different fatty acids drive prostate cancer cells once they've developed. Fats can accelerate the growth of tumors and increase their propensity to metastasize."

An ability of dietary fats to stimulate cancer growth in animals has been demonstrated for cancers of the breast, ovary, colon and uterus as well as for cancer of the prostate. While most fats have been implicated as cancer promoters in the laboratory studies, fats from fish—the so-called omega-3 fatty acids—have the opposite effect, suppressing cancer growth and metastases.

In the new study, researchers conducted careful assessments of the usual diets of the 47,855 participants who were free of recognizable cancer when the study began. In the next four years, 300 cases of prostate cancer, including 126 cases of advanced cancer, were diagnosed among these participants.

While no relationship was found between fat and prostate cancer overall, a definite link was established between consumption of animal fat and the likelihood of being diagnosed initially with advanced prostate cancer.

Among the various sources of animal fat, fat from red meat was most strongly linked to advanced cancer. Those who consumed the most red meat were two and a half times more likely to be found to have advanced cancer or to die of prostate cancer than those who ate meat infrequently. The investigators found a 10-fold difference in intakes of animal fat between low and high consumers, ranging from an average of 3.2 grams of fat from red meat each day to 30.5 grams a day.

Total fat intake was also associated with the risk of advanced cancer. Those who consumed an average of 88.6 grams of fat a day had a 79 percent greater chance of developing advanced prostate cancer than those who averaged 53.2 grams of fat daily. The greatest risk—nearly three and a half times higher—was associated with the highest intake of a monounsaturated fatty acid called alpha-linolenic acid. But Dr. Giovannucci said most of this fatty acid was derived from animal fats rather than vegetable oils in the men's diets.

Both the writers of the editorial and the authors of the new study pointed out that the relationship between fat intake and the promotion of prostate cancer was complex and in need of much further research. Dr. Giovannucci said, "The findings need to be confirmed in similar prospective studies in different populations, and more research is needed into how animal fats might promote prostate cancer."

But Dr. Ernst Wynder, director of the American Health Foundation, called for more aggressive intervention studies, in which men with early prostate cancer would be placed on a carefully controlled low-fat diet to see if it reduced their chances of dying of prostate cancer. Such a study is about to be begun by the foundation among 2,000 women who have been treated for early-stage breast cancer. Half the participants will be instructed to cut their usual fat intake by more than half, to just 15 percent of daily calories.

[JEB, October 1993]

New Cancer Tests: Diagnoses That Are Hard to Interpret

WITH a speed so rapid that many medical experts are taken aback, genetic tests that can tell if a person is likely to get cancer are entering the marketplace.

Those in favor of testing say people have a right to know if they are at increased risk and it would be unethical to deny them that knowledge. They say that people who harbor cancer genes may be helped by undergoing frequent screening for cancer so they could get early treatment. But opponents say that it is too soon, that the tests are still research tools, that it is not clear if patients will be helped or harmed by knowing their medical future and that in some cases it is not clear how to interpret the test results.

The tests look for mutated genes that can enormously increase a person's risk of getting breast cancer, colon cancer, melanoma, or thyroid cancer. Another gene points to an inherited predisposition to any of a variety of cancers, including breast cancer and brain tumors. The tests, which cost $800 for the first family member and $250 for each additional member, involve analyses of genes obtained from blood samples or, in the case of the melanoma gene, from swabbings of the inside of a patient's cheek.

The genes were discovered only recently. The melanoma gene was reported in September 1994, for example, and the breast cancer gene in October. And some researchers say they are only beginning to understand the consequences of inheriting one of these genes.

Dr. Francis Collins of the National Institutes of Health in Bethesda, Maryland, is the director of the Human Genome Project, the federal effort to map the entire human genetic sequence. Dr. Collins said the effort to market the genetic tests "is alarming."

"We are talking about treading into a territory which the genetics community has felt rather strongly is still research," Dr. Collins said. "Unanimously, the professional genetics community, the Human Genome Council and the National Breast Cancer Coalition have stated that these tests should not now be made available."

Dr. Neil Holtzman, the head of the Genetics and Public Policy Studies Department at Johns Hopkins Medical Institutions in Baltimore, said that "this is a critical issue" and that "it is already getting out of hand."

But Fred C. Follmer, the chief financial officer of the Preferred Oncology Network in Atlanta, a national association of hundreds of private cancer specialists, said the critics "had better get ready for this." The tests, he said, are already here. His group has signed an agreement with OncorMed Inc., a biotechnology company in Gaithersburg, Maryland, which will perform the tests. OncorMed has also advertised to doctors outside the network that it can now test patients for cancer genes. Members of the oncology network will begin offering the tests within the next month and expect that its patients will be helped.

Dr. Timothy Triche, the chief executive officer at OncorMed and the chief of pathology at Children's Hospital in Los Angeles, says that he recognizes the controversy but that it is too late to stop the testing. He said that because one test in particular, the one for the breast cancer gene, has become so contentious, the company will initially refer women who want it to a consortium of doctors at medical centers.

But Dr. Triche added that although OncorMed may be the first, it is far from the only company interested in marketing the tests, which are generally available through nonexclusive licensing agreements with the universities where the genes were discovered.

"Others are clearly going to enter this field," Dr. Triche said. "We're aware of at least three additional companies in the formative stages now," he said. "It's just a matter of how fast you do it and for how many diseases." At OncorMed, he added, "we've probably been more aggressive than most."

But Dr. Triche says he expects it will not be long before doctors begin using the tests routinely. "With time, of course, this will be available to every physician," he said.

Dr. Triche said the tests can benefit patients and help cut medical costs, and this could be especially useful to health maintenance organizations. "In a managed care environment, imagine 300,000 who just signed up," he said. "Ultimately, we know that one out of three will develop cancer," adding that 10 percent, or 10,000, of those will have a familial basis for doing so.

"So it is prudent not to try to screen 300,000 but to identify the 10,000 at extreme risk and manage them differently from the others," Dr. Triche said.

Computer programs that OncorMed has developed can help pick out those whose family histories indicate they may carry cancer-causing genes, Dr. Triche said. Then those who are identified can be offered genetic tests. If they inherited cancer genes, the doctors would urge them to be screened for cancer "on a much more regular basis at a much earlier age," than others without the genes, Dr. Triche said.

But some who have done the research leading up to the gene discoveries are wary. Dr. Barbara Weber, a breast cancer researcher at the University of Pennsylvania School of Medicine, said she regularly gets calls from women and their doctors asking for the breast cancer gene test. One problem, she and others say, is that the gene, called BRCA1, is large, with many possible mutations. If the investigators find a mutation they have not seen before, they cannot immediately tell whether that mutation causes cancer. If they do not find any mutations, they still cannot be completely reassuring, because the woman may have a mutation in a second, recently discovered breast cancer gene or she may have a mutation in a breast cancer gene that is as yet undiscovered.

And even if the investigators can say for sure that a woman has a mutation that will give her an 80 percent chance of developing breast cancer and a 60 percent chance of developing ovarian cancer, they cannot tell her what to do to protect herself.

Although large studies have shown that mammograms for women over age 50 can cut the death rate from breast cancer by 25 percent, it is not known whether these findings apply to women carrying a gene predisposing them to breast cancer. These hereditary cancers tend to occur when women are relatively young and to be very aggressive. Some women have had their breasts removed to avoid the cancer, but even that is not a guarantee, because the cancer can occur in the chest wall. Some women have their ovaries removed, but they still have a small chance of a cancer in their abdomen.

"Once we get this information, we are not able to help very much in terms of prevention," Dr. Weber said. "We will offer either more frequent mammograms or, if the women want it, prophylactic surgery, but we can't tell you that either will prevent you from dying from cancer."

Dr. Weber said she told women this and some decided they would rather not be tested. Many others, she said, say: "I can handle this. I want to know." But, Dr. Weber said, some are not prepared for the bad news when they get it. One woman tried to commit suicide when she learned she had the breast cancer gene.

The same caveats apply when the tests involve genes for other cancers, experts say. "As has happened in the past with genetics, the technology far precedes the response to what we're going to do with the technology," said Dr. Gail Vance, a molecular geneticist at the Indiana University School of Medicine. "The screening for any of these diseases is not wonderful."

Then there is the potential problem of discrimination by health and life insurance companies and by employers when people test positive for a cancer gene. "You've got information that can affect the outcome of people's lives," Dr. Vance said. "If you go to look for a job at age forty and you have the breast cancer gene, you know that by age fifty half the women with the gene will have cancer. What does that mean to an employer?" On the other hand, she added, as many as 15 percent of women with the gene never get cancer. So, she said, "you may be discriminating against someone who will never get the disease."

And there is the delicate question of testing children. OncorMed, in a letter on melanoma testing that it sent to dermatologists throughout the country, wrote, "Early screening with this easy and painless test is particularly useful when testing children." But many ethicists and cancer specialists say that they worry about testing children and labeling them as cancer-prone when there is little to be done to protect them from the disease.

The answer, for now, say those who want to go slowly, is to offer the genetic tests only in research settings, where patients would see expert genetic counselors before being tested and after learning the results of their tests and where they can participate in studies of what the genetic results mean clinically and whether intensive screening for cancer will help.

"Everybody has to be careful," Dr. Weber said. "People tend to say, What's the big deal? We tell people all the time that they have cancer." But she added: "This is telling people that they are going to get cancer. This is telling people that their kids will get cancer because of the gene they gave them."

Some experts say that the fears of testing are being overblown. Dr. Henry T. Lynch, the director of Creighton University's Cancer Center and an adviser to OncorMed, said he knew all about the caveats that go with genetic tests for cancer.

"I hear this all the time, from patients, physicians, ethicists—this is a favorite thing of ethicists," Dr. Lynch said. "They're looking for all the things that can do harm. But we've adopted the ostrich approach. We've got knowledge now through the brilliance of molecular genetics, and it's our duty as physicians to use it prudently. It's called medical judgment."

Dr. David Sidransky, a cancer researcher at the Johns Hopkins University School of Medicine and an adviser to OncorMed, said that he found many of the arguments against testing to be "bogus." It is unethical, he said, to prevent patients from having tests for cancer genes if they want them. It is not enough to say that patients can enter research studies, he said. "Not every patient can go on an academic protocol," he said. "Not everyone lives next to Hopkins.

"Information is neutral," Dr. Sidransky said. "We always have this question: Is it good or bad? We don't know until we use it. This is diagnostics, not a drug. The medical risks are zero. We're really talking about psychological issues."

And, Dr. Sidransky said, psychological reactions are hard to predict. He said those who want to stop the commercialization of the genetic tests are fighting a losing battle.

"If you don't offer the testing, the patients will get it anyway," Dr. Sidransky said. "They will go anywhere, to another country if they have to. There will be clinics set up to do it. Is that going to be better than having it available in the United States?"

[GK, March 1995]

Stages of Life—
Pregnancy and Birth

THE HUMAN LIFE CYCLE

What animal walks on four legs in the morning, on two legs at noon and on three at dusk? It was Oedipus who solved the Sphinx's deadly riddle about the ages of man, thus gaining the fateful crown of Thebes and the ensuing complications with the queen, later revealed to be his mother.

Modern medicine has not solved all the riddles of life's passages, but it has eased the complications in many ways. Pregnancy is safer; infant mortality has been much reduced, at least in developed countries; and the once-deadly infectious diseases of childhood have been kept at bay with public health measures and vaccines.

The discomforts that follow menopause can be treated with hormone replacement, and many of the frailties of age need no longer be regarded as inevitable.

This and the following three sections describe recent thinking about how best to traverse the passages of human life in full health.

Exercising Safely During Pregnancy

PREGNANCY is no longer a period of confinement. About the only thing that is "confined" during pregnancy these days is the unborn child. It is now commonplace to see pregnant women jogging, swimming, walking briskly and even skating and playing tennis, sometimes well into the last third of pregnancy.

Some women exercise after clearing their plans with their physicians, but many others never consult their doctors and instead take it for granted that activities they pursued before pregnancy are safe to continue. Still others are inspired by their pregnancy to start regular exercise.

Some join exercise classes designed for pregnant women and supervised by trained leaders, but most pregnant women exercise in an unsupervised fashion that can result in a choice of activities or intensity of exercise that is potentially harmful to them or their unborn babies.

How Exercise Helps

Contrary to common impressions, there is no evidence that an exercise program during pregnancy shortens or eases labor and delivery, although women who do aerobic activities like jogging, stationary cycling and swimming tend to gain less weight and get back into shape sooner.

More important is that exercise makes the nine months of pregnancy easier. It helps to counter common pregnancy-related discomforts like backache, constipation, fatigue, bloating and swelling of the extremities. By increasing muscle tone, strength and endurance, it can help with the physical stresses of pregnancy, especially carrying extra weight.

"The most consistent benefit of exercise during pregnancy is psychological," states the Melpomene Institute of St. Paul, Minnesota, which does research on women's health issues. "Regular exercise during pregnancy allows women to have control over their bodies at a time of profound bodily changes. It gives them a chance to relax and helps them maintain a positive self-image."

Desirable Activities

In general, activities you pursued before pregnancy can be continued, although as the pregnancy progresses the pace should be slowed and sometimes one activity should be modified or replaced by one more suitable for your new shape and weight. Contact sports, especially those that could result in abdominal trauma, should be avoided.

Swimming and water aerobics, if the water is neither very warm or cold, are ideal because the water supports your increasing weight and allows you to work out as vigorously in the ninth month as in the third. However, water skiing, scuba diving and surfing are too risky at any stage of pregnancy, and diving or jumping into the water should be avoided during the last three months. Jogging, brisk walking and tennis (especially doubles) can be continued but at an increasingly moderate pace.

As pregnancy progresses, difficulty maintaining balance makes bicycling, downhill skiing and ice-skating riskier than usual. In addition to the danger associated with falls, skiing at high altitudes can unduly compromise a pregnant woman's oxygen supply. A stationary cycle and cross-country skiing are much safer.

After the fourth month, avoid calisthenics that are done lying on your back, as well as full sit-ups, double leg raises and touching your toes with knees straight, which can strain the back. Partial sit-ups with knees bent are far less stressful and are good for strengthening abdominal muscles. If you wish to continue weight lifting during pregnancy, avoid weights that are so heavy they do not allow normal breathing, and be sure to breathe properly. Holding your breath may diminish blood flow to the uterus.

If you plan to join an exercise class for pregnant women, first observe a session and talk with the instructor and participants to be sure the class is sensibly run by a qualified person.

Precautions

Dressing properly and drinking enough water or other caffeine-free liquids are especially critical to comfort and safety. Becoming overheated is a serious risk that may cause birth defects early in pregnancy. Do not overdress; dress in layers, some of which can be removed, and choose exercise clothing that "breathes." During hot weather, exercise during the coolest part of the day. If you find yourself becoming overheated, modify the intensity of your routine. And, above all, drink a lot of fluids during as well as after your activity. Avoid exercising on a empty stomach.

Be sure to eat enough to gain between 25 and 35 pounds during your pregnancy. This is no time to diet or to exercise to lose weight. Melpomene Institute studies reveal that pregnant runners often shortchange themselves on calories, iron and calcium, all essential to a healthy pregnancy.

Devote at least five minutes at the beginning and end of your exercise session to warm-up and cool-down exercises, especially during pregnancy, when joints become lax and more susceptible to injury.

Never exercise to the point of exhaustion. Stop as soon as you begin to feel fatigued.

Women with certain conditions should not exercise during pregnancy, says the American College of Obstetricians and Gynecologists. These include pregnancy-induced hypertension, premature labor during a previous or the current pregnancy, persistent bleeding, incompetent cervix, evidence from a sonogram that the fetus is growing too slowly and premature rupture of the membranes. Any woman with a chronic medical condition, like cardiovascular or pulmonary disease, should be evaluated first by her physician to see what, if any, kind of exercise is suitable.

If you develop any of these symptoms, stop exercising: breathlessness; dizziness; muscle weakness; nausea; chest pain or tightness; pain in the back, hip or pubic area; vaginal bleeding; leakage of amniotic fluid; difficulty walking; a racing heart while resting; uterine contractions; or the loss of fetal movements.

Women who were sedentary before becoming pregnant should start out with very-low-intensity activities and build up gradually. Pregnancy is not the time to take up jogging.

Stretching and Calisthenics for a Comfortable Pregnancy

Moderate exercise, never to the point of strain and fatigue, is beneficial during pregnancy. Wear loose-fitting clothes, and always warm up before exercise and cool down afterward with exercises like walking in place or outside.

Stand with upper arms parallel to floor and forearms pointing toward ceiling. Slowly bring arms together in front; hold for 5 seconds, then slowly press away toward back, squeezing shoulder blades together. Do this 12 times.

Sit on floor with legs comfortably apart. Lean foward toward one foot. Hold for count of 10, then release. Do this five times with each leg.

Stand and place palms on wall. Bend elbows and move upper body toward wall. Hold for 10 seconds, then slowly push away from wall. Do this 10 times.

Stand with arms straight out, away from sides. Move both arms overhead, as if doing a jumping jack, then return them parallel to the floor. Do this 10 times.

Another important pelvic exercise is Kegel contractions, tightening and then releasing the same vaginal muscles that are used to cut off the urine stream. You can work up to doing this 100 or more times during the day.

Source: "L'eggs Exercise During Pregnancy Guide," Dr. Mona Shangold

Stand with arms straight out, away from sides. Move both arms in small circles for 60 seconds. Stop and relax. Repeat in reverse direction. Begin with three sets, work up to seven.

Stand, placing your palms on wall. Put one foot behind the other. With back leg straight, slowly lean foward, slightly bending front leg. Relax, then move back leg a little further from wall. Hold for 8 seconds. Repeat with other leg. Do this five times with each leg.

Lie on one side, lower leg bent slightly. Head can be up or down. Raise upper leg 12 or 18 inches, hold briefly, then lower. Begin with five lifts. Work up to 20 if it is comfortable. Repeat with other leg.

Stand with feet shoulder-width apart and knees slightly bent. Contract muscles of buttocks and abdomen. Gently thrust pelvis forward, rotating pubic bone upward. Hold for 10 seconds, then release. Do this five times.

Stand with one hand on wall and with other hand hold ankle. Using wall for balance, pull gently back until you feel a stretch. Hold for 30 to 45 seconds. Repeat with other leg. Do this three times with each leg.

To find further information, the staff and researchers at the Melpomene Institute have written a book, *The Bodywise Woman*, which includes a comprehensive chapter on exercise and pregnancy. The institute has also put together a packet of useful information on exercise and nutrition during pregnancy. The book ($13.95 plus $2 for shipping and handling) and the packet ($12 plus $2 for shipping and handling) can be ordered from the institute at 1010 University Avenue, St. Paul, MN 55104.

[JEB, February 1994]

New Thinking About
Fitness and the Fetus

I N recent years, the surging interest in physical fitness has led the medical profession to take a hard new look at the risks and benefits of both moderate and vigorous exercise for pregnant women and their unborn children. Gone are the days when doctors and mothers-in-law routinely told pregnant women to take it easy and avoid strenuous activity.

On the basis of findings of recent studies, the American College of Obstetricians and Gynecologists recently reconsidered recommendations it made in 1985 to restrict the intensity of exercise in pregnancy to what some fitness experts have called "old-lady limits."

That advice, which was deliberately conservative to apply to women of varying levels of fitness doing unsupervised exercise, was widely criticized for its suggested limits on time and intensity, which the experts said would make it difficult for a well-conditioned woman to maintain her desired level of fitness throughout pregnancy.

Now the nation's obstetrical leaders, after reviewing the latest data, state in a newly issued technical advisory that in otherwise uncomplicated pregnancies, women can let their own stamina and abilities be their guide. In such low-risk pregnancies, the college advisory says, "there currently are no data to confirm that exercise during pregnancy has any deleterious effects on the fetus."

According to the findings of various studies, pregnant women who exercise, including those who jog through most of their pregnancy, are no more likely to have babies with birth defects than are those who are sedentary. Although on average babies born to women who exercise are leaner at birth, weighing about half a pound less than babies born to sedentary women, birth weights are within a normal range and there is no increased risk of miscarriage or premature delivery associated with exercise in uncomplicated pregnancies.

In fact, the new advisory states, "There are no data in humans to indicate that pregnant women should limit exercise intensity and lower target heart rates because of potential adverse effects."

But Dr. Raul Artal, the main author of both the old and the new guidelines, said in an interview, "In my opinion, there is really no point in exercising strenuously, since a pregnant woman can maintain cardiovascular fitness through mild to moderate exercise."

Dr. Artal, the chairman of the Obstetrics and Gynecology Department at the State University of New York at Syracuse, defined "strenuous" as an exercise level during which a woman cannot converse normally.

In deciding not to place upper limits on exercise intensity, he said, "We've learned a whole lot since 1985, and the new technical bulletin reflects the state of knowledge today. Pregnancy should not be a state of confinement. A woman should not have to stop the life she lived before becoming pregnant."

By the same token, however, the college concluded, "No level of exercise during pregnancy has been conclusively demonstrated to be beneficial in improving perinatal outcome." In other words, babies born to mothers who exercise during pregnancy may have no particular advantage, although the college recognizes that "maternal fitness and sense of well-being may be enhanced by exercise."

The statement thus seeks to dispel the prevalent notions about the risks and benefits of exercise in pregnancy and to supplant them with facts reflecting both an improved understanding of the physiological changes that occur in pregnancy and the findings of an ever-growing number of studies of the results of pregnancy in women who exercise at varying levels.

In pregnancy, a woman's circulatory system undergoes profound changes. Blood volume increases, the heart pumps more blood with each beat, pulse rate rises and blood flows more easily through the body. At the same time, changes occur in the way the cardiovascular system responds to various body positions and levels of exercise.

For example, after the first three months of pregnancy, when a woman lies on her back there is a significant decline in the heart's output, a situation that could result in dizziness and diminished blood flow to the developing fetus. The problem is aggravated, Dr. Artal said, if a pregnant woman tries to exercise in that position.

Standing motionless results in an even greater decline in cardiac output than does lying on one's back during pregnancy. In fact, a study of nearly 1,900 women published in a recent issue of the journal *Epidemiology* found that women who had had a previous miscarriage and who stood for more than eight hours a day on their jobs faced an increased risk of miscarriage in a future pregnancy. But those whose daily activities were more strenuous and involved movement, like doing heavy housework or caring for young children, had a lower-than-average chance of miscarrying, whether or not they had already had a miscarriage.

Pregnant women also have less oxygen available for aerobic activity and are therefore more likely to get out of breath at a lower intensity of exercise. Even well-conditioned pregnant women are less able to exercise strenuously than they were before becoming pregnant, and as pregnancy advances, their tolerance for strenuous exercise declines.

Another caution issued by the college concerns body temperature. Studies have suggested that an increase in the mother's internal temperature above 102.5 degrees Fahrenheit raises the risk of neural tube defects like spina bifida in her unborn child. Pregnancy itself raises a woman's basal metabolic rate and the amount of heat her body produces.

A further important effect of exercise in pregnancy is an increased tendency for the blood to become more concentrated at a given level of exercise, which diminishes blood flow and the ability of the body to cool itself. Vigorous exercise itself generates body heat, and during pregnancy this could result in temperature rises that have been associated with an increased risk of birth defects. But the advisory pointed out that physically fit women are less likely than sedentary women to experience an extreme change in body temperature during strenuous exercise.

The college cautioned women against assuming that it was safe to continue their prepregnancy levels of exercise unless they were first examined by a doctor for possible complicating factors that could place their pregnancy or unborn child at undue risk. But in the absence of complications, the college concluded, "Women who have achieved cardiovascular fitness prior to pregnancy should be able to safely maintain that level of fitness throughout pregnancy and the postpartum period."

[JEB, February 1994]

Preventing Birth Defects
Even Before Pregnancy

IT is common for women to start paying serious attention to their health and nutrition once they know they are pregnant. Even women with the worst habits—eating haphazardly, smoking cigarettes, overindulging in alcohol, abusing drugs—often clean up their act when they realize that they are eating and living for two and one of the two is completely at the other's mercy.

But in recent years, a lot of new information has been gathered about the relationship between living habits before pregnancy and problems like miscarriage, birth defects, low birth weight and premature birth. As a result, there is now a new focus on all women of childbearing age.

The March of Dimes is spearheading a "Think Ahead" campaign to get women to start taking better care of themselves even before they conceive. The organization is urging women to pay closer attention to their health all the time, not just when they expect to become pregnant, since 56 percent of pregnancies in this country are not planned. All women who are either considering having children or at risk of becoming pregnant accidentally are asked to see their doctors beforehand so that any problems that can jeopardize a pregnancy can be cleared up before there is a fetus.

Of special concern are women who have been using birth control pills and those with poor eating habits, both of whom may be deficient in folic acid, a B vitamin that helps to prevent anencephaly and spina bifida, severe birth defects of the brain and spinal cord. Other issues that should be addressed before conception include an abnormally high or low body weight; the use of alcohol, tobacco, recreational drugs or medications; and preexisting health problems like infections, diabetes, hypertension and epilepsy.

Dr. William H. Herman, an epidemiologist specializing in diabetes at the federal Centers for Disease Control and Prevention, reported at a recent meeting of the American Diabetes Association that preconception care for women with diabetes could markedly improve the outcome for mother and child and reduce health care costs by about 80 percent.

To assess the extent of prepregnancy problems among women of childbearing age, the March of Dimes Birth Defects Foundation recently sponsored a Gallup survey of a national sample of 2,010 women from 18 through 45. The women, interviewed by telephone, were a fairly well-educated group, with 89 percent having completed high school and 55 percent having gone to college for at least a year.

Yet, among those who had been pregnant, 73 percent had waited to see the doctor until after they thought they were pregnant. Only 26 percent had talked to their doctors about pregnancy before it happened. The delay is risky because fetal organs begin to form within three days after the first missed menstrual period, before most women even suspect they are pregnant, and are completed by the 56th day after conception, said Merry-K. Moos, a nurse-practitioner at the University of North Carolina's School of Nursing and Public Health.

She noted that in the first three months of pregnancy, the fertilized egg increases 2.5 million times in mass and the risks of harm to developing tissues are far greater than during the rest of pregnancy, when the increase in mass is only 230 times.

Ms. Moos, a national leader in establishing model programs for prepregnancy health care, said: "For prevention to be truly preventive it has to be preconceptional. Far too many women don't get to the doctor within the first critical period of pregnancy, and too many babies and too many pregnancies don't end happily."

Dr. Lynn Bailey, a professor of nutrition at the University of Florida in Gainesville, noted that someone planning to drive across country "would certainly first take the car into a garage to make sure it is in working order." But, she said, the comparable message is not getting across to women having babies.

The survey revealed that women were well aware of the hazards to the unborn child of smoking, drinking alcohol and using drugs during pregnancy. But they are poorly informed about the importance of folic acid, the only known preventive of a serious birth defect.

Asked what vitamins or minerals were particularly important during pregnancy, 27 percent of the women listed iron and 26 percent said calcium but only 6 percent mentioned folic acid. Asked how the risk of birth defects could be reduced, most cited the need to avoid cigarettes and alcohol, but only 1 percent mentioned folic acid.

Nearly half the women questioned had never even heard of folic acid, and only 15 percent were aware of the Public Health Service recommendation that all women of childbearing age should consume four-tenths of a milligram (400 micrograms) of folic acid a day. Of those who had heard of folic acid, 90 percent did not know why it was important and only 6 percent knew specifically that it could prevent spina bifida, a gap in the spine that affects 10 to 20 of every 1,000 babies. Folic acid also helps prevent the fatal defect anencephaly, a failure of the brain and spinal cord to develop.

Dr. Bailey said that "during the first 28 days of pregnancy, even before the baby looks like a baby, millions of cells develop that make the brain, spinal cord and other organs, and at this time there is an enormous need for folic acid."

The main sources in the American diet of folic acid are dark green leafy vegetables and some fruits, especially orange juice. Yet, Dr. Bailey said, in a national assessment of food intake in 1986, 90 percent of women of reproductive age had not consumed a single dark green vegetable on any of the four days of the survey, and 50 percent of the women had consumed no citrus fruit or juice during that time.

Another national dietary assessment conducted from 1988 through 1991 revealed a slew of nutritional deficiencies among women of reproductive age. As a result of poor eating patterns, these women tended to consume too little folic acid, iron and calcium to ensure that they and their fetuses would not be shortchanged. The average woman consumed only about half the recommended amount of folic acid each day. Whereas the fetus will take whatever iron and calcium it can get from the mother, even at her expense, it apparently cannot compensate for a lack of folic acid.

Rather than trust to chance for an adequate dietary intake, most experts recommend that women of childbearing age take a daily vitamin supplement that supplies four-tenths of a milligram (400 micrograms) of folate, the biologically active form of folic acid.

Dr. Bailey noted that in the last revision of the Recommended Dietary Allowances, the daily level of folate was dropped to 180 micrograms, but she and others predict it will be raised back to 400 micrograms at the next revision.

[JEB, June 1995]

Fetal Monitoring
May Not Help Much

ELECTRONIC fetal monitoring during labor and delivery, used with a majority of births in this country, offers little significant benefit to justify its routine use, according to researchers reviewing the practice.

Researchers at the federal Centers for Disease Control and Prevention in Atlanta said a review of the most significant controlled studies of the effectiveness and safety of electronic fetal monitoring indicated that routine use of the procedure had no measurable effect on the death or illness of infants or mothers. But they said electronic monitoring was associated with a higher rate of cesarean deliveries, which increase surgical risks to mothers.

In view of the findings, they said, a review of the widespread practice of electronically monitoring fetal heart rate and contractions during labor is warranted. Electronic monitoring, introduced in the late 1960s, is now used during labor in three out of four pregnancies in the nation, they said, and studies are needed to determine who benefits from this kind of surveillance and who does not.

The researchers, led by Dr. Stephen B. Thacker of the centers' Epidemiology Program Office, reviewed 12 controlled trials of fetal monitoring published from 1966 to 1994. These studies included 58,855 women and 59,324 infants in both low- and high-risk pregnancies from 10 centers in the United States, Europe, Australia and Africa.

Fetal heart rate is a good indicator of stress on the fetus in labor and delivery, experts say. A normal heart rate suggests that the fetus is extracting enough oxygen from the woman's bloodstream through the placenta and umbilical cord. But variations in the heart rate can indicate decreased oxygen in the blood and tissues of the fetus, which can lead to potential damage to the brain, central nervous system and organs. In severe cases, this can result in death.

Most electronic monitoring is done with an ultrasound device attached to a belt put around the woman's abdomen. A computerized component of the device counts and interprets the signals to assess fetal heart rate and the contractions of labor.

Electronic fetal monitoring has been controversial for years, with some women's health groups charging that it was accepted as standard practice before its effectiveness was proven and that it was an unnecessary interference in childbirth, particularly in low-risk pregnancies. Some doctors also say the devices result in unnecessary cesarean sections because they can erroneously indicate that a fetus is in trouble.

The new study, published in the October issue of the journal *Obstetrics and Gynecology,* found that electronic monitoring was not measurably better in spotting distress and indicating that intervention was necessary than the traditional practice of intermittent auscultation. With this method, a nurse or midwife closely monitors the fetal heart rate with a stethoscope. If a problem is detected, the nurse can reposition the woman to relieve pressure that may be restricting the fetus's oxygen or give extra oxygen to the mother to increase the level in her bloodstream.

The American College of Obstetricians and Gynecologists, in guidelines issued in 1988 and revised this summer, recommends monitoring all labor either electronically or with auscultation, but leaves the decision to the woman and her doctor. But a federal health study group in the United States and a similar body in Canada recommend that electronic monitoring be reserved for high-risk pregnancies, such as cases when a woman enters labor prematurely, has a history of problem deliveries or has a complicating disease like diabetes or sickle-cell anemia.

Dr. Frank H. Boehm, a professor of obstetrics and gynecology at Vanderbilt University and a proponent of electronic monitoring, said the method had improved since its introduction and provides some benefits not mentioned in the latest study. The latest generation of monitoring equipment is more reliable and accurate than earlier models, he said, and as doctors and nurses gain more experience with electronic monitoring, they can more accurately interpret the information it provides.

The new study, whose other authors were Dr. Donna F. Stroup and Dr. Herbert B. Peterson, said the only significant benefit of electronic monitoring found was a reduction in neonatal seizures sometimes seen in the first month after birth. Such seizures are associated with about one-half of 1 percent of all births, Dr. Thacker said in an interview. But he said the only two studies done to date on the long-term effects of these seizures on infants indicated that they were minimal and rarely resulted in major adverse conditions, like cerebral palsy.

[WEL, October 1995]

A Drug for Babies at Risk of Being Born Prematurely

RARELY these days does an advance in medical technology end up saving dollars as well as lives. But one such development was enthusiastically endorsed recently by a panel of experts: a simple drug treatment administered to pregnant women to speed the development of fetuses in danger of being born prematurely.

The therapy, involving injections of corticosteroids that cost less than $10 a dose, can save the lives and health of large numbers of babies born prematurely, including many very tiny infants, the panel found after a year of study. The therapy can also reduce the time that such babies spend in hospitals by about one-third, the panel said. The study projected a "conservative" saving of $157 million a year in initial hospital costs alone, even if the treatment is used in only 60 percent of premature births.

Only about 15 percent of high-risk premature babies now receive steroid therapy, the panel said. It recommended that the treatment be used in nearly all pregnancies in danger of ending after 24 and up to 34 weeks of gestation, or 6 weeks before term. The treatment is not recommended for pregnancies more advanced than 34 weeks unless there is reason to believe the baby's lungs are not well developed.

The regimen involves giving pregnant women two intramuscular injections of the corticosteroid drug betamethasone or four injections of a related drug, dexamethasone. The drug crosses the placenta to the fetus, where it speeds maturation of the fetal lungs and blood vessels. Ideally, it should be given 24 hours or more before delivery. But even if given within 24 hours of birth, the treatment is beneficial, the panel said, adding, however, that it is pointless to use it when birth is imminent.

Theoretically, the treatment could benefit at least 287,000 babies who are born six or more weeks prematurely each year in this country. At greatest risk are those born weighing less than about two pounds. Many of those infants die soon after birth and many who survive face severe complications, like respiratory distress syndrome and bleeding in the brain, that require long hospital stays and costly treatments and can result in permanent disabilities.

The panel, which recently held a consensus development conference under the auspices of the National Institutes of Health, said its review of well-designed studies showed that nearly all premature babies could benefit from the treatment, with little or no risk to them or to their mothers. The studies indicated that well-timed steroid therapy could reduce infant deaths by about 40 percent and halve the incidence of respiratory distress syndrome and bleeding in the brain.

Dr. Duane Alexander, director of the National Institute of Child Health and Human Development, estimated that wide use of the therapy could save the lives of 6,000 to 7,000 premature babies each year. And there is also a $3,000 saving for every day that a premature baby does not spend in a neonatal intensive care unit.

The potential benefits of corticosteroid therapy administered to women in danger of giving birth prematurely were first demonstrated as far back as 1972, but the therapy has been very slow to take hold among obstetricians. Doctors were reported to be concerned about its overall effectiveness and the possible risks to both mother and infant. The benefits of corticosteroids were also overshadowed by the advent of pulmonary surfactants administered after birth to protect the lungs of premature infants.

However, the expert panel found that even when a surfactant was used, the steroid therapy had an added benefit, speeding the maturation of lungs prematurely forced to breathe on their own. The panel found no evidence of adverse effects on babies exposed before birth to the steroid therapy. Some of those babies have now been followed for 12 years, with no evidence of harm.

Nor did the panel find that the treatment placed mothers at risk of complications. Even women treated with drugs in an attempt to stop a threatened premature delivery should receive the steroid therapy, the panel said.

The 16-member panel was headed by Dr. Larry C. Gilstrap, a professor in the Department of Obstetrics and Gynecology at the

University of Texas Southwestern Medical Center in Dallas. The consensus conference was jointly sponsored by the National Institute of Child Health and Human Development, the Office of Medical Applications of Research, the National Heart, Lung and Blood Institute and the National Institute of Nursing Research.

[JEB, March 1994]

Using a Midwife

NOT that long ago, midwives were self-trained "grannies" who assisted women who could not afford or get to a doctor or hospital to give birth. But in the last two decades, midwifery in the United States and even more so in Europe has undergone a professional revolution that is bringing high-quality and highly personalized obstetrical and gynecological care to ever-growing numbers of women, pregnant and otherwise.

At the same time, the rise of consumerism and the women's movement have prompted many affluent women to choose to have their babies either outside or within hospitals aided by professionally trained and certified nurse-midwives, with doctors acting as consultants should a complication of pregnancy or delivery arise.

According to a recently issued analysis of 15 studies of births assisted by either certified nurse-midwives or doctors, the babies delivered by the midwives fared as well as or better than those delivered by doctors, even though those cared for by doctors were at no greater risk for a poor outcome. Babies who were considered to be at risk were not included in the study.

The analysis, undertaken by researchers for the American Nurses Association, revealed, perhaps not surprisingly, that the babies delivered by midwives were more likely to be born vaginally without induction of labor, fetal monitoring, forceps delivery or episiotomy (a surgical cut of the vaginal opening).

But midwife-delivered babies, the study found, were also less likely to be born prematurely or with an abnormally low birth weight and tended to have higher scores on the Apgar scale of several signs of a newborn's condition five minutes after birth. Women whose baby's births were assisted by midwives also had shorter hospital stays and were more than twice as likely to breast-feed their babies.

Roxanne Greenstein of New York, the daughter of a doctor, chose to have midwives deliver both her children at St. Luke's–Roosevelt Hospital. "For a healthy young person, it was the most natural way to go," she said in an interview. "The deliveries were very competently handled, and since they took place in a hospital, not at home, I knew there was no danger. Michael, my husband, was very much a part of it all, and the midwives made childbirth feel natural and comfortable for both of us."

Other parents complain about the high-tech atmosphere of many doctor-assisted hospital deliveries, which can strip a woman of her sense of dignity and responsibility and turn childbirth into an event that more closely resembles a medical emergency than a natural occurrence. Even though more than 87 percent of births attended by certified nurse-midwives occur in hospitals, the setting (often the labor room) and the techniques used by midwives tend to be far less clinical.

And for those who worry that they may be getting short shrift if assigned to a nurse-midwife instead of a doctor, a study published a year ago in the *American Journal of Public Health* should provide comfort. Midwives who practice in hospitals serve women who are at higher-than-average risk of birth complications, the study showed. These pregnant women tend to be younger and are more likely to be members of minority groups. They receive less prenatal care than pregnant women in general and are more likely to be unmarried and foreign-born.

Yet the report by Dr. Eugene R. Declercq of Merrimack College in North Andover, Massachusetts, stated, "Judged by birth weight and Apgar score, mothers and babies have distinctly better than average outcomes when births are attended by midwives, either in or out of hospitals."

Although midwives were traditionally self-taught or learned at the elbows of older midwives, modern midwives are nearly all registered nurses who have completed advanced training in gynecology and obstetrics. Those who are certified (known as CNMs) and licensed can practice midwifery in all 50 states. They must first pass a national examination and then attend continuing education programs.

Since 1975, the number of births in hospitals that were attended by certified nurse-midwives has increased sevenfold, from nearly 20,000 to nearly 142,000 in 1990. But this still represents only 3 percent to 4 percent of hospital-based births. Nurse-midwives attend about a third of deliveries at freestanding birth centers. And a growing number of obstetricians in private practice are hiring nurse-midwives to provide continuing care for their patients, as well as to see the women through labor and delivery.

And while midwives have traditionally cared only for pregnant women, today's nurse-midwives are trained to perform a broad range of gynecological services, including Pap smears; breast and pelvic examinations; contraceptive and menopausal counseling; prevention of teenage pregnancy; tests for infections of the vagina,

Choosing a Midwife

The American College of Nurse-Midwives suggests that women interested in using a midwife consult friends for recommendations or ask the college, which offers a directory of certified practitioners. To get the directory, send $9.95 to the college at 1522 K Street N.W., Suite 1000, Washington, DC 20005, or call (202) 289-0171 for the listings for your area.

■ To check on a midwife's qualifications, ask to see the midwife's certificate from the American College of Nurse-Midwives Certification Council Inc., or write the council at 8401 Corporate Drive, Suite 470, Landover, MD 20785; phone (301) 459-1321.

■ Ask the midwife or your medical insurance company, or both, about insurance coverage. Ask specifically about the settings in which the nurse-midwife's services would be covered. This is important because certified nurse-midwives may work in hospitals, birthing centers, health maintenance organizations, public health departments and physicians' offices and clinics; some practice independently, specializing in home births.

■ Determine what arrangements the midwife has for backup by a physician or hospital if there are complications.

■ Discuss the midwife's philosophy on matters like willingness to use anesthesia or analgesia for a delivery, should you want or need it.

■ If necessary, interview two or three midwives before making your selection.

pelvis and urinary tract; assistance with breast-feeding; and screening for menstrual irregularities, premenstrual syndrome and preconception problems. In more than half the states, certified nurse-midwives can independently prescribe medications like antibiotics and birth control pills.

For much of this century obstetricians regarded midwives as poorly trained competitors and backed laws to forbid them to practice in or out of hospitals, but in 1971 the American College of Obstetricians and Gynecologists helped pave the way for the current revolution by officially approving nurse-midwives. Now as third-party payers, including the federal and state governments, look for ways to reduce medical costs, midwives are expected to flourish.

The main problem today is that there are not enough nurse-midwives to meet the growing demand, according to Melissa D. Avery and Georgeanne T. DelGiudice, certified nurse-midwives in Minneapolis. The American College of Nurse-Midwives has called for the training and certification of 10,000 nurse-midwives by the year 2001, which would more than double the number now in practice.

And since the word "midwife" does not mean wife as in man and wife (rather, it is derived from the Middle English for "with woman"), there is no reason for men to exclude themselves from this growing and important profession.

[JEB, April 1993]

Sleeping Position and Sudden Infant Death Syndrome

IN a letter published recently in *The New York Times,* a distressed grandmother complained that she had been banished from babysitting for her six-week-old grandson after the parents caught her putting the baby to sleep on his stomach.

"Don't you know about SIDS?" the equally distressed father hissed, referring to the growing evidence that babies who sleep facedown are at increased risk of sudden infant death syndrome.

She did, and she knew of the current advice to avoid the prone position for all but a relative handful of babies. But she replied that she could not get the baby to settle down on his back and surely both baby and baby-sitter needed some rest.

She is not alone. Despite strong warnings, millions of American infants are being put to sleep in positions or on soft bedding now considered potentially hazardous. According to a recent survey, 45 percent of babies in the United States were still sleeping on their bellies. Many parents and caregivers have not heard the advice, others choose for various reasons to ignore it and still others are too poor to replace equipment now considered unsafe for their infants.

Meanwhile, in several countries where a vast majority of babies are now put to sleep on their backs or sides instead of their bellies, the rate of SIDS, or crib death as it was long called, has dropped by 50 percent or more.

The SIDS rate in this country, about 1 in 800 live births, is much lower than in these other countries, and experts here do not expect as large a drop in unexplained infant deaths if most American babies are switched from the prone position. But they insist that this is one of the simplest measures families and caregivers can adopt to reduce crib deaths, which each year claim the lives of about 6,000 infants in this country.

Many factors have been associated with an increased chance that a seemingly healthy baby might die without any apparent cause. Among them are exposure to tobacco smoke both before and after birth, lack of prenatal care, premature birth, a recent infection and bottle-feeding. The presence of any such factor adds to the risk that a baby sleeping on its stomach will succumb to the syndrome.

Concern about sleeping position, followed by concern about the surfaces babies sleep on, has been growing over the last two decades, but not until 1992 did the American Academy of Pediatrics advise parents to avoid putting babies to sleep on their stomachs. At the time, 75 percent of newborns here were sleeping facedown. Recently, with evidence mounting that prone sleeping was risky, a coalition of federal and private child health organizations began a national education campaign, "Back to Sleep," to persuade parents to put healthy babies to sleep on their backs.

Dr. Bradley T. Thach, neonatologist at Washington University in St. Louis, said, "Throughout history, most babies throughout the world have been placed on their backs, as was the case in the United States up until the 1930s." Then, he said, American experts, including Dr. Benjamin Spock, promoted prone sleeping, believing it would reduce the risk of babies' choking to death or developing aspiration pneumonia if they vomited while asleep. But there is no evidence for this, Dr. Thach said, and in Australia and England, where babies have now been switched to sleeping on their backs, there has been no increase in any cause of infant death, only a sharp decrease in crib death.

There is even a suggestion that babies who sleep on their backs are healthier than belly sleepers. Dr. Marian Willinger, a leading researcher in the field at the National Institute of Child Health and Human Development in Bethesda, Maryland, noted that in the Australian state of Tasmania, where sleep position has been intensely studied since 1988, the switch away from belly sleeping has been associated with a decline in visits to child health clinics, colds and vomiting after feeding.

Complicating the issue of sleep position, however, is the type of material on which the baby sleeps. The Consumer Products Safety Commission recently warned against putting babies to sleep on soft bedding, which the commission's studies indicated could be responsible for as many as 1,800 infant deaths a year. Although bereaved parents have long been reassured that their babies who died of SIDS did not suffocate, in fact many apparently do when sleeping facedown.

Dr. James Kemp, a pediatric pulmonologist at Washington University, has studied how various kinds of bedding materials might smother healthy infants. He has shown that soft bedding, like sheepskins, natural-fiber mattresses and quilts, placed under a baby sleeping on its belly can trap exhaled air and cause the baby to rebreathe it, resulting in a gradual rise in carbon dioxide in the baby's blood.

For various reasons, including defects in the arousal mechanism or damage to the part of the brain that detects rises in carbon dioxide, some babies may fail to wake up in time to take lifesaving breaths that are richer in oxygen, Dr. Willinger explained.

Very young infants lying facedown on a soft surface may be unable to raise or turn their heads enough to breathe fresh air. Dr. Kemp said that 20 percent to 50 percent of SIDS babies die with the nose and mouth sunk into soft bedding. And a new study of 200 SIDS infants in California revealed that while 66 percent had usually slept on the stomach, 80 percent of the victims had been found lying facedown.

Although the jury is still out on the role that prone sleeping may play in SIDS deaths here, there appears to be little reason not to abandon it for most babies. But there are important exceptions. The pediatrics academy says that premature infants with respiratory tract disease, those with reflux of food between the stomach and esophagus and infants with certain malformations of the upper airway should sleep on their stomachs.

Dr. Kemp said the safest sleeping surface for infants was a firm mattress covered by a tight-fitting sheet. A receiving blanket or quilt could be placed on top of the baby, but nothing should be placed underneath, he advised, nor should there be pillows or soft toys in the baby's bed.

When a baby is put to sleep away from home, an infant seat or portable crib is preferable to a quilt or rug. Also, babies should not sleep in bed with an adult or older child. Some studies have found a large increase in the risk of the syndrome among babies who sleep in their parents' bed, especially if one or both parents smoke.

The peak age for SIDS is from two to four months. After about five months, it may make no difference how babies are put to sleep, since many then learn to flip over on their own, Dr. Willinger observed.

The national "Back to Sleep" information campaign has established a toll-free number, (800) 505-CRIB (505-2742), for those seeking more information on sleeping positions for infants or free brochures developed for the campaign.

Several devices are now on the market to help keep infants sleeping on their sides, and parents who have used them for newborns report that they work. The products include Baby Sleep-EZ by Basic Comfort, Inc., of Denver and Prop-A-Bye Baby by DEX Products of Danville, California.

However, an unpublished study from New Zealand suggested that sleeping on the side is not as safe as sleeping on the back, and Dr. Kemp noted that the devices are made of foam, a soft material that he would rather not see in a baby's bed. Also, the pediatrics academy does not recommend putting babies to sleep on their sides.

[JEB, March 1995]

The Benefits of Breast-Feeding

BREAST is Best." This slogan promoting breast-feeding has been widely publicized. But the practice, which peaked among American mothers in 1982 after a decades-long decline, is far from commonplace.

According to periodic surveys, women who are young and unemployed, who live on low incomes and who lack a college education are the least likely to attempt breast-feeding and, if they do try, are the most likely to abandon it before their babies are six months old. Babies of such mothers face the highest risk of health problems that could best be countered by starting life on breast milk.

Even among immigrant mothers from countries where breast-feeding is nearly universal (and even when these same mothers nursed babies born when they were still living in their native land), their American-born babies are often bottle-fed.

These facts are especially discouraging to researchers who continue to uncover health-saving and possibly lifesaving benefits of mother's milk to the newborn child. But a 10-year slide in breast-feeding may be reversing, according to national surveys of tens of thousands of new mothers by Ross Laboratories, a baby formula company. In 1992, the last year for which data have been released, 53.9 percent of babies were breast-fed in the hospital and 20.1 percent were still being nursed at six months of age. The comparable figures in 1990 were 51.5 percent in the hospital and 19 percent at six months, significantly lower than in 1982, when breast-feeding in the hospital peaked at 61.9 percent. A preview of the 1993 data indicates that breast-feeding is continuing to regain popularity.

Yet the practice still lags among less affluent and less educated women, whose babies, for many reasons, including low vaccination rates and greater exposure to environmental contaminants like cigarette smoke, especially need the nutrients and protection against disease that mother's milk bestows. And many affluent and well-educated mothers continue to choose bottle-feeding for reasons of convenience or, for lack of support, give up nursing as soon as any difficulty arises.

The United States is still far from the goal established in 1990 by the Department of Health and Human Services that by 2000, 75 percent of mothers would nurse their babies at least in early infancy and 50 percent would continue to nurse until their babies are five or six months old.

In *Patient Care,* a magazine for physicians, Dr. Carole A. Stashwick, a pediatrician at Dartmouth Medical School, recently listed these reasons for the waning of breast-feeding: less emphasis on its benefits in lay publications; inadequate attention to nursing by professionals involved in newborn care; direct marketing of infant formulas to mothers; the common practice of hospitals' sending new mothers home with a sample of formula; and a general failure of modern society to pass on breast-feeding skills to new mothers, most of whose own mothers and grandmothers had chosen the bottle over the breast.

Most people assume, incorrectly, that breast-feeding comes naturally. Actually, it is a learned skill for both the mother and her infant. Although babies are born with a "rooting" tendency to nuzzle the breast and with an instinct to suck, neither baby nor mother knows instinctively how to breast-feed, Dr. Stashwick wrote. First-time mothers often need help in getting started with breast-feeding, but nowadays most leave the hospital within two days of delivery, before the mother's milk even comes in. Once they are home, there is no one to help when breast-feeding fails to go smoothly.

The first weeks of nursing can be a challenge. Some mothers become anxious when their babies cry a lot or seem to reject the breast or lose too much weight. Some mothers' nipples become cracked or sore, and others lack support for breast-feeding from their babies' fathers or grandparents.

As one 33-year-old first-time mother put it: "Nursing seemed to be going well in the hospital, but as soon as we got home, the baby refused the breast. She began crying incessantly and wouldn't even sleep. She was obviously hungry but still refused to nurse. So I gave up, and as soon as I gave her a bottle, she was happy."

The mother said that at the hospital, "three different people gave me conflicting advice: hold the baby this way, hold her that way, feed on demand, feed on a schedule, never give her a bottle, supplement with formula if she still seems hungry."

Then, too, there are important socioeconomic obstacles. Many new mothers must return to work—sometimes within weeks and often within three months of the birth—and decide, again mistakenly, that there is no point in nursing for so short a time. And in the case of mothers receiving federal aid under the Special Supplemental Food Program for Women, Infants and Children (WIC), infant formula is provided for those who bottle-feed, and additional foods but no monetary supplement are offered to those who nurse. In Quebec, to encourage breast-feeding, the comparable program now pays a cash allowance of $37.50 a month to mothers who breast-feed.

Breast-feeding specialists are founts of helpful advice. For example, it helps to change the baby's position from one feeding to another to ensure that milk is drained from all areas of the breast. Besides the traditional cradling position, try a football hold, with the baby tucked under one arm so she approaches the breast from the side, or try nursing lying down face to face with the baby.

Be sure that the baby latches onto the nipple properly. The entire nipple and most of the areola (the surrounding dark area) should be in the baby's mouth and the baby's lips should spread out around it. Women with flat or inverted nipples can wear plastic breast shields called "Swedish milk cups" for several hours a day at the end of pregnancy and at the start of nursing to help pull out the nipple.

As the baby begins to suck, the milk is "let down" from the breast ducts into the nipple. (Often some milk drips from the opposite breast at this time.) The baby's gulping noises are an indication that milk is being swallowed. During the first days of nursing, the mother often feels brief uterine contractions when the baby begins sucking.

In a society accustomed to precise measurements, many mothers who breast-feed worry about whether their babies are getting enough to eat. A baby will mostly empty a breast in about 10 minutes of nearly continuous sucking. Those who fall asleep after a few minutes of nursing need to be awakened and kept stimulated (for example, by tapping the feet) until they have eaten enough. To maintain a good milk supply and to ensure that the baby is getting enough, newborns should be nursed every two to three hours.

Success at nursing can be measured by whether the baby seems content afterward, produces at least six wet diapers and several fairly liquid, mustard-colored stools each day and wakes up at least every four hours around the clock to be fed. A baby who is gaining

Sources of Support

Breast-feeding is most likely to succeed when both mother and father are well informed. Many hospitals now have lactation specialists on staff; be sure to leave the hospital with a phone number to call if nursing difficulties begin at home. The hospital specialist may also be able to refer you to a local breast-feeding support group. Other useful resources include the following:

■ La Leche League International, 9616 Minneapolis Ave., Franklin Park, IL 60131; phone (800) LA LECHE (525-3243) or (708) 455-7730.

■ International Childbirth Education Association, Box 20048, Minneapolis, MN 55420; phone (612) 854-8660.

■ Lact-Aid International, Inc., Box 1066, Athens, TN 37371; phone (615) 744-9090.

weight normally is well fed, but experts advise against home baby scales, which are often inaccurate and can be anxiety-provoking instead of reassuring.

[JEB, April 1994]

The Value of Breast Milk

I N the decades since Dr. Paul Gyorgy bucked the tide of bottle-feeding more than 70 years ago by saying "Human milk is for the human infant; cow's milk is for the calf," scientists have discovered dozens of facts to substantiate his instinctive conclusion. The discoveries continue, indicating that no formula, no matter how intelligently devised, comes close to the known and potential benefits of nursing.

In the last few years, several studies have linked a woman's breast-feeding with lower risks of ovarian cancer and premenopausal breast cancer. In addition, it has long been known that the hormones of lactation help the uterus contract to prepregnancy size and help to space pregnancies by suppressing ovulation.

But it is the nursing infant who stands to gain the most from consuming its mother's high-fat, cholesterol-rich, antibody-laden milk. It has long been known that breast-fed infants have about one-fourth the risk of developing serious respiratory and gastrointestinal illnesses and one-tenth the risk of being hospitalized with a life-threatening bacterial infection.

And scores of studies have shown that the nutrient mix of mother's milk was tailored by evolution to provide exactly the right proportion and form of calories and essential nutrients to sustain a normal pace of growth. Although bottle-fed babies tend to gain weight faster, pediatric nutritionists, noting that obese adults are more likely to have been bottle-fed, question the wisdom of a too-rapid growth rate in early infancy.

In one of the newest findings, Dr. Joyce A. Nettleton, a nutritionist with the Institute of Food Technologists in Chicago, noted recently that human milk—but not infant formula—contains an omega-3 fatty acid, DHA, that is highly concentrated in the brain and retina. Studies in monkeys have shown that a deficit of this fatty acid in infancy results in "functional changes that may be irreversible," Dr. Nettleton reported in the *Journal of the American Dietetic Association*.

A woman can enrich her milk with DHA by consuming fish or shellfish two or more times a week before and after childbirth.

Two years ago, researchers at the Johns Hopkins Children's Center in Baltimore discovered that a protein called mucin in human milk suppresses the reproduction of rotavirus, a major cause of infant diarrhea.

Researchers are now exploring the developmental value of a host of bioactive compounds in human milk, from epidermal growth factor and various gastrointestinal peptides to prostaglandins and prolactin. For example, epidermal growth factor enhances maturation of the digestive and respiratory tracts and may largely account for the lower risk of life-threatening intestinal and respiratory disease in premature infants fed human milk.

Prolactin, for another example, appears to influence maturation of lymphocytes, white blood cells that fight infection. Premature infants with low levels of prolactin in their blood were found to spend more time on respirators and to grow more slowly.

In an interview, Lorie A. Ellis and Dr. Mary Frances Picciano of Pennsylvania State University said that most of these bioactive compounds are not present in soy-based formulas and are present only in "very low or undetectable concentrations in those based on cow's milk."

[JEB, April 1994]

Thumb Sucking and Pacifiers

THUMBS are out of style. Modern babies suck on pacifiers, now also a fashion accessory for teenagers, who wear them in psychedelic colors around their necks and sometimes actually put them into their mouths.

Sucking is an instinct essential to the survival of all mammals, which as newborns get all their sustenance by nursing. Human babies have been observed on sonograms to suck their thumbs even before they are born. But for most babies, the amount of sucking they do at the breast or on a bottle is not enough to satisfy the desire to suck. Sucking quickly becomes associated with satiation and security.

Little wonder that so many babies and young children turn to nonnutritive sucking whenever life seems uncertain or uncomfortable. In many ways, the oral habits pursued by many adults, especially smoking, nibbling and chewing gum, are simply an extension of the sucking reflex.

Left to their own devices, at least half of babies will suck on their thumbs or fingers for varying amounts of time when awake and asleep. The sucking impulse typically begins to fade between the ages of three and six months, but by then thumb or finger sucking can become habitual for babies whenever they feel insecure, tired, stressed or hungry.

Eventually, nearly all thumb suckers stop. But the numbers remain high in preschool years. About 40 percent of toddlers from one to three years old still suck their thumbs or fingers. A third of three-to-five-year-olds suck their thumbs, and only one in four five-year-olds still sucks a thumb or finger for some part of the day. Some children reared as infants on a pacifier switch to a thumb, but most seem not to.

But once children enter kindergarten or first grade, pressure is on them to stop lest they get teased or ostracized by their peers. A study of 40 first-graders in Nebraska, published in April 1993 in the journal *Pediatrics*, confirmed that children who suck their thumbs are considered by their peers to be less intelligent, happy, and likable and less desirable as a friend or neighbor. It is no surprise that most school-age thumb suckers try to give up the habit.

Parental concerns may start in the child's infancy, although non-nutritive sucking in the early months is natural and harmless. Parents worry not just about how sucking looks but also that the habit will distort the shape of their baby's mouth and cause teeth to grow improperly, possibly portending thousands of dollars' worth of orthodontic correction.

Enter the pacifier. This rubber or plastic nipple-shaped object has become a fixture obliterating half the face of millions of American infants. If a pacifier is introduced at the age of one or two months, many babies will suck on it instead of their thumbs or fingers. Many parents, unwilling to take the chance that their babies will find pleasure in their thumbs or fingers, introduce the pacifier soon after birth and use it whenever the baby whimpers. Parents may thus inadvertently create a dependency on the pacifier. An infant who depends on a pacifier to fall asleep may cry during the night for someone to retrieve it each time it falls out of the mouth. It should never be tied to a string, because it could choke the baby. Instead, Dr. Benjamin Spock recommends scattering several pacifiers around the crib, within easy reach.

There are two strong arguments in favor of pacifier over thumb. Because it is soft and in some cases specially designed to minimize pressure on mouth structures, the pacifier is less likely to result in distortions like buckteeth. But use of a pacifier is no guarantee of a trouble-free mouth or of preventing thumb sucking.

Parents also have more control over a child's access to a pacifier and can restrict its use or remove it entirely, whereas the thumb and fingers are the child's own to use however the child pleases. In fact, parents who actively try to discourage thumb sucking in preschoolers are likely to find that this approach backfires and becomes a power struggle that the parent inevitably loses.

First, parents should realize that there is nothing abnormal or harmful about thumb or finger sucking in infants and very young children. In fact, as long as the habit is relinquished before the permanent teeth begin to emerge at about age six, it rarely has a significant influence on mouth structures or tooth positions.

Parents can passively discourage thumb sucking in infants by trying to respond to their true needs. Is the baby hungry, tired, colicky, wet or simply in need of warmth and cuddling? Babies can also be nursed longer or given a water bottle to suck on between feedings or before sleep.

In their book *Good Kids/Bad Habits* (Prince Paperbacks, $6), Dr. Charles E. Schaefer, a psychologist at Fairleigh Dickinson University, and Theresa Foy DiGeronimo suggest that thumb-sucking toddlers be gently guided to alternative activities that occupy their hands and keep them involved. For preschoolers, parents can record the circumstances that trigger thumb or finger sucking, then respond more directly to the child's need; for example, by feeding a hungry child or cuddling a fearful one. Parents might also express their disapproval of sucking and praise preschoolers when they refrain from sucking.

But five-year-olds who still suck their thumbs or fingers usually need a more formal habit-breaking program. Most important is that the child must want to relinquish the habit. In her widely praised book *David Decides* (Reading Matters, $9.95), Dr. Susan M. Heitler, a clinical psychologist, provides a detailed guide for parents and a motivating story for youngsters.

Dr. Heitler and Dr. Schaefer both suggest a behavior modification program in which the child is made fully aware of the circumstances that lead to sucking, is helped to make behavior changes (like restricting activities that touch off the behavior, like watching television) and receives small incremental rewards for achieving the desired behavior of not sucking. Both psychologists suggest keeping a chart to mark the child's progress and caution against reproaching the child for backsliding. Parental attention must be focused on the desired behavior, with at most a gentle reminder when the child slips.

[JEB, June 1993]

Stages of Life—Childhood

THE VULNERABLE YEARS

For most of history childhood has been a mortally dangerous time in the human life cycle, and in many parts of the world it still is. In more fortunate countries, the ancient killers have been vanquished by vaccines, clean water and good nutrition.

Still, there are many secondary menaces that lurk along the passage from birth to adulthood. Vaccines are available but, in part because of parents' complacency, many American children do not receive the recommended shots during their preschool years.

Fluoride has proved a magnificent antidote to children's cavities, but here too parents' complacency has allowed tooth decay to creep back; even fluoride cannot fight floods of sugar and dental neglect.

Very young children can be wounded by unseen hazards, such as lead in the environment, and by socially inflicted ones such as pain, which some doctors are strangely reluctant to recognize and treat.

As children grow in confidence and stature, leaving the vulnerable years behind, they start to think of themselves as untouchable. When they neglect the steps to protect their bodies in play and organized sports, a parent's cautions can help avert strains and accidents.

Childhood is for most a time of natural good health, but the following articles show how much parents can contribute in providing the safest possible environment.

Vaccines and Childhood Killers

MOST parents of infants and preschoolers have no memory of summers when children were kept out of swimming pools for fear that they would catch polio. Indeed, a 1993 Gallup poll shows that nearly half of parents today are unaware that polio is a contagious disease. Nor do they know firsthand the terrors of breath-robbing whooping cough, the often fatal paralysis of tetanus or the sometimes fatal throat infection caused by diphtheria. Many do not know that measles can cause life-threatening encephalitis and mental retardation. Nearly all parents of young children today grew up when these serious infectious diseases were prevented by vaccines, which have saved more young lives than any public health measure since the purification of public water supplies.

This lack of firsthand experience has led to a frightening complacency about protecting infants and toddlers against the dangerous diseases that can be prevented by vaccines. While more than 95 percent of children are fully immunized by the time they enter school, a requirement in all 50 states, the protection of infants and toddlers is woefully inadequate.

Only 56 percent of children under age two get the immunizations recommended by public health officials and the American Academy of Pediatrics. Yet preschool children are most susceptible to these diseases. Although immunization rates are low among children from poor families, who depend on government-financed health care, a study among the employees of Johnson & Johnson, all of whom have good medical insurance, found that middle-class families are also often delinquent in immunizing infants and toddlers. As a result, the United States ranks 70th worldwide in preschool immunization rates.

While Washington has zeroed in on vaccines' cost, which has risen 10-fold in the last decade, as the reason so many youngsters are inadequately protected, experts cite other factors as equally or even more significant.

Perhaps most important is the failure of parents to appreciate the potential seriousness of the diseases. In the mid-1950s, when the Salk polio vaccine was first available, few parents needed prodding to present their children for the long-awaited shots. But the Gallup survey, reported recently on a poll of 1,000 parents of children under five, found that 47 percent did not know that polio is contagious, 36 percent did not know that measles could be fatal and 44 percent did not know that hemophilus B influenza is the leading cause of potentially fatal childhood meningitis.

Some parents figure that with so many vaccinated, there is no danger to their unvaccinated children because the diseases are rare. But parents who are counting on this so-called herd immunity are also seriously misled. As the measles epidemics of a few years ago sadly demonstrated, even when three-fourths or more of children are immunized, the unprotected ones can still get sick and die.

Some parents resist certain vaccinations because of the fear of side effects, particularly with the pertussis—or whooping cough—vaccine in the well-known DPT (diphtheria, pertussis and tetanus) shots given to infants. Rarely, an infant develops seizures, which can lead to permanent brain damage, following administration of the pertussis vaccine that is in common use in this country, and publicity about this effect has prompted some parents to take their chances with whooping cough. (A new and presumably safer pertussis vaccine is now available.)

To be sure, costs are a serious impediment for many families. Most insurance policies do not cover these costs, which usually include a physician or clinic fee. The cost of the vaccines alone now averages more than $230 in the private sector and more than $112 in the public sector for all the recommended shots. The charges include a congressionally mandated federal excise tax to cover the costs of vaccine-related injuries.

Out-of-pocket immunization costs have driven some middle-class parents to rely on already overburdened public clinics at a time when clinic hours and staff are being curtailed. Inconvenient hours and seemingly endless waits can mean no immunizations for many children whose parents have inflexible work schedules and who must make long trips to a clinic by public transportation.

Doctors also contribute to the problem by not taking advantage of every medical opportunity to check children's immunization status and by being overly conservative about giving vaccines to children with minor respiratory infections. Dr. Georges Peter, former chairman of the pediatrics academy's committee on infectious diseases, maintains that only a moderate or severe illness or allergic sensitivity to a vaccine component should preclude vaccination.

And experts who have studied reactions to the pertussis vaccine say the only children who should not get it are those over seven, those receiving immunosuppressive therapy and those with the following risk factors: a history of convulsions, a neurological disorder like epilepsy, a current fever or a history of a serious DPT reaction (allergic reaction, very high fever, collapse or shock, hours-long persistent crying or unusually high-pitched crying, convulsions or impaired consciousness). Physicians now recommend acetaminophen to prevent high fever after DPT shots.

Under the newest recommendations, children should be getting their shots at about 2, 4, 6 and 15 months, with some booster shots later. Included are the two newest vaccines, one for hepatitis B, which should be given in one shot at birth, another at 1 to 2 months and a third at 6 to 18 months; and four shots for hemophilus influenza (Hib), starting at 2 months. Then come the old standbys: DPT shots should be given in four shots, starting at 2 months; the oral polio vaccine should be given in three doses, starting at 2 months; and the combined mumps, measles and rubella (MMR) vaccine should be given at 15 months. The Hib vaccine has now been combined with DPT to reduce the number of shots.

Why is this early start so important? In 1992, according to data from the United States Public Health Service, more than 2,000 cases of measles, more than 2,000 cases of mumps and more than 3,000 cases of whooping cough afflicted American children; many of the victims were incompletely immunized toddlers.

In the coming years, the cost of some vaccines is expected to drop. To encourage more vaccinations than ever, access to the clinics providing immunizations will have to improve greatly, with more staff and extended hours, perhaps evenings, weekends and holidays. New vaccines and improved ways to administer old ones are also expected. Meanwhile, parents must assume the primary responsibility for getting their preschoolers fully immunized.

[JEB, August 1993]

Whooping Cough Vaccine Deemed Necessary and Safe

IN a new study that may help diminish a long-standing dispute about the safety of the standard vaccine against whooping cough, researchers have found that the vaccine does not lead to increased risk of serious neurological illness.

The federally financed study, the largest of its kind in the United States, involved 218,000 children up to 24 months old in Oregon and Washington who were studied for a one-year period, beginning August 1, 1987.

The dispute centers on whether the vaccine, which is injected into millions of children around the world, increases the risk of permanent brain damage. The vaccine for whooping cough, also known as pertussis, is usually given in combination with immunizations against diphtheria and tetanus as DPT shots.

All major vaccine advisory groups in the United States, Canada and Britain have concluded that the benefits of protection against whooping cough, a bacterial infection, clearly outweigh the potential risks of the vaccine. The findings from the new study provide reassuring evidence that the vaccine is safe and support current recommendations, the authors write in a recent issue of *The Journal of the American Medical Association*.

Whooping cough was once a common disease of children, reaching a peak reported incidence of 265,269 cases in 1934. The infection used to kill 5 of every 1,000 children born in the United States. Within 10 days of exposure to the bacterium that causes whooping cough, a child comes down with sneezing, red eyes and a mild cough that lasts about a week. The child may then develop prolonged paroxysms of violent coughing. As the child gasps for breath and vital oxygen, the face can turn blue. Untreated, the infection can lead to death.

The incidence of whooping cough fell sharply as use of the vaccine became widespread after the 1940s. But in 1976 a British study of all children 2 to 36 months old in Britain suggested the vaccine was responsible for some cases of brain damage that followed inoculation by a few days. After many parents then refused to have their children immunized against whooping cough, outbreaks of the infection followed in several countries, including Britain and Japan. But other researchers criticized the methodology of the British study, and smaller studies later found no increased risk of brain damage.

The new study was not intended to give a definitive answer to the question of whether whooping cough vaccine causes neurological illness, said the team from the Centers for Disease Control and Prevention—a federal agency in Atlanta—and the University of Washington in Seattle. It would take a study several times larger and would be extremely expensive to rule out any possibility of an association between vaccination and brain damage, the researchers said. But even a larger study, they said, might not settle the dispute because of the rarity of adverse effects.

"It is reassuring that if there is any risk associated with the vaccine, its absolute magnitude is so low that it cannot be detected in a study of this size," said Dr. James L. Gale of the University of Washington, who headed the team of researchers.

His team found 424 cases of neurological illness among the 218,000 children studied. The illnesses identified included acute inflammation of the brain and seizures. The conclusion about a lack of increased risk of serious neurological illness was reached after the researchers matched each of these cases with two children of the same sex who were born in the same county on the same date.

[LKA, January 1994]

Making Sure That Children Play Safely

EVERY day millions of young people participate in sports like baseball, football, basketball and soccer and in activities like skating, cycling, swimming and running. And every day, several thousand are treated in emergency rooms for sports-related injuries.

While accidents can happen to anyone, even the most cautious and best prepared, all too often safety issues are ignored by children, their parents and their coaches. As a result, activities that should be fun, stimulating and health-promoting can readily become the opposite.

Distressed by the more than 775,000 hospital visits each year by children aged 5 through 14 with sports injuries, orthopedic and sports medicine specialists have combined forces to promote safety measures for young athletes. The American Academy of Orthopaedic Surgeons, the Pediatric Orthopaedic Society of North America, the Canadian Orthopaedic Association and the American Academy of Sports Medicine have begun a "Play It Safe" campaign, with safety and exercise guidelines that should be adopted by every youthful participant, parent and coach.

Adults need to be reminded that children are not miniature adults. Their bones, muscles, tendons and ligaments are still growing and are weaker than an adult's. Developing bodies are more vulnerable to injury. What may be just a bruise or sprain in an adult can be a serious injury in a child and result in impaired bone growth. Children are also more susceptible to the effects of heat and dehydration.

They are, by definition, mentally and emotionally immature. Under the stress of competition or pressure from parents and coaches, they often fail to heed warning signs like pain or fatigue. Many suffer overuse injuries because they do not know when to stop or they are afraid they will disappoint adults.

Youngsters often think of themselves as invulnerable, and many shun wearing protective equipment. And lacking an adult's experience and judgment, they are more likely to ignore rules and take undue risks.

Children do not grow or develop at the same rate, but in organizing sports activities for children, parents and coaches typically group them by chronological age rather than by physical size and skill level. As a result, children who are smaller or less skilled are sometimes placed at a serious disadvantage, especially in contact sports.

When it comes to children's sports, parental responsibility goes beyond being a cheering squad for Little Leaguers. That responsibility includes ensuring that children are physically prepared and properly equipped to participate safely, that coaches have appropriate qualifications and sensible attitudes, that equipment and facilities are well maintained and that children know and follow the rules of the game. Parents should also inform coaches of any physical limitations or health problems a child may have, like asthma or diabetes, that might be affected by exercise.

The following guidelines will help children avoid injury:

- *Warm up and stretch.* Children's tendons, ligaments and muscles are even more vulnerable than an adult's to injuries from the stresses of physical activities. Every game and practice session, even a casual game of street hockey, should be preceded by warm-up exercises and stretches that reduce the risk of a sprain or strain.

- *Wear protective equipment.* Each sport has its own paraphernalia. For baseball, that includes wearing a batting helmet when at bat, waiting to bat or running the bases; wearing molded, cleated baseball shoes (not steel spikes); and preferably using the new, softer baseballs. The outfit for in-line skating should include wrist guards, hard-shell knee and elbow pads and a helmet. A bicycle helmet, which should always be worn when cycling, is fine protection for skaters. Soccer players should wear shin guards and shoes with molded cleats or a ribbed sole (save screw-in cleats for wet fields with high grass). Goals should be well padded and securely posted. On wet fields, synthetic nonabsorbent balls should be used. Children who wear glasses should have a pair with shatterproof lenses and sturdy

Stretching Young Muscles

The American Academy of Orthopaedic Surgeons has developed stretching exercises for young people to use before participating in athletics.
First warm up, by running in place, for instance. Then do the exercises, which should take no longer than 10 minutes

**Seat
Straddle
Lotus**

Place soles of feet together and drop knees toward floor. Place forearms on inside of knees and push knees to the ground. Lean forward, bringing chin to feet. Hold for five seconds. Repeat three to six times.

Seat Side Straddle

With legs spread, place both hands on same ankle. Bring chin to knee, keeping leg straight. Hold for five seconds. Repeat three to six times. Repeat on opposite leg.

**Seat
Stretch**

Sit with legs together, feet flexed, hands on ankles. Bring chin to knees. Hold for five seconds. Repeat three to six times.

**Lying
Quad
Stretch**

Lie on back with one leg straight, the other leg with hip turned in and knee bent. Press knee to floor. Hold for five seconds. Repeat three to six times.

Knees to Chest

Lie on back with knees bent. Grasp tops of knees and bring them out toward the armpits, rocking gently. Hold for five seconds. Repeat three to five times.

Foward Lunges

Kneel on left leg, and place right leg forward at a right angle. Lunge forward, keeping the back straight. Hold for five seconds. Repeat three to six times. Repeat on opposite leg.

Crossover

Stand with legs crossed. Keep feet close together and legs straight. Touch toes. Hold for five seconds. Repeat three to six times. Repeat with opposite leg.

Standing Quad Stretch

While standing against a support, pull foot to buttocks. Hold for five seconds. Repeat three to six times.

Side Lunges

Stand with legs apart, and bend the left knee while leaning to the left. Keep the back and the right leg straight. Hold for five seconds. Repeat three to six times. Repeat on opposite leg.

frames. Tennis players should wear protective sports glasses, and swimmers should wear goggles.

- *Learn basic skills and proper techniques.* These not only make participation in sports safer, they also make it more enjoyable. A skater who does not know how to slow down and stop is an accident waiting to happen. Cyclists should know how to handle wet or sandy surfaces. Participants in field sports should know how to adapt to wet or muddy surfaces. Children who become pitchers should avoid sidearm pitching—it can severely damage tissues in the elbow—and should be limited to throwing no more than 70 overhand pitches in a game and 40 pitches in a practice session. Tennis players, too, should learn proper strokes to reduce the risk of tennis elbow, a painful tendinitis.

- *Maintain a healthy attitude.* The value of participation in sports includes reaping the physical and emotional rewards of exercise, fostering coordination and cooperation and releasing the excess energy of childhood in a healthful and socially acceptable way. Parents and coaches who emphasize winning at all costs place children at serious emotional and physical risk, prompting some to continue playing when they are injured and causing mental anguish if they lose. Dr. Michael J. Goldberg, a pediatric orthopedic surgeon at Tufts School of Medicine in Boston, says that parents and improperly trained coaches who insist that winning is what counts are practicing "sports abuse," which he considers a form of child abuse.

- *Do not work or play through pain.* Exercise-induced muscle soreness should disappear after two days; if any sports-related pain persists beyond that, the child should see a doctor.

- *Protect against environmental assaults.* Children face a greater risk than adults do of suffering heatstroke and dehydration. Children and adults alike should drink lots of water during games and practices. It is best to start out well hydrated by drinking one or two eight-ounce glasses of water before starting the activity and half a glass every 20 to 30 minutes during exercise. If there is no nearby fountain, provide the child with a quart-size water bottle (or two). For outdoor activities in the sun, sunscreens and a hat are a must. Sunglasses or tinted goggles are also helpful.

For a free copy of the "Play It Safe" brochure, send a stamped, self-addressed business-size envelope to Play It Safe, American Academy of Orthopaedic Surgeons, P. O. Box 1998, Des Plaines, IL 60017, or call the academy at (800) 824-BONE (824-2663).

[JEB, May 1995]

Fluoridation Does Not Justify Complacency

MANY adults in this country are justifiably envious of young people, who grew up drinking fluoridated water, using fluoride toothpastes and rinses and having sealants applied to protect the chewing surfaces of their teeth.

Children and young adults today have far fewer cavities than members of the prefluoride generation, many of whom spent a significant part of childhood in dentists' offices and now spend a significant part of their incomes trying to hang on to teeth that have rotted to the roots. Indeed, no less a source than the National Institute of Dental Research has repeatedly rejoiced in the findings of a 1986–87 survey of oral health among schoolchildren. Half of the nation's schoolchildren have never had a cavity, the federal agency concluded.

But is this really true? And is this proudly proclaimed finding prompting parents and health care agencies to overlook the real and often serious dental needs of millions of American children?

Two professionals at the Harvard School of Dental Medicine, Dr. Burton L. Edelstein and Dr. Chester W. Douglass, maintain that the 50-percent-cavity-free claim is a myth derived by ignoring decay in baby, or primary, teeth and by averaging the decay in permanent teeth among children from 5 to 17 years old. If decay in primary teeth is included, these experts report, 42 percent of kindergartners have been affected by tooth decay, half of 7-year-olds have had at least one decayed tooth and children younger than 9 have an average of nearly four decayed or filled tooth surfaces.

And if the progress of decay is tracked through the childhood years, the Harvard experts say, 84.4 percent rather than 50 percent of the nation's 17-year-olds have had decay in one or more permanent teeth. Only one in six 17-year-olds can legitimately say, "Look, Ma, no cavities."

The 50-percent-caries-free statistic was derived by averaging the decay experience of all children with at least one permanent tooth, from preschoolers who have not had their permanent teeth long enough for them to decay to high school seniors who have had plenty of time for decay to develop. With each passing year of age, "250,000 additional children are afflicted with tooth decay," Dr. Edelstein and Dr. Douglass wrote in *Public Health Reports*.

The 50 percent figure may be breeding complacency about the extent of dental disease in children, which is still major, the Harvard researchers say. They, among many other experts, point out that the problem of tooth decay is almost entirely preventable if parents and society do their jobs right. As Dr. Michael J. Till, a pediatric dentist at the University of Minnesota, put it: "Dental decay is an elective disease. You can choose to have it or not."

Baby teeth that are going to fall out in a few years may seem unimportant. But a decayed baby tooth can spread infection into the permanent tooth that will take its place or into the surrounding dental tissues, resulting in a painful and possibly dangerous abscess as well as feeding and sleeping problems.

Primary teeth help to align the emerging permanent teeth properly; a decayed tooth can change the spacing of teeth and may be lost prematurely. This, in turn, can interfere with speech and cause permanent teeth to come in crooked, necessitating costly orthodontic work later on.

A major cause of decay in primary teeth is nursing bottle syndrome: rampant decay on the tongue side of the front teeth caused by the pooling of milk or juice in the mouths of infants and toddlers who fall asleep with a bottle. Despite widespread warnings about this problem dating back to the early 1970s, pediatric dentists have noted a recent increase in nursing bottle syndrome. Especially at risk are children from low-income families. For example, about a third of children in Head Start programs in the Southwest have the syndrome, and more than half of Navajo children have decayed front teeth before their third birthday.

Dr. Till cautions that a bottle of milk or juice should not be used as a pacifier and that unless the bottle is filled with plain water, babies and toddlers should not be given a bottle at bedtime or naptime.

With regard to solid foods, many parents today try hard to avoid cultivating a child's sweet tooth. But parents who think that their children's teeth are safe because the youngsters only rarely eat sweets are sadly mistaken. While sugars of all kinds, including honey and the "natural" sugars in dried fruits, are the favored foods of decay-causing bacteria, sugar-coated and unsweetened carbohydrates, especially those that stick to tooth surfaces, are also a problem. Children who snack between meals on dry cereals, pretzels, crackers or bagels are also providing fodder for decay-causing bacteria.

Children need not be denied sweets, but these are best given as dessert with meals, after which the teeth should be brushed. Sweets that stick to the teeth are most damaging; liquid sweets are less of a problem. Preferable snacks include fresh fruits and vegetables, dairy products, popcorn, nuts, unsweetened peanut butter and potato and other vegetable chips.

To maximize resistance to decay, every child needs dietary fluorides. Only about half the population has a fluoridated water supply, and many children who consume well water do not benefit from this public health measure. If the household water does not have adequate amounts of fluoride, babies should be given supplements of the mineral starting at birth, with the amount tailored to the level of natural fluoride in the water, Dr. Till said.

Fluorides are most effective in preventing decay on the smooth surfaces of the teeth, according to Dr. Philip R. Lee and Dr. Robert J. Collins of the United States Public Health Service. As a result, most of the decay in children's teeth now affects the grooved surfaces; this can be prevented by the use of dental sealants. Together, fluorides and sealants have the potential to eliminate dental caries as a public health problem, these experts say. Yet sealants, which should be applied as soon as the permanent teeth start coming in, are still underused.

And even the most diligent parents are often neglectful about cleaning a baby's mouth, which collects decay-promoting plaque just as the mouths of adults do. Start by wiping an infant's gums and first teeth regularly with a gauze pad. As soon as the baby has several teeth, start brushing them daily with a soft brush. Once a child has two teeth that make contact, they should be flossed daily as well. Because young children lack the needed dexterity, parents should be the primary cleaners of children's teeth until the age of seven, eight or nine. After that, parents should supervise the child's own efforts.

Finally, children should start seeing the dentist regularly no later than the age of two, with visits every six months.

[JEB, February, 1996]

Children and Low-Fat Diets

CHILDREN with high cholesterol levels can safely be placed on low-fat diets to reduce their risk of future heart disease, a new study shows. Over a three-year period, children in the study lowered their blood cholesterol levels without interfering with their growth, nutritional status or emotional well-being.

The study, reported in a recent issue of *The Journal of the American Medical Association,* is the first large, controlled clinical trial to examine the benefits and possible risks of a cholesterol-lowering diet among prepubertal children. Since such children are in a phase of rapid growth, there has been considerable concern that limiting their diet might somehow interfere with normal physical and psychological development.

The children, 636 elementary school pupils from six regions, were divided into two groups, in one of which the children were encouraged to eat less total fat, less saturated fat and less cholesterol than they normally would. Over a three-year period, those in the group that was given intensive dietary guidance reduced their total cholesterol levels by about 3.5 milligrams more than the comparison group of children who received the usual medical care.

Although the decline was not large, the researchers say they believe that even small decreases in the level of harmful cholesterol during childhood could have a significant effect on the chances of suffering a heart attack years later. And, they say, small changes in cholesterol levels in the population at large could save thousands of lives that might otherwise be lost to premature cardiovascular disease.

Moreover, the decline in cholesterol levels that the researchers observed among the study's participants represented an average among all the children in the intervention group, about a third of whom are believed not to have followed the dietary advice and another third of whom made only about half the recommended changes.

"This is probably what we can expect from the way life is for children in this country," said Dr. Ronald M. Lauer, the study's director. Dr. Lauer, a professor of pediatrics and preventive medicine at the University of Iowa in Iowa City, noted that "other forces play on children than the forces we place on them," adding, "We could do a lot better if the forces within our society improved, such as the offerings in school lunch programs and peer pressures about where to eat."

Dr. Russell V. Luepker, head of epidemiology at the University of Minnesota School of Public Health in Minneapolis, who wrote an editorial applauding the study's findings, said in an interview: "It's difficult enough to get adults to adhere to a cholesterol-lowering diet. Kids are a particular challenge, especially at an age when they have more free choice. They have allowances, and they do what their friends do."

The goal for those in the intervention group was to limit their total dietary fat to 28 percent of calories, saturated fat to less than 8 percent of calories and polyunsaturated fat to no more than 9 percent of daily calories. In addition, the children were supposed to limit their cholesterol intake to less than 75 milligrams for every 1,000 calories they consumed, as long as they did not go above 150 milligrams a day. These levels are about a third lower than the amount of fats and cholesterol normally consumed by children in the United States.

If the diet were stricter, Dr. Luepker said, it probably would result in a greater reduction in blood cholesterol. But there is a trade-off: "The lower in fat the diet becomes, the poorer the adherence is likely to be."

All the study's participants were drawn from an initial population of 44,000 prepubertal schoolchildren whose blood cholesterol levels were tested. Those found to be in the upper 25 percent of cholesterol readings but below the top 2 percent were selected for possible participation in the study. The researchers excluded certain children, among them those already on special diets or taking medication that might affect their growth or cholesterol level. The final participants were randomly assigned to either the intervention group or a comparison group that was given only a booklet on healthful eating.

The intervention included frequent group sessions at which the children and their families were taught about the sources and effects of dietary fat, especially saturated fat and cholesterol. The intervention group was also given guidance in shopping, reading labels and dining out healthfully.

In addition, at family sessions with nutrition counselors, individual food preferences were considered and families were taught how to select and prepare foods differently to curb dietary fat and cholesterol.

The researchers intend to follow the study's participants until the children are 18 to assess their final growth and development.

[JEB, March 1995]

How to Safeguard Children from Lead Exposure

DESPITE growing concern about the damaging effects of even low lead levels on the brains of young children, millions of American infants, toddlers and preschoolers continue to live and play in environments that are seriously contaminated with lead. And despite national recommendations that every preschool child be tested annually for lead, federal public health officials say most young children, including those most heavily exposed to lead, have not been tested even once to see if their bodies are harboring dangerous amounts.

Many affluent parents are unduly complacent because they assume incorrectly that lead poisoning is a ghetto disease or that it is not a problem in the area where they live. In poor neighborhoods, where lead is indeed a more serious problem, parents are often preoccupied with challenges that are more obvious or have greater immediacy than the subtle effects of lead on their children's developing brains.

Those who are concerned about lead sometimes remove it in ways that introduce even further hazards. Or they rely on home test kits that may or may not provide an accurate assessment of the amount of lead in their children's environment. Until and unless a federal analysis of these kits suggests otherwise, it is best to use a certified professional to assess the lead hazards in a child's environment. In many areas, the local health department will test homes for lead-containing paint, soil and water or else recommend a professional tester.

Experts say that 75 percent of the lead children take in comes from paint dust in their homes and 20 percent comes from drinking water. A new federal law will soon require that the potential occupants of all housing units built before 1980 be notified of known or possible lead hazards in them. Of the 57 million private dwellings involved, 14 million are believed to contain lead paint in unsound condition and 3.8 million of these deteriorated units are occupied by at least one young child.

If a child is tested more than once and found to have blood lead levels consistently above 10 micrograms per deciliter, the best treatment is to identify the sources of lead in the child's environment and eliminate them. When lead levels exceed 45 micrograms, in addition to environmental cleansing, most lead experts recommend chelation therapy, the use of oral or intravenous drugs that carry lead out of the body.

By far the best solution is to prevent lead accumulation in the first place, said Dr. Sue Binder, a lead expert at the Centers for Disease Control and Prevention in Atlanta.

All homes built before 1980 are likely to contain leaded paint, with the highest concentrations of lead in homes built before 1960. The same goes for day care centers and nursery schools. When such paint flakes or is disturbed during even minor renovations, the home becomes filled with lead-containing dust. Sweeping or vacuuming can spread the dust to furniture, toys and food, from which it is readily transferred to the hands and mouths of infants and toddlers.

Lead paint should be removed only by a licensed abatement contractor, someone trained and certified by the Environmental Protection Agency. When abatement or renovations are undertaken, all pregnant women and small children should stay out of the home until the job is completed. Professional lead removal includes a thorough cleanup with an industrial HEPA, or high-efficiency particle accumulator, a filtered vacuum and a wet mop dipped in a hot-water solution of a phosphate polymer such as powdered dishwasher detergent.

Lead-based paint should be removed with a chemical stripper, not torched, sanded or scraped off. Lead paint that is not flaking does not necessarily have to be removed. The paint can be covered with an impervious material like wallboard, plywood, ceramic tile or vinyl-coated fabric. Regular wallpaper or painting the wall over with a lead-free paint is considered a quick fix, not a permanent solution, according to the New York Public Interest Research Group in its booklet "Get the Lead Out."

If soil surrounding a child's home contains a lot of lead, the soil should be removed and replaced or else covered with grass or a layer of mulch, or planted with shrubbery to discourage children from playing in the area.

Drinking water should be tested for lead. Two samples are needed, one when the cold-water faucet is first turned on after six or more hours of nonuse and the second after the water has been running for one or two minutes. When the first test reveals more than 15 parts per billion of lead or the second has more than 5 parts per billion, either a reverse-osmosis filter or a distiller can be used to remove the lead. There are also inexpensive two-quart countertop units with replaceable carbon and resin filters that remove most of the lead from drinking water.

Never use water from the hot tap for cooking or for mixing drinks or infant formula, and do not soften drinking water; hot water and soft water can leach excessive amounts of lead from pipes. In general, it is wise to let the cold water run for a few minutes before using it for cooking or drinking.

If anyone in the household works at a lead-related job or hobby, children must be protected from the worker's lead-contaminated clothing and shoes. Workers should change clothes and shower before returning home. Hobbies using lead, like stained-glass making, are best pursued outside the home.

The hands of anyone preparing food and of infants, toddlers and preschoolers should be washed often, particularly before handling food. Food and drinks should never be served, cooked or stored in decorative ceramic containers or lead-based crystal. Imported pottery is best checked for lead content before it is used for food. Avoid imported canned foods; the solder may contain lead.

Make sure children consume adequate amounts of iron, calcium and protein; deficiencies in these nutrients increase the absorption of lead.

The American Academy of Pediatrics recommends that all children be routinely screened for lead. Testing should start at about 6 months of age, with repeat tests at 12 and 24 months and every year afterward through 6 years old. Waiting to test for lead when a child is ready to start school is a little late; serious damage may already have occurred, since the developing brain is most vulnerable to lead damage between birth and the age of 3, said Dr. John Rosen, who runs a lead screening and treatment program at Montefiore Hospital in the Bronx.

Dr. Rosen suggests an initial screening on a drop of blood drawn from a finger stick, after the finger is thoroughly cleansed to remove any traces of lead dust. If that level is below 10 micrograms, nothing further needs to be done. If it is higher than 10 micrograms, a second test is done on a small amount of blood taken from a vein.

Even if a child's blood lead level is higher than 10 micrograms, Dr. Rosen says: "This is not something to panic about. Rather, it is something to address in a systematic, productive way."

For further information, "Get the Lead Out," a 54-page handbook for preventing lead poisoning written by Catherine McVay Hughes and Chris Meyer for the New York Public Interest Research Group Fund, can be obtained by sending $7 to NYPIRG Publications, 9 Murray Street, 3rd floor, New York, NY 10007-2272.

The handbook lists two sources of home test kits as reliable, although they are generally not available in stores. Pace Environs Inc. in Scarborough, Ontario, Canada, (800) 359-9000, produces the Frandon Lead Alert kits to test surfaces and drinking water. Lead-check swabs by Hybrivet of Framingham, Massachusetts, (800) 262-LEAD, can be used to test all painted surfaces, ceramics, dishes, crystal, soil and dust.

For a fuller treatment of the lead problem, consult the newly published paperback book *Lead Is a Silent Hazard* by Richard M. Stapleton (Walker & Company, $11.95).

[JEB, March 1995]

Protecting Children from the Sun

SCHOOL is almost out, and millions of youngsters will be outside playing from dawn to dusk. But while they frolic in the summer sun, many will be overexposed to the sun's skin-damaging ultraviolet rays.

Although wrinkled, leathery skin and skin cancers may seem too remote to matter to a 5-year-old, the aging effects of sunlight are cumulative, and children spend three times as much time in the sun as adults do. Eighty percent of the typical American's lifetime exposure to cancer-causing ultraviolet radiation occurs before the age of 20.

Unless sun-related attitudes and habits change, one of every six children will eventually develop skin cancer. Cases and deaths, growing steadily for years, are expected to continue increasing as the earth's protective ozone layer thins and millions of sun worshipers reach their 40s and beyond, when the sun's toll typically becomes obvious.

It is never too soon to start worrying about skin cancer. Parents and anyone else who cares for children must be sure they play it safe in the sun and develop lifelong habits that will protect their skin from ultraviolet damage.

Experts estimate that the consistent use of sunscreen with a sun protection factor (SPF) of 15 during the first 18 years of life could reduce the lifetime risk of developing nonmelanoma skin cancer by 78 percent. (A recent study in mice that questioned the value of sunscreens in preventing melanoma is not considered by some experts to be relevant to human sun exposure.) Suffering just one blistering sunburn as a child or teenager is associated with a doubling of the risk of eventually developing melanoma.

Along with feeding, diapering and bathing infants, parental responsibilities include keeping babies out of the sun. The skin of newborns has little or no ability to protect itself from sun damage, and sunscreens are not recommended for babies under six months old. Shade is their best protection. Carriages and strollers should be fitted with hoods or umbrellas, and babies should always wear hats with brims.

But even when shaded from above, skin can be attacked from below by ultraviolet rays reflected off sand, water and concrete (as well as snow and ice). So it is best to protect babies with clothing that covers them when they are going to be outdoors for any length of time. And never put baby oil onto a baby's skin before taking the baby outdoors; it makes skin translucent and renders solar rays even more damaging.

For children who are six months old or older, a sunscreen with an SPF of 15 or higher should be applied 30 minutes before the child goes out, which allows time for the protective ingredients to interact with the skin. Reapply sunscreen every two hours, and more often if the child goes into the water or sweats a lot, even if the sunscreen is supposed to be water-resistant. Wearing a T-shirt in the water offers some protection, depending on the tightness of the weave; the skin under it should still be coated with sunscreen.

Even when dry, many garments let a lot of ultraviolet light through, so it is best to coat the child's entire body, especially areas that will be covered by sheer clothing. Dermatologists recommend sunscreens with a cream or lotion base for young skin and a stick sunscreen or lip balm with an SPF of 15 for the hands, face, ears and lips of babies and toddlers. (It is not known whether sunscreens with higher SPF ratings are any more effective.)

Teenagers with acne should ask their doctors to recommend a sunscreen that is unlikely to aggravate their condition. Children who burn very easily can use zinc oxide on sensitive areas like the nose and ears.

To avoid attracting insects, use a product that has no scent. And to prevent sensitivity reactions, do a patch test before using a new sunscreen. Apply the sunscreen to the inside of the child's wrist a day or more before you will need to apply it widely; if the test site develops an irritation or rash, switch to a product with a different active ingredient (for example, look for one that is PABA-free) and do another patch test. Certain medications, like tetracycline, can result in a heightened sensitivity to the sun, so check with your child's doctor if your child is taking any medication before taking the child out in sunlight, even with sunscreen protection.

Do not assume that because you or your child has dark skin, no protection is needed. Blacks can get sunburned and also get skin cancer, though not as often as light-skinned people. Those most vulnerable are people with blue, green or gray eyes, fair skin or freckles, as well as redheads, blonds and those with light brown hair. Any child who burns before tanning or who never tans is also at greater-than-average risk. And children born with birthmarks called congenital nevi, which look like big freckles, or who develop dysplastic nevi, skin blemishes that show abnormal changes, seem to be particularly vulnerable to developing melanoma.

Try to avoid outdoor activities year-round between 10 A.M. and 3 P.M., when the sun's ultraviolet rays are most intense. As Dr. Perry Robins, dermatologist at New York University Medical Center and president of the Skin Cancer Foundation, cautions in *Play It Safe in the Sun,* a resourceful and entertaining book for children five years old and older: "It's safer to play outside in the early morning or late afternoon. Play inside or in the shade during the middle of the day."

Make sure anyone who cares for your children is knowledgeable about the sun. That includes day care workers, teachers, baby-sitters, coaches and relatives. Studies have shown that few teachers apply sunscreen to their charges or encourage children to wear hats when they go out to play.

Finally, set a good example by always using sunscreen and wearing a hat, sunglasses and protective clothing when out in the sun. One company, Sun Precautions in Seattle, makes lightweight sun-blocking garments with an SPF of more than 30 for children and adults. The garments are marketed by mail. The company can be reached by phone at (800) 882-7860 from 6 A.M. to 7 P.M., Pacific time, Monday through Friday, or 9 A.M. to 1 P.M. on Saturdays.

There are times when even the best-intentioned caretaker errs and a child suffers a painful sunburn. Dr. Mary Spraker, a pediatric dermatologist at Egleston Children's Hospital in Atlanta, and others recommend the following:

• Do not apply first-aid cream or sunburn spray, which may cause an allergic rash and will not help to heal the burn. Neither should you apply ointments, butter or any other greasy substances, which seal in the heat and make matters worse. Do not use any medicated cream, like hydrocortisone or benzocaine, unless it is recommended by the child's doctor.

- Apply cool compresses or place the child in a cool bath. But avoid showers, as these can sting and intensify sunburn pain. Do not apply alcohol.

- If you have an aloe vera plant or aloe vera extract (available in most health food stores and many drugstores), apply the juice directly on the burned skin.

- Give the child acetaminophen or aspirin to relieve pain and fever.

- Give the child lots of water or diluted fruit juices to replace lost body fluids.

- Call the child's doctor if the sunburn is severely painful and widespread or blisters, if the child's eyes hurt when looking at lights, if the child develops a fever of 101 or higher or faints, or if the child is lethargic or appears to be very sick.

For more information, the book *Play It Safe in the Sun* by Dr. Perry Robins, illustrated by 10-year-old artist Michael Podwal, can educate both children and their caretakers about being sensible in the sun. To order, send a check or money order for $12.90 (shipping included) to: The Skin Cancer Foundation, 245 Fifth Avenue, New York, NY 10016.

The foundation has also produced two pamphlets for parents, "Sunproofing Your Baby" and "For Every Child Under the Sun: A Guide to Sensible Sun Protection." Single copies are available free from the foundation.

A more comprehensive discussion of sun protection for people of all ages is *Safe in the Sun: Your Survival Guide for the 90s* by Mary-Ellen Siegel (Walker & Company, $21.95 hardcover, 13.95 paperback).

[JEB, June 1994]

Drugs to Treat Children's Pain

CHILDREN'S aspirin has been on the market for decades, joined more recently by children's acetaminophen. Both are mild pain relievers, although mainly used to reduce fevers. But when it comes to quelling severe pain—the kind, for example, associated with sampling bone marrow, setting a broken arm or sewing up a bad cut—children have long been therapeutic orphans.

Drug companies feel that the pediatric market does not offer enough economic incentive to warrant the costly testing and approval process required to license pain medication in a form suitable for small children. Most potent painkillers are administered by injections that are themselves painful and frightening for children. And when doctors want to reduce anxiety in children undergoing painful medical procedures, they are often forced to reformulate into an oral preparation a drug called Versed that is marketed only in an intravenous form.

The drug companies' reluctance to develop pediatric analgesics has been tacitly supported by doctors, who have long harbored many myths about pain in children, including the notions that they do not feel pain as much as adults, that they do not remember their pain and that they might become drug addicts if given narcotics. Such beliefs account for the longstanding failure of doctors to use painkillers when circumcising newborn boys.

Too often, instead of being given pharmacological or other forms of relief, frightened children about to undergo painful procedures are simply restrained physically, a practice pain specialists call barbaric. Infants may be unable to verbalize pain and small children may be afraid to, but there is no longer any doubt that children suffer as much as adults, and it is clear from their response to repeated procedures that they remember the pains of the past all too well.

In fact, as noted by Dr. Lynda J. Means, an anesthesiologist at James Whitcomb Riley Hospital for Children in Indianapolis, "infants may actually have a heightened response to pain because inhibitory mechanisms, while present, have not fully matured."

Dr. Kathleen M. Foley, chief of the pain service at Memorial Sloan-Kettering Cancer Center in New York, said pain in children might be worse than pain in adults because children are often unable to understand that "the pain may be short-lived, that relief is possible or that the pain associated with treatment or diagnostic procedures can have long-term benefits." Dr. Foley added, "Some children, especially those with chronic disease, become desperately afraid of needles and those who wield them."

Furthermore, anxiety and unrelieved pain can complicate recovery, prolong hospitalization and even increase the risk of dying from a medical procedure, said Dr. Myron Yaster, a pediatric anesthesiologist at Johns Hopkins Hospital in Baltimore.

The nervous system circuitry for feeling pain is present in fetuses from 30 weeks of gestation onward. There are several ways to measure the pain of children too young to describe accurately how they feel. Pain profiles have been developed for infants based on such physical symptoms as breathing and heart rate, skin color and facial expression. Babies as young as 18 months can express pain and tell where they hurt.

For preschoolers there are facial scales, like the "Oucher" Scale, that allow them to point to a picture that best describes how much they hurt. Other scales use poker chips or colors that help young children indicate the intensity of pain.

Recently a small company, the Anesta Corporation in Salt Lake City, won approval for the first potent analgesic specifically designed for and tested in children. The drug, fentanyl, an opiate, acts fast but is short-lived, making it an ideal medication for providing relief during painful medical procedures. It has the added virtue of being absorbable through the mucous membranes in the mouth and so could be formulated in a "lollipop" that makes it easy and painless and not frightening to administer. This form also enables doctors to remove the remaining drug from the child's mouth when a sufficient dose has been absorbed.

But Fentanyl Oralet, as the analgesic lollipop is called, has yet to be used for most of the procedures for which it is intended. That is not because it is unsafe or ineffective but because some outspoken doctors have raised concerns about possible subsequent drug abuse by patients who receive it, as well as objections to the link it establishes between candy and opiates and its potential for abuse as a street drug.

Dr. Yaster maintains that these are empty arguments that simply deprive children of the kind of comfort readily provided to adults undergoing painful medical procedures. In a recent editorial in the journal *Pediatrics,* he pointed out, for example, that "most orally administered medications are made palatable for children so that they can be better tolerated—'a spoonful of sugar helps the medicine go down.' " He also noted that addiction and drug abuse do not result from "the judicious use of analgesics" and that the frightening situations under which children would be given the opiate lollipop "are not the type of life experiences that children will want to voluntarily repeat."

There is another new medication to reduce the pain and resulting fear of needle injections and other external procedures for adults as well as for children. It is a topical anesthetic called EMLA Cream, manufactured by Astra Pharmaceutical Products Inc. of Westborough, Massachusetts. It combines two local anesthetics, lidocaine and prilocaine, and rather than being injected, it is first smeared on the skin; the area is then covered for one to two hours until the drug is absorbed. It temporarily deadens nerve endings, providing pain relief for several hours after the cream is removed. It has been shown to reduce pain significantly in children undergoing insertion of an intravenous line, a spinal tap or aspiration of bone marrow. It may also help to diminish the distress associated with immunizations and circumcision.

For children six and older who are experiencing chronic or prolonged pain, there is now also the option of using patient-controlled analgesia. Patients give themselves medication by triggering a microprocessor-controlled infusion pump that is designed to prevent overdosages. This technique allows drug doses to be individualized, prevents anxiety-inducing delays in relieving pain and gives children a sense of involvement in and control over their own care.

Experts in pediatric pain urge parents to be aggressive in ensuring that their children do not suffer unnecessary pain during medical treatment. They say that children's complaints of pain should always be taken seriously and treated with the same respect and care that an adult would receive.

[JEB, October 1995]

Treating Children's Pain
with Play and Imagination

PAIN is always real, and each person experiences it differently. For children as well as adults, physical, emotional, cultural and social factors influence how pain is experienced and how they respond to different methods of pain control.

Mary K. Kachoyeanos and Margaret Friedhoff, nurses who specialize in the management of pain at Children's Hospital of Wisconsin in Milwaukee, have found that helping children to cope with pain gives them a sense of mastery and self-control that they can apply to other stressful situations as well as to future health problems involving pain.

Experts in controlling pain in children condemn the common practice of restraining children who resist painful treatments. Restraint, they say, only increases a child's anxiety and fear and the stressful reactions induced by pain, which in turn can complicate and delay recovery.

While most people think first of drugs to curb or prevent the perception of pain, children are often highly responsive to pain control strategies that involve their imagination and sense of play. The Milwaukee nurses, who summarized behavioral and cognitive strategies for reducing children's pain in the journal *Maternal-Child Nursing,* point out that not only are these methods completely safe and effective, but they also "cost nothing to implement and actually save staff time."

Behavioral and cognitive methods can also be used as supplements to drugs, reducing the amount of pain medication needed to comfort the child. Many of the techniques the Milwaukee nurses describe can also be applied by parents both in medical settings with the aid of health professionals and on their own at home when a child is in pain.

Some of the most effective methods of minimizing children's pain capitalize on a child's natural imaginative skills and high degree of suggestibility. These approaches usually work with children three years old and older. The simplest technique, and probably the one most often used instinctively by parents, is to distract the child from the pain by telling a story, either with the child or to the child.

A young child can often defuse momentary pain, like that associated with an injection or removal of a wound dressing, by turning off an imagined "pain switch" just as the child might turn off a light switch. Or the child might "blow away the pain." Children are taught to blow out as hard as they can at the first sensation of pain; this distracts them by forcing them to concentrate on responding to the pain signal.

Another method for calming a child who faces a painful experience is controlled breathing: the child is taught to take slow deep breaths through the nose and then to let the breath out slowly, through pursed lips.

Children are very susceptible to the power of suggestion, which makes the "magic glove" technique especially effective. An imaginary glove is placed on the child's hand, finger by finger. Then the child is told that the glove can help to lessen the discomfort of a medical procedure. If pain is widespread, a "magic blanket" might be used to cover the painful area.

A related technique, tactile transference, is already likely to be used in its most basic form by most parents, who would naturally try to comfort a child by touching or stroking. In a more sophisticated form, the child's hand is stroked at the same time as the parent or health professional strokes the area where pain will be inflicted, for example where a needle is about to be inserted. The child is told that when the needle goes in, the hand will be stroked. The child is usually able to transfer the soothing experience of the stroking from the head to the area where the pain is actually being inflicted.

A child's favorite hero or heroine or one of the Ninja Turtles might be invoked to help "wipe away the pain." A child can also be passively distracted by a television program or soothed by soft, low-pitched instrumental music, which has been shown to help reduce stress-related responses for those undergoing orthodontic procedures and bone marrow aspirations.

Other "active distraction" techniques include having the child blow bubbles or count the tiles on the ceiling or the instruments in the examining room. Grasping a comforting parent's hand is also helpful if the child is told to squeeze hardest when it hurts the most.

Even infants can be distracted to minimize a painful situation, for example, by giving the infant a pacifier to suck on while undergoing a heel stick to extract tiny amounts of blood for medical analysis.

Behavioral techniques enable children to work through an anticipated painful or anxiety-provoking medical procedure before undergoing it. These methods can be used alone or in conjunction with the cognitive methods described above.

Desensitization techniques that have been developed for ridding people of phobias can also be applied to reduce the anxiety and pain associated with a medical procedure. The child is gradually exposed step by step to the anxiety-provoking procedure through play. In effect, the child plays doctor or nurse. For example, a child who is about to receive an injection might first be shown a syringe. Then the child might be allowed to handle the syringe, then fill it with water and finally give an injection to a doll or stuffed animal.

A related approach involves "modeling," or learning about the procedure and ways of mastering the experience either through observing it firsthand or by watching a videotape of another child going through the experience. By becoming familiar with the experience, the child is better able to prepare for it and is likely to be less frightened.

For example, the nurses described a situation in which a "model child" demonstrates how a cast is removed: the model child is first shown touching the instrument that will be used to cut the cast. The child is then shown sitting still as the technician cuts and removes the cast.

"As children observe that the model child survives the experience without bodily harm, chances for these children's cooperation during the procedure increase," the nurses wrote. "Behavioral rehearsal helps children learn about the impending experience by 'pretending'—becoming familiar with, and preparing for, the painful event through play."

The Milwaukee nurses also point out that "there is no exact recipe" for helping children through a painful experience, nor are the techniques they suggest always limited to a particular age group. For example, they say they have successfully used the magic glove technique with preschoolers, school-age children and adolescents.

Sometimes trial and error is necessary to find the most effective techniques for a particular child. But, the nurses assure, one or more nondrug methods will be found to help a child in any situation. And the rewards of using these methods are considerable, they say.

[JEB, November 1995]

Stages of Life—Menopause

THE DIMINUENDO OF
THE HORMONES

Biologists who study evolution suggest that the reason for menopause may be to preserve the mother's energies; being unable after the hormonal change to bear more babies, she is better able to look after her existing children.

Whatever the truth of that speculation, modern women now have the chance to reverse the less welcome side effects of menopause by taking hormonal supplements to replace those their bodies no longer make.

The supplements offset a major natural risk that befalls women after menopause, that of heart attacks, and they also counteract osteoporosis, the thinning out of the bones.

On the other side of the ledger is a possibly increased risk of breast cancer, one which physicians are still trying to assess. So far it is known that estrogen alone can increase the risk of endometria cancer, but that the combination of estrogen and progesterone appears to be without risk.

In general, the benefit of hormone replacement therapy in reducing heart disease is far larger than the possible risk of increasing breast cancer. But that judgment may differ for women at particular risk of this cancer.

Men too experience a shift of hormonal gears in middle age. The change is not as dramatic as menopause, just a gradual ebbing of the hormonal fires. Experiments are under way in which testosterone levels are banked up to youthful levels. Many men say they feel more vigorous, but the long-term safety of the procedure is far less assured than is the case with hormone supplements in women.

Hormone replacement therapy is in a sense a grand experiment with nature's design. For women, the therapy now seems effective and fairly safe; for men, many unknowns must be resolved before the therapy can be widely recommended.

The Truth About Menopause

MENOPAUSE: Rarely has a subject emerged from the closet and so quickly assumed center stage. With 40 million American women now in or past menopause and another 20 million due to reach that stage of life in the next decade, its management has become a major national health concern.

Women, including many who are nationally prominent, now discuss their own experiences with menopause openly with friends, family, coworkers, bosses and even the general public. The subject is being discussed in popular books and periodicals, in the offices of the National Institutes of Health and on the floor of Congress as well as in gatherings of women of a certain age.

Given the damaging mythology of decades past, everyone can benefit from the truth, and women in particular can be liberated by it. The following are some common beliefs about menopause:

- *Menopause makes women crazy.* This myth probably developed because some women do experience mood swings, not unlike premenstrual symptoms, when their hormonal cycles become erratic during the four years or so as they enter and pass through the menopause. But the more serious psychological symptoms that have been associated with menopause are more likely to result from night sweats, or hot flashes, which disrupt sleep. In a recent PBS series on the subject Dr. Judith Reichman, of Cedars-Sinai Medical Center in Los Angeles, recalls a recent study in which men were awakened every time they lapsed into the deep sleep during which dreaming takes place; after three days of being deprived of dream sleep, the men showed distinct signs of psychosis.

- *Menopause precipitates depression.* This myth may arise from the fact that women in midlife may experience the death of parents, the breakup of a marriage or the loss of a job or may suddenly find their nest empty, all of which may lead to depression. Women are far more likely to be hospitalized for depression during their premenopausal years, when they may buckle under the combined pressures of child rearing, job demands and financial, family and household stresses.

- *Menopause spells the end of a satisfying sex life.* In fact, freed of worry about unwanted pregnancy and fears of interruption by children, many women find that their enjoyment of sex *increases* after menopause. Rather than a hormonally precipitated loss of sex drive, the decline in libido some women experience is more likely to result from the lack of an interesting or interested partner or from discomfort during intercourse caused by vaginal dryness. Vaginal dryness can be treated with lubricants, estrogen therapy or both. And the libido of those who are affected by the decline in ovarian hormones can usually be revived by small doses of testosterone.

At the turn of this century, the average life expectancy for a woman in America was 50 years. Today it is nearly 80 years, meaning that women in America can expect to live a third of their lives after menopause. During those postmenopausal decades, a woman's risk of developing two costly, life-threatening diseases—heart disease and osteoporosis—rises sharply, a fact that is forcing medical researchers to take a serious look at the health consequences of menopause and how they might be stemmed.

After the age of 50, women have a 31 percent chance of dying from heart disease in their remaining years; heart disease kills four times more women than breast cancer does. At 55, heart disease becomes the leading cause of death among women; women are more likely than men to die after a heart attack or cardiac surgery.

When the amount of estrogen declines at menopause, a woman's blood level of heart-protecting HDL cholesterol often falls and heart-damaging LDL cholesterol rises. At the same time, women's arteries become narrower and less elastic and blood clots form more easily. There is also a change in the distribution of body fat, with more fat accumulating around the abdomen, as happens in men who gain weight at any age, instead of around the hips. All these changes add up to a significant increase in coronary risk.

As for osteoporosis, Dr. Reichman points out that one postmenopausal woman in three is developing or already has severe bone loss, a silent, preventable $10-billion-a-year problem that results in 1.3 million fractures and thousands of deaths each year.

The most rapid bone loss occurs in the first five years of menopause, and close attention to preventive measures is urged, particularly for those at highest risk: thin white women, women who smoke or drink excessively and those who have a family history of osteoporosis, as well as women who enter menopause with thin bones or whose menopause occurs early, in their 30s or early 40s, perhaps as a result of surgery or chemotherapy.

Menopause can be accompanied by a loss of muscle tone in the pelvic region, resulting in stress incontinence (urine leakage when one coughs, sneezes, laughs or exercises vigorously) and a discom-

The Physical Risks of Menopause

Many of the problems associated with declining estrogen levels can be helped by appropriate changes in things like diet and exercise as well as by hormone replacement, if both the woman and her doctor find it advisable on the basis of individual characteristics.

■ **CARDIOVASCULAR DISEASE** Levels of cholesterol change with estrogen levels; protective HDL cholesterol drops and damaging LDL cholesterol rises. Arteries become narrower and less elastic and blood clots form more easily. Fat distribution changes, with more of it around the abdomen. All these changes raise coronary risk.

■ **OSTEOPOROSIS** Rapid bone loss occurs during the first five years of menopause, increasing the risk of fractures. The risk is highest for thin white women who smoke and/or drink excessively and who have a family history of osteoporosis and for women who enter menopause early.

■ **OTHER PROBLEMS** Loss of muscle tone in the pelvic region can result in stress incontinence or a drop in pelvic organs. Skin thins and becomes more lax and wrinkled. The relative increase in testosterone may result in growth of facial hair and thinning of scalp hair.

forting drop of the pelvic organs. Skin thins out and becomes more lax and wrinkled when estrogen production declines, and the relative increase in testosterone (also produced in the ovaries) may result in a growth of facial hair and thinning of scalp hair.

Dr. Reichman says the most important approach to menopause is to take action: assess your personal and family medical history for health problems that are related to menopause; stop health-damaging habits like smoking, abusing alcohol, and overconsuming caffeine; and adopt health-promoting habits like regular weight-bearing exercise and a low-fat diet rich in vegetables, fruits, grains, and calcium-rich foods.

Then there is the option of hormone replacement. The pendulum, which has swung back and forth about estrogen supplements in recent decades, is now clearly on the side of taking them, at least for most women. Only 15 to 20 percent of menopausal women are now on estrogen. Some are against what has been called "the medicalization of menopause" and question the wisdom of monkeying with nature. Others have health concerns, like a history of breast cancer, that preclude its use. Still others are afraid that menopausal hormones might increase their risk of getting cancer. Before making a decision, it pays to weigh the existing evidence.

[JEB, December 1993]

Deciding Whether and How to Treat Menopause

EVERY woman, if she lives long enough, goes through menopause, when her ovaries stop releasing eggs, her menstrual cycles cease and production of estrogen and other ovarian hormones falls sharply. The average age at menopause for American women is now 51, and those who reach this age will live on average 30 more years, or 10 years longer than women of the same age were likely to live at the turn of the century.

Thus, unless she receives hormone replacement therapy, the typical American woman spends more than a third of her life without the considerable benefits of estrogen to her heart, bones, skin and other tissues. Yet only about one menopausal woman in seven chooses to take replacement hormones. Critics often cite these objections to this therapy:

- Some women consider it unnatural to tamper with the body's chemistry. But as Dr. Rogerio A. Lobo, an expert in the field, pointed out at a recent conference on hormone replacement, "Neither is it natural from an evolutionary standpoint for a woman to live to 80."

- Hormone replacement often sets off cyclical or irregular bleeding, which postmenopausal women often find distressing and occasionally frightening.

- Many women fear that hormone replacement therapy will increase their risk of developing breast or uterine cancer or will promote the growth of a preexisting cancer.

- And when progestin is given to prevent cancerous changes in the uterus, some women react adversely to this synthetic hormone, with side effects like bloating, depression and irritability that prompt them to abandon hormone treatment.

When hormone replacement first became popular three decades ago, women were given rather large doses of estrogen every day, an approach later found to result in a ninefold increase in the risk of uterine cancer.

To protect the uterus against cancer, the regimen was changed in the last decade to lower doses of estrogen for 25 days a month, progestin for the last 10 of those 25 days and nothing for 5 days. This approach, known as cyclical hormone therapy, usually results in a continuation of menstrual-type bleeding for years beyond menopause. Bleeding is the main reason women who begin replacement therapy often drop it after they have passed through menopause and no longer have disturbing menopausal symptoms. Many women have been reluctant to continue taking the replacement hormones for seven or more years to achieve the known benefits to the heart and bones.

Now there is a veritable cafeteria of choices: different dosages, different hormone combinations and different methods of administering them, so replacement therapy can be better tailored to individual needs.

As Dr. Leon Speroff, of the Oregon Health Sciences University in Portland, put it, "If a woman has an undesirable response to one approach, there is often a choice that could improve the therapy." He advises women not to abandon hormone therapy with the first problem but to seek an alternative regimen.

For example, women who experience bad reactions while on larger cyclical doses of Provera, the most commonly prescribed progestin, might switch to its continuous use in a lower dose of 2.5 milligrams daily or substitute 0.35 milligram of norethindrone, the mini–birth control pill.

Women who, despite hormone therapy, experience an undesirable decline in their sex drive at menopause can have their libido enhanced by the addition of small doses of an androgen, like testosterone, which is naturally produced by premenopausal ovaries.

For those who are uncomfortable taking a pill each day or who respond poorly to Premarin, the leading menopausal estrogen product, another estrogen drug, Estinyl (ethinyl estradiol), could be substituted in the form of a skin patch on the lower abdomen and replaced twice a week, to provide a steady dose of estrogen.

But Dr. Speroff and Dr. Lobo, who are both reproductive endocrinologists, pointed out that all the needed facts about the various options were not yet available. None of the regimens, including the now-standard cyclical therapy, have yet been tested adequately for long-term benefits to the heart, blood vessels and bones and for long-term complications.

It is still uncertain whether adding progestin to the regimen to protect the uterus will also protect the breasts against cancer or will perhaps blunt the benefits of estrogen to the heart or whether the estrogen patch will confer the cardiovascular benefit of a 50 percent reduction in coronary mortality associated with oral estrogens.

As for breast cancer, studies have had conflicting results, with some showing no increased risk associated with hormone replacement and others showing a rise of about 35 percent in the risk.

Dr. Speroff and others noted that heart disease is a far more common killer of postmenopausal women than is breast cancer, and hormone replacement appears to cut the risk of a fatal heart attack in half. So even if the hormone therapy somewhat increases the risk of breast cancer, there would still be a substantial overall benefit.

In weighing the various options, a woman and her doctor should consider her personal and family medical history. If heart disease or osteoporosis is common in a woman's family or if she herself has a high risk of either, hormone replacement might be more strongly recommended than for a woman without such risks.

On the other hand, for a woman with a family or personal history of breast cancer, doctors are reluctant to prescribe estrogen and may instead emphasize the importance of healthful living habits like a low-fat diet and regular exercise.

Dr. Speroff said a treatment alternative for such women might be tamoxifen, an estrogenlike drug that has favorable effects on cholesterol levels and prevents bone loss at the same time that it protects the breasts against cancer. But tamoxifen does increase the risk of uterine cancer, and women taking it would be wise to undergo periodic examinations to check for uterine changes that could herald this cancer, which is highly curable when detected early.

Properly designed studies are now under way to answer the various questions about the long-term risks and benefits of hormone replacement, but results will not be available for about 10 years, by which time another 20 million women of the baby-boom generation will have entered menopause and grappled with a decision about whether and how to treat it. The best approach, experts agree, is for each woman and her doctor to review her risk factors, concerns and therapeutic options and together come to an informed decision.

For further information, a comprehensive and up-to-date reference for those seeking detailed information on menopause and hormone replacement therapy is the newly revised edition of *Menopause: A Guide for Women and Those Who Love Them* by Dr. Winnifred B. Cutler and Celso-Ramon Garcia (in paperback by W. W. Norton, $12.95).

Another helpful book is *Estrogen Replacement Therapy: The Johns Hopkins Guide to Making an Informed Decision* by Dr. Howard Zacur and Dr. Roger Blumenthal (Johns Hopkins University Press, 1993). To order the book, a check payable to Johns Hopkins University for $4.95, which includes postage and handling, should be sent to Johns Hopkins University Women's Health Center, 550 North Broadway, Suite 1100, Baltimore, MD 21205.

[JEB, December 1993]

Combination Therapy for Menopause Reduces Risks

A three-year study of nearly 900 women may result in a significant refinement in hormone replacement therapy after menopause. The study found that a mixture of the two hormones estrogen and progestin is better than estrogen alone, protecting women not only against the risk of uterine cancer but against heart attacks as well.

The findings, described at a meeting of the American Heart Association in Dallas, should help resolve a vexing issue facing the more than 40 million American women past menopause. While estrogen alone was known to significantly reduce a postmenopausal woman's risk of cardiovascular disease, it also increased her risk of uterine cancer.

In recent years doctors have prescribed a second hormone to offset the uterine cancer risk, but studies indicated that the cardiovascular benefits then decreased. The new study goes a long way toward resolving that dilemma. The researchers stressed, however, that much remains to be studied, including the effect of these hormones on bone strength and the role of hormone replacement in the development of osteoporosis.

The study also found that the best overall cardiovascular effect—nearly equal to that from taking estrogen alone—was found when a little-used form of the natural hormone progesterone was substituted for progestin. The form is known as micronized, or finely ground, progesterone.

The first findings of the study, called the Postmenopausal Estrogen and Progestin Interventions Trial, were reported by Dr. Trudy Bush and Dr. Elizabeth Barrett-Connor to the annual meeting of the heart association in Dallas. Dr. Bush, an epidemiologist at Johns Hopkins School of Hygiene and the University of Maryland in Baltimore, and Dr. Barrett-Connor, a hormone expert at the University of California at San Diego, concluded that the various combinations of estrogen and progestin or progesterone tested in the trial appeared to be "very safe," at least with regard to the uterus and heart.

Also reassuring, especially to women who worry about gaining weight, was the finding that hormone replacement therapy that includes progestin did not result in as much weight gain as taking no hormone therapy at all.

Dr. Claude Lenfant, the head of the National Heart, Lung and Blood Institute, the federal agency that paid for the research, said in a recent interview that it was "a major study that has the potential to have very significant individual and public health impact." The results were surprising because of the magnitude of the benefit, he said.

But Dr. Lenfant cautioned that the therapy "is not for all women." The decision to treat should be made according to a woman's risk factors for heart disease, just as doctors tailor prevention therapy for men according to their risk factors, such as a family history of heart attacks, high blood pressure and results of blood tests.

Although the study has been completed, many of the women will be followed for three additional years for ethical reasons to determine whether any complications occurred. Although there was no evidence of an increased risk of breast cancer in the study, additional studies are needed to measure that risk, Dr. Lenfant said.

Physicians have long known that estrogen raises blood levels of protective HDL cholesterol, lowers levels of harmful LDL cholesterol, reduces the tendency of the blood to form clots and helps to keep artery walls elastic. But when estrogen is given alone to women who have a uterus (almost one-third of American women have had their uterus removed by the age of 60), they face a ninefold increased risk of developing cancer of the endometrium, the tissue that lines the uterus.

Preliminary studies indicated that adding progestin to the hormone regimen could protect the uterus from the growth-stimulating effects of estrogen and thus would presumably greatly reduce the cancer risk. But several small studies also suggested that progestin might erase the heart-saving benefits of estrogen.

Recently announced findings, based on a carefully designed and executed trial conducted at seven clinical centers with money from the National Institutes of Health, confirmed the potentially harmful effects on the uterus of taking estrogen alone. Nearly half the women who had a uterus and who were taking estrogen alone had to be taken off the therapy in the course of the study because of excessive endometrial growth, Dr. Bush reported. No such problem was found among the women taking combinations of estrogen and progestin or progesterone.

In addition to estrogen alone and a look-alike placebo, or dummy, also taken alone, the regimens tested were a continuous daily combination of estrogen and progestin (0.625 milligram of Premarin and 2.5 milligrams of Provera); daily estrogen and progestin for 12 days of the month (the same dose of Premarin and 10 milligrams of Provera on each of the 12 days); and the same daily dose of estrogen plus 200 milligrams of micronized progesterone.

All the regimens, except the placebo, lowered harmful LDL cholesterol by about the same amount, Dr. Bush reported. The levels of protective HDLs were higher among those taking any of the hormone regimens than in the group on the placebo. They were highest in women taking estrogen alone, but almost as high in those women on estrogen and micronized progesterone.

Dr. Rita Redberg, a cardiologist who is codirector of a woman's health center at the University of California at San Francisco, said it was the first randomized, controlled study of the combination of estrogens and progestin and their effects on the blood fats that are important in heart disease.

"The study will have an impact on prescribing practices and also on patient acceptability because a big problem now is that there is poor compliance with hormone replacement therapy, partly because women do not think that heart disease is as much of a threat as it is and partly because of the side effects," Dr. Redberg said. "It will increase women's awareness of the benefits of hormone replacement therapy and of the risks of heart disease."

There is only a limited commercial supply of micronized progesterone in this country, which is used for a variety of conditions, including premenstrual syndrome. Susan Wulfsberg, pharmacist at Madison Pharmacy Associates in Madison, Wisconsin, said the Upjohn Company in Kalamazoo, Michigan, derives the finely particled progesterone from soybeans and sells it to pharmacies as a bulk powder. Pharmacies can then formulate it into capsules, tablets, suspensions or suppositories in various dosages according to a physician's prescription. Ms. Wulfsberg said 200 milligrams of micronized progesterone is "a moderate dose" and added, "Doses of 1,200 milligrams are commonly prescribed for premenstrual syndrome."

The micronized progesterone used in the postmenopausal study was obtained from Europe by the Schering-Plough Corporation in Madison, New Jersey, Dr. Bush said. She said the soybean-derived hormone is widely marketed in Scandinavia, where studies have indicated that it has no harmful effects on blood cholesterol.

To the researchers' surprise, all the hormone regimens tested increased the women's blood levels of triglycerides, fatty substances which some experts consider a risk factor for heart disease, especially in women. Dr. Bush suggested that women taking postmenopausal hormones should have their triglyceride levels checked.

Women in all the treatment groups gained weight—on average, about five pounds, the researchers reported. Those taking estrogen alone gained significantly less weight than women on the placebo, and those taking a combination of estrogen and progestin or progesterone gained an intermediate amount.

[JEB, November 1994]

But Even Combination Therapy May Carry Some Risk . . .

RESEARCHERS at Harvard Medical School have found in a large study that women who continue to use hormone replacement therapy for five or more years after menopause are 30 percent to 40 percent more likely to develop breast cancer than women who have never used menopausal hormones.

The finding is the latest in a series of conflicting studies on the relationship between hormones and breast cancer. Although estrogen has long been known to be able to promote the growth of some existing cancers, its possible role in causing breast cancer has been highly controversial.

The new study, reported in a recent issue of the *New England Journal of Medicine,* considered only the relationship between hormones and breast cancer, not the rather substantial benefits of postmenopausal estrogen documented in previous studies. Past studies have shown, for instance, that hormone replacement therapy sharply reduces the risk of developing heart disease, the leading killer of American women; and osteoporosis, a loss of density in the bones that can lead to debilitating or life-threatening fractures.

Thus, one of the authors said, the new study should not be the sole basis for a woman's decision on whether to use postmenopausal hormones. And other experts argued that even with the new findings, estrogen's benefits to the heart more than outweighed any risk of breast cancer.

The study of 122,000 nurses was mainly intended to see if adding progestin to estrogen replacement therapy would block estrogen's effects on the breast. Although previous studies have shown that including progestin in hormone replacement therapy can protect the uterus against estrogen-induced endometrial cancer, no such protection was found for the breast in the new study.

Among those who were taking estrogen alone and had done so for five or more years, the risk of breast cancer increased 30 percent, and among those who used a combination of estrogen and progestin, the risk was 40 percent higher, a difference that was not statistically significant.

To put this risk into perspective, instead of the 7 cases of breast cancer that would be expected to occur over 10 years among 200 women who were initially 55 years old, 10 such cancers would be found if all the women used postmenopausal hormones.

The study, directed by Dr. Graham A. Colditz of Brigham and Women's Hospital and Harvard Medical School in Boston, documented 1,935 newly diagnosed cases of invasive breast cancer that occurred among the women from 1978 to 1992. The participants were all enrolled in the Nurses' Health Study, a continuing observational study of 121,700 female nurses who were 30 to 55 years of age when it began in 1976.

Among the women studied who were 60 to 64 and who naturally have a higher rate of breast cancer than women in their 50s, current use of hormone replacement was associated with a 70 percent increase in the risk of breast cancer for reasons researchers cannot explain, the Harvard team reported. The study also found a 45 percent higher death rate due to breast cancer among participants who had taken postmenopausal estrogen for five or more years.

But other researchers in the field said that focusing on breast cancer risk alone distorted the overall value of hormone replacement by failing to take into account the reduced risk of developing heart disease and osteoporosis.

For example, Dr. Trudy Bush, an epidemiologist at the University of Maryland at Baltimore who has conducted several studies on hormone replacement and heart disease, said estrogen's benefits to the heart more than outweighed any risk to the breast. In fact, in previous reports from the same Harvard study, the researchers showed that the risk of developing heart disease was reduced by 50 percent and deaths from all causes were reduced by 11 percent among current users of postmenopausal estrogen. In a clinical trial at a number of medical centers, Dr. Bush and her colleagues recently showed that adding progestin to the replacement regimen did not significantly reduce the benefits of estrogen to the heart.

"It's of no service to women to talk only about breast cancer," Dr. Bush said in an interview. Instead of helping women arrive at a reasoned decision about whether to take postmenopausal hormones, she said, "it only frightens and confuses them."

One of the study's authors, Dr. Meir J. Stampfer, agreed that "from a public health perspective it would be more useful to summarize all the risks and benefits of taking postmenopausal hormones," adding that he and his colleagues were working on such a report.

"My view is that for the average woman, the benefits outweigh the risks," Dr. Stampfer said. "But there are plenty of women for whom the reverse is true. Ideally, before deciding whether to take hormones, a woman's risk profile should be identified for all the diseases related to estrogen: heart disease, breast cancer and osteoporosis."

In the past, estrogen therapy was mainly prescribed to control the symptoms of menopause over a period of a few years, but now women are being advised to take it for many years, if not indefinitely, to prevent heart disease and osteoporosis.

The new study also found that when women stopped using postmenopausal hormones, the increased risk of developing breast cancer disappeared within two years. In fact, among women who stopped hormone therapy, there was actually a somewhat lower risk of breast cancer than in women who had never used the therapy. And among women in the study who continued using hormones for more than five years, no further increase in cancer incidence was found.

"These findings are consistent with estrogen's role as a cancer promoter rather than as a direct cause of breast cancer," Dr. Bush said. In other words, she suggested, "estrogen may have promoted the growth of tumors already present but not yet clinically detectable."

She added: "If hormone replacement caused a true increase in tumors, I think we would have seen it more clearly by this time. There have been so many studies with findings on one side or the other; if there is a real increase in risk, it's not a very big one."

Critics of the new study also questioned whether initial differences between the women in the study who took hormones and those who did not might account for all or part of the risk that the Harvard team attributed to hormone replacement. Among those differences was the fact that hormone users were more likely to have had mammograms, which might have resulted in a greater rate of cancer detection among them.

Dr. Leon Speroff, a professor of obstetrics and gynecology at the Oregon Health Sciences University in Portland, said that only a controlled clinical trial, in which women were randomly assigned to receive either hormone therapy or a dummy medication, could ensure that there were no initial differences between the women who took hormones and those who did not. In studies like the Nurses' Health Study, in which women themselves choose whether or not to use hormone replacement, there may be differences between the two groups that influence their risk of developing breast cancer, Dr. Speroff explained.

Although the Harvard researchers tried to take such differences into account in their statistical analysis of the data, it is not possible to consider every conceivable influence on the risk of breast cancer. For example, Dr. Stampfer of Harvard noted that estrogen users tended to be better educated than nonusers and that, for unknown reasons, better-educated women are more likely to get breast cancer.

Dr. Speroff has prepared a critical review of the many studies exploring the relationship between postmenopausal hormone therapy and breast cancer. The review, which is to be published in the journal *Obstetrics and Gynecology*, concludes that available evidence "on the impact of combined estrogen-progestin treatment on the risk of breast cancer is still too limited" and that "neither a protective nor a detrimental effect has yet to be convincingly demonstrated."

[JEB, June 1995]

. . . Or Maybe It's Completely Safe After All

JUST one month after a study found that women who took hormone replacement therapy after menopause had an increased risk of breast cancer, another study has found no such effect.

The new study, published in *The Journal of the American Medical Association,* compared some 500 women aged 50 to 64 who had newly diagnosed breast cancer with a similar group of healthy women. The authors found no link between use of the hormones and breast cancer. In fact, they found that women who had used hormones for eight years or longer had, if anything, a lower risk of breast cancer than those who had never taken them. The latest development, scientists say, is good news tinged with great uncertainty.

The previous study, published on June 15, 1995, in the *New England Journal of Medicine,* followed 122,000 nurses for 14 years and found that hormone replacement therapy increased the risk of breast cancer by 30 to 70 percent.

Researchers say the conflicting results of the two highly regarded studies underscore the fact that this is science in progress: they are nowhere near obtaining a completed picture of the risks and benefits of taking hormone replacement therapy after menopause.

Other researchers are sharply divided in their interpretation of the studies. Some think the cancer risk from hormone therapy is nonexistent or virtually so. Some, on the other hand, are convinced that the hormones do slightly increase the risk of breast cancer. But, they say, because this increase is small, as a matter of chance some studies will detect it and some will not, which may be why the new study saw no effect. Indeed, the author of the study of nurses responded to the new research recently by saying that its results might have been skewed because the study was smaller than his own and because some prospective subjects had declined to be interviewed.

In the meantime, women going through or anticipating menopause are facing the momentous decision of whether to take hormones for the rest of their lives. It is already established that hormone replacement therapy reduces the risk of heart disease and bone fractures from osteoporosis. As a result, many doctors encourage women to take hormones. In fact, Wyeth-Ayerst's postmenopausal estrogen, Premarin, is the nation's best-selling prescription drug. Nonetheless, many women are troubled by the idea of taking a drug that, whatever its benefits, might increase their risk of breast cancer.

The lead author of the new study, Dr. Janet L. Stanford, an epidemiologist at the University of Washington in Seattle, said she and her colleagues had begun the research specifically to see whether the sort of hormone replacement therapy now in vogue conferred any increased cancer risk.

In that therapy, which has grown popular during the last decade, many doctors have switched from prescribing estrogen alone to prescribing a combination of estrogen and another hormone, progestin. The reason is that estrogen taken alone increases a woman's risk of developing cancer of the lining of the uterus. The addition of progestin appears to alleviate that risk.

But progestin also stimulates the growth of breast cells in women who have not gone through menopause, causing some concern that it might increase the risk of breast cancer if it is taken after menopause. That concern was sharpened by studies showing that the use of estrogen after menopause seemed to increase breast cancer risk slightly. But other estrogen studies have not found that increased risk, and, until the study of nurses was published, there had been no major American research on risk associated with the estrogen-progestin combination.

In their study, Dr. Stanford and her colleagues found no effect on breast cancer risk in taking either estrogen alone or estrogen plus progestin. In the previous study, Dr. Graham Colditz of the Harvard Medical School and his colleagues found a 30 to 70 percent increased risk of breast cancer whether women took estrogen alone or an estrogen-progestin combination.

Dr. Stanford said she thought there really was no increased risk of breast cancer in women who use hormone replacement therapy. She said the previous study, of nurses, might have been biased because women taking hormone replacement therapy "are more likely to be in contact with the health care community and more likely to be receiving mammograms and breast exams," with the resulting greater likelihood of a breast cancer diagnosis.

Dr. Colditz, on the other hand, said Dr. Stanford's study might have missed an effect because it was smaller and because as many as 30 percent of the women who were prospective subjects had declined to be interviewed. "That makes it hard to know how much of the difference is due to selection," he said.

Others, like Dr. Louise Brinton, chief of the Environmental Studies Section at the National Cancer Institute, think the hormones do increase breast cancer risk. "It's not a huge risk, but it's fairly consistent" across studies, Dr. Brinton said.

Dr. Nanette Wenger, a cardiologist and professor at the Emory University School of Medicine in Atlanta, said she could not state whether there was an increased risk of breast cancer with hormone replacement therapy. The two studies had very different designs, Dr. Wenger said, and each had its limitations. The growing body of studies on the effects of hormone replacement therapy "is information in development," she said. As of now, she added, "there really is no bottom line."

Just as experts differ on whether the data show an increased risk of breast cancer, so they differ on whether they would advise women to take hormones. A coauthor of the new study, Dr. Noel Weiss, an epidemiologist at the University of Washington, said that even if there was more breast cancer in women who take the hormones, "you still have to do this balancing act: which is more important, the risk or the benefits?"

It is clear, Dr. Weiss said, that estrogen lowers a woman's risk of heart disease, the number one killer of elderly women. "There are probably a dozen studies, all of which are consistent," he said. And estrogen lessens the chances of developing osteoporosis. Even with a greatly increased risk of breast cancer, he said, these benefits alone would argue that women are better off taking hormones.

Dr. Colditz and Dr. Brinton are less certain. They see ways for women to reduce their chances of developing heart disease and osteoporosis that carry no cancer risk. For example, women can ex-

---

SIDE BY SIDE

Two Studies of Hormones and Cancer

Nurses' Health Study

Conducted by Dr. Graham A. Colditz of Harvard Medical School and colleagues. Published in the *New England Journal of Medicine*, June 15, 1995.

SUBJECTS 121,700 female nurses.

METHOD Nurses filled out questionnaires, starting in 1976, and every two years afterward, telling what medications they were taking and whether they received diagnoses of breast cancer. They were followed until 1992.

RESULTS Women using estrogen or a combination of estrogen and progestin showed a 30 to 70 percent increased risk of developing breast cancer.

University of Washington Study

Conducted by Dr. Janet L. Stanford of the University of Washington and colleagues. Published in *The Journal of the American Medical Association*, July 12, 1995.

SUBJECTS 537 women, 50 to 64 years old, living in King County, Washington, who were diagnosed with breast cancer from January 1, 1988, to June 30, 1990, and 492 randomly selected women of the same ages, living in the same area of Washington, who did not have breast cancer.

METHOD Women were questioned in detail and in person about hormone use in previous years.

RESULTS No difference in hormone use was found between the women who had breast cancer and those who did not. About 1 in 5 women in both groups used the hormones.

---

ercise, avoid smoking, watch the fat in their diet, maintain a normal weight and take aspirin.

With hormone replacement therapy, Dr. Brinton said, "the thinking in clinical medicine is that the benefits are known but the risks are less clearly known." So, she said, the hormones "are pushed because of the benefits." She disagrees with that approach.

Dr. Wenger takes a middle ground. She agrees that many women can reduce their risk of heart disease and osteoporosis without taking hormones. For example, she said, a recent study found that postmenopausal women who had adequate calcium in their diets, who exercised and who averaged one alcoholic drink a week had bones that were just as strong as those of women who took hormones. "So there are alternatives," Dr. Wenger said.

But, she said, what about a woman whose parents both died prematurely of heart disease, whose cholesterol level is very high or who has high blood pressure and diabetes? "These are things over which you have no control," Dr. Wenger said. She said a woman's chance of developing heart disease at some time after menopause is 31 percent. Her chance of developing breast cancer is 3 percent, and her chance of developing osteoporosis is 3 percent.

"We will never say all women should or all women should not" take hormones after menopause, Dr. Wenger said. For now, she added, researchers are trying desperately "to define the women most at risk and those most likely to benefit."

[GK, July 1995]

The Truth About Depression at Menopause

IN her newly published memoir, Barbara Bush reveals that in the mid-1970s she was overcome by depression so severe that she feared she might purposely end her life by crashing her car. The former first lady attributed her emotional distress to the hormonal changes of menopause compounded by the stress of her husband's job as director of the Central Intelligence Agency.

By linking her depression to menopause, Mrs. Bush perpetuates a centuries-old belief that the hormonal swings that accompany this life stage can touch off what had long been called involutional (a term referring to the body's changes at menopause) melancholia.

Popular literature and the clinical experience of psychiatrists have convinced many laypeople and professionals that menopause increases the risk of depression in women who were never before clinically depressed and whose depression was not attributable to any other life event.

Numerous studies among American women have concluded that

in otherwise emotionally healthy women, menopause by itself does not cause depression. In fact, the studies show, there is no particular link between menopause and depression; if anything, it is far more common among younger women than in those from 45 to 55, when most women enter menopause.

For example, a community survey of 511 women in New Haven, Connecticut, beginning in 1967 and repeated in 1969 and 1976, found no evidence of an increase in depressive symptoms in the menopausal years. The rates of depressive symptoms were highest in women under 35 and decreased gradually with age, according to one author, Dr. Myrna M. Weissman, professor of psychiatry and epidemiology at Columbia University. A much larger follow-up study among 18,000 men and women in five urban areas confirmed that "depression is now occurring in women at younger ages and the rate decreases at menopause," she said.

But she added that the same study had since been done in nine other countries and that the data, now being analyzed, might show that a relationship between menopause and depression was not a myth in countries where women still had more traditional roles.

Dr. Weissman does not discount the possibility that Mrs. Bush's depressive episode was related to menopause, but she questions whether hormonal factors were responsible. "Barbara Bush had led a traditional family life with her major role being raising children," she said. "As her children left home, the loss of this role may have made her more vulnerable to depression at that time. When women are not in the workforce, depression may be more common at menopause, reflecting the woman's stage of life, not necessarily her hormones."

Some women acknowledge that depression at menopause is directly related to feelings that they are getting old and fears that they will become less attractive and sexually undesirable. It is also possible that for women prone to depression, a major life event like menopause can set off a depressive episode.

For example, after a hysterectomy, in which a woman's uterus and hormone-producing ovaries are removed, depression is far more common than with other operations. While depression might not be unexpected after such traumatic surgery, women who are depressed are more likely to have such surgery, according to Dr. Winnifred B. Cutler, coauthor of *Menopause* (W. W. Norton, 1993, $12.95) and founder of the Athena Institute for Women's Wellness in Haverford, Pennsylvania. She says it is not necessarily accurate to attribute depression to hormonal changes. Nonetheless, Dr. Weissman said, studies of the role of hormones in women's emotional stability have been poor at best, a situation she hopes will be corrected by the new Women's Health Initiative of the National Institutes of Health.

To be sure, menopause can be an emotionally challenging time for some women who experience symptoms much like those associated with premenstrual syndrome: mood swings, irritability, anxiety, irrational anger and weepiness. Such symptoms have been associated with the premenstrual decline in estrogen, a mood-elevating hormone, which may also account for similar symptoms at menopause if estrogen levels drop precipitously. When such women take replacement hormones, their moods commonly lift and they feel more in control.

Among those who become depressed at menopause, their negative emotional state may result more from physical factors than psychological ones. According to Dr. Lonnie Barbach, a San Francisco psychologist who is the author of *The Pause* (Dutton, 1993, $20), studies at the American Institute for Research in Cambridge, Massachusetts, showed that women who felt ill, reporting that they had two or more distressing physical symptoms of menopause, were four times as likely to be depressed as women who reported having no more than one symptom. Depressing symptoms might include vaginal dryness, hot flushes or night sweats.

"The worse you feel physically and the more anxious you are about your physical health, the more likely you are to feel depressed," Dr. Barbach wrote. "Some women also feel angry that the bodies they trust and depend on are letting them down. If there is no outlet for this anger, it can be turned inward and experienced as depression."

Do not follow Barbara Bush's example of muddling through on your own. See a doctor without delay if you experience four or more of these symptoms of major depression for two weeks or longer: feelings of deep despair and worthlessness, debilitating fatigue or loss of energy, loss of interest in activities that used to give you pleasure, inability to get to sleep and/or early-morning awakenings, agitation, inability to concentrate, diminished interest in sex, social withdrawal, extreme changes in eating patterns or suicidal thoughts.

Whether or not you have suffered from depression in the past, you may respond well to hormone replacement—not because it cures depression but because of its effect on the other symptoms of menopause. An antidepressant might also be prescribed. Self-help groups and regular physical exercise are also helpful.

When hormone replacement is prescribed, estrogen is usually combined with synthetic progesterone (progestin) to protect the uterus from cancer. But some women have adverse reactions to progestin, similar to the symptoms of premenstrual tension. For them, estrogen alone, with periodic tests to check on the uterine response, may be better.

Women for whom any hormone supplement is medically inadvisable or unwanted might try consuming more foods with effects that mimic those of ovarian hormones. These include the various forms of soybeans like tofu and textured vegetable protein, yams and ginseng.

[JEB, September 1994]

Midlife Hormone Declines in Men

ALTHOUGH a decade ago specialists were still insisting that men retain throughout life the sex hormone levels reached in young adulthood, there is now no longer any doubt that starting at about the age of 40 or 50, blood levels of the so-called male sex hormone testosterone gradually fall, dropping to a third to a half of their peak by the age of 80.

There is also no question that aging is accompanied by changes that can be signs of insufficient testosterone: muscle size and strength decline, body fat increases, bones slowly lose strength-giving calcium, and sexual performance wanes.

But it is still uncertain whether these bodily changes represent a condition in need of treatment or whether they are physiologically normal aspects of the aging process that men just have to accept, said Dr. Peter J. Snyder of the University of Pennsylvania School of Medicine. It is an issue of growing importance as men now living into their 70s, 80s and beyond strive to maintain as high a quality of life as possible.

Here is a case where far more is known about women's health than that of men. In women, the hormonal change at menopause is abrupt and its adverse effects on body organs are well documented. In women, both the immediate and the long-term benefits of providing hormonal supplements are also fairly well established, although the possible risks are still incompletely explored. But for men it will probably be years before doctors know whether they, too, can profit from hormone replacement and, if so, at what price.

Well-designed studies of hormone replacement for normal, healthy aging men are just getting under way. For example, in about three years Dr. Snyder and his colleagues will have completed a scientific study of 100 men aged 65 and older who were randomly assigned to be treated with either a testosterone patch or a look-alike dummy medication. The researchers are trying to determine whether raising the men's testosterone level to that of a 40-year-old will result in an enhanced sense of well-being and improved bone calcium levels, muscle mass and strength.

At the start of the study, both groups of men had testosterone levels of about 350 nanograms per deciliter of blood, which is at the low end of normal for a young man. Those being treated daily with a testosterone patch that adheres to the scrotum are reaching hormone levels of about 570, which is in the middle of the normal range. All the men are being checked periodically for possible harmful effects, including prostate enlargement, prostate cancer, sleep apnea, high red blood cell counts and potentially harmful changes in blood cholesterol and other circulating fats.

"If we prevent the decline in testosterone with age, will that do more good or more harm?" Dr. Snyder asked. "In three years, we'll have the beginning of an answer, but it will be just the beginning."

There are thousands of men, meanwhile, with a far more serious problem with testosterone than the gradual decline in hormone levels with age. Among them are adolescent boys and adult men whose bodies, for one reason or another, have never produced enough testosterone to induce such characteristics of male maturity as a beard and body hair, a muscular physique, adult-size genital organs, a libido and sexual potency to match.

Dr. Richard F. Spark, a specialist in male hormones and sexuality at Beth Israel Hospital in Boston, explained that these men may have either primary hypogonadism, in which testicular cells fail to produce testosterone, or secondary hypogonadism, in which the pituitary gland fails to produce adequate levels of the hormones that stimulate the testes to release testosterone.

There is a second group of men with acquired hypogonadism who are equally if not more distressed: they have lost the ability to produce enough testosterone to maintain their libido and sexual potency and sometimes their secondary sex characteristics. This loss can result from an accident, an illness or a medical treatment that irreparably damages the testes or pituitary gland.

At a meeting of the Endocrine Society in June, various researchers presented evidence for major improvements in hypogonadal men treated with either injections of testosterone every two or three weeks or daily application of testosterone patches to the scrotum or to other parts of the body.

Both techniques have their pluses and minuses, but overall the patch has so far proved superior to injections in terms of patient acceptance and the ability to induce near-normal levels of testosterone throughout the day, day after day. With the injections, there is a sudden testosterone surge immediately afterward and a serious dip toward the end of the period before the next injection is given. With the scrotal patch, it is necessary to shave the hair on the scrotum for the patch to stick, and some men are embarrassed about having the patch when undressing in front of other people.

The effects of a scrotal patch called Testoderm, manufactured by the Alza Corporation of Palo Alto, California, on a 66-year-old man with a subnormal testosterone level is typical. After three months of therapy, the man reported a "definite increase in energy level and a definite improvement in mood," his doctor said. The patient said his sexual interest increased, his desire returned and his sexual relationship with his wife improved and reached a new level of intimacy.

In clinical studies using a still-experimental body patch called Androderm, produced by Theratech Inc. of Salt Lake City, researchers from the University of Utah in Salt Lake City, the Karolinska Institute in Stockholm and Johns Hopkins University in Baltimore showed that several groups of men achieved normal hormone levels, which resulted in improved mood and sexual function. Use of the patch resulted in virilization in five men who had never gone through puberty, including a 51-year-old man who developed pubic and facial hair and an enlarged penis for the first time in his life.

In discussing the effects of testosterone replacement on sexual potency, Dr. Spark said that men with "clearly subnormal levels of testosterone of 200 nanograms per deciliter of blood or less respond well to replacement hormone," adding, "However, those whose levels are not subnormal may experience an improvement in mood, but testosterone is not likely to affect their erectile function."

Even among men with clearly subnormal testosterone levels, there are some who do not respond well to treatment for impotence, Dr. Spark said. These include heavy smokers, who have damaged the small blood vessels within the penis; men who are morbidly obese, whose metabolism results in low blood levels of testosterone even when normal amounts are produced; and men with diabetes, who often have damaged blood vessels and nerves in the penis.

[JEB, August 1995]

Stages of Life—Aging

COPING WITH AGE

Is it possible that old age, often viewed as a time of fading mental and bodily powers, has gotten an unjustly bad rap?

Many more Americans than once expected are avoiding disability and chronic illness in their old age. The reason may be better nutrition in their youth and better education, which goes with healthier habits.

As for the long-held idea that the aging brain inexorably loses its functions, some of the studies on which that thesis rested included people with Alzheimer's disease. When these are excluded, the picture brightens considerably. Many people retain mental clarity and acuity into their 90s.

Meanwhile researchers are busily ferreting out the factors that promote longevity. Lack of stress and close family ties are a help. So, curiously, is conscientiousness, according to one study. As in other stages of life, attention to exercise and diet is important, and the elderly have different nutritional needs.

The age-old search for the fountain of youth still continues, though in more sophisticated ways. Now that supplies of natural substances like growth hormone have become available, scientists are testing whether extra doses, to counteract the falling quantities produced in old age, may bring back the vigors of youth. The prospect is pleasing, but then nature in its wisdom may have good reason for sparing the aging body from hormonal overstimulation.

Old age and health are far from opposites; there is much that common sense can do to bring them together.

Elderly Minds Don't Necessarily Lose Their Agility

THE conventional image of the aging brain is that people lose neurons the way balding men lose hair. Brain cells are supposed to start falling away around the age of 20, with everything downhill from there. Some people go bald, or senile, early. Some lucky and unusual ones keep their hair, or their wits, about them into their 90s and beyond.

Science has precious little good news about hair loss, but new findings on the death of brain cells suggest that minoxidil for the mind is unnecessary. Data from men and women who continue to flourish into their 80s and 90s show that in a healthy brain, any loss of brain cells is relatively modest and largely confined to specific areas, leaving others robust. In fact, about 1 of every 10 people continues to increase in mental abilities, like vocabulary, through those decades.

New imaging techniques, like the PET (positron-emission tomography) scan and magnetic resonance imaging (MRI), have shown that although the brain does gradually shrink in life's later decades, it does not shrink as much as had been thought. Furthermore, the shrinkage of a healthy brain does not seem to result in any great loss of mental ability.

"We used to think that you lost brain cells every day of your life everywhere in the brain," said Dr. Marilyn Albert, a psychologist at Massachusetts General Hospital in Boston. "That's just not so—you do have some loss with healthy aging, but not so dramatic, and in very selective brain areas."

The new imaging techniques have also enabled neuroscientists to discover a flaw in many earlier studies of the aging brain: those studies included findings from people in the early stages of Alzheimer's disease. Now, both by scanning the brain and by screening for cognitive function more carefully, most people with Alzheimer's are excluded from such studies.

Researchers measure brain shrinkage by keeping track of the fjordlike spaces that crease the wrinkled surface of the cerebral cortex, the topmost brain layer, which is critical for thought. These small crevasses are called ventricles and sulci, and the amount of space in them gradually increases with age, reflecting a loss in the overall mass of the brain.

From age 20 to 70, the average brain loses about 10 percent of its mass, said Dr. Stanley Rapoport, chief of the neuroscience laboratory at the National Institute on Aging in Bethesda, Maryland. But that loss "seems related only to subtle differences in cognitive abilities," Dr. Rapoport said. "We think the brain's integrity is maintained because the massive redundancy of interconnection among neurons means that even if you lose some, the brain can often compensate."

Compensation is precisely what studies of the "successful" elderly show. When neuroscientists weed out people with cognitive decline that is a sure sign of illness, the shrinkage is still there, but performance on mental tests is good. And what analyses of healthy old brains show is that old people might use different parts of the brain from young people to accomplish the same task. In some ways, a healthy old brain is like a pitcher whose fastball has faded but who can still strike a batter out with other pitches.

Some of the data come from autopsies of 25 men and women from 71 to 95 years old who had volunteered to be part of a control group in a 16-year study of Alzheimer's disease. Dr. John Morris, a neurologist at Washington University in St. Louis who did the study, said the brains of the mentally alert group showed some of the neuron tangles that, more than shrinkage, seem to be the main problem in Alzheimer's disease. But these tangles were in the hippocampus, a structure involved in memory, rather than in the centrally important cerebral cortex.

Dr. Morris said his data suggest that "there may be a pool of people who not only have no important cognitive declines but no brain changes of consequence for mental function, even into their eighties and nineties." Changes in the hippocampus might impair only the rate of retrieval from memory, he said, not its accuracy.

Similar findings have been made by Dr. Brad Hyman of Massachusetts General Hospital. "We've found no appreciable neuronal loss in people from their sixties to nineties who had retained their mental clarity until they died," said Dr. Hyman, who studied two specific regions of the cortex. "The dire picture we've had of huge cell losses is wrong for a healthy person, whose brain remains structurally intact into old age."

Apart from a reduction in the number of brain cells, another aspect of aging in the healthy brain seems to be a drop in the number of connections among them. Dr. Albert at Massachusetts General said her studies of brain tissue had uncovered specific structures deep in the brain that did show more neuronal loss, even with healthy aging. These include areas important for memory, like the basal forebrain.

But, Dr. Albert said, "It's important for mental abilities that most of the neurons in the cortex are retained—they store information once you've learned it."

Some of the most intriguing evidence for the resourcefulness of the aging brain comes from PET scans of the brain at rest and while engaged in mental tasks. In one study using PET scans that compared people in their 20s with those 60 to 75, Dr. Cheryl L. Grady, a neuroscientist at the National Institute on Aging, found that the younger people were indeed quicker and more accurate in recognizing faces and used more areas of their brains during the task than the older people.

But in similar studies at the institute comparing people from 20 to 40 with those 55 and older, those in the older group were able to recognize the faces with about the same accuracy, though they needed more time to do so than the younger group, Dr. Rapoport said. Images of the brains of the older group showed less activity in visual areas of the brain but more activity in the prefrontal cortex, suggesting increased mental effort.

Dr. Rapoport said that in older people, there seemed to be some loss of the circuitry involved in visual memory. "So the brain has to recruit other circuits to get the task done," he said. But recruit it does. The prefrontal cortex, which is the brain's executive area for intellectual activity, appears especially crucial in compensating for areas that no longer function so well in mental tasks.

Still, all is not rosy. The number of people who do end up with Alzheimer's disease and fall into senility is still quite large.

"There are three very different groups among the elderly," said Dr. Guy McKhann, director of the Zanville and Krieger Mind Brain Institute at the Johns Hopkins Medical School. "One does remarkably well, aging very successfully into their eighties and nineties.

The second group slides a bit, having some problems with memory and recall, but the problems are typically more aggravating than they are real."

Dr. McKhann said that the third group, which largely consists of people with Alzheimer's disease, suffered inexorable losses in mental function, leading to senility. That group accounts for about 15 percent of those in their 70s and 30 to 40 percent of those in their 80s.

But for those without disease, the brain can withstand aging remarkably well. "Some people stay very good at intellectual tasks all their lives," said Dr. Judith Saxton, a neuropsychologist at the University of Pittsburgh Medical Center, who is analyzing data from a two-year follow-up of more than 700 men and women from 65 to 92.

Dr. Saxton added, "I'd guess up to ten percent of people above seventy fall in this range." The question that interests many people who are headed toward 70, as well as some new and unconventional researchers, is how and why one ends up in this 10 percent. Is a person's neurological fate predetermined? Or is there something that can be done to stay healthy and mentally alert?

[DG, February 1996]

More Elderly People Are Retaining Their Good Health

THEY called it the failure of success. As medical scientists got better and better at treating people with fatal diseases—but not curing them—the nation would be burdened with an accumulation of elderly people who were living longer and longer but were crippled with pain and riddled with disabilities.

It was a notion that called into question what medicine had wrought. But, to nearly everyone's surprise, the predicted pandemic of pain and disability has not materialized. Instead, new information, some not yet published, on studies involving people at all socioeconomic levels show that not only are Americans living longer, but they are developing less chronic disease and disability. And the reasons may have as much to do with changing social circumstances, including events that occur in the first few decades of life, as they have to do with medical advances in treating diseases.

The National Long Term Care Surveys, a federal study that regularly surveys close to 20,000 people aged 65 and older, finds that every year there is a smaller and smaller percentage of old people who are unable to take care of themselves, comb their hair, feed themselves or take a walk.

The surveys use the Medicare population, which includes about 99 percent of all Americans, regardless of their income levels, who are 65 and older. Data from 1994 have just been compiled and analyses have not yet been published, but these data continue to support the picture of the healthier old.

Although the annual declines in disability rates are only about 1 to 2 percent a year, they have continued unabated since 1982, when the survey began, until 1994, the most recent survey. At the same time, the percentage of old people with chronic diseases, like high blood pressure, arthritis and emphysema, has steadily declined.

For example, the proportion of people over 65 with high blood pressure fell to 39.5 percent in 1989 from 46 percent in 1982. In that period, the proportion with arthritis dropped to 63.1 percent from 71.1 percent, and the proportion with emphysema fell to 6.4 percent from 8.9 percent.

The implications are profound, said Dr. Richard Suzman, who directs demography research at the National Institute on Aging. "This plays to the general question of what's going to happen as the older population, and especially the oldest old, mushrooms in size over the next fifty years," Dr. Suzman said.

It could mean that the growing elderly population may not be quite the economic drain that it was projected to be. The longer people live, Dr. Suzman said, the longer they will need programs like Medicare. But the new findings indicate that Medicare costs might be much less than expected in the coming years, even with the increased life spans of Americans.

For example, Dr. Kenneth Manton, a demographer at Duke University who analyzed the National Long Term Care Surveys, calculates that declining disability rates from 1982 until 1995 have saved Medicare $200 billion. He explained that if the disability rates of 1982 had held steady into 1995, there would have been nearly

300,000 more disabled people aged 65 to 74 in the population in 1995 than 13 years ago. Instead, there were nearly 121,000 fewer disabled people in 1995 than in 1982 in this age group, resulting in the Medicare savings.

Although some demographers have been wary of the new evidence that disease and disability rates are declining, many now say they believe the decline is real. "The evidence is limited, but different people have shown, with different sources of data, the same thing," said Dr. Douglas Wolf, a demographer at Syracuse University. "The preponderance of evidence seems to show that this is true."

There is little doubt that the elderly population is exploding, in large part because death rates from many chronic diseases are plummeting. The annual mortality rate for Americans of all ages from strokes dropped by 65.2 percent (from 79.7 deaths per 100,000 to 27.0 deaths per 100,000) from 1960 to 1990, and the death rate from heart disease dropped by 46.9 percent (from 286.2 per 100,000 to 152.0 per 100,000) in that period, Dr. Manton said.

But the true picture of the steady improvement in these old people's lives comes from studies that ask about how well they go about their daily activities. The best national data, Dr. Wolf and others said, are from the National Long Term Care Surveys. The surveys follow people enrolled in the Medicare program, asking where they live, what their diseases are and whether they are able to care for themselves. The surveys, Dr. Manton said, are "the closest thing we have to a national population registry."

The picture of a robust elderly population that emerges from these surveys is confirmed by a different kind of study, one that looks at the ability to work. Dr. Eileen Crimmins of the University of Southern California has been analyzing data from a representative sample of about 12,000 Americans aged 50 to 69 for the last 11 years. The people in the study are asked whether their physical or mental health affects their ability to work.

Over the course of the study, Dr. Crimmins and her colleagues found that fewer and fewer people said their ability to work was impaired. For example, in 1982, about 27 percent of men aged 67 to 69 said they were unable to work. But in 1992, just 20 percent of men in that age group could not work. "We regard the ability to work as an indicator of disability," Dr. Crimmins said.

The study was sponsored by the Social Security Administration.

Dr. Crimmins said the declines in reported disability that she observed applied equally to blacks and whites and to the rich and poor.

All these findings lead demographers and researchers on aging to ask why it is that older Americans are less frail and less feeble than ever before. One answer seems to be that people either are not developing the diseases that cripple and disable or are getting them at older ages, Dr. Manton said. In his survey, he asked about 16 diseases, including diabetes, heart disease, cancer, chronic lung diseases and arthritis. The number of diseases afflicting people over 65 declined by more than 11 percent over the last decade, Dr. Manton said. The largest declines were in the number of people with arthritis or joint problems, high blood pressure and heart disease.

Of course, saying people are healthier because they have fewer diseases begs the question *Why* do old people have fewer diseases today than in previous years? One possibility, Dr. Suzman and others said, is that the changes are an effect of education. In study after study, educational level is associated with better health. However, higher levels of education are also associated with greater wealth, and it has not been demonstrated that education itself produces beneficial effects.

"Education is one of the most powerful and mysterious variables," Dr. Suzman said. It is associated with health "throughout life and late in life." And there has been a dramatic increase in the educational levels of the elderly.

Dr. Samuel Preston, an economist at the University of Pennsylvania, calculated that in 1980 more than 60 percent of Americans from 85 to 89 had fewer than eight years of schooling. But by the year 2015, that figure will have dropped to 10 to 15 percent.

"We are at the cusp of a rapid increase in the educational status of the oldest old," Dr. Manton said. And, he said, people who are better educated tend to be more likely to change their diets to improve their health, to be nonsmokers and to seek out treatments, like hip and knee replacements, that can prevent disability.

Another possible explanation for the improved health of the elderly, researchers said, is that old people are reaping the benefits of improvements in public health that occurred when they were young. This might mean that people today would enter old age without the subtle lifelong burdens that afflicted earlier generations, who were more likely to have been affected by marginal nutrition, poor water quality and poor hygiene.

Then, Dr. Suzman said, there is the contribution of medical advances, like hip replacements, lens replacements for people with cataracts, angioplasty for heart disease and drugs to slow the bone loss of osteoporosis. These could delay or prevent the terrible burdens of chronic diseases that afflicted previous generations.

For now, researchers say they are uncertain which factors are most important in changing the picture of old age in America. But they are convinced that the picture has indeed changed.

[GK, February 1996]

Good Habits Outweigh Genes in Healthy Aging

HOW most people fare in old age may not be a matter of fate or genes, as many people believe. The way people age—whether in their 70s and 80s they end up sick, demented and sexless or vigorous, sharp and libidinous—is mostly a matter of how they live.

"Only about thirty percent of the characteristics of aging are genetically based; the rest—seventy percent—is not," Dr. John W. Rowe, director of the MacArthur Foundation Consortium on Successful Aging, said. The research team has found that staying active both physically and socially contributes to successful aging.

"People are largely responsible for their own old age," said Dr. Rowe, a gerontologist and president of Mount Sinai Medical Center in New York.

The MacArthur research team—which also included Dr. Gerald E. McClearn, a gerontological geneticist at Pennsylvania State University; and Dr. John R. Nesselrode, a psychologist at the University of Virginia—found that genetics played the greatest role in health characteristics early in life.

"But by age eighty, for many characteristics there is hardly any genetic influence left," Dr. McClearn said.

By examining what they call the positive side of aging rather than people who are already sick, the interdisciplinary, interuniversity team is finding not only that most old people are doing well physically and mentally but also that much can be done to foster a healthy and productive old age in the millions of Americans who might otherwise not age well.

In 1985 the MacArthur Foundation established the research team as a joint project among several universities and hospitals to study an often-overlooked segment of the elderly population: people who enter their eighth decade healthy and independent. The studies have shown that the serious losses in physical and mental functioning commonly attributed to age are neither inevitable nor immutable.

The MacArthur studies have already identified several factors that predict successful aging, including regular physical activity, continued social connections, resiliency—the ability to bounce back readily after suffering a loss—and self-efficacy, a feeling of control over one's life.

These factors, the researchers say, are ones that can be changed by people as they age, putting their well-being under their own control. The researchers also maintain that society has a crucial role in helping older people achieve these characteristics.

"We can no longer afford to ignore the link between social policies and health," said Dr. Lisa F. Berkman, a member of the MacArthur team who is a social epidemiologist at the Harvard School of Public Health. On the basis of findings of the research she directed, Dr. Berkman said that by improving access to physical activity and promoting social engagement instead of isolating or ignoring the elderly, much could be done to enhance physical and intellectual abilities in later life.

In a related study of older people in the community, gerontology researchers at Penn State, Dr. Warner Schaie and Dr. Sherry Willis, who are not part of the MacArthur group, found that while many people did not decline mentally in any significant way with age, those who did could minimize the fall and even improve cognitive functions through "intellectual" training or doing crossword, find-the-word and jigsaw puzzles.

"Our goal is to increase the health span, not the life span," Dr. Rowe said. Through community studies, he added, "our team has established that most old people are aging very successfully." The research showed that more than 90 percent of those living outside institutions reported that they were not sick. On the basis of tests of physical and cognitive abilities developed by the MacArthur group, the team found that a vast majority were functioning quite well.

By repeatedly testing people over a period of years, the researchers found that verbal intelligence did not necessarily decline with age but could actually increase. Dr. Marilyn Albert, a neuropsychologist at Massachusetts General Hospital in Boston, has found that certain aspects of intelligence, mainly information-processing speed, do fall off with age, but if older people are given enough time, they do as well as younger people on tests of cognitive ability.

Dr. Berkman has observed that declines in memory with age are linked to lesser degrees of physical activity. But how could physical activity enhance cognitive functions? Experiments in rats by Dr. Carl Cotman, a neuroscientist at the University of California at Irvine, have shown that treadmill exercise raises levels of brain-derived neurotrophic factor, or BDNF, a nerve growth factor that keeps neurons healthy.

"Surprisingly, the increase in BDNF occurred not just in the motor areas of the brain but also in the areas involved in learning, memory and cognition, the very areas that are attacked in dementias," Dr. Cotman said. "It appears that the brain keeps itself operative with activity." He believes the same mechanism operates in humans as in rats.

Many studies have shown that better-educated people are healthier in old age. This may, of course, be a result of higher income or of better health care because of their higher income. But other, more direct roles have been suggested. Dr. Albert has argued that by stimulating the brain, education may establish more neuronal pathways early in life as well as prompt people to remain cognitively active throughout life.

It is not just formal education that works. Even among people who are self-educated, said Dr. Schaie, director of the Penn State gerontology center, "those who led very active lives—traveling, reading books, taking courses—maintained intellectual function much longer than those who became couch potatoes."

He said his wife, Dr. Willis, a professor of human development, had demonstrated that "you can bring back people who have declined and you can teach old dogs new tricks." Dr. Willis gave five hours of training in spatial orientation and reasoning to people over 65 and found that two-thirds of them showed mental improvement.

Dr. Willis said there were many activities people could do on their own to maintain or improve cognitive functions. She suggested games like chess or jigsaw puzzles to foster spatial orientation. Such games can also stimulate inductive reasoning, which helps in figuring out patterns or sequences.

The significance of education has so intrigued researchers that some have thought it might offer some protection against the ravages of Alzheimer's disease. But one effort to pin down this effect, in a study of 93 nuns in the School Sisters of Notre Dame, showed no effect of education. Instead it hinted that Alzheimer's disease might be a lifelong illness, like atherosclerosis, already affecting brain function as early as the age of 20.

In people who do not suffer from Alzheimer's, cognitive function is influenced by social circumstances, like support from family and friends, as well as by intellectual activity. Dr. Teresa E. Seeman, a social epidemiologist at the University of Southern California in Los Angeles, found that "people who have more emotional and instrumental support have a better self-image, which in turn is related to better cognitive and physical functioning." Her studies suggest that a high level of social support results in lower blood levels of stress-induced hormones that can promote disease.

Dr. Seeman tested older people in a simulated driving situation, which became increasingly challenging until the drivers eventually had "accidents" they could not avoid. She found that "those with stronger self-confidence showed much less of an increase in stress hormones when put in this stressful situation." She suggested changes in social policies to "help older people participate more in group activities that enable them to maintain a network of social and emotional support."

But when it came to doing things for older people, she said the findings were more equivocal. "People who get too much instrumental help are at greater risk of experiencing a decline in physical functioning and in the kinds of things they can do on their own," she said. In other words, while it is beneficial to make it easier for older people to do things for themselves, it can be harmful to do the tasks for them. She concluded that "older people should not be discouraged from doing what they think they can do."

Resilience, the ability to bounce back from distressing events, also separates those who age successfully from those who experience sharper physical and cognitive declines. Dr. Robert Kahn, who at 77 describes himself as "the grand old man" of the MacArthur project, pointed out that successful old people "do not have some kind of marvelous genetic immunity that allows them to wander through life untouched." They are not blessed by having escaped bad events like illness, bereavement and job loss, he said.

Rather, Dr. Kahn said, "what differentiates the successful from the unsuccessful is the ability to come back from 'hits' of various kinds that for some people have long-lasting, even permanent effects."

Dr. Kahn has also demonstrated that people who continue to be productive after retirement are more likely to age successfully. He described productive activities as those that "generate valued goods or services as opposed to monetary gain," like taking care of a family or a child, gardening, participating in volunteer work and doing housework and home maintenance.

[JEB, February 1996]

Strength Workouts Can Help Keep Aging at Bay

I N just 10 weeks of a strength-training program, 50 frail men and women in their 80s and 90s were able to increase their weight-lifting ability by 118 percent, their walking speed by 12 percent and their stair-climbing ability by 28 percent, according to a recent study in the *New England Journal of Medicine*. This study and previous work by the same researchers at Tufts University show that strength training can help the elderly be more active and remain more independent.

Impressive though these accomplishments are in stemming some of the costly and debilitating incapacities of old age, they pale in comparison with what strength training can do for younger people who want to maintain or improve their physical prowess even as their biological clocks keep ticking toward decline.

Strength training is a fancy way of describing the process of building muscle power by lifting free weights or working out against resistance—using equipment like Nautilus or Universal machines or working against large elastic bands. While "aerobics" was the exercise catchword of the 1970s and 80s, strength training is the trend of the 1990s, hailed as a critically important complement to aerobics in a total fitness program. In 1990, the American College of Sports Medicine revised its exercise guidelines to recommend a more balanced fitness program that includes both aerobic workouts and strength training.

Before you start thinking, "Enough already—I have no time for any more activities," consider these established benefits of strength training: improved performance in other sports, like tennis, golf, basketball and even swimming; greater endurance and stamina in both recreational activities and the chores of daily life, like carrying groceries, children or a suitcase; loss of body fat and gain of lean muscle tissue, resulting in a dramatic improvement in body composition; more energy and self-confidence; a greater sense of power, both physical and emotional, and well-being; and a reduced risk of heart disease, diabetes, osteoporosis, back problems and joint injuries. Strength training can help reduce total cholesterol levels and raise the level of the desirable HDL cholesterol, keep blood sugar in balance and build bone strength better, it is thought, than weight-bearing exercises like walking.

Probably most enticing of all, strength training can make it easier to shed unwanted pounds and lose the inches you need to slip into those slender jeans. By helping you build muscle tissue and lose body fat, strength training revs up your metabolic rate, so you burn more calories whatever you are doing, even when sitting and sleeping. More muscle and less fat also mean fewer inches and smaller sizes, because fat takes up more room than the same weight of muscle tissue. After age 45 or so, sedentary people—and even many who do aerobic exercise—rapidly lose muscle mass and, consequently, strength. For every pound of muscle lost, the resting metabolic rate drops by nearly 50 calories a day. The lost strength largely accounts for the difficulty many elderly people have in rising from chairs, climbing stairs and carrying groceries.

You may not have to add any minutes to your current exercise schedule to make room for strength training. The current recommendation to achieve balanced fitness calls for aerobic workouts four times a week with strength training on the remaining three days.

The beauty of strength training is that it can be done by almost anyone, no matter how old or feeble, in a wide variety of circumstances and at little or no added expense. To do most of the recommended exercises, you need nothing fancier than a few full cans from the supermarket or plastic bottles filled with water or sand. And while women who work out with weights or against resistance can gain strength and muscle tone at the same rate as men, they need not worry about developing bulging muscles unless they also dose themselves with an extra shot of testosterone.

The goal is to work different muscle groups to achieve overall fitness and balanced muscular strength. Muscular imbalance increases the risk of injury. For example, cycling builds the quadriceps at the expense of the hamstrings, running strengthens the hamstrings at the expense of the quads and neither does anything for the upper body. To correct imbalances by using strength training, you should work on the muscle groups that are otherwise neglected.

You can use a set of free weights, like barbells, dumbbells or add-on ankle and wrist weights; cans of different weights; elasticized exercise bands, which come in different resistances; a home gym; or the calibrated resistance machines found in commercial gyms. Experts say you can get a full workout in just 30 minutes. The basic rule is to start light and gradually increase the stress on your muscles so they will grow stronger.

Through trial and error, pick a weight that you can lift 10 to 15 times but no more. Or pick the heaviest weight you can lift once and then drop back to one that is 60 to 80 percent of that maximum weight. In each workout, begin with the large muscle groups of the legs, chest, back and shoulders, then move to the smaller ones of the arms and abdominals. Figure on doing at least 8 to 10 different exercises each session.

Start each session with a 5- or 10-minute warm-up (perhaps jogging in place) and gentle stretching, then do two or three sets, each with 10 to 15 repetitions, for each type of exercise, resting a bit between sets of the same exercise. After a few weeks, increase the weights you are working with by 10 to 25 percent. You may have to drop down to 8 to 12 repetitions, which is fine. As your strength increases, continue to add more weight.

People with high blood pressure or heart disease should avoid working with heavy weights or resistance, and anyone with a chronic illness—arthritis, diabetes, heart disease, and so on—should consult a physician before starting a strength-training program.

Be sure to breathe evenly throughout the exercises, exhaling at the point of maximum exertion. Holding your breath can cause a dramatic rise in blood pressure. Lift the weight smoothly and release it gradually so your muscles, not the weight itself, do the work. If anything causes pain, stop doing it right away, but muscle soreness the day after a workout is to be expected, especially if you are a beginner or have just increased the weights you are using.

Muscles grow by being torn—microscopically—and rebuilt, so they need a day between strength-training workouts to recover. It is best to space out your workouts, interspersing them with aerobic activities.

[JEB, August 1994]

More of the Elderly Seek the Benefits of Exercise

WHEN it comes to adopting health-promoting exercise habits, growing numbers of older Americans are putting their younger counterparts to shame. While the overall share of adults who are physically active has not increased in about a decade (about 30 percent are completely sedentary, and nearly 60 percent participate in fewer than three 20-minute exercise sessions a week), men and women 65 and older are gradually getting the message and becoming more active. In fact, on the basis of the latest federally sponsored state-by-state analysis of physical activity among older Americans, they are coming closer than younger adults to achieving the surgeon general's goals for the year 2000.

One of the national health objectives established by the surgeon general in *Healthy People 2000* is to reduce to 22 percent the share of adults 65 and older who engage in no leisure-time physical activity. In 1987, when 32 states and the District of Columbia began collecting annual data about residents' exercise habits, 43.2 percent of older people were completely sedentary. Five years later, in 1992, the percentage of older residents who engaged in no physical activity had dropped to 38.5 percent. These promising findings come from the Behavioral Risk Factor Surveillance System of the federal Centers for Disease Control and Prevention; the results were reported in September 1995 in the CDC's *Morbidity and Mortality Weekly Report*.

In 19 states that gathered annual data, there was a moderate overall improvement in the share of older residents who reported some leisure-time physical activity. In three states—New York, Maryland and New Mexico—and in the District of Columbia, there was a consistent annual decline in the share of respondents who were completely sedentary. In no state did the percentage of sedentary older residents increase each year during the five-year period. The greatest improvement occurred in Rhode Island, where the percentage of completely sedentary older residents dropped from 59.5 percent in 1987 to 38 percent in 1992. Massachusetts, Ohio, New Mexico and Maryland all reported declines of more than 10 percentage points.

However, in projecting activity trends to the year 1997, researchers concluded that only three states—Massachusetts, Rhode Island and Minnesota—would meet the *Healthy People 2000* objective and that Americans overall would fall significantly short of the national goal for the year 2000.

Perhaps older people are more willing to take up exercise because many have retired and have more time. But the most common excuse younger adults give for not exercising—"I don't have time"—is belied by the fact that 84 percent watch at least three hours of television each week.

Regular physical activity comes closer to being a fountain of youth than anything modern medicine can offer. Researchers have documented many improvements in the health and well-being of older Americans who take up exercise and have found that it is never too late to start. The major areas of benefit are these:

- *Heart disease and stroke:* Physical activity can halve the risk of developing heart disease or suffering a stroke. Exercise helps to reduce the risk of these vascular diseases by lowering blood pressure, raising the level of protective HDL cholesterol, reducing the risk of developing blood clots and diabetes and countering weight gain.

- *Cancer:* Exercise lowers the risk of developing cancer of the colon, one of the leading causes of cancer deaths among men and women. In animals, exercise protects against breast cancer.

- *Osteoporosis:* At any age at which exercise is begun, it can increase the density of bones and reduce the risk of fractures. Furthermore, there is growing evidence that exercise need not be weight-bearing to foster bone density; stationary cycling and water aerobics may help as well. Older people who become active also experience improvements in balance, strength, coordination and flexibility, which all help to prevent the falls that can result in debilitating fractures.

- *Diabetes:* Older people who are physically active are less likely to develop diabetes than sedentary people. Physical activity increases the sensitivity of cells to insulin, which, in turn, lowers blood sugar and the need for insulin.

- *Weight:* Exercise helps people maintain a normal body weight or, when combined with a moderate reduction in caloric intake, fosters weight loss. Most important, exercise helps people lose fat and gain muscle. That makes it easier to maintain weight loss because muscle tissue burns more calories than fat does. Even in those of normal weight, exercise can counter the age-related loss of lean muscle tissue and the deposition of body fat, especially the heart-damaging accumulation of abdominal fat.

- *Immunity:* Exercise increases the circulation of the immune cells that fight infections and tumors. Physically fit people get fewer colds and other respiratory infections than people who are not fit.

- *Arthritis:* Nearly everyone over 65 has some arthritic symptoms. Studies suggest that regular moderate exercise combined with stretching can reduce arthritic pain and the need for medication.

- *Depression:* Exercise has long been known to help people overcome clinical depression, so it is not much of a stretch to conclude that it can help to prevent the depression that is so common, albeit often hidden, in older people. The emotional benefits of exercise are likely to be greatest if the chosen activities bring older people into contact with others.

- *Gastrointestinal bleeding:* Regular physical activity significantly decreases the risk of severe gastrointestinal hemorrhage in older people, probably by improving circulation to the digestive tract.

- *Memory:* Even brief periods of mild exercise can result in immediate improvements in memory in older adults. Exercise also fosters clearer thinking and faster reaction time by helping to speed the transmission of nerve messages.

- *Sleep:* A study by researchers at Stanford and Emory Universities showed that in older adults who were initially sedentary, regular exercise, like brisk walking, improved sleep quality and shortened the time it took to fall asleep.

Anyone over 40 who decides to increase his or her level of physical activity should first have a thorough medical checkup. Even if one is given a clean bill of health, it is wise to start slowly and build up gradually.

With the guidance of the President's Council on Physical Fitness and Sports, the American Association of Retired Persons has published a 32-page illustrated guide to fitness activities for older adults. Called "Pep Up Your Life: A Fitness Book for Mid-Life and Older Persons," the booklet can be obtained, at no charge for single copies, by writing to the American Association of Retired Persons, Fulfillment Department, 601 E Street N.W., Washington, DC 20049.

The National Association for Human Development has prepared three booklets on exercises—basic, moderate and advanced—for people over 60. Each one costs $3 and can be obtained from the association at 1424 16th Street N.W., Washington, DC 20036.

Yablon Enterprises Inc., in collaboration with Creative Fitness Inc., a company that develops fitness programs for older adults, has produced "Senior Shape-Up," which consists of two audiotapes and a 41-page manual and is available for $36 postpaid from Yablon Enterprises Inc., P. O. Box 7475, Steelton, PA 17113.

[JEB, October 1995]

The Secret of Long Life?
Be Dour and Dependable

SCORE one for those pious voices of prudence: being cautious and somewhat dour is a key to longevity, according to a 60-year study of more than 1,000 men and women.

Those who were conscientious as children were 30 percent less likely to die in any given year of adulthood than their most free-wheeling peers. But those who were ebullient in childhood fared less well in life's roulette wheel; they were about 6 percent more likely to die in any given year than the least cheerful children.

"We don't really know why conscientious people live longer—it's not as simple as wearing your sweater when it's cold outside," said Dr. Howard S. Friedman, a psychologist at the University of California at Riverside who did the research. "And despite assertions that optimism and a sense of humor are healthy, we found no evidence for this claim. Cheerfulness predicted a shorter life, perhaps because it indicated an unrealistic optimism, which led people to ignore risks to their health."

The findings were based on research with 1,178 California boys and girls who in the early 1920s, at an average age of 11, were first studied by Lewis Terman, an inventor of the IQ test. All the children were bright, with an IQ of at least 135. Dr. Terman and later psychologists interviewed them at regular intervals throughout their adult lives, from the 1920s until the 1980s, when most were in their 70s.

At the age of 11, the children were evaluated by their parents and teachers on measures that Dr. Friedman summarized into five personality traits: sociability and extroversion; self-esteem and confidence; physical energy and activity level; conscientiousness; and, last, "cheerfulness," a combination of optimism and sense of humor. Successive evaluations showed that these traits, though first measured in childhood, held fairly steady through the course of life.

The most conscientious children were "the kids you can depend on to do their homework, lock the doors, put their bikes away," Dr. Friedman said. Although they grew up to be adults who smoked and drank less than their peers, the statistical link between conscientiousness and longevity held beyond such healthy habits.

To his surprise, Dr. Friedman found that traits like sociability and self-esteem had no relationship to how long people lived. Perhaps the biggest surprise was that optimism in childhood had a negative impact on longevity; other studies have shown an optimistic outlook to have positive benefits for health, at least in short-term situations like recovery from surgery. But those studies defined optimism differently, as a sense of control over events in life.

Other psychologists whose study of personality traits includes conscientiousness are not surprised by Dr. Friedman's finding. "The lives of the conscientious are more cautious in general," said Dr. David Watson, a psychologist at the University of Iowa. "They do less drinking, less exploration of drugs, they're more circumspect in their sexuality."

Among the traits that mark people as conscientious, said Dr. Watson, are thinking things through before acting, being dependable in following through on their commitments, adopting conventional norms of morality and being neat and orderly. "They often have ambitious long-term goals and work hard to fulfill them," Dr. Watson said. "They are not risk takers."

But avoiding risks did not explain the longevity of the conscientious. In an as-yet-unpublished finding, Dr. Friedman examined the death certificates of those in the Terman study and found that the more unconscientious men and women did not have an appreciably higher rate of death from accidents.

Still, prudence has obvious health payoffs. "People who are not conscientious do things now and worry about the consequences later," Dr. Watson said. "They're more impulsive, less organized, and willing to assume greater costs and risks to get more fun and pleasure in their lives."

Dr. Watson added: "Conscientious people don't live in the moment. They're guided by what's appropriate, by a sense of duty and their long-term goals. But they don't live longer because they're happier."

[DG, November 1993]

Stress and Isolation Erode the Chances of Longevity

STRONG new evidence shows that high levels of stress combined with a lack of close friends or family can significantly reduce life expectancy.

Data from a new Swedish study show that 50-year-old men who had recently endured high levels of emotional stress without social support were three times as likely to die within the next seven years as those whose lives were placid.

While those who were socially isolated and identified themselves as lacking emotional support and friends suffered fatalities from stressful lives, those who experienced similar stress but said they had ample emotional support and relationships in their lives had no increase in mortality. The life events most strongly related to dying were having serious concerns about a family member, being forced to move, feeling insecure at work, having serious financial trouble and being the target of a legal action.

"Men with adequate social support seem to be protected" from the damaging effects of life's stresses, said an article published recently in the *British Medical Journal* by a team of scientists at the University of Göteborg in Sweden.

In the Swedish study, a random sample of 50-year-old men living in Göteborg were given a physical examination and psychological evaluation. Seven years later, researchers searched official records to determine which of the men had died.

Of those men who at 50 had reported three or more recent upsetting life events, 11 percent had died. All had identified themselves as lacking family or social support. Of those who reported no such disturbances, just 3.3 percent had died.

The researchers propose that stress, if not buffered by emotionally reassuring relationships, may lower resistance to disease, though they do not suggest any physiological mechanism that might be involved.

"Other people may help you handle your emotional reactions to the stress that triggers biological mechanisms that can lead to disease," said Dr. David Spiegel, a psychiatrist at the Stanford University School of Medicine. "They can help you see the situation differently, so it looms as less threatening, or can suggest helpful ways of responding that you may not have thought of. Or simply because they care about you, even though this terrible thing is happening to you, may make it seem not so bad."

There has been much research since the 1970s on links between stressful life events and ill health. But taking advantage of the national health system in Sweden, this is the first study to examine the link prospectively with a group representative of the whole population, for whom deaths from all causes can be traced.

"There's ample research evidence now that having a rich social network protects health somehow," said Dr. Lisa Berkman, an epidemiologist at the Yale University School of Medicine. "The question is how this might work." She suggested that it might simply be that people with many social ties also have healthier habits in general. "Or the mechanisms may be more subtle," she said, "operating through the neuroendocrine and immune systems."

Dr. Berkman was among the first to find a link between social isolation and mortality. In an epidemiological study of more than 7,000 men and women in Alameda County, California, in the late 1970s, she and Leonard Syme, an epidemiologist at the University of California at Berkeley, found that over the course of nine years, people with the fewest social ties were twice as likely to die as those with the strongest ties.

"Friends and family help you put your stress in perspective," Dr. Spiegel said.

[DG, December 1993]

Nutritional Needs of the Elderly

IF you are 60 or over, you may not be eating enough protein—or fiber, calcium, zinc, B vitamins, vitamins A, D, C and E, selenium and carotenoids.

It may sound like a tall order to keep track of all these nutrients, but deficiencies in one or more of them can increase your risk of suffering a heart attack or stroke; developing cancer, osteoporosis or vision-robbing eye disorders; or contracting a serious infectious illness like pneumonia.

But researchers disagree about what should be done about this problem. Some, like Dr. Jeffrey Blumberg, a nutrition researcher at Tufts University, take an aggressive public health stance. He maintains that the existence of widespread dietary deficiencies among older Americans and the evidence, albeit incomplete, that nutritional augmentation can be helpful is sufficient to justify recommending multinutrient supplements for older people.

"Supplements of the one-a-day type are safe and inexpensive, and the evidence suggests that improving nutritional status in older people will reduce their risk of developing chronic diseases and boost them in the direction of optimal health," Dr. Blumberg said after a recent United Nations–World Health Organization conference on healthy aging. He defined healthy, or successful, aging as "being able to operate at maximal levels of physiological functioning—muscle strength, cognition, bone density—and achieving the greatest reduction in risk of chronic disease."

Except for vitamin E, Dr. Blumberg is not recommending megadoses of any nutrient. The goal, he said, should be to consume one to two times the current Recommended Dietary Allowance through a combination of foods and supplements. For vitamin E, which acts as a potent antioxidant that may counter atherosclerosis, carcinogenic assaults on cells, cataracts, macular degeneration and premature aging of cells throughout the body, he suggests a dose of 100 to 400 international units daily. Although these amounts are many times greater than the RDA, Dr. Blumberg said they present no health risk for a vast majority of people.

Others, like Dr. Julie Buring, preventive medicine specialist at Harvard Medical School and Brigham and Women's Hospital in

Boston, are more cautious, pointing to beta-carotene studies as a warning of what can happen when preliminary evidence forms the basis for a public health recommendation. In two large studies, both of which admittedly had limitations, those who took beta-carotene supplements developed more cancers than those who did not.

"Before we recommend supplements," Dr. Buring said, "we should do clinical trials to see if the supplements are both safe and effective. Can we achieve through supplements the benefits seen from eating a diet rich in fruits and vegetables? Is it the nutrients themselves, or is it the kind of people who choose such a diet, that explains why they do better?"

But Dr. Blumberg worries about waiting for so-called definitive evidence. "The rapidly growing number of older people has created a demographic imperative to do something now," Dr. Blumberg said. "We cannot afford to wait until the baby boomers get sick. There is enough evidence already on which to base a judgment that the potential benefits of supplements will outweigh by a large degree the potential risks."

While it is always best to improve health by eating more nutritious foods, this is not always practical for older people. As people age, a restricted diet and nutritional shortfalls can result from factors like social isolation, limited mobility and dexterity, tight budgets, chronic illness, dentures and digestive difficulties. Also, since older people need fewer calories, they must get more nutrients from less food. In such cases, supplements can help to fill in important gaps.

Protein

With advancing age, the body becomes less efficient at using protein, and many experts now believe that the RDA for protein—50 grams a day for women and 65 grams a day for men over 50—is inadequate. The consequence may be an accelerated loss of lean muscle tissue. The most concentrated sources of high-quality protein, providing 24 to 34 grams in 4 ounces of cooked food—chicken and turkey breast (skinless), well-trimmed pork tenderloin and beef round steak, fish and shellfish—are costly and in some cases hard to chew. Less expensive alternatives that may be easier to eat, though not always as rich in protein, include canned tuna and salmon (22 to 30 grams in ¹/₂ cup); cooked dried beans, peas and lentils (13 to 17 grams per cup); nonfat yogurt (13 grams in 8 ounces); skim milk (8 to 10 grams in 8 ounces); and two egg whites (7 grams). An 8-ounce can of a liquid nutrition supplement like Ensure or Sustecal supplies 8 or 9 grams of protein.

Vitamins and Minerals

Leading the list of nutrient deficiencies among older Americans are folate, vitamins B-12 and D and calcium. A low intake of folate, a B vitamin prominent in fortified cereals and vegetables like spinach, okra, asparagus, dried beans and peas, can result in a high blood level of homocysteine, which raises the risk of heart disease and stroke. About 400 micrograms of folate a day is recommended for older people.

Deficiencies of B-12, which is found only in animal foods, can result in neurological problems like poor balance, impaired memory and dementia. The elderly are less able to absorb B-12 from foods and may do better taking a supplement, which is more readily absorbed. Dr. Robert Russell, nutrition researcher at Tufts, suggests 25 micrograms a day of B-12, about four times the current recommended amount.

Vitamin D, found in fortified milk but not in yogurt, enables the body to use calcium. Shortages in older people result from a diminished ability of the skin to form vitamin D in sunlight and a limited amount of time spent outdoors. Also, with age, there is a declining ability to form vitamin D into the hormone that aids calcium use. At least 400 international units (but not more than 800) should be consumed daily, from milk, fatty fish or a supplement.

At the same time, an increase in calcium intake—to 1,500 milligrams a day for older men and women—is necessary to reduce bone loss and resulting fractures. Calcium is best absorbed from foods, particularly dairy products. Other good sources include collard greens and canned salmon and sardines eaten with the bones. Among calcium supplements, calcium carbonate (found in Tums) is inexpensive but less well absorbed than calcium citrate. The elderly may also need a small increase in zinc, which aids immune functions and wound healing. Zinc is prominent in meats, poultry, shellfish, dairy products, beans and fortified cereals. Supplements should not contain more than 15 milligrams.

[JEB, May 1996]

After 70, Cholesterol May Not Be So Bad for You

CHOLESTEROL levels, which so accurately predict risk of heart disease in middle-aged people, appear to have no such predictive value in the elderly, a new study has found.

The study, by investigators at Yale University, included 997 men and women 70 years old or older who were followed from 1988 until the end of 1992. It is one of the very few studies of cholesterol to focus on people over 65, and in fact the average age of the study participants was 79. The researchers report that although a third of the women and a sixth of the men had high cholesterol levels, these people did not have any more heart attacks during the study period than those whose cholesterol levels were normal or even low, nor were they more likely to die from heart disease or from any cause.

The study appeared in a recent issue of *The Journal of the American Medical Association.*

"This is good news for old people," said Dr. Stephen B. Hulley, the chairman of the Department of Epidemiology and Biostatistics at the University of California at San Francisco. He said the study showed that after about the age of 70, "they can take it easy and relax" and stop worrying about cholesterol. Dr. Hulley, who wrote an editorial accompanying the paper, said that the findings were "very important" because there has been virtually no information on cholesterol's effects in the very old. Although this study by itself is unlikely to be definitive, he said, its findings are bolstered by those of the Framingham Heart Study, now in its 46th year, which also found no effect of cholesterol in the elderly.

Dr. Michael Criqui, an expert on cholesterol and heart disease at the University of California at San Diego, said the Framingham data showed, in fact, that cholesterol levels taken at the age of 50 were a better predictor of heart disease risk at 70 or 80 than cholesterol levels at 70 or 80.

Dr. Harlan M. Krumholz, the study director, a cardiologist and epidemiologist at the Yale University School of Medicine, said many old people were alarmed by their cholesterol readings and were trying desperately to get them down, with diet or often with cholesterol-lowering drugs. But Dr. Krumholz, Dr. Hulley and others say that since there is no evidence that lowering cholesterol helps in people over 70, doctors should not even take cholesterol measurements in old but otherwise healthy patients.

Dr. Hulley explained: "At least for people in their late seventies and beyond, we don't know what's a good cholesterol level. We actually don't know whether you're better off with a high one or a low one, so there is no point in measuring it." He added that there was especially no point in treating old people with cholesterol-lowering drugs and said he was deeply concerned because many people in their late 70s and older were taking those medications.

At first glance, the questioning of cholesterol's effects may sound odd, heart disease researchers said. After all, if large amounts of cholesterol in the blood encourage the buildup of artery-clogging plaque in middle-aged people and even in people as old as 65, why would they not do the same in the very old?

One possible explanation, said Dr. David Kritchevsky, a cholesterol researcher at the Wistar Institute in Philadelphia, is that anyone who reaches 80 or so with a high cholesterol level and no evident heart disease may be immune to cholesterol's effects. "The bullet has missed you," he said.

But Dr. Kritchevsky said many people did not want to hear that they could ignore cholesterol after reaching a certain age. "What has happened is that the risk factor has become the disease," he said. High cholesterol levels themselves have come to be viewed as a pathology.

Dr. Kritchevsky said many old people and their doctors were so convinced that high cholesterol levels were dangerous at any age that the question of whether to measure them or try to lower them if they were high might never come up. "My own father, who is eighty-two, announced to me that he was going to stop eating eggs," Dr. Kritchevsky said. "I told him, 'Eating eggs is what got you here.'"

Until very recently, nearly all studies that looked at whether high cholesterol levels were a risk factor for heart disease focused on people under 70, and most looked predominantly at men under 65. And the studies that showed that lowering cholesterol could prevent heart attacks focused on middle-aged men, in whom the relationship between high cholesterol levels and heart disease is strongest.

The National Heart, Lung and Blood Institute is starting a study that may eventually involve as many as 40,000 people over 60, looking into whether reducing cholesterol levels and blood pressure prevents heart disease. But the study is in its earliest stages, and the results will not be known until after the year 2000. In the meantime, researchers have been forced to extrapolate from studies of the middle-aged in giving advice to the elderly.

Dr. Basil Rifkind, a senior scientific adviser to the heart institute's vascular research program, said studies had consistently shown that as people grew older, the relationship between cholesterol levels and heart disease risk steadily weakened. Eventually, he said, "there is some point where the return is not worth the effort, where benefits are not likely to be seen." But the problem is deciding at what age that point occurs.

Dr. Rifkind said that when the heart institute's cholesterol education panel tried to decide what to recommend to old people with high cholesterol levels, "they did not come up with a blanket recommmendation." Essentially, they said doctors should use their judgment in treating people over 65; for example, asking if the person was healthy and vigorous or chronically ill. Nonetheless, Dr. Rifkind said, there has been "a shift toward being more aggressive about treating cholesterol in the elderly."

Some think that is appropriate. Dr. William P. Castelli, director of the Framingham study, one of the largest observational studies ever done, said his data showed that cholesterol remained a risk factor at any age, for men and women.

In an analysis published in 1992, he reported that total cholesterol levels predicted heart disease risk in 992 men 50 to 64 years old and in 1,295 women 50 to 79 years old. But, he said, he could predict heart disease in older men if he looked at a particular fraction of the cholesterol-carrying proteins, the ratio of total cholesterol to the cholesterol carried by high-density lipoproteins, or

HDL, which are the proteins that carry cholesterol away from blood vessels.

Using this ratio is a way of correcting for the fact that people who have high levels of HDL cholesterol, the so-called good cholesterol, are at lower risk than those whose HDL levels are low.

Dr. Castelli focused not on death from heart disease but on heart attacks and chest pain, signs that arteries are becoming blocked. He said his findings showed why doctors should aggressively treat old people: not to prevent deaths from heart attacks, since few die the first time they have a heart attack, but to prevent the heart attack in the first place.

"I want to slow the progress down so you will not shut down an artery and have a heart attack from which you will not die but the quality of your life will go downhill," he said.

But others say the case is not so clear-cut. Dr. Hulley argued that Dr. Castelli had not, in fact, shown that cholesterol or the cholesterol ratio was important after 79, so that his results were actually consistent with those from the new study. And another investigator, using the Framingham data, looked at heart disease deaths and found no relationship to cholesterol levels among the very old.

Dr. Richard Kronmal, a statistician at the University of Washington in Seattle, found that the relationship between cholesterol levels and risk of death from heart disease diminished as people grew older, eventually becoming nonexistent.

The new study, by Dr. Krumholz, found no relationship between cholesterol and deaths from heart attacks or between cholesterol and symptoms of heart disease in the elderly whether he looked at total cholesterol or at the ratio between total cholesterol and HDL levels.

Dr. Anthony Gotto, chairman of the Department of Internal Medicine at Baylor College of Medicine in Houston and a past president of the American Heart Association, said he still felt that high cholesterol levels in the elderly should be treated because some studies showed that artery-clogging plaque regressed in the elderly when they reduced their cholesterol levels.

"As a matter of fact," he said, "we have seen patients treated with angioplasty and bypass operations when they are in their eighties and when they have severe symptoms. If it's worthwhile treating with invasive therapy, then surely it's worth preventing."

But, Dr. Kronmal said, that sort of statement "requires several leaps of faith." He explained: "You have to believe that treating old people will work. And there are no data one way or the other. You have to believe it is safe to treat. And what is safe in young people may not be safe in old people. And you have to say that the benefit is substantial enough to make a difference. If you save people from a heart attack, they may suffer the ravages of another disease soon thereafter."

In the end, definitive answers will come only from studies that test treatments in the elderly. Dr. David Gordon, the heart institute's main adviser on its new study, said that for now he was "a little more comfortable recommending treatment to old people who actually have heart disease." But, he added, he cannot say how high cholesterol levels should be before treatment should begin. "There's not a lot of hard data to base that on," he said.

[GK, November 1994]

No Proof Yet That Extra Hormones Can Reverse Aging

WHY do some people in their 80s look, act and feel vigorous and energetic while others need help just to get through the chores of daily living? A good part of the answer may lie in their hormones. If studies now under way bear out their initial promise, hormone treatments for people over 60 may help to turn back the clock and, though without extending life, greatly enhance its quality.

Researchers are exploring the rejuvenating effects of several hormones that are known to undergo rather striking declines with age. These include, but go beyond, replacing estrogen, which declines sharply in women after menopause. The safety of estrogen replacement, particularly with regard to the risk of breast cancer, is hotly debated and raises a cautionary note about the wisdom of replacing other hormones that fall with age.

A major focus of the new research is growth hormone, a product of the pituitary gland that gradually declines with age and until recently was not thought important to older people. Researchers are considering replacing testosterone loss in older men. There is also keen interest in a hormone of the adrenal cortex called DHEA, or dihydroepiandrosterone, which is said to enhance immune function and life span in rats.

Whether or not nature has some hidden agenda for the ebbing of these various hormones with age, for example in slowing people down as the life span wanes, it is now recognized that as people live to their 80s and beyond, the effect of declining hormones may contribute significantly to chronic, debilitating and costly illnesses.

"For every major hormone system that's been studied, we find age-related changes that suggest they could have meaning to the aging process," said Dr. Marc R. Blackman, chief of endocrinology at the Johns Hopkins Bayview Medical Center in Baltimore. Among the well-known attributes of aging that hormone loss may bring about are the loss of muscle mass and strength, an increase of body fat, particularly fat around the abdomen, a weakening of the bones, a decline in immune responses and a general loss of energy.

While no one expects to turn a frail 80-year-old into an iron man, the hormonal effects under study could help to save old people from some of the burden of illness and to preserve their independence. More than 7 million Americans now need long-term care costing tens of billions of dollars a year because they are no longer able to perform daily activities without help. Without an antidote for age-associated disabilities, by the year 2030 nearly 14 million people will need such care.

Several years ago, the National Institute on Aging in Bethesda, Maryland, made available some $2 million for exploring hormone replacement in people 60 and older. Nine research teams are now midway through their studies, which focus on growth hormone and other "trophic factors," substances that promote growth or maintenance of tissues.

"Trophic factors may not be the 'fountain of youth,' as some have suggested, but they may have promise for halting or reversing degenerative changes in bones, muscles, nerves and cartilage, which lead to frailty," said Dr. Stanley Slater, deputy associate director for geriatrics at the institute. Some form of growth hormone therapy, if its early promise is sustained, might help people "stay stronger, leaner and more mobile" in their later years, he said.

But it would be wrong to make too much of these early findings, researchers caution. Dr. David Clemmons, an endocrinologist who studies growth hormone at the University of North Carolina at Chapel Hill, said: "Just because you make a person's hormone profile more youthful does not mean you will arrest or reverse aging. You'll still have wrinkles and gray hair."

Growth hormone, along with the special factors that trigger its release or carry out its effects on the tissues, is the star of current antiaging studies. The hormone was once thought to be important in making the body reach its final stature, though of no great consequence afterward. But several important studies have showed that this is not the whole picture.

European researchers, following up patients who had lost their pituitary gland, found that when growth hormone was added as well other pituitary hormones, there was a much greater improvement in muscle and bone mass and psychological well-being. The hormone also promoted a healthful loss of body fat, especially belly fat, which raises the risk of heart disease.

In this country, a team led by the late Dr. Daniel Rudman at the Medical College of Wisconsin in Milwaukee gave growth hormone three times a week for six months to 12 healthy men aged 61 to 81. They found that the men gained muscle, lost fat and developed thicker skin, while a comparison group did not.

The interest in growth hormone picked up significantly after advances in genetic engineering made it possible to synthesize the hormone in bacteria. Until then it had to be extracted from the pituitary glands of cadavers and was in very short supply. As a result of recent studies, much has been learned about the physiology of this potent natural messenger.

"A gradual but inexorable decline in growth hormone release starts in one's thirties and forties, and by the time people reach seventy and beyond, two-thirds to three-fourths of them have experienced a substantial decline in growth hormone," Dr. Blackman said.

Many factors contribute to this loss, including changes in sleep patterns with age, he explained. Growth hormone is secreted in pulses predominantly during the evening hours and especially during the phase of sleep known as slow-wave, or deep, sleep. This is just the phase that becomes truncated with age and can also be disrupted by medications and illness.

Another contributing factor is the tendency for older people to become sedentary, he said. Physical activity, particularly aerobic exercise, sets off the release of growth hormone in people of all ages, and, Dr. Blackman said, "sedentary people who become physically active frequently have bursts of growth hormone release." In fact, it may be no coincidence that the known benefits of physical exercise mimic those now observed for growth hormone.

But what might such changes mean to overall well-being? Will supplements of growth hormone and other factors lead to greater independence, fewer fractures and heart attacks and more of a zest for life? And can the hormone treatments be administered in a way that is safe, convenient and cost-effective? These are some the questions the National Institute on Aging is addressing.

In one of its nine projects, at the Johns Hopkins Bayview Medical Center, Dr. Blackman, Dr. Mitchell Harman and their colleagues are treating men and women over 65 for six months with one of three regimens: growth hormone alone, growth hormone plus the appropriate sex hormone (testosterone for men, estrogen for women) and an inactive dummy medication.

In another project, Dr. Mark L. Hartman and colleagues at the University of Virginia Health Sciences Center in Charlottesville are looking into the interactive effects in people over 60 of a year of growth hormone treatment with and without aerobic exercise or strength training. Perhaps most telling, Dr. Hartman said, will be the effects on everyday function, like how well the participants climb stairs, walk at a normal pace and maintain their balance.

At the University of Washington in Seattle, Dr. Robert S. Schwartz, Dr. George Merriam and their colleagues are looking at growth hormone–releasing hormone, or GHRH, the brain chemical that prompts the pituitary gland to release growth hormone into the bloodstream.

"Our preliminary findings include significant changes in body composition—a decrease in body fat and increase in lean body mass due to the hormone and in some cases to exercise—and a complete absence of side effects," Dr. Merriam said.

Treating a person with the brain's releasing factor for growth hormone instead of with growth hormone itself, he explained, should better mimic the body's natural pulsed output of the hormone and diminish possible side effects, like swelling of tissues and aggravation of diabetes and congestive heart failure. "We're still learning how to give growth hormone to older adults," Dr. Hartman said. "The original dose, based on body weight, turned out to be too high."

Other researchers are looking at the effects of the sex steroids testosterone and estrogen in older people. Dr. Peter J. Snyder of the University of Pennsylvania School of Medicine explained that although men do not experience the precipitous decline in sex hormones that women do at menopause, "by age eighty, healthy men have roughly one-half to one-third the amount of free testosterone they had at age twenty."

In a study of 100 normal, healthy men over 65, he and his colleagues are testing the effects of skin patches that raise the blood level of free testosterone to that of men in their 30s and 40s. After three years of treatment with either a testosterone or a placebo patch, the researchers will look for hormone-related improvements in muscle mass and strength, bone calcium and sense of well-being.

A different and more mysterious hormone, the DHEA produced by the cortex of the adrenal gland, is being studied by Dr. Samuel S. C. Yen at the University of California in San Diego. Production of DHEA starts at about the age of 7 and peaks between the ages of 25 and 30. It then slowly declines to 10 to 15 percent of peak levels by the age of 70.

In a small study of 16 middle-aged to elderly people who received either DHEA or a placebo for one year, Dr. Yen said there was a 75 percent increase in overall well-being among those receiving the hormone. He reported at a recent conference in Washington that his subjects coped better with stress, got around more easily and slept better. Men, but not women, also gained muscle and bone and lost body fat, although neither reported any change in libido.

Dr. Blackman said that other research had pointed to important effects of DHEA on cardiovascular function and the risk of heart disease, especially among men, and on immune function, which normally declines significantly with age.

One of the messengers of growth hormone, too, may have important immunological benefits. Dr. Ross Clark, an endocrinologist, and Dr. Paula Jardieu, an immunologist, at Genentech Inc. in San Francisco, are finding that an insulinlike growth factor called IGF-1, produced in the liver and elsewhere, can stimulate production of both B cells and T cells, which are vital in producing antibodies to infectious organisms and in fighting off cancers.

In animal studies, Dr. Clark found, "the thymus gland, which shrinks to one-half to one-quarter of its youthful size with age, can be made to bloom again by IGF-1." The thymus is a major source in the production of immune cells.

There are, to be sure, a few naysayers among hormone cognoscenti about stoking the healthy elderly with hormones. For example, Dr. Clemmons of the University of North Carolina believes the most effective use of growth hormone therapy will be on a short-term basis to speed recovery in elderly people who have sustained injuries or suffered illnesses that result in a prolonged convalescence. He pointed out that like all drugs, hormone treatments have side effects, and the risks would be more acceptable in people who have a lot to gain.

Furthermore, there are many problems to solve before growth hormone or its related growth factors can be used practically in millions of people, even on a short-term basis.

At present, both growth hormone and the brain hormone that sets off the release of growth hormone as well as IGFs must be administered by injection either daily or several times a week. Furthermore, the cost is now prohibitive—on the order of $14,000 a year for growth hormone therapy in a typical older person.

But several major pharmaceutical companies are in hot pursuit of surrogate substances that could be administered as a pill or skin patch. These smaller molecules, called secretagogues, could make it much easier and cheaper to supply the elderly with more youthful levels of growth hormone.

[JEB, July 1995]

The Hazards of Falls

ALTHOUGH winter may be the prime season for falls, among older people falling is a year-round hazard that is costly, frightening, debilitating and sometimes even life-threatening.

As people age, the risk of falling rises linearly and the risk of injury from a fall rises exponentially. One in three adults 65 or older falls each year. Among those over 75 who live independently, a quarter of the falls result in a serious injury. Falls are the immediate reason for 40 percent of all admissions to nursing homes, and they are the sixth leading cause of death for people over 70.

Even when an older person who lives alone is not hurt by a fall, the resulting fright can prompt a voluntary restriction of activity and a loss of mobility, self-confidence and independence. Restricted activity also leads to a decline in physical strength, which further increases the risk of falling, as well as the chance that the next fall will result in a serious injury.

Even in a nursing home or other adult care center, where the environment has been arranged for the safety of people with limited physical ability and agility, the risk of falling persists.

Researchers at the State University of New York at Buffalo studied the incidence of falls at one center that provides custodial care for relatively well elderly people. Of the 348 residents who lived in the center during a three-year period, falls were reported for 95, or 27 percent. What the researchers learned can help make living safer for those in special residences as well as for older people who live independently or in another person's home.

The researchers, Dr. Beth Erasmus Fleming and Dr. David R. Prendergast, both rehabilitation physiologists, were astonished to find that even in a center arranged with the safety of elderly residents in mind, half the falls were attributable to "environmental hazards." Elderly residents tripped over furniture, slipped on polished floors and fell over their walkers, which are designed to help the frail remain upright.

Furthermore, nearly 60 percent of the accidents occurred in the most familiar environment, the elderly person's own room, with only about 14 percent occurring in the person's bathroom and 4 percent on steps, which are generally considered the most likely places for an older person to fall.

"Clearly, aspects of the environment that appear to be safe for fully functioning individuals present hazards to an ambulatory, but frailer, older population requiring custodial care," the researchers wrote in their report, which was published recently in the *Archives of Physical Medicine and Rehabilitation*.

Not surprisingly, nearly a quarter of the falls occurred at night, usually when the people had left their beds to use the toilet.

As for personal frailties, nearly a quarter of the falls were attributable to physical conditions like arthritis, loss of balance, dizziness and "collapsed" knees, the term used when a knee buckled for some reason. Many older people have poor vision or one or more chronic ailments—like heart disease, high blood pressure, diabetes, Parkinson's disease or the residual effects of a stroke—that can contribute to the risk of falling either directly or indirectly, through the side effects of the drugs used to treat them. In addition, medications given to many elderly people to counter depression or insomnia can result in disorientation, grogginess or coordination difficulties that add to the risk of falling.

In another analysis, the researchers found that those who fell had significantly weaker muscles than those who did not fall. They also found that many residents for whom walkers had been prescribed did not use them because they considered them more of an impediment than an aid to mobility.

Many measures to help prevent falls are easy to put into effect. To fall-proof the environment, cover floors with tacked-down carpets; keep walking areas clear of obstacles like shoes, footstools, toys and wastebaskets; avoid slippery fabric on beds, chairs and sofas; wipe up all spills on floors immediately and thoroughly; equip bathrooms with grab bars around the toilet and tub or shower; cover the floor of the tub or shower with glued-on nonslip strips; keep stairways well lit and covered with nonskid treads; mark top and bottom steps with glow-in-the-dark tape; place night-lights along the route from the bed to the bathroom; and leave a light on in the bathroom during the night.

Pajamas and knee-length nightgowns, robes and coats are safer than longer ones for someone who is likely to climb stairs while wearing them. All shoes and slippers should have nonslip rubber soles, and rain and snow boots should have nonslip treads.

Symptoms like dizziness and loss of balance should be brought to a physician's attention. If the symptom is due to illness, getting proper treatment may reduce or eliminate it, and if it is due to medication, changing the dosage, administration schedule or type of drug will often help. The correction of sensory defects, like vision-impairing cataracts or hearing loss, is also helpful.

But perhaps the best way to prevent falls and fall-related injuries is to minimize the loss of muscle strength and flexibility that occurs with age and infirmity and to rebuild the strength and flexibility of older people. Studies have shown that even healthy people show a significant loss of muscle strength after the age of 50, particularly in the muscles needed for climbing stairs, rising from a chair and walking.

A person is considered to run an especially high risk of repeated falls if he or she has difficulty rising from an armless chair or walking a straight line by placing one foot in front of the other, with the heel of the forward foot touching the toe of the one behind. Reduced grip strength and weakness of the muscles in the legs and around the hips are associated with falls in older people.

While many older people have taken up some form of aerobic exercise, like walking or dance therapy, to improve cardiovascular function and lift their spirits, this type of activity does little to build muscle strength. However, older people—even those with multiple chronic ailments—can significantly increase their mobility, strength and balance in just six weeks through physical therapy and strength training, Dr. Prendergast and his colleagues showed. Muscles are strengthened by working them against resistance, which includes activities like lifting weights or working out on Nautilus-type equipment.

[JEB, January 1994]

Diagnosing Depression in the Elderly

THE patient was a 70-year-old grandmother who lived alone in an apartment building for the elderly. The doctor was asked to see her because she had twice been taken to the emergency room in danger of a diabetic coma.

But when the doctor examined her, he found the pressing problem was not her diabetes, which could be controlled by diet and medication. Rather, it was depression, which rendered the woman apathetic about taking care of herself.

"A brother to whom she was close had died the year before, and in her grief she didn't bother to take her insulin or eat right," said

Dr. Gene Cohen, who was called to treat her. After six months of psychotherapy for depression, the woman did very well, and her diabetes was back under control.

A new finding, that depression among men and women 65 and older nearly triples the risk of a stroke, underscores the need to treat depression in the elderly—not just to raise their spirits but also to protect them better against other diseases.

The study of more than 10,000 elderly men and women, all told by their doctors that they had hypertension and all with blood pressure readings higher than 160/95 or on medication for hypertension, found that over a three-year period, those with symptoms of depression suffered strokes at up to 2.7 times the rate of those being treated for hypertension but without depression.

"If elderly people have depression, it complicates their medical risk across the board," said Dr. Eleanor Simonsick, an epidemiologist at the National Institute on Aging, who published results of the stroke study in a recent issue of the journal *Psychosomatic Medicine.*

Other studies have found that elderly people with depression fared worse in recovering from heart attack, from hip fracture and from severe infections like pneumonia and had more difficulty regaining functions like walking after being stricken by diseases of all kinds.

One obvious reason for the higher risk of stroke among the depressed, Dr. Cohen said, is that "if you're depressed, you're less motivated to be diligent in staying on top of eating right or treating your hypertension."

For some, these lapses in treatment may be a "covert suicidal act," he said. For such patients, despairing thoughts, like "So what—nobody cares what happens to me anyway," can lead to a failure to take essential medications.

Another increased medical risk is biological. "Prolonged depression interferes with the functioning of the immune system," Dr. Cohen said. "If you have a broken hip or an infection, the depression slows the rate of recovery, which can in turn worsen the depression."

Of the 32 million Americans 65 and older, about 6 million suffer from some level of clinical depression, said Dr. Barry Liebowitz, chief of the Mental Disorders Among the Aging Research Branch at the National Institute of Mental Health. Of these, the depression of at least 75 percent is undiagnosed and goes untreated, even though a large share are routinely treated for other illnesses by doctors who fail to recognize that they are depressed, he added.

"The major reason depression is not diagnosed is that doctors don't ask," said Dr. Deborah Marin, director of geriatric psychiatric at Mount Sinai Medical School in New York. "And older people don't divulge it unless they're probed, because for their generation there is such great stigma to having a psychiatric problem."

Studies of elderly people who committed suicide as a result of depression have found that three-quarters visited a doctor within a week of their deaths, but in only one-quarter of those cases did the doctor recognize that the patient was depressed.

"People around a depressed older person don't see the depression as a disease that should be treated," Dr. Cohen said. "They just think it's part of aging: 'Oh, you'd be depressed, too.' Or they don't know it can be treated successfully at just about any age."

Among the symptoms of depression that can be discounted or misinterpreted, Dr. Cohen said, are sudden irritability and fault-finding, or pessimism and little hope for the future, which may be seen as personality changes that come with aging. "But the personality does not ordinarily change with age," he said.

The physical symptoms of depression, like low energy, apathy, loss of appetite or lack of interest in former pleasures, can be seen simply as a sign of frailty, Dr. Cohen added.

Depression in older people is commonly a side effect of medications, like those for heart disease. When the medications are changed, such depression typically lifts.

The prognosis for elderly patients whose depression is diagnosed and treated is good. "We know that treatment works in eighty percent of cases where patients receive appropriate treatment," Dr. Liebowitz said.

[DG, September 1995]

INDEX